LUKE'S PEOPLE

Luke's People

The Men and Women Who Met Jesus and the Apostles

THOMAS J. F. STANFORD

WIPF & STOCK · Eugene, Oregon

LUKE'S PEOPLE
The Men and Women Who Met Jesus and the Apostles

Copyright © 2014 Thomas J. F. Stanford. All rights reserved. Except for brief quotations in critical publications or reviews, no part of this book may be reproduced in any manner without prior written permission from the publisher. Write: Permissions, Wipf and Stock Publishers, 199 W. 8th Ave., Suite 3, Eugene, OR 97401.

Wipf & Stock
An Imprint of Wipf and Stock Publishers
199 W. 8th Ave., Suite 3
Eugene, OR 97401

www.wipfandstock.com

ISBN 13: 978-1-62564-196-0

Manufactured in the U.S.A.

For Mary

Contents

Acknowledgments | ix
Abbreviations | x
Introduction: The Aim and Scope of the Study | xv

CHAPTER 1
Methodology | 1
1.1 Authorship | 1
1.2 The Intended Reader | 8
1.3 The Socio-Historical Background | 11
1.4 The Narrator's Standpoint | 29
1.5 Rich and Poor, High and Low Status | 31
1.6 The Use of Historical Data | 43

CHAPTER 2
The House of Herod | 49
2.1 Introduction | 49
2.2 Context: The History of the House of Herod | 50
2.3 Luke's Antetext: Mark | 61
2.4 Luke's Two-Volume Work | 64
2.5 Summary | 75

CHAPTER 3
The Roman Authorities | 77
3.1 Introduction | 77
3.2 Context | 78
3.3 Soldiers of the Roman Army in Luke-Acts | 87
3.4 Roman Governors | 92
3.5 Municipal Authorities | 104
3.6 Summary | 107

CHAPTER 4
The Jewish Authorities | 109
4.1 Introduction | 109
4.2 Context | 110

4.3 Luke's Character Groups | 122
4.4 The Chief Priests | 126
4.5 The Pharisees | 131
4.6 Summary | 150

CHAPTER 5
The Male Local Elites and Non-Elite | 152
5.1 Introduction | 152
5.2 The Local Elites | 157
5.3 The Penētes in the Gospel | 163
5.4 The Penētes in Acts | 168
5.5 The Destitute and the Sick | 179
5.6 Summary | 186

CHAPTER 6
Women in the Introduction to the Gospel | 188
6.1 Introduction | 188
6.2 Overview of the Women in Luke-Acts | 215
6.3 Anna | 218
6.4 Mary and Elizabeth | 234

CHAPTER 7
Other Women in Luke-Acts | 238
7.1 Introduction | 238
7.2 The Hellenist Widows | 239
7.3 Providers of Diakonia | 255
7.4 Providers of Witness or Testimony | 264
7.5 Other Women | 268
7.6 The Plausibility of Our Interpretation | 276
7.7 Summary: Chapters 6 and 7 | 289

CHAPTER 8
Summary and Conclusions | 291
8.1 Introduction | 291
8.2 Methodology | 294
8.3 The Author | 294
8.4 The Male Characters | 295
8.5 The Female Characters | 299
8.6 Peter and Paul | 300
8.7 The Church after Luke's Time | 300
8.8 In Conclusion | 301

Appendix I: Members of the House of Herod Significant for Luke | 303
Appendix II: *Chēra* (widow) and cognates in the Septuagint | 305

Bibliography | 309
Scripture Index | 323

Acknowledgments

My thanks are due to my PhD supervisor, Bill Telford, for his unfailing provision of advice, constructive criticism, and encouragement as needed.

My interest in exegesis was stimulated many years ago by John Sawyer at Newcastle University Adult Education courses and later encouraged by Jon Davies. I am grateful to them. I would also thank the examiners for my dissertation and thesis, Loveday Alexander, Gerard Loughlin, and Justin Meggitt for their encouragement.

Early versions of the material in chapters 6 and 7 were presented to a seminar at the Department of Religious Studies of Newcastle University in January 2001 chaired by Nicholas Sagovsky and on various occasions at the British New Testament Society between 2001 and 2013, usually at the Acts seminar chaired by Steve Walton. My thanks are due to the chairs and to the participants for their stimulating and helpful contributions to the discussions.

The work draws on the work of many scholars whom I have not met, but I would particularly thank Peter Rabinowitz, who provided the framework upon which it is built and Elisabeth Schüssler Fiorenza. My interpretation of Luke-Acts differs very substantially from hers, but could not have been started if she had not broken the ground.

I would also thank the librarians at the Universities of Newcastle and Durham, at Newcastle City libraries, and at Tyndale House whose assistance was invaluable.

Above all my thanks are due to my wife, Mary Lorigan, who not only put up for many years with the demands of the work, but read each draft and made innumerable helpful suggestions to correct errors, obscurities and infelicities. Needless to say, any remaining failures are fully my responsibility.

Abbreviations

Books of the Old Testament and Septuagint

Gen	Genesis
Exod	Exodus
Num	Numbers
Deut	Deuteronomy
Judg	Judges
1–2 Sam	1–2 Samuel
1–2 Kgdms	1–2 Kingdoms (LXX)
1–2 Kgs	1–2 Kings
3–4 Kgdms	3–4 Kingdoms (LXX)
1–2 Chr	1–2 Chronicles
Jdt	Judith
Tob	Tobit
1–2 Macc	1–2 Maccabees
3–4 Macc	3–4 Maccabees
Ps(s)	Psalms
Prov	Proverbs
Eccl	Ecclesiastes
Song	Song of Songs
Job	Job
Wis	Wisdom
Sir	Sirach (Ecclesiasticus)
Hos	Hosea
Amos	Amos
Mic	Micah
Joel	Joel
Zech	Zechariah
Mal	Malachi
Isa	Isaiah

Jer	Jeremiah
Lam	Lamentations
Ezek	Ezekiel
Dan	Daniel

Books of the New Testament

Matt	Matthew
Mark	Mark
Luke	Luke
John	John
Acts	Acts
Rom	Romans
1–2 Cor	1–2 Corinthians
Gal	Galatians
Eph	Ephesians
Phil	Philippians
Col	Colossians
1–2 Thess	1–2 Thessalonians
1–2 Tim	1–2 Timothy
Titus	Titus
Phlm	Philemon
Heb	Hebrews
Jas	James
1–2 Pet	1–2 Peter
1–2–3 John	1–2–3 John
Jude	Jude
Rev	Revelation

Quotations, unless otherwise stated, are from NRSV for the New Testament and from NETS for the Septuagint. NETS names 1–4 Kingdoms as 1–4 Realms and 1–2 Chronicles as 1–2 Supplements. References other than quotations are given to books as described in NRSV and any significant variations between NRSV and the Septuagint are described in the text.

The Greek text of the New Testament is taken from NA^{27} and the Septuagint from the Rahlfs edition—see below under LXX.

Apostolic Fathers

1 Clem.	1 Clement
Ign. *Eph.*	Ignatius, *To the Ephesians*
Ign. *Magn.*	Ignatius, *To theMagnesians*
Ign. *Smyrn.*	Ignatius, *To the Smyrnaeans*
Ign. *Phld.*	Ignatius, *To the Philadelphians*
Ign. *Rom.*	Ignatius, *To the Romans*
Ign. *Pol.*	Ignatius, *To Polycarp*
Ign. *Trall.*	Ignatius, *To the Trallians*

Translations and Greek text from Holmes, M. W., *The Apostolic Fathers.* Grand Rapids, MI: Baker.

Josephus

Life	*Life of Josephus*
Apion	*Against Apion*
War	*The Jewish War*
Ant	*Jewish Antiquities*

Translations and Greek text from *The Works of Josephus.* 9 vols. Translated H. St. J. Thackeray et al. Loeb Classical Library, London, Heinemann, various dates.

Other ancient authors are included in the Bibliography.

Works of Reference

ABD	*Anchor Bible Dictionary.* 6 vols. Edited by David Noel Freedman. New York: Doubleday, 1992.
BDAG	Walter Bauer, Frederick W. Danker, W. F. Arndt, and F. W. Gingrich. *A Greek-English Lexicon of the New Testament and Other Early Christian Literature,* 3rd ed. Chicago: University of Chicago Press, 2000.
BDF	Friedrich Blass and Albert Debrunner. *A Greek Grammar of the New Testament and Other Early Christian Literature.* Translated and revised by Robert W. Funk. Chicago: University of Chicago Press, 1961.
EDB	*Eerdmans Dictionary of the Bible.* Edited by David Noel Freedman. Grand Rapids, MI: Eerdmans, 2000.
EDNT	*Exegetical Dictionary of the New Testament.* 3 vols. Edited by Horst Balz and Gerhard Schneider. Grand Rapids, MI: Eerdmans, 1990–1993.
FCAA	*A Feminist Companion to the Acts of the Apostles.* Edited by Amy-Jill Levine. London: T. & T. Clark, 2004.

FCL   A Feminist Companion to Luke. Edited by Amy-Jill Levine. London: Sheffield Academic, 2002.
IMGL   An Intermediate Greek-English Lexicon: Founded upon L&S. Oxford: Oxford University Press, 1963.
L&S   Henry George Liddell and Robert Scott. A Greek-English Lexicon. 7th ed. Oxford: Clarendon, 1890.
NJBC   The New Jerome Biblical Commentary. Edited by Raymond E. Brown et al. London: Chapman, 1989.
OBC   The Oxford Bible Commentary. Edited by John Barton and John Muddiman. Oxford: Oxford University Press, 2001.
OCD   The Oxford Classical Dictionary. 3rd ed. Edited by Simon Hornblower and Antony Spawforth. Oxford: Oxford University Press, 2003.
ODQ   The Oxford Dictionary of Quotations. 5th ed. Edited by Elizabeth Knowles. Oxford: Oxford University Press, 1999.
OED   The Compact Edition of the Oxford English Dictionary. London: Book Club Associates, 1979.
STS   Searching the Scriptures: A Feminist Commentary. 2 vols. Edited by E. Schüssler Fiorenza. London: SCM, 1995.
TDNT   Theological Dictionary of the New Testament. 10 vols. Edited by Gerhard Kittel and Gerhard Friedrich. Translated by Geoffrey W. Bromiley. Grand Rapids, MI: Eerdmans, 1964–1976.
TGAC   The Gospels for All Christians: Rethinking the Gospel Audiences. Edited by R. Bauckham. Edinburgh: T. & T. Clark, 1998.

Bible Versions

AV   Authorised Version. Cambridge: Cambridge University Press, n.d.
Barclay   The New Testament: A New Translation. London: Collins, 1968
Douay   Douay-Rheims. Challoner revision of 1752.
ESV   English Standard Version. Wheaton, IL: Crossway, 2001.
GNMM   The New Testament in Today's English Version. 3rd ed. London: Fontana, 1973.
ISV   International Standard Version. Santa Ana, CA: ISV.
JB   The Jerusalem Bible. London: Darton, Longman & Todd, 1966.
LXX   Septuaginta. Edited by A. Rahlfs. Stuttgart: Deutsche Bibelstiftung, 1935.
McReynolds Word Study Greek-English New Testament. Carol Stream, IL: Tyndale, 1999.
NA^{27} Novum Testamentum Graece. Stuttgart: Deutsche Bibelgesellschaft, 1993.
NASV   New American Standard Version. La Habra, CA. Lockman, 1995.
NCV   New Century Version. Fort Worth, TX: Worthy, 1987.
NEB   The New English Bible. Oxford: Oxford University Press, 1970.
Newberry Interlinear Greek-English New Testament. Various publishers.
NETS   A New English Translation of the Septuagint. New York: Oxford University Press, 2000.
NIV   The New International Version of the Holy Bible. Copyright International Bible Society, 1973–1984.
NJB   The New Jerusalem Bible. London: Darton, Longman & Todd, 1990.

NLT		New Living Translation. Carol Stream, IL: Tyndale, 2007.
NRSV		The New Revised Standard Version of the Holy Bible. Copyright Division of Christian Education of the National Council of the Churches of Christ in the United States of America, 1989.
OSB		Orthodox Study Bible. Nashville: Nelson, 1982.
Phillips		*The New Testament in Modern English*. Rev. ed. London: Fontana, 1973.
Rieu		*The Four Gospels*. Harmondsworth: Penguin, 1952.
		———. *The Acts of the Apostles*. Harmondsworth: Penguin, 1957.
RSV		The Revised Standard Version of the Holy Bible. Copyright Division of Christian Education of the National Council of the Churches of Christ in the United States of America, 1946–1957.
The Message		*The Message: The Bible in Contemporary Language*. Colorado Springs: NavPress, 2002.
TNT		*Translator's New Testament*. Publication details not given.
UBS⁴		*The Greek New Testament*. 4th Rev. Ed. Stuttgart: Deutsche Bibelgesellschaft, 1994.
Youngs		*Youngs Literal Translation*. Originally published 1898. Various editions.

Introduction

The Aim and Scope of the Study

This book seeks to learn more about and thus better understand the men and women who met Jesus and the apostles as they are described in the Gospel of Luke and in the Acts of the Apostles. It aims to do so in the way intended by the writer of these two works, both written by the same individual known as Luke, and together referred to as Luke-Acts. In this, it differs from most other studies of Luke-Acts (or the New Testament generally) in that it does not try to understand the actual historical figures described by Luke, does not try to get behind his narrative to "real history," but rather seeks to understand what he himself wished to convey about these people. This is fundamental to the study: "We should inquire *what the author thought* took place before we ask what took place. We should ask *why the author narrates* it as he does before we ask whether it is true as he narrates it."[1]

The focus is on those men and women who are portrayed in Luke's narrative as meeting Jesus and the apostles. It does not deal with Jesus himself, nor, except tangentially, with the Baptist or the male apostles (a term which includes Paul, Barnabas, Stephen, and Philip). However, our argument does address traditional misunderstandings about Luke's presentation of Peter (in the story of the selection of Matthias) and Paul (in the story of his dash to Pisidian Antioch). It deals with all the significant women in Luke's narrative, including Mary, the mother of Jesus, but her part in this study is relatively small. This focus on minor characters can provide new and important insights into Luke-Acts.

This is a socio-historical literary examination of the texts, literary in that it considers the text itself, socio-historical in that it considers the text in the light of the time when it was written. Recent research by secular scholars

---

1. Cadbury, *Making of Luke-Acts*, 362 (emphasis added).

has cast new light on various aspects of those very different times, and we describe important aspects of that background. Above all, this study aims to clarify and understand the author's intentions. We have made one fundamental assumption—that is, that Luke selected his words, and that, in choosing those words, he intended to convey a specific meaning. We have not accepted explanations of what he said along the lines of "it was in his sources" or "he could not omit it." Luke could, and did, both change what he found in his sources and omit material. To argue that any element of his work is there other than by the writer's choice is to run a grave risk of misunderstanding significant aspects of the narrative. This is not to say that Luke did not make mistakes and it is, of course, also possible that any part of the extant text could be corrupt (some early corruptions of the text are discussed in 7.6.6). In some instances we have been unable to understand why Luke wrote that which he did write, and have fallen back on editorial fatigue or carelessness, or ignorance on our own part. Other scholars may find better explanations.

The objects of the study are minor characters in Luke's narrative and this examination risks building too much on slight foundations, but he had a purpose in writing about them which can only be discovered by examining his words. However, his main purpose was undoubtedly theological and was achieved through his descriptions of the actions of Jesus and his followers. If our understanding of his minor characters is consonant with this theological purpose (outside the scope of this study), there is less risk of major error.

It is also necessary to form a view as to what can be known about Luke, who, so he says, was one of the characters who met the apostles, especially Paul. The main source of information is to be found in the parts of Acts where Luke refers to himself as a participant, usually known as the "we" passages, as Luke figures only as one person among "we" or "us." Many scholars have considered the "we" passages, but almost all are concerned to form a view of what one might call the history behind Acts. We have a different, literary, focus, and are concerned to understand what Luke intended to convey when he wrote these passages, and therefore consider not the "we" passages, but the "we" words and phrases. This is discussed further in 1.1.2, which attempts to understand what Luke actually wrote about his three voyages with Paul, but it may be helpful to state here that we conclude that Luke may have been a child at the relevant time. This hypothesis has the advantage of rendering less cogent many of the traditional objections to the idea that Luke was a companion of Paul's, objections which form the basis of much scholarly skepticism about Luke's historical reliability.

This study compares not only individuals, but also some groups (such as the Pharisees) who share similar characteristics, who may be called group-characters. The individuals rarely feature in both Gospel and Acts, but group-characters appear in both books. Our approach has been to bring together in a single chapter those individuals and groups who share certain characteristics, for example, the house of Herod in chapter 2, and we have dealt separately with men and with women. We believe that to understand the way in which Luke portrays one character or group, it is necessary to compare them with other characters or groups throughout the two-volume work. To help achieve this there are frequent cross-references between different parts of our text.

In chapter 1 we explain the methodology and tools we use, describing the social and economic background to Luke's work and the literary influences which help us to understand what he intended to communicate to his readers. The chapter concludes by considering how recent discoveries by secular scholars about Pisidian Antioch can help us to understand Luke's portrayal of that city and of Paul himself. We then examine individuals and groups of characters in chapters 2 through 7. Chapter 2 deals with the house of Herod, chapter 3 with the Roman authorities, chapter 4 with the Jewish authorities, and chapter 5 with other male characters. Female characters are discussed in chapters 6 and 7. Chapter 6 begins by demonstrating that a number of patriarchal interpretations, accepted by many feminist scholars as representing Luke's intentions, are not supported by the text. It goes on to provide an overview of women in Luke-Acts, and to consider the women who feature in the beginning of the Gospel. Chapter 7 considers other women in Luke-Acts and finishes by identifying evidence of a general attempt around the end of the first century to subordinate women and promote exclusively male patriarchal governance. Finally, in chapter 8, we summarize our findings and draw conclusions.

CHAPTER 1

Methodology

1.1 AUTHORSHIP

1.1.1 Introduction

We make certain assumptions about the authorship of Luke-Acts, shared by the majority of scholars. These are:

1. The same person (whom we call Luke) wrote both Gospel and Acts.

2. He (or she—we make no assumption as to gender, but use "he" for brevity)[1] wrote both volumes after the fall of Jerusalem (CE 70). Most scholarly opinion places both works between about 80 and 90,[2] or, to use a chronology familiar to Luke, during the first part of the reign of Domitian (81–96), with the work perhaps begun during the preceding reign of his brother, Titus (79–81). We attempt to understand Luke from the perspective of his own time, so this dating is important to our interpretation[3]—we find that a date in the early 80s illuminates aspects of the text.

3. He was familiar with the Septuagint, the Greek translation of the Hebrew Bible.

---

1. A masculine participle is used of the writer in the introduction to the Gospel (Luke 1:3) but this male persona does not necessarily preclude a female writer—see Telford, *Theology of Mark*, 7. However, there are other reasons to believe that Luke was male, considered in 1.1.2.

2. E.g., Kümmel, *Introduction*, 151 (70–90), Fitzmyer, *Luke I-IX*, 57 (80–85), Johnson, *Gospel of Luke*, 2 (80–85), Green, *Gospel of Luke*, 14 (latter decades CE), Barrett, *Critical and Exegetical Commentary*, 2:xlii (80–early 90s), Bovon, *Luke 1*, 9 (80–90).

3. A number of scholars, e.g., Pervo, *Acts*, 5, date Luke-Acts in the second century.

4. He used two written sources for his Gospel, the Gospel of Mark (substantially as we now have it) and Q, which is no longer extant. Both sources were also used by Matthew.

5. Luke wrote two related volumes. It has long been accepted that Acts was written as a sequel to the Gospel, and in recent years there has been a widespread acceptance that when the Gospel was written Luke already had the successor volume in mind.[4]

We accept the hypothesis that Luke attempted to be a reliable historian, that is, tried to describe events as he thought that they had happened. He did this from his own perspective and in accordance with the standards of his day. His perspective shaped his narrative, but in this Luke does not differ greatly from other historians of his time or ours, except that, like the authors of the Septuagint, his perspective was fundamentally theological. Historians of his day did have different standards, perhaps most obviously in the putting of speeches in the mouths of their characters, as Luke does in Acts.[5] Thucydides provided the classic description:

> My method has been, while keeping as closely as possible to the general sense of the words that were actually used, to make the speakers say what, in my opinion, was called for by each situation.[6]

We also adopt two principles of interpretation, first that Luke was a skilled writer whose words conveyed what he wanted them to convey to his intended readers.[7] That is to say, we do not accept that he included material because it was "in his sources," or because it was too well known to omit. The second principle is that Luke (strictly, the Lukan narrator) endeavored to align his views with those of the Lukan Jesus. As a result, the words and actions of the Lukan Jesus are of special importance in interpreting Acts.

---

4. See 1.3.4.

5. The speeches of the Lukan Jesus may differ, but this does not need to be addressed in this study.

6. Thucydides, *Peloponnesian War* 1.22.

7. The concept of the intended reader is described in 1.2.

1.1.2 The Autobiographical Material

1.1.2.1 The "We" Passages

In Acts Luke uses the first person plural (the "we" passages)[8] on a number of occasions. Many scholars doubt that he was himself present on these occasions, because of differences between the narrative of Paul's journeys in Acts and that which can be deduced from the authentic Pauline letters, and also because of perceived theological differences between Paul (as revealed in the letters) and Luke,[9] especially regarding Christology, natural theology, the concept of law and eschatology.[10] Some theological differences are to be expected in view of the time-lapse (some twenty years) between Paul's imprisonment in Rome and the time when Luke wrote. In particular, during that time Jerusalem, including the temple, was destroyed, a catastrophe which was of great theological importance to Luke and to his Jewish and Christian contemporaries. As to Christology, this clearly developed during this period, perhaps most evidently in the idea of the virginal conception, not known to Mark (who wrote around 70) but adopted by Matthew and Luke[11] who both wrote around 80. Mikeal Parsons has addressed the theological differences between Acts and the authentic Pauline letters and argues that as regards atonement, natural theology, and law, the differences are relatively minor. He also finds that an audience familiar with Paul's letters would have seen various aspects of Luke's portrait of Paul as very familiar, in particular his use of rhetoric, his miracles, and his suffering endurance in his apostolic mission.[12] We would add that there are close parallels between the understanding of prophecy as shown by Paul in 1 Corinthians and that in Acts.[13]

Most modern commentaries are agnostic on the "we" passages, either not discussing them or leaving the matter open. However, accepting doubt about Luke's veracity in this matter raises questions about his veracity generally, and there have been a number of attempts to find plausible reasons why Luke would have used "we" about events at which he was not present, although none have met with general acceptance. As noted above, for the

---

8. Acts 16:10–17; 20:5–15; 21:1–18; 27:1—28:16.

9. See Fitzmyer, *Acts*, 98–103 (the "we" passages), 129–47 (Paul).

10. Ibid., 147.

11. Luke's treatment of the virginal conception and its relationship to that of Matthew is discussed in 6.3.12.

12. Parsons, *Story Teller*, 134–38.

13. See 6.1.4.

purposes of this study we adopt the hypothesis that Luke was reliable, that is, if he says he was there, he was there.

We distinguish between the "inscribed author,"[14] that is the self-revelation in the text of the author, who may, or may not, have a relationship to the real flesh and blood person who wrote the material,[15] and the "deduced author," about whom we can learn something through the combination of the material revealed in the text and our other information about the period. For example, Acts tells us that the inscribed author arrived in Rome with Paul at a particular time. We know from other information that Paul had, not long previously, written a letter to the Romans, sending greetings to, among others, Prisca and Aquila. It would be confusing to suggest that the inscribed author might have met Prisca and Aquila in Rome, but it makes sense to consider whether the deduced author might have done so. Such considerations can help to form a judgment about the "real author of Luke-Acts," the actual person who wrote or dictated the two volumes and who some scholars argue lived in the second century and never met Paul. We attempt to understand what the material says, and do not evaluate the reliability and veracity of the autobiographical material or the relationship between the deduced and the real author—this will be considered in chapter 8.

The autobiographical material in Luke-Acts is in two parts. First, there are the two prologues, Luke 1:1–4 and Acts 1:1, written in the first person singular, forming introductions to the two volumes and describing what the author is attempting to do. Second, the author writes in the first person plural about parts of three journeys undertaken in company with Paul, in what are known as the "we" passages.

These three journeys are: from Troas to Philippi (Acts 16:11–40), from Philippi to Miletus and on to Jerusalem (Acts 20:5–15; 21:1–25),[16] and from Caesarea to Rome (Acts 27:1—28:16), and on each of these journeys he tells us that he accompanied Paul. It is important to understanding Luke's autobiographical material to note that, on the first of these journeys, Paul, Silas, and Luke arrived at Philippi (Acts 16:12),[17] but only Paul and Silas left Philippi (Acts 16:40). Later, in Luke's description of the second journey, we see Paul arriving in Philippi (Acts 20:3–5),[18] and then Paul and Luke leaving

---

14. Closely related to the implied author and usually equivalent to the narrator.

15. E.g., the inscribed author of the Deutero-Pauline and Pastoral epistles is Paul, but the flesh and blood author may not be.

16. The last mention of "we" is at Acts 21:18, but Luke implies that he was among those present at the meeting described in Acts 21:19–25.

17. Silas was among the company (Acts 15:40).

18. The text has Paul in Macedonia, but it seems clear from the context (20:5–6) that Philippi is meant.

Philippi (Acts 20:5–6).[19] Luke intends us to understand that he spent the period between the first and second journeys in Philippi, although this has rarely been referred to in the commentaries.[20]

Luke describes Philippi as: "a leading city of the district of Macedonia and a Roman colony" (Acts 16:12). The original wording of the text is problematic, but "Philippi was not the capital of Macedonia or of any part . . . of it"[21] and "there certainly does seem to be some pride involved in Luke's description of the 'honor rating' of the city";[22] this may be because of his personal connection with the place, having lived there for some six or seven years. His pride had some foundation: "[Philippi] . . . prospered and outstripped other cities in this district of Macedonia, including . . . the capital of the district, Amphipolis."[23]

Luke's journeys were taken in the company of Paul and there has been a great deal of interest in the dating of Paul's life. J. D. G. Dunn has summarized recent scholarly opinion;[24] There is fairly broad[25] agreement on the dates relevant to Luke's journeys, between the start of Paul's Aegean mission (Acts 16:40) between 48 and 53, and his arrival in Rome (Acts 28:16) between 59 and 62. Adapting Dunn's own Pauline chronology[26] we would see Luke's first journey in 49, his second in 56 and his third in 59–60.

Looking at the "we" words, the majority merely include Luke among those present, one of those traveling with the group or listening. There are a few possible exceptions. On the first journey he tells us that: "We sat down and spoke, *elaloumen*, to the women who had gathered there" (Acts 16:13). It seems very possible that Paul, as the spokesperson of the group, was the

---

19. This is the usual reading, but Richard Pervo differs: "Formally this 'we' excludes both Paul and the seven persons of v. 4" (Pervo, *Acts*, 509). On this reading it is difficult to understand who "we" might be, unless Luke was, as we suggest below, a child accompanied by one or both of his parents.

20. An exception being F. F. Bruce: "Luke was apparently left behind to continue the work in Philippi, where he reappears in xx.5. His stay in Philippi may sufficiently account for his interest in the place" (Bruce, *Acts*, 323). Barrett notes, but does not discuss, this possible interpretation (Barrett, *Critical and Exegetical Commentary*, 2:949). Dunn notes it and concludes that "Luke had much richer sources of information [in Philippi] than in any of the preceding episodes" (Dunn, *Beginning from Jerusalem*, 676, including n82).

21. Barrett, *Critical and Exegetical Commentary*, 2:779.

22. Witherington, *Acts*, 487.

23. Ibid., 488.

24. Dunn, *Beginning from Jerusalem*, 499.

25. Broad agreement in that a difference of a few years usually matters little for our purposes.

26. Dunn, *Beginning from Jerusalem*, 511–12.

only, or at least, principal speaker, and in Acts generally Paul's companions are not shown as speaking. Indeed, Paul's capacity to monopolize the opportunity to speak is described later when he spoke from the breaking of bread to midnight, and then again, after healing Eutychus, until dawn (Acts 20:7–11). So, Luke's use of *elaloumen*, the first person plural, need not imply that he spoke personally, but may mean no more than that he was among Paul's companions while Paul spoke.

On his second journey Luke was among those who prayed at Troas (Acts 21:5) and also among those who tried to dissuade Paul from going on to Jerusalem (Acts 21:12–14). Luke was present but not necessarily leading the prayers or speaking. On his third journey, Luke was again part of a group, but was personally and actively involved in an incident when the ship in which he was traveling met a severe storm:

> By running under the lee of a small island called Cauda we were scarcely able to get the ship's boat under control, *ischusamen molis perikrateis genesthai tēs skaphēs* (Acts 27:16).

Luke, because of the use of "we," seems to have been assisting the sailors in this endeavor—he describes the activities of the sailors using "they" on all other occasions including one of the preceding verses (Acts 27:13)[27] and that immediately following, also dealing with the ship's boat (Acts 27:17).[28] We agree with Bruce that: "The 1st pers. *ischusamen* suggests that Luke himself helped (any landlubber could haul on a rope)."[29]

This is the only action recorded in Acts which we can be sure was carried out by Luke as an individual, here helping the sailors in an emergency. We can draw some tentative conclusions about Luke himself from this incident. First, that he was male; there were 276 people on the ship (Acts 27:37) and it is not at all likely that, in such circumstances, a woman would have helped with the ropes in this way. Second, it tells us something about his age. It seems probable that he must have been at least twelve, probably a few years older, and perhaps ten or twenty years older. If he was less than twelve, we suggest, he would not have been able to help, indeed, would have been in the way. If he was much older than thirty, it is less likely that he would have been involved. The interpretation which we provisionally adopt is that Luke was a child when he first met Paul in 49 and an adolescent or young adult when he arrived in Rome in 60. We cannot be more precise because

---

27. 27:15 also uses "we," in that case for the whole ship's company, but does not refer to a particular activity.

28. Conzelmann notes: "The transition to the third person in this verse is striking. Is this intentional, or is it carelessness?" (Conzelmann, *Acts*, 218).

29. Bruce, *Acts*, 459.

he tells us almost nothing about his own role in the events he describes, but by indicating the occasions when he himself was present, adding to the authority of his narrative for his intended readers.

1.1.2.2 Education

We can also learn something about the inscribed author from the way in which he wrote. "[Luke] was deeply versed in his Bible and knew it like the Greek rhapsodes knew Homer or Dante knew Virgil":[30]

> It is hard to understand in social terms where Luke could have learned to write "biblicizing Greek" as well as he does as an adult Gentile convert to Christianity ... Luke's use of biblical language goes much deeper than mere quotation or explicit allusion. The obvious locus for acquiring such deeply-embedded linguistic patterns is a school ... There is a substantial element of Luke's language that is *not* clear biblical allusion, but simply shares lexical and/or syntactic features with Jewish Greek texts which were never read in synagogue ... texts like the books of the Maccabees and Ben Sira.[31]

But Luke did not only write "biblicizing Greek." Alexander also compares his language with the classical Greek used by literary writers and finds that it "is a direct continuation of standard Hellenistic prose ... untouched by classicism but ... significantly more 'Attic' [i.e., classic] in character than everyday spoken Greek."[32] The combination of standard Hellenistic prose with biblicizing features fits well with our hypothesis that Luke was a child who spent six or seven of his formative years in Philippi, in the household of Lydia, "a dealer in purple cloth" (Acts 16:14). His Greek education would have been that appropriate for a member of Lydia's household, while his missionary parents would have seen to his education in the Septuagint.

1.1.3 The Source Q

There is a widely-held hypothesis that Luke used the source Q, but this has recently been subject to a sustained critique by Mark Goodacre,[33] who

---

30. Wifstrand, "Septuagint," 41, cited Alexander, *Ancient Literary Context*, 243.
31. Alexander, *Ancient Literary Context*, 246.
32. Ibid., 240, summarizing Wifstrand.
33. See Goodacre, *Synoptic Problem*; Goodacre, *Case against Q*; and Goodacre and Perrin, *Questioning Q*.

argues that the literary evidence for Q can be explained to a substantial degree by Luke's use of two extant written sources, Mark and Matthew, so that there is no necessity for a hypothetical source, Q. These arguments have not been accepted by mainstream scholarship and the issue is of minor importance for much of this study. Accordingly, we have assumed that Luke used Mark and Q,[34] but have on occasion referred in footnotes to the possibility of a Matthean source. The infancy narratives of Luke and Matthew are not generally regarded as being influenced by Q, but our reading raises the possibility that Luke could have used part of the Matthean infancy narrative[35] as a source.[36] This possibility is addressed in 6.3.12.

1.2 THE INTENDED READER

Our aim is to understand as far as possible what Luke conveyed or wished to convey to his intended readers. Our methodology is based on the concept of the "authorial audience"[37] developed by Peter Rabinowitz, and used in New Testament studies by C. H. Talbert:

> To read as authorial audience is to attempt to answer the question: If the literary work fell into the hands of an audience that closely matched the author's target audience in terms of knowledge brought to the text, how would they have understood the work? This type of reading involves trying to adopt the perspectives of the authorial audience so that one may become a member of the author's original audience's conceptual community. To do this, modern readers must gain an understanding of the values of the authorial audience and the presuppositions upon which the original text was built.[38]

This is not a new approach in New Testament studies, being implicit in much exegesis. A somewhat similar concept[39] has been articulated by John Darr:

> If our treatment of Lukan characters and characterization is to be truly *text-specific*, then the audience to which we refer should

---

34. Luke's use of Mark and Q is discussed in 1.3.5.
35. Matt 1:18—2:1.
36. This could have been Matthew, or a written or oral source also used by Matthew.
37. Robert Tannehill has also used the term "authorial audience" ("Freedom and Responsibility," 274).
38. Talbert, *Reading Luke-Acts*, 15.
39. For a comparison of these concepts, see below.

fit the cultural profile of the readers for whom the account was written. That is, we must reconstruct—to the fullest extent possible—the extratextual repertoire, literary skills and basic orientation of the original audience.[40]

The concept developed by Rabinowitz provides additional clarity, although as well as "authorial audience" he also uses "intended reader,"[41] a term we prefer:[42]

> The intended reader—the hypothetical person who the author hoped or expected would pick up the text—may not be marked by or "present in" the text at all but may rather be silently *presupposed* by it. The intended reader, therefore, is not reducible to textual features but can be determined only by an examination of the interrelation between the text and the context in which the work was produced. The intended reader, in other words, is a *contextualized* implied reader, and studies of reading that start here have the potential to open up new questions of history, culture, and ideology.[43]

He has elsewhere addressed the relationship of the intended reader and the author:

> The notion of the authorial audience is clearly tied to authorial intention . . . my perspective allows us to treat the reader's attempt to read as the author intended, not as a search for the author's private psyche, but rather as the joining of a particular social/interpretive community; that is, the acceptance of the author's invitation to read in a particular socially constituted way that is shared by the author and his or her expected readers.[44]

Although the concept used by Darr (original audience) and that used by Rabinowitz (authorial audience) seem similar, there is an important difference. Darr attempts to understand the actual people who would have read or listened to Luke's account. Rabinowitz is concerned with the audience Luke intended to address: that is, the focus is on the author, not the audience. Luke wrote some twenty to thirty years after the events he described in the second half of Acts. It is likely that he expected some of the people

---

40. Darr, *Character Building*, 25–26.
41. These terms are equivalent (Rabinowitz, "Whirl without End," 85).
42. Although Luke-Acts was written to be read aloud, that is, heard, our argument makes little use of this, so we refer to the intended reader, not audience.
43. Rabinowitz, "Whirl without End," 85.
44. Rabinowitz, *Before Reading*, 22.

who feature in his narrative to have still been alive and to have been among, or of interest to, his intended readers.[45] Some examples are given in 1.3.1.1.

The author usually takes considerable pains to ensure that the intended reader understands what is being said and implied:

> [In] the New Testament . . . just as in the Old Testament every word has been selected deliberately and has been given its place in relation to many others, directed by a creative and controlled narrative art. Here, too, every detail serves the whole composition.[46]

Where Luke has a known source and has amended it, we have additional evidence as to his intended meaning. We may not always understand the author's purpose, but we may be sure that there is one, and our understanding of that purpose increases as scholarship develops.

In order to read as the intended reader would have done, we need to understand the "socially constituted way" shared with the author: "Learning to read authorially involves learning historical and cultural norms"[47] and in this chapter we identify certain of these historical and cultural norms. In 1.3 we address the broad socio-historical background beginning with the identification of the appropriate "social/interpretive" community. We then describe tools developed by Joel Green, context, intertext, and co-text, and explain the way in which we have used Luke's identified written sources, Mark and Q, which we have termed his antetext.[48] We next turn to the original method of transmission and reception of the text and then identify methods of interpretation which are not valid for understanding Luke's time or intended readers. In 1.4 we consider the appropriate standpoint from which to assess the objects of our study, that is, the narrator's point of view. In 1.5 we evaluate the criteria for deciding whether a character or character group is to be regarded as of high or low status, rich or poor, and finally, in 1.6, we use a specific example, Pisidian Antioch, to consider the possible use of the historical information available to us in order to interpret the Lukan text.

---

45. Others were alive but were not likely to have been among his intended readers.
46. Fokkelman, *Reading Biblical Narrative*, 188–89.
47. Rabinowitz, *Before Reading*, 138–39.
48. 1.3.5. Henceforth, we use the term "source" for material other than Mark, Matthew, and Q which, perhaps, was available to Luke. This material may have been written or oral.

1.3 THE SOCIO-HISTORICAL BACKGROUND

1.3.1 Introduction: The Social/Interpretive Community

1.3.1.1 A Specific Community?

This study seeks to understand Luke-Acts as a narrative in the light of the socio-historical realities of the time when he wrote. The term socio-historical needs clarification. A number of scholars have attempted to deduce from Luke's narrative the socio-historical realities of a specific community for which he wrote, a monograph by Philip Esler[49] being particularly influential. Esler finds the clearest evidence for the view that Luke wrote for a specific community in "Paul's prophetic address to the elders of the Ephesian *ekklēsia*" (Acts 20:17–35), which describes how "'fierce wolves' will invade the flock and men will rise up from within it . . . to mislead the disciples." In particular he finds the use of the word flock (*poimnion*),[50] also used at Luke 12:32, suggestive:

> The context Luke establishes for these troubles is the local Christian community, the "flock," with clear boundaries between itself and the outside world . . . This repeated use of the flock image suggests that Luke found it appropriate to the circumstances of his own readers . . . members of a small Christian community beset by difficulties from within and without.[51]

We do not agree: the image is extremely generalized and cannot support Esler's conclusion. *Poimnion* is a rare word, used in only one New Testament passage outside Luke-Acts,[52] but of its cognates, *poimnē* (also meaning "flock") is used in four passages,[53] *poimēn* (shepherd) is used seventeen times (four times in Luke)[54] and *poimainō* (to herd, to tend) eleven times.[55] In addition there are some 38 other references to sheep.[56] Moreover, the attacks from inside and outside do not necessarily signify a particular community. Luke has throughout Acts shown us the church under both

---

49. Esler, *Community and Gospel*.
50. Esler does not refer to the Greek word.
51. Esler, *Community and Gospel*, 26.
52. Twice in 1 Pet 5:2, 3.
53. Matt 26:31; Luke 2:8; John 10:16; 1 Cor 9:7 (twice).
54. Luke 2:8, 15, 18, 20.
55. Including Luke 17:7 and Acts 20:28, which is part of Esler's passage.
56. And over thirty references to "lamb" in various Greek forms.

internal[57] and external[58] attack, and these instances provide more than enough reason for the Lukan Paul to refer to such attacks in this speech,[59] "Paul's last will and testament,"[60] which sets out the "way that Luke wants Paul to be remembered."[61] The Lukan Paul expects that attacks (described in stereotyped language)[62] like those which he has faced, and will face again, will continue to trouble the Ephesian community.[63]

Similar attempts to describe a Lukan community have been made by other scholars, including a number of those[64] included in a survey by Thomas E. Phillips,[65] who notes that:

> Many scholars construct a reader whose unique insights, knowledge, experiences or location provide an interpretive lens through which to view the diversity. The characteristics of these constructed readers vary significantly.[66]

The fact that different scholars interpret readers in a hypothetical Lukan community in a number of different ways is an indication of the difficulty of the enterprise—they cannot all be right. Indeed, the idea that the Synoptic Gospels were written for specific communities has been cogently criticized by Richard Bauckham.[67] We must, indeed, "ask why the author narrates it as he does"[68] but we should do so without assuming that Luke wrote for a specific community, such as that described by Esler. "A 'readership' may

---

57. Acts 5:1–11; 15:1–2, 5.

58. Acts 7:54—8:1; 8:2–3; 9:23–25; 12:1–19; 13:8–12, 45, 50; 14:2, 5, 19; 16:19–24; 17:5–9, 13; 18:6, 12–17; 19:9, 23–40; 21:27—26:32.

59. Luke was, he implies, present at this speech.

60. Fitzmyer, *Acts*, 674.

61. Ibid., 675.

62. For example, "ravenous wolves" is used by Matthew, who describes the same people as "false prophets" (Matt 7:15; cf. Acts 13:6). Barrett gives references to similar imagery in Didache, Ignatius, 2 Clement, etc. (Barrett, *Critical and Exegetical Commentary*, 2:978).

63. "What is actually striking about Paul's address . . . is how generalized the language is" (Bauckham, "For Whom," 21n22).

64. Degenhardt, *Lukas Evangelist*; Schmithals, "Lukas—Evangelist der Armen"; Karris, "Lukan Sitz im Leben"; Stegemann and Schottroff, *Hope of the Poor*; Seccombe, *Possessions and the Poor*; Schmidt, *Hostility to Wealth*; Koenig, *New Testament Hospitality*; Kim, *Stewardship and Almsgiving*; and Garrett, "Beloved Physician."

65. Phillips, "Recent Issues," 237–51.

66. Ibid., 260.

67. Bauckham, "For Whom."

68. Cadbury, *Making of Luke-Acts*, 362.

be general, diverse in interests or background, and widely diffused."[69] We envisage Luke's intended readership as a much broader social/interpretive community, that is, the Greek-speaking world of his time, and such a readership would be familiar with the situation in the Greek part of the Roman Empire.[70] Luke intended to write history, and was successful and, therefore, we base our interpretation, as far as possible, on what has been called "palpable, actual first-century history."[71] "If it is true that Luke has engendered in the reader a belief . . . in the historical accuracy of his work,"[72] this is not only due to what has been called "his rhetorical superiority,"[73] but also to his story's grounding in first-century events as known by his intended readers;[74] any major errors (or lack of plausibility) in his narrative could have led to its rejection.

Nevertheless, many of Esler's insights can be adapted to the wider readership we envisage. For example, he argued that Luke's community was Christian,[75] included Jews, god-fearers who were not Jews,[76] and both rich and poor.[77] He bases these views in part on the inclusion of matter which would seem to be directed at specific elements of his posited community, such as knowledge of the teaching of Jesus and of the Septuagint,[78] and also his emphasis on higher status people and almsgiving.[79] We too see Luke's intended readers as including Christians, Jews, and god-fearers, rich and poor.[80]

Although we have rejected the idea of a community specifically addressed by Luke in these two volumes, we believe that Luke may have

---

69. Telford, *Theology of Mark*, 15.

70. Even if Luke wrote in Rome, as tradition has it, he wrote in Greek, and there was much communication between Rome and the East, so that, for example, "writing to Rome, a city he had not yet visited, Paul knew by name at least twenty-six people there" (Thompson, "Holy Internet," 64).

71. Penner, "Madness in the Method," 229.

72. Ibid., 246.

73. Ibid.

74. History for our purposes includes stories told by Josephus, the historical truth of which is not always accepted by modern scholars—see 2.2.1.

75. Esler, *Community and Gospel*, 25.

76. Ibid., 30–45.

77. Ibid., 183–87.

78. Ibid., 25, 45.

79. Ibid., 184–87.

80. In a similar way, Richard Bauckham rejects a proposed Johannine community but applies the insights derived from such a proposal to Christian communities generally who would have received the Johannine corpus (Bauckham, "For Whom," 22–24).

included some details in his narrative which would have been of importance to individuals or small groups whom he saw as part of his intended audience. In this Luke follows the example of his ante-text, Mark, who identified Simon of Cyrene as the father of Alexander and Rufus (Mark 15:21), although neither of these plays any part in his narrative and their identification does not seem to serve any narrative purpose. The prime examples in Luke-Acts are the dedications to Theophilus (Luke 1:1–4 and Acts 1:1), but our understanding of the historical background suggests that the mention of Lysanias of Abilene (Luke 3:1)[81] may have been of particular interest to some part of his intended audience. But, of course, individual characters in the narrative will have been of interest, not only to themselves, but also to their associates. If Luke wrote in the early 80s, many will still have been living.

1.3.1.2 *Background Knowledge*

The background knowledge presupposed by Luke-Acts is, as for any substantial text, very great. Various aspects have been summarized by Joel Green, and, although he used a different methodology (discourse analysis) his findings are relevant for our approach:

> Discourse analysis brings to the fore for investigation the social and linguistic webs within which speech occurs and derives its significance. These "webs" are of various kinds and can be outlined with reference to the relationship of a given text to its co-text, intertext, and context. *Co-text* refers to the string of linguistic data within which a text is set, the relationship of, say, a sentence to a paragraph or a pericope in Luke's Gospel to the larger Lukan narrative. *Intertext* refers to the location of a text within the larger linguistic frame of reference on which it consciously or unconsciously draws for meaning; for example, Luke's narrative builds especially on the Greek version of what we have come to call the OT (i.e., the LXX). *Context* refers to the sociohistorical realities within which the Lukan text, for example, is set.[82]

Co-text, *intertext*, and *context* are each part of the "socially constituted" way of reading which we seek to deploy. To these we add *antetext*, Luke's identified written sources which were not available to his intended readers

---

81. In Luke's time Abilene was part of the territory of Agrippa II. Abilene is discussed in 2.2.7.
82. Green, "Discourse Analysis," 226.

but which can help us to understand his intentions. In 1.3.2 we consider *context*, an understanding of the social background and of certain aspects of the history of the time. In 1.3.3 we turn to *intertext*, Luke's references to other texts (predominantly the Septuagint), and in 1.3.4 *co-text*, cross-references or allusions within his own two-volume work. These are part of the background that Luke shared with his readers, presupposed by his text. In 1.3.5 we describe our use of the *antetext*. These are our main tools, but we also, in 1.3.6, review what is known about the methods of transmission and reception of the original text. Finally, in 1.3.7 we outline certain modern approaches to the understanding of texts which should be set aside in developing our interpretation of Luke-Acts.

We, therefore, primarily use the tools of context, intertext, co-text, and antetext to understand how Luke's narrative was to be interpreted by his intended reader. The extent to which we use each of these tools varies from chapter to chapter, depending on the subject matter. Context is important for all chapters, as would be expected in seeking to interpret a text over 1900 years old. Intertext is of little importance in the chapters dealing with the house of Herod and the Roman authorities, who do not feature in the Septuagint, but of major importance in the chapters dealing with the Jewish authorities and with women. Co-text is important in all chapters, as is antetext, especially where Luke's material is derived from the Gospel of Mark.

1.3.2 Context: The Social and Economic Background

The social and economic background to the New Testament writings has been the subject of much scholarly analysis over the last twenty or thirty years. Of particular relevance to our study are the economic conditions in Palestine and the cities of the eastern empire (the settings of the Gospel and of Acts) and the social realities (honour/shame, patron/client, etc.) with which people lived their lives. The more important aspects of the economic and social situations of the groups we are to examine are set out in 1.5 but we shall refer to other elements in the appropriate chapters as they become relevant to our argument.

Luke and his first readers lived at the same time and in much the same part of the world, and they will have shared much of the same knowledge of the people and events relevant to Luke's story, part of the social background shared by the intended reader. Most of these people and events are the common currency of New Testament scholarship, but we believe that certain aspects of such knowledge, for example, deriving from recent scholarship or relating to the house of Herod, have been overlooked; the importance of that house in Luke's narrative is demonstrated by the number of references to members of it in both Gospel and Acts,[83] and we summarize its history in 2.2. The historical context of Luke's presentation of women has been generally misunderstood; in 6.1.1 we briefly describe the role of women in the first century CE and in 7.6 we set out evidence about the context of early Christian communities which demonstrates the historical plausibility of our interpretation.

1.3.3 Intertext: The Septuagint

1.3.3.1 Septuagintal References

> The phenomenon of intertextuality—the imbedding of fragments of an earlier text within a later one—has always played a major role in the cultural traditions that are heir to Israel's Scriptures: the voice of Scripture, regarded as authoritative in one way or another, continues to speak in and through later texts that both depend on and transform the earlier.[84]

Luke used the Septuagint[85] to "achieve his goal of presenting the Jesus-story and its sequel as a continuation of biblical history,"[86] using Septuagintal references to illuminate his text. It is useful to distinguish between various forms of reference, that is, quotations, allusions, and echoes:

> Previous studies on the Old Testament in the New have often divided references into quotations, allusions and echoes. There [are] no agreed definitions but generally, a quotation involves a self-conscious break from the author's style to introduce words from another context . . . Next comes allusion, usually woven into the text rather than "quoted," and often rather less precise in terms of wording . . . Lastly comes echo, faint traces of texts that are probably quite unconscious but emerge from minds soaked in the scriptural heritage of Israel.[87]

---

83. And also to the number of references to people who had served, or could have served, members of that house: Joanna (Luke 8:3), Manaen (Acts 13:1), and, we argue, Julius (Acts 27:1), and perhaps other soldiers (see 3.2.2).

84. Hays, *Echoes of Scripture*, 14.

85. The term "Septuagint" refers to the ancient Greek versions of the Hebrew bible, described in Dines, *Septuagint*, 1–3. There are many variant readings of the text, usually of little importance for our study.

86. Fitzmyer, *Acts*, 92.

87. Moyise, "Intertextuality and Study," 18–19.

A quotation makes it clear that reference to the specific text is intended, but there may be doubt as to whether Luke also intended to refer to the co-text in which the original passage occurred. However, Luke was clearly familiar with much of the Septuagint, his mind was, indeed, "soaked in the scriptural heritage of Israel," and we believe that the original co-text (especially the immediate co-text) will often illuminate Luke's intentions. For a reference or allusion this is more problematical, especially as allusions may be to a single word or phrase, or perhaps to a concept, but Luke often intended such references[88] and examination of the original co-text, if identifiable, can elucidate his meaning.[89] "If a subtext[90] is well known, the slightest of allusions is sometimes sufficient to evoke its presence."[91]

1.3.3.2 *Criteria for Interpretation*

However, "if . . . a reader begins with the supposition that there might well be a hidden pattern . . . the chances are that one will be found, whether intended or not."[92] Although this was said about modern fiction, it is also true of the search for Septuagintal references, and we need strict criteria to determine whether we should use such references to understand what Luke intended to convey, or whether they should be regarded as coincidental. Richard Hays, writing about the Pauline letters, suggests seven criteria, "rules of thumb," to decide whether "to treat a particular phrase as an echo and whether to credit my proposed reading of it."[93] These are:

1. Availability: "Was the proposed source of the echo available to the author and/or original readers?"

2. Volume: "The volume of an echo is determined primarily by the degree of explicit repetition of words or syntactical patterns, but other factors may also be relevant: how distinctive or prominent is the precursor

---

88. Some references may not have been specifically intended, but the overtones of the Septuagintal language Luke chose cannot be ignored.

89. "Luke's scriptural allusions frequently depend on the literary trope of *metalepsis*, a rhetorical and poetic device in which one text alludes to an earlier text in a way that evokes resonances of the earlier text beyond those explicitly cited" (Hays, "Liberation of Israel," 105).

90. By "subtext" Moyise appears to mean the predecessor text which can be identified by traces or echoes in the successor text.

91. Moyise, "Intertextuality and Study," 19.

92. Rabinowitz, *Before Reading*, 181.

93. Hays, *Echoes of Scripture*, 29.

text within Scripture, and how much rhetorical stress does the echo receive in Paul's discourse?"

3. Recurrence: "How often does Paul elsewhere cite or allude to the same scriptural passage?"

4. Thematic Coherence: "How well does the alleged echo fit into the line of argument that Paul is developing?"

5. Historical Plausibility: "Could Paul have intended the alleged meaning effect? Could his readers have understood it?"

6. History of Interpretation: "Have other readers, both critical and pre-critical, heard the same echoes?"

7. Satisfaction: "Does the proposed reading make sense? Does it illuminate the surrounding discourse? Does it produce for the reader a satisfying account of the effect of the intertextual relation?"[94]

Joel Green, commenting on Luke, a narrative not a letter, specifically uses the criteria of "availability" and "volume," but with slightly different definitions which seem more appropriate to narratives. By "availability" he means "the presence in the presupposition pool shared by Luke and his audience of the text(s) from which his narrative is alleged to have drawn" which does not seem to differ from Hays's meaning. He defines "volume" as:

> The presence within the Lukan narrative of any of a wide array of evidence that Luke's vision has been drawn to a particular OT figure and/or text . . . Evidence might take the form of linguistic similarities, common motifs, the actual naming of OT figures, parallel patterns, and the like.[95]

Green looks at the narrative as a whole, and his "volume" seems to incorporate Hays's "recurrence." It also differs from Hays's "volume" in explicitly taking account of a range of evidence, and does not mention "explicit repetition," the primary criterion used by Hays. We find that, as Green suggests, Luke uses "linguistic similarities, common motifs, the actual naming of OT figures, parallel patterns," etc.[96]

Hays describes his sixth criterion, "History of Interpretation," as "one of the least reliable guides."[97] The presence of such a history would be important evidence but we would not necessarily regard its absence as carrying great weight. Secular historians have made new discoveries and in

---

94. Ibid., 29–31.
95. Green, *Gospel of Luke*, 13–14.
96. We see such uses as exemplified in the description of Anna—see 6.3.
97. Hays, *Echoes of Scripture*, 31.

recent years there has been a substantial increase in scholarly interest both in Luke's presentation of women and in his use of the Septuagint, and such developments can be expected to lead to new insights. We see all the other criteria as important, but the seventh, "satisfaction," is crucial. To merit consideration the "echo," as Hays calls it, or "allusions" or "reverberations," terms used by Green, must illuminate Luke's text. Of Hays's other criteria, the first, "availability," can for much of the Septuagint be taken for granted,[98] and the third, "recurrence" can be regarded as a subset of the second, "volume"—does Luke show elsewhere in his narrative that he is familiar with the words, figures, or ideas in a particular Septuagint passage?

It is not always easy to demonstrate that Hays's fourth and fifth criteria, "thematic coherence" and "historical plausibility," are met. He applies thematic coherence in the context of Paul's letters, where it can be tested against Paul's arguments in the text. In the aspects of the Lukan narrative which we consider, it has to be assessed in a different way: does the reference supplement Luke's portrayal of the character in a way that is coherent when taken with the rest of the Lukan description of that character or the thrust of his narrative? There may be little more than a word or two about an individual character and it may be difficult to determine whether or not a reference is coherent, but in many instances such a character can be seen as a member of a larger character group, and can be compared to Luke's portrayal of other members of that group or contrasted with members of other groups. We consider characters using such comparisons and look for thematic coherence in that context. Our interpretation of Luke's presentation of women differs radically from traditional interpretations and we shall attempt to demonstrate both the thematic coherence and the historical plausibility of the interpretation we put forward.[99]

Volume, particularly in the introduction to the Gospel (chapters 1–4), may include linked references.[100] Fearghus Ó Fearghail has identified a number of these:

> Luke uses an eclectic method of composition. In the case of Elizabeth, for example, elements are used from various Old Testament stories of barren women who conceive through divine intervention—Sarah (1:7, 18, 25a, 58), Rachel (1:25b),

---

98. We endeavor, in footnotes, to support the availability of those books of the Septuagint less commonly used by Luke. There may be doubt about whether Luke knew 4 Maccabees, referred to in 6.3.9.

99. See 7.6 and 7.7.

100. Details of many Septuagintal references in Luke 1 are given in Litwak, *Echoes of Scripture*, 66–115. Our understanding of Luke's description of Anna (see 6.3) is based on such linked references.

Rebecca (1:41, 44, 57) and Hannah (1:5–7, 24). Added to these are elements from the stories of Deborah (Lk 1:42), Araunah (1:43) and Noah (1:6). For Zachary elements from the stories of Noah (1:6), Abraham (1:7, 18), Elkana (1:23–24) and Daniel (1:9–13, 19–20, 64–65) are found . . . In the case of John one can identify elements from the stories of Isaac (1:13–17), Ishmael (1:13, 80a), Naaman (1:15), Elijah (1:17), Elisha (1:17) and Samson (1:15); in that of Jesus, elements associated with Isaac (1:37), Ishmael (1:31–33; 2:40a), Samuel (2:22b, 40b, 52) and David (1:27, 32–33; 2:4, 8, 11); in that of Mary, elements associated with Sarah (1:37), Abigail (1:38a), Laban (1:38b), Gideon (1:26–38), Jael (1:42), Hannah (1:30, 47–55; 2:48), David and Daniel (2:19, 51b).[101]

To sum up, we see four criteria as necessary to confirm the acceptability of a proposed Septuagintal reference in Luke-Acts:

1. Volume: Is there evidence[102] that Luke's vision has been drawn to a particular Septuagint motif or text?

2. Coherence: Does the alleged allusion fit well with Luke's presentation of the character or the thrust of his narrative?

3. Plausibility: Could Luke have meant and his intended readers accepted the alleged allusion?

4. Satisfaction: Does the proposed reading make sense?

Such Septuagintal references are of great importance to Luke and to the intended reader:

> The implied readers knew the LXX and the concepts it presents, and not simply the wording of the text of the various books. That is, they had insight into the texts . . . [They] also accepted the Scriptures of Israel as authoritative theologically.[103]

1.3.4 Co-Text

We also consider co-text, sometimes called intra-textuality, including the literary techniques used by our author. As in most literary narratives, the

---

101. Ó Fearghail, "Imitation of the Septuagint," 72.

102. "Of linguistic similarities, common motifs, the actual naming of OT figures, parallel patterns, and the like" (Green, *Gospel of Luke*, 14, cited above).

103. Litwak, *Echoes of Scripture*, 60.

beginning and ending of the two volumes merit close consideration. The beginning sets the scene and identifies matters of importance, while:

> There is . . . a widely applicable interpretive convention that permits us to read [the ending of a text] in a special way, as a *conclusion*, as a summing up of the work's meaning.[104]

The beginning includes not only the infancy narratives, but the words of Jesus in Nazareth at the start of his ministry. Alexander (cited below) sees the conclusion of Acts (the narrative epilogue) as comprising chapters 27 and 28, which also form the conclusion of the two-volume work.[105] However, we are considering two separate, albeit related, works, and therefore the ending of the Gospel and the beginning of Acts are also especially important. We also so regard the ministry of Jesus, from its beginning (in the synagogue at Nazareth) to its ending (at the Last Supper). We make frequent reference to both, especially the words of Jesus about service (Luke 22:24–27).

Luke uses a number of literary techniques, but the most important for our purpose are intra-textuality, repetition, analepsis, and prolepsis. *Intra-textuality* refers to the use in one part of the narrative of references, echoes, of other parts of the narrative. Luke's echoes can be verbal, that is, the recurrence of a particular word, or conceptual. Intra-textuality does not only refer to readings within a single volume of Luke's work—he also cross-refers between the two volumes, and to fully understand some of these references requires repeated readings:

> There is also a tendency to hold over certain narrative details from the gospel to Acts[106] which suggests that Luke already had Acts in view when he was writing the gospel . . . In particular, major themes introduced in the narrative prologue to the gospel (Lk chs. 1–4) reappear in clearer definition in the narrative epilogue to Acts (Acts 27–8). For a reader who did not know the story in advance, it would not be possible to predict the ending of Acts from the beginning of the gospel. Readers who make it to the end of Acts, however, will be sent back to reread the beginning of the gospel with new eyes, and will have

---

104. Rabinowitz, *Before Reading*, 160.

105. She also sees the narrative prologue as comprising Luke 1–4—see the citation in the next paragraph.

106. That is, details in Mark omitted from the parallel passage in the Gospel may be included in a different context, perhaps in Acts.

a new appreciation of the prophetic significance of the Nazareth episode . . . and of Simeon's "light to the Gentiles."[107]

These references are not seen only in the prologue and epilogue, as Tannehill points out:

> My concern with Luke-Acts as a unified narrative leads me to note many internal connections among different parts of the narrative. Themes will be developed, dropped, then presented again. Characters and actions may echo characters and actions in another part of the story, as well as characters and actions of the scriptural story which preceded Luke-Acts.[108]

Repetition is used by Luke as a plot device in two main ways, the first being a series of similar, but different, scenes, such as the banquets to which Jesus is invited. These "type-scenes" are important both for their similarities and their differences—both are emphasized by the technique.[109] Rather similar is the use of a word or a concept several times in the course of a passage, which always adds emphasis.[110] Most significant is the repeated description of a single event which always occurs in matters important to the story Luke tells. Well-known examples are the stories of Paul's conversion and the vision of Cornelius, told three and four times respectively,[111] and in both cases the first telling of the story is when the incident occurs in the time-frame of the narrative, and the subsequent tellings are retrospective. In addition to specific repetition, there may be reference or allusion back to a previously encountered repetition, adding further emphasis.[112]

Such a repeated account of an event is similar to *analepsis* in that the later telling occurs after the event, but the term analepsis is better restricted to a single description of an event at a time in the narrative subsequent to its occurrence. An example of this in the Gospel is where Herod said: "John I beheaded" (Luke 9:9). The event had taken place earlier, but we only hear of it when the narrator wants us to know of it, perhaps because, as in this instance, it explains a point in the later narrative.[113] Both analepsis and varia-

---

107. Alexander, "Acts," 1029.

108. Tannehill, *Narrative Unity*, 1:3.

109. See, e.g., the successive challenges by the Pharisees (4.5.2).

110. See the repeated references to god-fearers at Pisidian Antioch (5.2.2) or the four heavenly interventions in the story of Lydia (6.1.5.1).

111. Paul, Acts 9:1–19; 22:6–16; 26:12–18; Cornelius, Acts 10:1–6, 22, 30–32; 11:13–14.

112. E.g., the instruction of the risen Jesus to the disciples (see 6.1.2.3) and Mary's acceptance of the word of God (see 6.4.3).

113. This example is discussed in 2.4.2.

tions in a reiterated description of events ensure that we obtain information at a later point in the narrative which can change our understanding of the original incident. We believe that Luke intended his narrative to be read and re-read, so that later readings could be informed by information obtained during previous readings.

Luke also on occasion tells us about an event before it occurs—*prolepsis*. One example of this is when Judas is identified as "Judas Iscariot, who became a traitor" (Luke 6:16).[114] The purpose is to ensure that the reader is aware of the subsequent event during his first reading of the narrative, in this instance, perhaps to ensure that the reader regards the apostles and disciples with a somewhat skeptical eye. Prolepsis is also seen, in a slightly different form, when Jesus, or a prophet, tells what is going to happen. The prophecy is fully understood only when the narrative shows how (or if) it is fulfilled. Such prophecies not only help to build or maintain narrative tension, but also stress themes of particular importance.

1.3.5 The Antetext: Luke's Written Sources

We do not believe that Luke's intended readers were familiar with his identified written sources, Mark's Gospel and Q. Although he frequently amends Mark, he does so without emphasis. Richard Bauckham[115] has argued that the writer of the Gospel of John expected his readers to know Mark, whose narrative is expanded and explained in the text of John. We see no evidence of a similar intention in Luke, and indeed, the usually accepted dates for Mark and Luke[116] give little time for Mark to find a wide readership before Luke wrote his Gospel. So Luke's sources are not part of the *intertext*, shared with his readers, but rather an *antetext*. Luke drew upon Mark: if his narrative differs from that of his Markan source, it is because he changed it and we can often deduce that Luke intended to convey something which differed from that which Mark conveyed,[117] so these changes help us to understand Luke.[118] They are in some instances purely syntactical or verbal, reworking or omitting an individual pericope, but he sometimes alters the order of the Markan narrative. Both kinds of change may be important for understanding Luke's purpose. More often, Luke incorporates Markan passages without

---

114. We see such prolepsis in the story of Lydia (see 6.1.5.2).
115. Bauckham, "John for Readers of Mark," 147–71.
116. Mark, after 70; Luke, 80s.
117. Luke sometimes changes Mark to a more polished Greek.
118. We see this in the way that Luke changed Mark in his description of the Pharisees—see 4.5.

significant change. This may be because he intended to convey what Mark conveyed, but we must allow for the possibility of inertia or fatigue. In interpreting Luke's intentions, a passage taken directly from Mark may carry slightly less weight than an amended passage.

Luke also used Q, but as this is not extant it is less useful as a guide to Luke's intentions, especially as the general view of scholarly opinion is that Luke made fewer changes to Q than did Matthew. As a result, differences between Luke and Matthew do not often allow us to deduce that Luke has altered Q, so it is rarely possible to use such differences as a definitive aid to interpreting the text. However, in some instances our argument suggests that Luke may have altered his antetext, whether it was Q or Matthew—we show such possible changes as footnotes.

Luke's attitude towards his predecessors has been examined by Mikeal Parsons from a rhetorical perspective. Luke describes how: "Many have undertaken, *epecheirēsan*, to set down an orderly account of the events that have been fulfilled among us" (Luke 1:1). Parsons notes that elsewhere[119] Luke uses *epecheireō* of undertakings that failed and argues that Luke's intention to write "an orderly account" (1:3) "seems to imply some criticism of previous attempts."[120] He notes a number of rhetorical failings in Luke's predecessors, and our own examination suggests that Luke had little hesitation in amending his antetext when he thought it necessary.

1.3.6 Transmission of the Text

At the time that Luke-Acts was written, the most common method of ensuring the circulation of a literary text was for the author to make it available for copying,[121] so that further copies could then be made. Bauckham has described the way in which the early churches communicated and transmitted texts,[122] and although much of his evidence is from a generation or two later than Luke, the descriptions of travel in Acts, and in the letters of Paul some twenty to thirty years earlier, suggest that the methods of transmission he describes would have been available to Luke. If so, the text could soon have been frequently copied[123] and made available relatively widely.[124]

---

119. Acts 9:29; 19:13.
120. Parsons, *Story Teller*, 47.
121. Alexander, "Ancient Book Production," 88–89.
122. Bauckham, "For Whom," especially 38–41.
123. The many textual variations including those in what is known as the Western text (discussed 7.6.6) support this view.
124. Bauckham points out that the early missionaries traveled widely ("For Whom,"

"The primary means of publication in Greco-Roman antiquity was *oral performance*,"[125] and "the general—indeed, from all evidence, the exclusive—practice was to read aloud."[126] We can assume that Luke's volumes were read (and intended to be read) aloud and very often to a group of people, which is, of course, the only way that his text could have reached the illiterate.[127] In such circumstances, the oral clarification of readings from scripture (for Greek-speakers, the Septuagint) was common (e.g., Luke 4:21). We believe that Luke expected his works to be read aloud, discussed, and explained, including the identification and exposition of important intertextual references (or other material) perhaps not familiar to the auditors. He, therefore, was able to avoid lengthy explanations or elaboration and write on the basis that his intended audience shared much of his own knowledge, both of the Septuagint and of historical events which illuminate his text. For example, Luke assumes that his readers understand his method of dating using temporal references to political figures (Luke 1:5; 2:1-2; 3:1-2), and apart from this rarely provides other explanatory information.[128] His intended reader did not need it.

In Lukan times texts were not punctuated, indeed, there were no gaps to indicate word endings, and runovers (changes from line to line in the middle of a word) were common and were not signaled. Abbreviations were also used. Sight reading must have been difficult, and the public reading of a text required careful preparation. Jesus in the synagogue at Nazareth was able to find the place in the scroll of Isaiah and read (Luke 4:17), but this shows that he was familiar with Isaiah, as, in a similar situation (Acts 8:30-35), was Philip.[129]

33-44) and argues that the Gospel writers would also have traveled (36). Luke, of course, claims to have done so.

125. Alexander, "Ancient Book Production," 86.

126. Achtemeier, "Omne Verbum Sonat." For further discussion of reading aloud, in the context of Mark's Gospel, see Telford, *Theology of Mark*, 15-16.

127. See Burridge, "About People," 142.

128. He provides brief geographical information for some towns: Capernaum (Luke 4:31), the country of the Gerasenes (Luke 8:26), Arimathea (Luke 23:51), Emmaus (Luke 24:13), Lydda (Acts 9:38), Philippi (Acts 16:12), and Phoenix (Acts 27:12). Except for Philippi, itself not large but important to Luke personally (see 1.1.2), these were all very small places which Luke could reasonably have thought needed further information.

129. That in each case the text was Isaiah indicates its enduring importance—see Sawyer, *Fifth Gospel*.

1.3.7 Modern Methods of Interpretation

1.3.7.1 Reading Female Characters

As well as taking account of the socio-political situation and the literary background of Luke and his intended readers, we should also attempt to set aside modern approaches to the interpretation of literary narratives which would not have been shared by Luke and those readers. One of these is the understanding of the role of women. Rabinowitz, addressing nineteenth- and twentieth-century British and American novels, describes what he calls the rule of the "dominant negative": readers "should give priority to the most negative qualities [of female characters]."[130] We see something similar in modern interpretations of Luke-Acts, perhaps most evident in the common understanding that the woman who was a sinner (Luke 7:37) was a prostitute,[131] and the, now somewhat rarer, tendency to identify that woman with Mary Magdalene:

> It is curious how much attention commentators give to speculation about Mary Magdalene's illness or supposed sinfulness. By contrast, they never expostulate about the nature of Peter's sinfulness, even though Luke clearly stresses this in his call story (5:8).[132]

Similarly, some scholars still read generic masculine plurals (e.g., *adelphoi*,[133] *mathētai*) as referring solely to males. A more pervasive "dominant negative," of importance for our thesis, is to see women as passive: we shall attempt to demonstrate that in Luke-Acts the opposite is usually true.[134] This tendency in interpretation may be in part because modern readers "have a well-developed arsenal of techniques for drawing out symbolism latent in male experiences and the objects of male interest"[135] but lack this for women. We should not assume that this was the case for Luke and his intended readers, among whom were women. Indeed, in the absence of contrary evidence, we may assume that they made up about half of his intended audience,[136] and were also among those whom Luke expected

---

130. Rabinowitz, *Before Reading*, 206.
131. See 7.4.3.
132. Reid, *Choosing*, 134.
133. For *adelphoi*, see 6.2.4.
134. See chapters 6 and 7.
135. Rabinowitz, *Before Reading*, 222.
136. For women in the early church, see 7.6.

to read his text, and, where necessary, explain it.[137] His omission of female characters from much of his narrative may seem surprising, but in this Luke resembles his antetext, Mark, who, until the very end of his Gospel (Mark 15:40), makes no mention of the women who follow Jesus in Galilee and on to Jerusalem. Moreover, as noted above, Luke was a historian and:

> Tal Ilan concludes that, "in the minds of the ancient historians [such as Josephus and Nicolaus of Damascus],[138] real history was enacted in the male realm, while women were confined to the field of fiction."[139]

Ilan refers to Jewish historians, but Luke was also a Jewish historian, at least in his theological approach. However, Luke's secular near contemporaries also rarely treated of women in their histories. "The recorded history of women, as opposed to the imagined history of women, is a history of exceptionalism."[140] But, insofar as they did so, nearly all the women were held up for public obloquy.[141]

> When women are represented in Roman[142] sources as taking a public role, this tends to be accompanied by allusions to female spite, treachery, or lack of self-control. References to women's political action are intended to discredit the men associated with them.[143]

1.3.7.2 Modern Standards of Behavior

Another approach to be set aside is judging a character using modern standards of appropriate behavior. This is especially important in understanding the Roman governors and administrators described in chapter 3. The Romans (and Greeks) did not believe in equal justice for all before the law,[144] and the way they saw the role of the state in maintaining civic order would

---

137. Like, for example, Priscilla (Acts 18:26).
138. Kraemer's gloss. Josephus was a contemporary of Luke. Nicolaus was born ca. 64 BCE and lived to assist Archelaus in obtaining his inheritance from Augustus—see Meister, "Nicolaus of Damascus."
139. Kraemer, "Jewish Women," 52.
140. Mantel, "War against Women," 4.
141. In the Gospels one might point to Herodias and Salome.
142. Greek sources differ little.
143. King, "Women," 1624.
144. See 3.4.4.

not be acceptable by modern western standards.[145] Luke, whose views would have been influenced by the Septuagint, believed in equal justice, but knew that Roman magistrates did not. He, and his intended readers, would have known, even if they did not share, this view of the role of the emperor and the state. In describing the Roman governors he shows where they do, and do not, act in accordance with their own ethos, while also ensuring we understand the narrator's judgments of their actions.[146]

We should also be aware of Luke's style:

> Luke offers no continuously advancing course of action. Instead he portrays the events as a sequence of individual episodes that normally lack any or have only minimal connection to the context . . . Almost never does the action of one episode affect another event . . . The episodes of Acts were written above all as dramatic scenes, as living, vivid illustrations, concise and purposefully put together.[147]

In this instance the modern reader, accustomed to similar treatment in on-screen drama, may find it easier to understand Luke. The action is shown in discrete episodes, but one episode does illuminate another.

1.3.7.3 Second-Century Lenses

Moreover, we should not try to interpret Luke's writings using second century lenses. We argue in 7.6 that around the end of the first century there was a wide-spread attempt to promote a patriarchal culture in the church. Christianity was also changing in other ways at about this time, including a degree of separation from its Jewish roots, perhaps responding to the anti-Judaism promoted by Vespasian and his successors.[148] Later (second century) changes were in response to the development of gnostic and ascetic ideologies, and a number of scholars have attempted to place Luke-Acts in this period,[149] often identifying such ideologies as aids to understanding. As the Lukan narrator was present at events in the mid-50s we do not find this plausible.

---

145. Under the Principate "day-to-day law enforcement . . . remained the responsibility of private citizens acting on their own behalf" (Cornell, "Police," 1205).

146. See 3.4.

147. Plümacher, "Luke," 400.

148. Described Goodman, *Rome and Jerusalem*.

149. E.g., Pervo, *Acts*, 5.

1.4 THE NARRATOR'S STANDPOINT

For the most part we are concerned not with the main themes of the Lukan narrative, but rather with the authorial standpoint or point of view regarding the individuals who featured in his narrative, each of whom can be regarded as a member of one of the various socio-economic groups. In Luke's work there is little evidence of a distinction between the authorial and the narrator's point of view, and we shall seek to determine that of the narrator. This is reliable, that is, the intended reader can and should accept and share that viewpoint. It is aligned with the standpoint of Jesus, of the Baptist and the Septuagintal prophets, of those filled with the Holy Spirit, so that statements by the Lukan Jesus, or those filled with the Holy Spirit, can help us to understand the narrator's point of view. To put it another way, the Lukan narrator attempts to align his views with those of the Lukan Jesus, which, of course, the narrator had depicted.

However, whereas Jesus, the Baptist, and angelic messengers are always reliable, other prophets in Luke's narrative and those said to be inspired by the Holy Spirit can be seen as inspired only when that inspiration is made explicit, and we cannot assume that, after once receiving the Holy Spirit, a person is thereafter always reliable. For example, Barnabas and Saul were sent out together by the Holy Spirit (Acts 13:2–4). Was their subsequent separation (Acts 15:39) similarly inspired? It seems probable that it was not. An even clearer example is Simon Magus, whose simony followed immediately after he received the Spirit (Acts 8:17–19). So we may only rely on prophets or figures inspired by the Holy Spirit when, without contradiction, we are told of their inspiration at the time. We should also be aware that individuals, even when inspired, may misunderstand the message they have received, or may be misunderstood by their auditors.[150]

Characters who are not identified as reliable may, nevertheless, give information which is correct. The devil told Jesus that authority over all the kingdoms of the world had been given to him (Luke 4:6). He was not a dependably reliable source of information, but this may, nevertheless, be a true statement as Jesus, to whom it was made, did not contradict it, and, indeed, the purpose of the devil was to tempt Jesus, not to deceive him. Such statements by unreliable characters must be considered with special care—this important statement by the devil is considered further in 2.4.1.

Our thesis examines the portrayal of characters in the narrative. Luke tells us about character either by specific description, or, more often, by showing us the character in action. Luke's contemporary, the Latin writer

---

150. See 6.1.4.4.

Tacitus, said that: "It seems to me a historian's foremost duty to ensure that merit is recorded, and to confront evil deeds and words with the fear of posterity's denunciations."[151] Indeed, such "was also the trend of ancient historiography as a whole, with its epic, tragic and moralising background."[152] One of our findings is that Luke took a similar view, amending his sources so as to clarify the responsibility for evil deeds, as for example, in the alterations to material about the Pharisees in his antetext, Mark,[153] making it clear that they did not share responsibility for the death of Jesus.

We examine the characters in whom we are interested in the light of their words or actions, and also take into account any descriptions of them by the narrator or other characters, especially where those other characters are themselves reliable. On that basis we assess the point of view of the narrator towards them. For the relatively peripheral characters considered in this survey,[154] there is one overwhelmingly important indicator of the narrator's point of view, that is, whether they hear and accept Jesus or the apostles, who, of course, are the messengers of Jesus.[155] For the characters at the beginning of the narrative Luke provides an equivalent criterion by describing the characters by words such as "righteous" or showing them acting when inspired by the Holy Spirit.

However, there are some other important distinctions, particularly evident in the description of the Roman governors.[156] Only Sergius Paulus believed, but Luke shows Festus in a much better light than Pilate, Felix, or Gallio, in that he apparently seeks to serve the emperor, while Pilate and Felix manifestly do not. Characters like Festus, some municipal authorities and the Pharisees, are mistaken, but seek to carry out what they see as their duty. They are distinguished from self-serving characters like Pilate, Felix and the chief priests in Jerusalem.

---

151. Tacitus, *Annals* 3.65.

152. Grant, "Translator's Introduction," xxvi.

153. See 4.5. He also seems to clarify material which he found confusing.

154. We deal to some extent with Mary, the mother of Jesus, who is not peripheral, but our examination is limited.

155. "To an extraordinary degree, intermediate agents in Luke-Acts are assessed on the basis of their interaction with the protagonists, especially Jesus" (Darr, *Character Building*, 41).

156. See 3.4.

1.5 RICH AND POOR, HIGH AND LOW STATUS

1.5.1 Introduction

In this section we consider the general social and, particularly, economic situation of people in the Roman Empire of the first century, especially in the Greek eastern provinces, including a brief description of some of the cities which feature in the narrative, an important aspect of the social and economic background against which Luke wrote. Further contextual information is given in the appropriate chapters: that about the ruling elites of Herodians and Roman governors and about the local elite in Jerusalem is given in chapters 2 through 4 and the particular circumstances of other Lukan local elites and the non-elite are considered further in chapter 5. The role of women in general in the first century is discussed in 6.1.1 and that of women in the early churches in 7.6.

1.5.2 Senators and Equestrians

Luke and his intended readers lived in a Greco-Roman society that was rigidly stratified both formally and in practice. In seeking to understand how Luke and his readers viewed the status of the individuals and groups in his narrative, we use categories which would have been familiar to them.[157] In the Roman Empire of the first century there was a codified system of status:

> The "orders" (*ordines*) or "estates" of imperial Roman society ... were clear-cut, legally established categories. The two most important and enduring ones were the senators and the knights ... In addition, the families whose members had served or were eligible to serve in the councils or senates of the provincial cities constituted a local order in those places ... These three top *ordines* comprised considerably less than 1 percent[158] of the population.[159]

---

157. Most modern scholars (including those discussed below) considering the social and, especially, economic status of his characters use modern categories. This is a literary study and it is appropriate to use categories which would have been recognized by Luke and his intended readers.

158. Other scholars differ slightly on the percentage. For example, Steven Friesen calculates 1.23%, including wives and children. He gives details of his calculations (Friesen, "Poverty in Pauline Studies," 340).

159. Meeks, "Social Level of Pauline Christianity," 200–201.

The highest ranking order was the senatorial. At any one time there were some 600 senators,[160] but senators would have had families, although it appears that some who were "qualified by birth and wealth for senatorial careers . . . refused the honour."[161] The members of the order, with their families, perhaps numbered 2,000 to 3,000 in an empire of 50–60 million. Senators were subject to a strict minimum property qualification of one million sesterces, that is, 250,000 denarii,[162] although many senators were much richer. "The younger Pliny . . . did not consider himself rich, but is estimated to have been worth over 20,000,000 [sesterces]."[163] Income from land was conventionally reckoned at 6%,[164] so that a senator with the minimum qualification might have had an annual income (unearned) of some 15,000 denarii. This is substantial if we compare it to the income of a laborer, one denarius a day, some 200–300 a year, or the income of an ordinary legionary, 225 denarii a year, but it was no more than the annual salary of a senior centurion,[165] also 15,000 denarii.[166] A senator with this minimum qualification would not have felt rich. Indeed, there is evidence that 8 million sesterces was seen as the "appropriate capital for a senator,"[167] providing an annual income of some 120,000 denarii.

Before the accession of Vespasian in 69 very few senators came from the east, and "the reigns of Domitian and Trajan have been seen as the real turning point for easterners."[168] One early senator from the east was Sergius Paulus (Acts 13:7) of Pisidian Antioch. By the reign of Domitian he had been succeeded (or joined) by his son and by another prominent senator from the same city, Caristanius Fronto. The implications of this are discussed in 1.6.

The second order was the equestrian (knights), which required a minimum property qualification of 400,000 sesterces. There were many more

---

160. Hopkins, "Elite Mobility," 103; Jones, *Domitian and the Senatorial Order*, 2n9.

161. Hopkins and Burton, "Ambition and Withdrawal," 167.

162. A denarius was equivalent to one Greek drachma or four sesterces.

163. Wells, "Roman Empire," 805. For a list of private fortunes attested in ancient sources see Duncan-Jones, *Economy of the Roman Empire*, 343–44. Ten such attested first century fortunes were 200 million sesterces or more.

164. Duncan-Jones, *Economy of the Roman Empire*, 33 and n2, providing references to primary sources. Also Finley, *Ancient Economy*, 104. The interest rate on loans relating to land was also 6% (Duncan-Jones, *Economy of the Roman Empire*, 133).

165. *Primus pilus*, see 3.2.2.

166. MacMullen, *Roman Social Relations*, 94.

167. Duncan-Jones, *Economy of the Roman Empire*, 18.

168. Levick, "Senators, Patterns of Recruitment," 1388.

equestrians than senators; Strabo[169] found that in a late Augustan census there were five hundred men of equestrian standing at Gades (Cadiz) and the same number at Patavium (Padua),[170] in Cis-Alpine Gaul. The equestrian class in Rome from the late second century BCE "came to be defined *de facto* to include all non-senators with a minimum property of 400,000 sesterces."[171] Fergus Millar sees this definition as later extending to the whole of the empire: "The wider class of *equites* from whom imperial officials and new entrants to the senate were recruited was formed by men of free birth and the necessary census."[172] They also had to be Roman citizens,[173] which restricted eligibility in the east. Although in Italy, Spain and North Africa the elites of most cities were Latin speaking and citizenship was widespread among the wealthy, as, for example, in Gades and Patavium, this was much less the case in Greek speaking areas.[174]

The minimum property qualification of an equestrian would have provided an income of 6,000 denarii a year, less than the annual salary of the top ten centurions in a legion (7,500 denarii).[175] Equestrians with the minimum qualification would not have seen themselves as rich, and both senators and equestrians were usually ambitious to obtain remunerative positions outside Rome:

> Aristocrats had to maintain their status by competitive ostentation without recompense from public office . . . In order to make large fortunes, or even in some cases in order to support their extravagance, ambitious senators had to go away from the capital to govern provinces, and make money there.[176]

1.5.3 Local Elites in the Eastern Empire

The provincial cities of the eastern empire which feature in Acts were very diverse in character, but most were ruled by local elites with shared characteristics—Jerusalem is a special case, discussed in chapter 4. The way of life

169. Cited Sherwin-White, *Roman Citizenship*, 343n3.
170. About 1% of the inhabitants of Padua (MacMullen, *Roman Social Relations*, 89).
171. Finley, *Ancient Economy*, 46.
172. Millar, Emperor in the Roman World, 283–84.
173. Ibid., 280.
174. See 1.5.3.
175. MacMullen, *Roman Social Relations*, 94.
176. Hopkins and Burton, "Ambition and Withdrawal," 175.

of the elites of these cities is illuminated by the writings of Dio Chrysostom, a contemporary of Luke[177] from the city of Prusa (Bursa) in Bithynia, "a typical middle-sized city of the early empire."[178] His writings deal with the affairs of a number of cities including Athens, Tarsus, and Rome.

Chrysostom's "mother and her father were Roman citizens," as was his own father, having perhaps received their citizenship through their links with the Roman colony of Apamea.[179] For those with sufficient wealth, if Millar is correct, this will have included equestrian status. This may not have been regarded as important unless an equestrian career was intended, but there is evidence of such careers for men from the east, based on the army,[180] although such cases may have been exceptional in our period.

The ruling elites of these cities, members of the ruling council, also had to meet a minimum property qualification which varied from place to place, although many would have been much richer.[181] In Dio's Prusa the minimum qualification for the council was 100,000 sesterces,[182] which would produce an annual income of some 1500 denarii.[183] However, in the larger and more prosperous city of Tarsus, the entrance fee for membership of the second echelon of municipal government, the assembly, was 500 denarii.[184] That is, this one-off payment was equivalent to four months' income for a member (with the minimum holding) of the highest echelon at Prusa.

Cities differed in many respects, but in all there were substantial expenses associated with being a member of the council. *Liturgies* (the

---

177. First extant work, 68 or later, died 110 or later (Jones, *Roman World*, 133, 140).

178. Ibid., 5.

179. Ibid., 7.

180. Millar cites two Greek legionary tribunes, from Cos and Ephesus, under Claudius (Millar, *Emperor in the Roman World*, 86). Further, we discuss Caristanius Fronto in 1.6.2 and Tiberius Julius Alexander in 2.2.8, and Luke describes Claudius Lysias (Acts 22:24—23:30), all of whom had held military positions requiring equestrian status.

181. An Athenian magnate of the first century was said to have a fortune of 100 million sesterces (Duncan-Jones, *Economy of the Roman Empire*, 344).

182. Referring to a decurion (a member of a local elite) with 25,000 denarii, the amount we have cited for Prusa, Esler comments that: "The immensity of these amounts can be seen by comparison with the daily wage earned by labourers—one *denarius*" (Esler, *Community and Gospel*, 171). The "immensity" depends on the point of view—the decurions (who would have scorned comparison with a laborer) would not have seen the resultant annual income, 1,500 denarii, perhaps some five times that of a laborer, as "immense."

183. In comparing such an income with the Roman equivalent we should note that prices in the provinces were much lower than in Rome (Duncan-Jones, *Economy of the Roman Empire*, 345).

184. Members of this tier were not regarded as being of the elite.

provision of buildings, games or other benefits for the city) were expected, and those sent as ambassadors to the emperor or to other cities frequently had to pay their own expenses. The high cost of office-holding later became a major problem, with those eligible refusing office, but: "There are . . . no firm indications of a malaise in municipal government in the last quarter of the first century,"[185] although Dio Chrysostom himself tried to avoid election and the consequent expense.[186] Nevertheless, within our period the local elites met their obligations, and:

> Continuity within the ruling class . . . becomes far more the rule than the exception as one moves eastward . . . The monopolizing of leadership by a narrow circle, generation after generation, is cause for no surprise. Given the high cost of office-holding . . . we should expect nothing else.[187]

1.5.4 The Non-Elite

1.5.4.1 Introduction

The remainder of the population included slaves and freed men and women, and also the majority of the population, those born free—we include all of these groups under the term "the non-elite."[188] Although the view of some scholars is that "those devoid of political power, the non-élite, over 99% of the Empire's population, could expect little more from life than abject poverty,"[189] this seems to somewhat overstate the case.[190] Other scholars see the proportion in such poverty as much lower:

> In fourteenth- and fifteenth-century Europe . . . one person in three lived in habitual want, that is, he devoted the vast bulk of each day's earnings to his immediate needs and accumulated no property or possessions to speak of. I would be surprised if the indigent of the Roman empire constituted much smaller a part of the total population.[191]

---

185. Garnsey, *Cities, Peasants and Food*, 6.
186. Jones, *Roman World*, 22–24.
187. MacMullen, *Roman Social Relations*, 101.
188. A term used by Justin Meggitt, *Paul, Poverty and Survival*, 50.
189. Ibid.
190. The economic position of the Pauline communities, seen as predominantly non-elite, is discussed further in 5.1.
191. MacMullen, *Roman Social Relations*, 93.

This figure, say 33%, does not include slaves: "In Italy . . . possibly a quarter of the whole . . . In the provinces . . . closer to a tenth."[192] These together approach 50–60% which would make the (slightly) more prosperous rather more than 40%. Friesen, in a more sophisticated but perhaps no more soundly based analysis,[193] has calculated that some 7% of the population had a moderate surplus and some 22% lived above subsistence level in a stable way. He sees some 40% at subsistence level and 28% below.[194] Moses Finley has estimated that: "The slave-owning section of the population in antiquity was proportionately greater than the estimated twenty-five per cent in the southern states [of the United States]."[195] Setting aside the elites, all of whom were slave-owners but who were few in number, this would perhaps make other slave-owners rather more than 25%, close to the 29% calculated as above subsistence level by Friesen. If those above subsistence level were about 29–40%, the majority owned slaves.

Although none of the above percentages can be relied upon, there is a near consensus that below the ruling elites there was a substantial number of people living above subsistence level, who did not have to devote all of their earnings to meeting their immediate needs (see the following subsections). There was a further substantial number, probably greater even excluding slaves, living at or below subsistence level.[196] We describe such people in terms familiar to Luke and his audience; those above subsistence as *penētes*, and those at or below subsistence as *ptōchoi*.[197] Using these terms avoids the error, castigated by Meggitt,[198] of seeing some of these people as constituting a middle class.

1.5.4.2 Prosperous Peasants and Merchants

There were landowners who were not of the elite, and there were tradespeople and artisans who made a reasonable living, some of whom have left traces in the literature: for example, the assembly-members who had the

---

192. Ibid., 92. It is not clear whether these figures include those in bondage for debt, which could be a temporary condition. Cf. Matt 18:23–35.

193. Primarily based on medieval Florence. Such a comparison is of doubtful value—the differences between these societies, including slavery and the massive bureaucracy comprising the Roman army and administration, were very great.

194. Friesen, "Poverty in Pauline Studies," 347.

195. Finley, *Ancient Economy*, 79.

196. See 1.5.4.4.

197. These terms are used in a similar way by Stegemann and Stegemann, *Jesus Movement*, 88–95, and *ptōchoi* by Finley, *Ancient Economy*, 73.

198. Meggitt, *Paul, Poverty and Survival*, 7.

property qualification or could pay the fee;[199] the ship-owners of Ephesus and Nicomedia;[200] the Egyptian village elders who were required to have a minimum annual unearned income of from 200 to 800 *drachmai*;[201] the richer peasants in Syria, with larger houses.[202] We have information on property holdings in three Egyptian villages, one African[203] village, and two areas of Italy: the great majority of the holdings are small.[204] The freedmen who seem to have dominated economic activity in the west, perhaps financed by their former masters, did not do so in the east,[205] so that their economic functions were performed by others, perhaps less well financed and operating on a smaller scale. Dio Chrysostom gives an often cited picture of economic activity in an eastern city, describing the periodic assizes at Apamea[206] (whose transport and economic links with the Lukan territories of Pamphylia and Pisidia he had praised):

> [At the assizes] a countless number of people gathers here, litigants, jurors, speakers, magistrates, servants, slaves, pimps, grooms, merchants, whores, craftsmen, so that retailers sell their wares at the highest prices, and nothing in the city goes idle, animals, horses, or women.[207]

1.5.4.3 Retired Soldiers

To these better off peasants and merchants must be added large numbers of those settled in Roman colonies, retired soldiers[208] and some civilians, "possibly about 150,000 . . . in the Roman republican period . . . and . . . perhaps another 200,000 in the period of Caesar and Augustus,"[209] some of

---

199. Jones, *Roman World*, 96–97. "Above [the humbler trades] was the class corresponding roughly to membership of the assembly, less poor but still 'banausic' [mechanics or artisans]" (ibid., 6).

200. Pleket, "Urban Elites and Business," 134–35.

201. MacMullen, *Roman Social Relations*, 14. This presumably refers to the Egyptian drachma, worth about a quarter of a Greek drachma.

202. Tate, "Syrian Countryside," 67.

203. That is, in the province of Africa.

204. MacMullen, *Roman Social Relations*, 95–97.

205. See 1.5.4.4.

206. The great Phrygian city, not the Roman colony of the same name referred to earlier.

207. Cited Jones, *Roman World*, 67.

208. Retired centurions would have been among the local elites—see 3.2.2.

209. Whittaker, *Land, City, and Trade*, Art. II, 74.

whom would have had assets not far short of those of local elites.²¹⁰ Most of these colonies were in the west, but they included a number of cities which feature in Acts.²¹¹ After about 12 BCE retired soldiers were rarely settled in colonies, but instead received a retirement gratuity. "In A.D. 6 . . . provision for soldiers on retirement was settled on a fixed basis as a right and no longer as a privilege." The scale of gratuities gave "legionaries 3,000 *denarii* after twenty years' service."²¹² There is no evidence of similar retirement gratuities to auxiliaries, but a number of scholars believe that they also would have received such a gratuity. On that basis Richard Duncan-Jones has estimated that some 3,600 legionaries would have retired each year, and, his calculations imply, a further 4,900 auxiliaries.²¹³ Over a twenty-year period the total numbers so retiring would therefore have been some 170,000, and over the fifty years between the introduction of the retirement gratuity and Paul's arrival in Rome, some 425,000. These are substantial numbers (especially when considered with those settled in colonies as described above) and with a gratuity of 3,000 denarii,²¹⁴ together with their compulsory savings,²¹⁵ they would have been able to acquire a land-holding²¹⁶ which, when worked, would have been sufficient to keep a family²¹⁷ in reasonable comfort, although it would hardly have allowed them to live without working.

---

210. "A man who had served with Caesar in Gaul . . . could have retired with considerable cash reserves (50,000 sesterces or more)" (de Vos, *Church and Community Conflicts*, 103–4).

211. See 1.5.4.5.

212. Watson, *Roman Soldier*, 147.

213. 47,900 *alares* and 176,240 *cohortales* in service, of whom 2.18% [1,044 *alares* and 3,845 *cohortales*] would retire each year, equivalent in cost, at a ratio of 5:6 for *cohortales*, to 4,245 [precisely, 4,248] legionary equivalents (Duncan-Jones, *Money and Government*, 33–36).

214. Duncan-Jones uses a ratio of 5:6, that is, 2,500 for *cohortales*.

215. A legionary was required to save a substantial part of his earnings. "The long-term effect would be to build up a considerable nest egg which would be useful for his retirement" (Watson, *Roman Soldier*, 107). Moreover the Baptist told soldiers to be content with their pay and not to extort money (Luke 3:14), which suggests that the warning was necessary—extortion was practiced. This is probably what Tacitus meant when he described troops from Syria during the reign of Nero as "flashy moneymakers who had soldiered in towns" (Tacitus, *Annals*, 13.35). Nevertheless, a soldier during the principate would have been unlikely to do as well as the veteran of Caesar's army described above.

216. Some may have used the funds to set up a business.

217. During service "the men were unofficially married and were raising families" (Watson, *Roman Soldier*, 135).

In addition to those soldiers who retired or were settled by the emperors, Herod established military colonies in Trachonitis,[218] settled 6,000 colonists, including "disbanded soldiers" at Sebaste,[219] and settled veterans at Caesarea.[220] There may have been other such settlements, by Herod and by other rulers. These veterans obtained their holdings without debt. No doubt some veterans, or their descendants, became rich and joined the local elites,[221] while others lost their land and joined the impoverished, but over the relatively short time-span between the settlements (for example, Antioch and Lystra in 25 BCE) and the time about which Luke wrote in Acts (the 50s CE), it seems very probable that the majority of veteran families would have retained their land and should be regarded as among the relatively prosperous non-elite. These colonies were mainly in the west, but there were a number in the east which feature in Acts, and some veterans would have settled in the east independently.

1.5.4.4 *The Destitute: Slaves, Freedmen, and Free Born*

However, the majority of the population were not prosperous and they had few, if any, economic resources. They included slaves, some freedmen and women and the freeborn poor, many of whom, in rural areas, were tied to the land in some fashion. They scratched a living, with no resources to fall back on in hard times. Among these were the sick and infirm, who were often dependent upon their families or the charitable gifts of others as any illness which prevented someone from working could soon bring them to destitution.[222]

A great deal more information is available about Rome and the western part of the empire than there is about the east. In many respects conditions were similar, but there are two major differences which should not be overlooked. The first is the position of freed slaves. In the west freedmen were citizens, and were frequently financed in business ventures by their former owners, to whom they continued to be bound by ties of patronage. They were upwardly mobile and, especially in Italy and Africa, rich freedmen formed a special class, the *augustales*.[223] In the east freed slaves were

218. Tate, "Syrian Countryside," 59.
219. Schürer, *History of the Jewish People*, 162.
220. Levine, *Caesarea under Roman Rule*, 16.
221. See the description of the leading families of Pisidian Antioch in 1.6.
222. Charitable giving was a custom confined to the Jews—elsewhere the destitute had to rely on their friends and kin. See the description of peer support below.
223. Sherwin-White, *Roman Citizenship*, 327. For examples of substantial public

not citizens,[224] and their situation has been examined by Keith Hopkins, who considered a series of "roughly one thousand recorded acts of slave manumission, involving over twelve hundred slaves."[225] These were at the religious shrine of Delphi, in the centre of mainland Greece, and include only about one hundred from the first century but his findings are confirmed by a further series from the first century on Calymna, an island near Cos and about seventy miles from the Lukan city of Ephesus.

At both Delphi and Calymna the freed slave was required to pay a fee, but frequently had to continue to serve the former owner until death. This continued service was, in some cases, for not merely the life of the former owner, but sometimes for both the life of the former owner and that of another person, spouse, son, or daughter. Freed slaves could also be required to provide one, or more, children to form a new generation of slaves. At Calymna, out of a total number of sixty-eight freed slaves only twelve were released without conditions. Indeed, fifty were required to stay and serve their masters, and twenty-eight were required to provide one or two children as slaves.[226] The situation was similar at Delphi where:

> Many ex-slave parents succeeded in securing their children's full or partial freedom only by the successive manumission of family members (father, then mother, then child). It must have taken years of struggle.[227]

A second important difference between east and west was patronage, a constant and prevailing condition of life in the west and also important in Roman colonies in the east. However, "among the Greeks . . . a patronage system did not operate and patronal relationships were generally avoided."[228] Patronage was seen as shameful in a democratic society, and:

> There was a system of peer-loans, *eranoi*, such that a man in financial difficulty collected small contributions from each of his *philoi* and relatives until he had enough for his needs. It was expected that these loans would be repaid as soon as practical.[229]

---

gifts by *augustales*, see Duncan-Jones, *Economy of the Roman Empire*, 152–53.

224. "Greek freedmen became metics [resident non-citizens], not citizens; their nomenclature did not reveal freedman status as did the Roman" (Finley, *Ancient Economy*, 78).

225. Hopkins, *Conquerors and Slaves*, 133–71, this citation 133.

226. Ibid., 170.

227. Ibid., 166.

228. de Vos, *Church and Community Conflicts*, 89.

229. Ibid., 90.

This phenomenon was also found in rural areas where "the ideal of complete household autarky being a mirage, peasants were enmeshed in complicated interpersonal support networks."[230] Such support may have been more effective in urban areas, where the risk of wide-spread financial difficulty (such as crop failure) was lower. This kind of peer support has been identified by Meggitt as a feature of the Pauline communities which he calls "mutualism."[231]

1.5.4.5 *The Cities*

Cities form the background to most of the narrative of Acts, and it is helpful to understand the ways in which they differed, one from another, especially as Luke's account tends to confirm that he was aware of their distinctive characters. Each city was a Greek *polis*, partly self-governing in either the Greek or Roman fashion, and, except for Herodian cities,[232] controlling the surrounding rural area as part of its own territory. Luke wrote about larger cities and Roman colonies—there are few small Greek cities in his narrative—and they were all on important trade routes.[233] The Greek cities usually contained Jewish groups. There is usually little information about these groups, although Meeks tells us that "estimates run from 10 to 15 percent of the total population of a city."[234] This seems high, but suggests that Luke's description of the influence of the Jewish opponents of Paul would have been regarded as plausible by his intended readers. In some cases the proportion of Jewish residents can be estimated and this can be helpful in understanding Acts, as the information is likely to have been known, in broad terms, to Luke and, therefore, to his intended readers.

But all the Greek and Roman cities in the narrative shared some characteristics. They were very independent, and although subject to the Roman governor, tried to avoid his interventions. They were also extremely status conscious, and each city promoted itself in whatever way it could—Luke shows us the town clerk of Ephesus telling the crowd: "Who is there that does not know that the city of the Ephesians is the temple keeper of the great Artemis and of the statue that fell from heaven?" (Acts 19:35). Indeed, the cult of Artemis was very important for the city's prosperity, so much so that

---

230. De Ligt, *Fairs and Markets*, 131.
231. Meggitt, *Paul, Poverty and Survival*, 155–78.
232. Levine, *Caesarea under Roman Rule*, 17.
233. For the importance of travel and the trade routes through the cities of the Pauline mission see Meeks, *First Urban Christians*, 16–19.
234. Ibid., 34.

"around AD 44, the proconsul of Asia [took measures to eliminate any risk of] the bankruptcy of the temple of Artemis."[235]

We saw in 1.5.3 that office holders in the cities were expected to spend money for the benefit of their cities,[236] but any wealthy resident was also expected to play their part in beautifying and glorifying their city.[237] This was also the case for rulers such as the Herodians. Caesarea had been completely rebuilt "on a most magnificent scale"[238] as a port city by Herod and was his provincial capital. Tiberias, founded by Antipas, and Caesarea Philippi, founded by Philip, were similar cities in their form of government, as perhaps was Bethsaida, renamed for a time as the city of Julias,[239] also founded by Philip.[240] Tiberias was essentially a Greek city, mainly populated by gentiles. Sepphoris differed in that "in Jesus' day [it] was a thoroughly Jewish city."[241] Bethsaida remained a fishing village with a large Jewish population,[242] the newly built city of Julias being a mile or so away.[243]

All of these cities were part of the Roman Empire and a substantial element of perceived status was the reflected glory of a Roman connection. This could be an important role in the imperial cult, such as that performed by Paul's friends, the officials of the province of Asia (Asiarchs—Acts 19:31),[244] or status as part of the Roman administration or as a Roman colony—Luke specifically tells us that Philippi "is a leading city of the district of Macedonia and a Roman colony" (Acts 16:12).[245] A much rarer distinction in Luke's time was for an eastern city to provide members of the Roman senate. The importance of this for Pisidian Antioch is discussed in 1.6.

---

235. Rogers, *Sacred Identity of Ephesus*, 11.

236. "The kings of the Gentiles lord it over them; and those in authority over them are called benefactors" (Luke 22:25).

237. The role of women in this regard is discussed in 6.1.1.

238. Schürer, *History of the Jewish People*, 116.

239. Cities often reverted to their original names. Caesarea Philippi began as Paneas, had five other names, and then again became Paneas (ibid., 169–71).

240. Its identification with the "Bethsaida of the New Testament" may not be secure (ibid., 172).

241. Evans, *Jesus and His World*, 26.

242. See 4.2.1.2.

243. Strange, "Bethsaida," 692–93.

244. Kearsley, "Asiarchs," 495–96.

245. Antioch of Pisidia, Lystra, Corinth, and Troas were also colonies.

1.5.4.6 High and Low Status, Rich and Poor

In the Roman Empire, east and west, wealth and status were closely linked. Senators, equestrians and the ruling members of the house of Herod were all of very high status and wealthy. Although among them there were degrees of status and wealth, these are of relatively little importance for our purposes. The local elites, of lower status and wealth, were important in their own cities, and richer than those among whom they lived. Although some of them were Roman citizens, and even equestrians, in the east this was relatively rare and was probably seen as of less importance than their position in the local community. These groups together constituted the elite of the empire, which they governed in their own interests.

Lacking such wealth and despised by the elite were all those who had to work for a living. Some were relatively successful and acquired some resources, a little more than was required for daily living—these we have called the *penētes*. They varied greatly in the level of resources available to them, a few were rich by most standards, but none had significant political power. Those without such resources we have called the *ptōchoi*. They included beggars and day-laborers, people who rarely knew where their next meal was coming from. Many were destitute. Of similar status were slaves (although they may have been economically better off in that their owners provided food and shelter); those former slaves who obtained their freedom had skills which ensured that they were included among those whom we have called *penētes*. Each of these groups included women, but they were always considered to be of lower status than men of equivalent wealth. Many women derived their status and economic resources from their husbands—nearly all others did so from the family into which they were born.[246]

1.6 THE USE OF HISTORICAL DATA

1.6.1 Criteria for Interpretation

Before beginning our examination of the texts themselves we should consider how far the historical information we set out above and in subsequent chapters can be used to interpret them. In considering whether to take account of Septuagintal references, we identified four criteria: volume, coherence, plausibility, and satisfaction.[247] The criteria of coherence, plausibility, and satisfaction seem as relevant to historical events as to literary refer-

---

246. See 6.1.1.
247. See 1.3.3.2.

ences, but it is difficult to see how the criterion of "volume" could be applied to the former. We can be sure that Luke was aware of the important social and economic circumstances of the time and places in which he lived, and this is clearly reflected in, for example, the descriptions of rich and poor in his narrative.[248] The position about particular items of historical knowledge is less clear. Luke knew a great deal more about many of the events of the first century than we do, but there are, no doubt, some matters of which he was ignorant, but which we know about today. However, to exclude from our consideration material which we know, on the grounds that it cannot be demonstrated that Luke knew it, is likely to result in a failure of understanding. We suggest that only the three criteria of coherence, plausibility, and satisfaction should be applied in considering whether a historical fact should be taken into account in our interpretation. So, if we are aware of a historical circumstance, Luke also could have been aware of it, and we should examine its implications for the understanding of his text. If doing so provides a coherent, plausible, and satisfying reading of the text, we should consider it. As a result, the date of composition is important. If, as we assume, the work was written in the early 80s, Luke's intended reader would have had knowledge of events of what was then the recent past. If he wrote in the second century, twenty or more years later, this is less plausible.

1.6.2 Caristanius Fronto

We can use as a practical example the relationship of Sergius Paulus[249] with Pisidian Antioch. A century ago a paper by G. L. Cheesman was published about the Caristanius family which found that the daughter or granddaughter of Sergius Paulus, "who believed" (Acts 13:7–12) was probably married to Caristanius Fronto, a view which was accepted for many years. He was an important official:

> Caristanius was adlected[250] into the Senate with the rank of ex-tribune ... [perhaps] in A.D. 73–74. Promotion continued to be rapid. Caristanius was immediately advanced to praetorian rank and sent by Vespasian to Britain as legate of the ninth legion ... After the governorship of Lycia-Pamphylia, which he held

---

248. See Esler, *Community and Gospel*, 195–200.
249. The family is usually referred to as Paullus. We follow the New Testament spelling, Paulus.
250. Appointed by the emperor.

under Titus and Domitian, Caristanius returned to Rome and became one of the suffect[251] consuls of the year 90.[252]

His family had been connected with Q. Sulpicius Quirinius, the governor of Syria (Luke 2:2), who was titular *duumvir* (magistrate) of Antioch in Pisidia, and for whom a member of the family acted as representative.[253] It was rare for private individuals to hold such titular positions,[254] and Levick suggests that they were often "friends, *protégés*, or relatives by blood or marriage of Tiberius,"[255] who was to become emperor, and Quirinius was such a friend or *protégé*.[256] He chose as his representative a prominent member of the local community, as is shown by a statue in the city of the man he selected.[257]

This raised the question of whether Paul's dash to Pisidian Antioch after the conversion of Sergius Paulus, proconsul of Cyprus, should be interpreted in the light of the Caristanius connection. If there was such a connection it might also explain Luke's mention of Quirinius, who died in 21 CE[258] and by Luke's time, sixty years later, was a forgotten figure.

1.6.3 The Sergii Pauli

However, more recent scholarship disputes Cheesman's findings. A further inscription has been found which shows that Caristanius Fronto married Calpurnia Paula,[259] a member of a distinguished family in Antioch and that Cheesman's inscription is better read as referring to Calpurnia Paula, not Sergia Paula.[260] On the other hand, it is now clear that Sergius Paulus himself had very strong connections with Pisidian Antioch.[261]

251. A consul appointed to serve out the balance of a term.

252. Levick, *Roman Colonies*, 112. See Cheesman, "Caristanii," with reproductions of many of the inscriptions which provide this information. Caristanius was living, and a senator, during the whole of the period within which Luke wrote.

253. Ibid., 255.

254. Ibid., 256.

255. Levick, *Roman Colonies*, 81n6.

256. Potter, "Quirinius," 588–89.

257. Levick, *Roman Colonies*, 111.

258. Potter, "Quirinius," 589.

259. Possibly related to Sergius Paulus (Mitchell, "Geographical and Historical Introduction," 10).

260. Christol and Drew-Bear, "Sergii Pauli," 180.

261. However, although in Paul's time there was a senator called Sergius Paulus, there is little evidence outside Acts that he was ever in Cyprus and none that he became

> Si la famille est originaire d'une autre région d'Anatolie, c'est à Antioche qu'elle s'est rapidement installée, et c'est à partir d'Antioche que son élévation s'est produite ... [Le proconsul de Chypre] devait s'y trouver encore une partie de sa domesticité, des clients aussi, des compatriotes plus généralement. Son nom n'y était pas oublié. Son influence y demeurait réelle.[262]

Although not published until 2002, Christol's paper was given in 1997 and influenced a book published in 1998:[263]

> On his first journey Paul travelled directly to Antioch from Paphus in Cyprus, where he had converted the Roman proconsul Sergius Paullus. This was the very man whose home was Pisidian Antioch and who was to become consul at Rome around AD 70 ... It is an elementary inference that he advised or encouraged Paul to make the trip up-country into Asia Minor, following the *via Sebaste* from Perge, where Paul and Barnabas docked, to Antioch.[264]

Mitchell had earlier found that:

> It is overwhelmingly likely that Paul, who had almost certainly adopted the Latin name in place of the Hebrew Saul in recognition of the meeting with Sergius Paulus, was directed to Antioch by his recent convert.[265]

1.6.4 Two Senatorial Families

In Antioch in Luke's time there were two senatorial families, the Sergii Pauli[266] and the Caristanii. It was a small town and there were not many families wealthy enough to aspire to equestrian status:[267]

---

a Christian (ibid., 186–89).

262. Ibid., 186.
263. Mitchell, "Geographical and Historical Introduction," 17n59.
264. Ibid., 12.
265. Mitchell, "Antioch of Pisidia," 264. For a similar view, see Pearson, "Antioch (Pisidia)," who notes that: "Roman Antioch in the mid-first century was a wonder to behold" (32).
266. Four generations have been identified in the first century (Christol and Drew-Bear, "Sergii Pauli," 184).
267. The reason for the mention of Quirinius may lie in the web of marital and patronal relationships of Antioch.

We must conclude that there were few [fellow citizens of equestrian census]; that wealth was concentrated in the hands of a few landowners; that class distinctions in the colony were sharp; that the aristocracy was not broadly based, but, as one might expect, was an alien growth, artificially fed and maintained.[268]

Is it plausible to suggest that Luke knew of these two senatorial families? He was a contemporary of both the senators Sergius Paulus and of Caristanius Fronto and wrote in Acts about places where Caristanius lived and worked: Antioch of Pisidia,[269] his home-town, and Lycia[270] and Pamphylia,[271] where he was governor, probably while Luke was writing his two-volume work. Luke was also interested in the Roman administration generally, writing about five governors, including Sergius Paulus. There were very few eastern senators (and holders of senatorial posts) up to or during the time of Domitian,[272] and to have three[273] from one small town was remarkable and probably widely known, especially by someone like Theophilus.[274]

The matter has significance for the understanding of Acts. We address Luke's presentation of the "devout women of high standing" of Pisidian Antioch in 7.5.2, but it also helps to understand the Lukan portrait of Paul. He changes his name and dashes to Antioch in order to build on his success with the proconsul, but the mission is a failure, at least as far as the Antiochene elite are concerned. Yet although described in the ABD article cited above (but not that on Paulus, Sergius),[275] the connection of Sergius

---

268. Levick, *Roman Colonies*, 120.
269. Acts 13:14–52; 14:21–24.
270. Acts 27:5, and also Patara, a town in Lycia, 21:1.
271. Acts 2:10; 13:13–14; 14:24; 15:38; 27:5.
272. "It seems . . . Vespasian admitted between six and thirteen new men of eastern origins, Domitian perhaps as many as twenty-four" (Jones, *Emperor Domitian*, 172).
273. There is very strong evidence for the first senator Sergius Paulus and for Caristanius Fronto. That for the second Sergius Paulus is not as strong, but even two senators from one small eastern town is remarkable.
274. He was called *"kratiste"* (Luke 1:3), a "strongly affirmative honorary form of address" BDAG, 565. Luke uses it of two governors, Felix (by Claudius Lysias, Acts 23:26) and Festus (by Paul, Acts 26:25). A person so addressed, Greek-speaking, would surely be aware of three senators from a single small eastern city.
275. Martin, "Paulus, Sergius."

Paulus with Pisidian Antioch is not mentioned in the later commentaries of Barrett[276] or Fitzmyer,[277] although it is reflected in that of Witherington.[278]

The scholars cited were addressing the historical circumstance, that is, whether the historical Paul did change his name and dash to Antioch because of Sergius Paulus. This is a literary study, concerned with Luke's intentions, and we find that Luke knew of the senatorial families of Antioch, as did his intended readers. Luke has tailored his narrative to indicate, to the intended reader, that Paul *did* change his name and dash to Antioch because of Sergius Paulus.

In the following chapters we attempt to understand Luke's view of people, men and women, of high or low status, wealth or destitution, as it would have been understood by his intended readers, aware of the history of their times and capable of recognizing his Septuagintal references. We derive additional insights from Luke's changes to his sources, principally Mark; these changes help us to understand what he was trying to convey. Our tools of context, intertext, co-text, and antetext are not new—all of them have been used under different names by many scholars. However, by confining our subject matter to the minor figures of the narrative and taking account of recent scholarship we find new insights which are helpful in determining Luke's meaning.

We begin our detailed examination by considering members of the house of Herod in chapter 2, and in chapter 3 the Roman authorities, including all those involved in the administration of the Roman Empire. In chapter 4 we consider the Jewish authorities, including the Pharisees, and in chapter 5 other men, including the non-elite and members of local elites (apart from those in Jerusalem). We consider women in chapters 6 and 7 and then draw our conclusions in chapter 8.

---

276. Barrett, *Critical and Exegetical Commentary*, vol. 1.

277. Fitzmyer, *Acts*.

278. Witherington, *Acts*, 403–4. Johnson also refers to "the implied patronage of Sergius Paulus" without going into detail (Johnson, *Acts*, 227). Pervo dismisses the idea (Pervo, *Acts*, 320n11), but he dates Acts in the second century. On this assumption there would be little likelihood of the intended reader knowing of the Sergius Paulus connection with Antioch.

CHAPTER 2

The House of Herod

2.1 INTRODUCTION

In both Gospel and Acts Luke introduces a number of members of the house of Herod. At the time he wrote they had been a ruling family in Judaea and the surrounding area for well over a hundred years. Moreover, the members of the family whom we meet in Acts were descended from the Hasmonean royal house, which had begun to rule Israel some 250 years before Luke wrote, and whose history featured in the Septuagint. The members of the house of Herod described by Luke were both extremely wealthy and of very high status, and the history of the house of Herod is an important part of the context within which Luke wrote. We shall argue that Luke was aware of at least part of that history,[1] as were his intended readers, and we too need to take it into account if we are to understand his meaning. Accordingly a substantial part of this chapter deals with the history of the house of Herod as told by secular historians, largely dependent upon Josephus.

Luke drew upon information about the house of Herod which influenced what he wrote both directly and indirectly. It did so directly in that his sources provided information which he used, and indirectly in that the information so provided influenced the way in which he dealt with material from his antetext, Mark. In this chapter we shall first set out in some detail this aspect of the context within which Luke wrote, that is the history of members of the house of Herod (2.2), then examine the changes which Luke made to his antetext, the Gospel of Mark (2.3). We next consider Luke's own text (2.4), and finally summarize our findings (2.5). In this chapter we make most use of context, but also use co-text, particularly in respect of Antipas.

1. The house of Herod could be described as notorious.

2.2 CONTEXT: THE HISTORY OF THE HOUSE OF HEROD

2.2.1 Introduction

The relationships of the family of Herod are complicated, both because of the large number of intra-familial marriages and because many individuals shared a small number of names. Appended is a list of members of that house who are significant for understanding Luke's work (Appendix I).[2]

In the text we generally refer to individuals by the names commonly used in New Testament scholarship, any further necessary identification being given by description, e.g., Salome, the sister of Herod the Great, instead of Salome I, and Salome, without addition, for the dancer in Mark 6, referred to in the list as Salome III. There are substantial disagreements between historians about many of the facts relating to some of these individuals, and even their names. Where important for our purposes these are discussed in the text but, for clarity, they are ignored for the purposes of the list, which represents the generally accepted view, based on Josephus. We shall argue that both Luke and Josephus had links to the courts of Agrippa II: because of this, the historical accuracy of a story may be less important than the fact that Josephus accepted it.[3] If a story was current and plausible enough to be used by Josephus, it may have been available to Luke, and is a potential aid in understanding his text.[4]

2.2.2 Herod the Great and His Sister Salome

Ancestry was of great importance to the house of Herod, and it is necessary to know something about the Hasmonean dynasty.[5] The Hasmonean king Judas Aristobulus died in 103 BCE without children, and his widow, Salome Alexandra, married, following levirate rules, his brother Alexander Jannaeus, who became king. In 76 BCE, following his death, she became

---

2. The list is based on the tables prepared by K. C. Hanson and members of the family are numbered for purposes of identification (Salome I, Salome II, etc.). following the usage of Hanson ("Herodians, Part 1," 78–81) although Hanson used Arabic numerals.

3. The reliability of Josephus as a historian is questioned by Steve Mason (*Josephus, Judaea*, 7–43).

4. The evidence for a Herodian source for Josephus is addressed in 2.2.8 and for Luke in 2.3.2.

5. For the Hasmonean dynasty, see Saldarini, "Jewish Responses," 317–21, and Mandell, "Hasmonaeans," 556.

ruling queen of the kingdom of Judaea, although she then had two adult sons. Following her own death in 67 and after a brief civil war between her sons, the younger, Aristobulus, became king. Antipater, the father of Herod the Great, sided with the other son, Hyrcanus, and after a further period of strife both sides appealed for help to the Romans who, under the leadership of Pompey, deposed Aristobulus and took control of the kingdom in 63. Hyrcanus was appointed as high priest "with Antipater as the real power behind the throne."[6] The influence of Antipater and his son Herod increased, and in 40 Herod was appointed king.[7] He was already betrothed to Mariamme, the grand-daughter of both Hyrcanus and Aristobulus,[8] and duly married her. Herod was an Idumean whose ancestors had been converted to Judaism, probably by force, in the time of his grandfather.[9] He married a total of some ten wives,[10] the second being Mariamme, the Hasmonaean, and his other wives included a first cousin and a niece. Herod died in 4 BCE.

Salome, the sister of Herod, is regarded as responsible in large measure for the strife and the many executions among the family of Herod, including the killing of both her first husband, Joseph, and her second, Costobarus.[11] She was also regarded as largely responsible for the death of Mariamme, Herod's Hasmonean wife,[12] and of Mariamme's sons Alexander and Aristobulus[13] (Aristobulus being her own son-in-law), and was implicated in the execution of another of Herod's sons, Antipater.[14] Herod had previously executed Mariamme's maternal grandfather, Hyrcanus, her mother and her brother,[15] but had also arranged the marriage of one of his sons by Mariamme (Aristobulus I) to Salome's daughter (Berenice I)—their descendants, including all those members of the house who feature in Acts, are

---

6. Saldarini, "Jewish Responses," 357.

7. For Herod and his descendants, see Richardson, *Herod: King of the Jews*.

8. Endogenous marriages (children of brothers), although frowned on by Romans and, in the first century, Greeks, were permitted by Jewish law and custom (Hanson, "Herodians, Part 1," 77). He documents a number of marriages by members of the house of Herod to the father's brother.

9. Kokkinos, *Herodian Dynasty*, 350.

10. It is not clear to what extent, if any, his marriages were polygamous.

11. Kokkinos, *Herodian Dynasty*, 178, 182.

12. Ibid., 179.

13. Ibid., 188.

14. Ibid., 189.

15. Her father and paternal grandfather had been executed long before by Pompey (*War* 1.184–85).

marked (H) in Appendix 1. They seem to have taken their Jewishness more seriously.[16]

Salome received a very substantial legacy of land on the death of Herod, subsequently added to by Augustus, but in her own will, "left her entire landed wealth to the Empress Livia,"[17] that is, her children did not inherit this very substantial landed wealth. This may have been because of the strong patron/client relationship between the Julio-Claudian and Herodian dynasties. As an example of this, Herod had left an extremely substantial legacy to Augustus, but Augustus seems to have subsequently given as much or more back to his family.[18] There is no record of similar gifts from Livia to Salome's family, but as noted in 2.2.5, Livia's daughter-in-law, Antonia the younger, made a very substantial loan to Agrippa I, Salome's grandson. His mother Berenice (Salome's daughter) at the time of Salome's death was widowed and living an aristocratic life in Rome, and was friendly with Antonia,[19] the mother of the emperor Claudius and grandmother of Gaius (Caligula).

2.2.3 Archelaus and Philip

Herod died in 4 BCE, leaving a will disposing of his territories, albeit subject to the approval of Augustus. He had changed the will often, and had executed three sons who had been beneficiaries in previous wills. His final will divided his kingdom between three of his other sons, Judaea going to Archelaus, Galilee to Antipas, and Trachonitis and the adjoining regions to Philip. Herod had been much hated and on his death, before Augustus had confirmed the will, the crowd in Jerusalem made a number of demands of Archelaus, who was acting as regent. He sent in troops to clear the temple and three thousand were killed.

Archelaus then went to Rome to secure from Augustus his succession to the throne of Herod. He was followed by his brother Antipas, Salome the sister of Herod, and other family members who all opposed such an appointment. They in their turn were followed by a delegation from Judaea who asked that the country be made a Roman province. Augustus, however, largely following Herod's will, divided the kingdom in three, Archelaus getting the greater part including Judaea, Antipas getting "Galilee" (Luke 3:1) and Peraea, and Philip a group of territories including "Ituraea and

16. Kokkinos, *Herodian Dynasty*, 342–52.
17. Ibid., 192.
18. Hanson, "Herodians, Part 3," 18–19.
19. Kokkinos, *Herodian Dynasty*, 189–91, including n64.

Trachonitis" (Luke 3:1). Josephus gives the annual revenue of these territories as 400 talents for Archelaus, 200 for Antipas and 100 for Philip. In addition, Salome the sister of Herod received land whose annual revenue was 60 talents.

Archelaus was deposed by Augustus in the year 6 CE, "au terme d'un règne brutal qui avait scandalisé les Juifs de toutes les façons possibles,"[20] and his territories then became a Roman province. So, during the ministry of Jesus, Judaea was a Roman province governed by Pontius Pilate (Luke 3:1), Galilee was ruled by Antipas and Philip's territories included Bethsaida in Gaulanitis and Caesarea Philippi in Paneas, both of which figure in the Gospels.[21] Bethsaida, in Gaulanitis, was important to Luke (see 2.4.2) and it is not clear why he mentioned Trachonitis (which does not figure in Luke-Acts), and not Gaulanitis, in 3:1. These territories were contiguous and there may have been confusion, perhaps shared by Josephus, himself a Galilean, whose lists of Philip's territories differ, in one mentioning both Gaulanitis and Trachonitis,[22] but in another only Trachonitis.[23]

Archelaus had divorced his first wife (probably a niece)[24] and married Glaphyra, the widow of his half-brother Alexander (who had been executed by Herod the Great) to whom she had borne children. This marriage to his brother's widow, not being covered by the levirate custom, was a serious offence against Jewish laws and was recognized as such by Josephus,[25] but did not have anything to do with his deposition—Josephus tells us that he was deposed by Augustus because of accusations of "cruelty and tyranny" by "the leading men among the Jews and Samaritans."[26]

Philip seems to have been an unusual ruler:

> In his conduct of the government he showed a moderate and easy-going disposition. Indeed, he spent all his time in the territory subject to him . . . whenever anyone appealed to him for redress along the route, at once without a moment's delay . . . he took his seat and gave the case a hearing. He fixed penalties

20. Sartre, *L'Orient Romain*, 31.

21. The "Ituraea" mentioned as part of Philip's territories would normally mean Chalcis, the center and former capital of the Ituraean kingdom, but it could mean any part of the area inhabited by Ituraeans, a vast region from the North of Lebanon almost to Damascus. Luke's Ituraea may have been Paneas (including Caesarea Philippi), which was part of the former kingdom of Ituraea (Richardson, *Herod: King of the Jews*, 24).

22. Josephus, *Ant* 17.189.

23. Ibid., 17.319.

24. Kokkinos, *Herodian Dynasty*, 227.

25. Josephus, *Ant* 17.341.

26. Ibid., 17.342.

for those who were convicted and released those who had been unjustly accused.[27]

He married, late in life, Salome the daughter of Herodias, and had no children.[28]

2.2.4 Antipas and Herodias

Herod Antipas ruled Galilee and Peraea for over 40 years, being deposed by Gaius at the instigation of Agrippa I in 39 (see 2.2.5). He first married a daughter of Aretas, king of Nabataea, but divorced her to marry his niece Herodias, the wife of his brother, whom Mark calls Philip. However, according to Josephus,[29] her first marriage was not to Philip but to another brother of Antipas called Herod. Hanson calls this man Herod Philip I and Philip, the ruler described in 2.2.3, Herod Philip II. Although Hoehner follows this usage, other scholars argue that the first husband of Herodias had no name but Herod, and to call him Herod Philip is required only by the desire to preserve the New Testament's reliability.[30] So also Kokkinos[31] who, however, argues that Herodias married first her uncle Herod, then her uncle Philip, the tetrarch, and finally her uncle Antipas: he explains how ambition could plausibly have led to this sequence, and rejects the idea that Antipas could have become infatuated with Herodias when she was "about 48."[32] However that story is not implausible; compare the undoubted infatuation of Titus with Bernice, who was of a similar age.[33]

According to Josephus, Herodias had a daughter, Salome, by her first husband, Herod:

> After whose birth Herodias, taking it into her head to flout the way of our fathers, married Herod [Antipas], her husband's brother by the same father, who was tetrarch of Galilee; to do this she parted from a living husband.[34]

27. Ibid., 18.106–7.
28. Ibid., 18.137.
29. Ibid., 18.110.
30. Richardson, *Herod: King of the Jews*, 308n59.
31. Kokkinos, *Herodian Dynasty*, 223.
32. Ibid., 267. This age is doubtful: Hoehner has Herodias born about 8 BCE (*Herod Antipas*, 154) and married to Antipas about 29 CE (350), and thus about 37 at that time.
33. "Over forty when Titus fell in love with her" (Graves, *Twelve Caesars*, 299n).
34. Josephus, *Ant* 18.136.

This marriage of Antipas, like that of Archelaus, was contrary to Jewish law. Condemnation of the marriage by the Baptist is given as the reason for his execution by Mark and Matthew and, for his arrest, by Luke. Josephus gives a different reason, which is discussed further in 2.3.1:

> When others too joined the crowds about [the Baptist], because they were aroused to the highest degree by his sermons, Herod became alarmed. Eloquence that had so great an effect on mankind might lead to some form of sedition, for it looked as if they would be guided by John in everything that they did. Herod decided therefore that it would be much better to strike first and be rid of him before his work led to an uprising, than to wait for an upheaval, get involved in a difficult situation and see his mistake.[35]

2.2.5 Agrippa I

Agrippa I married his first cousin and had five children, including Agrippa II, Bernice and Drusilla. He ran through at least one fortune in his youth and found refuge at the court of his uncle, Antipas, who was married to his sister, Herodias. He quarreled with Antipas and made his way to Rome, borrowing a large sum (200,000 drachmas) from Alexander the Alabarch of Alexandria,[36] steward to Antonia the Younger,[37] who herself lent him a larger sum (300,000 drachmas) in Rome.[38] It is not clear how he intended to repay these loans. In Rome he became friendly with Gaius (the grandson of Antonia), but was jailed by Tiberius. On the death of Tiberius, Gaius, the new emperor, gave the former territories of Philip to Agrippa, also giving him the title of king. This aroused the jealousy of Herodias, who persuaded her husband, Antipas, to go to Rome to seek a similar royal title. Agrippa there brought charges against Antipas, and Gaius deposed him and added his former territories to Agrippa's kingdom. Despite this gift, Agrippa successfully opposed in person Gaius's plan to erect a statue of himself for veneration in the temple at Jerusalem[39]—if true, this demonstrated great courage. After the death of Gaius, Agrippa was of assistance in arranging the succession of Claudius (Antonia's son), who added Judaea and Samaria

---

35. Ibid., 18.118.
36. Ibid., 18.159-60—actually lent to his wife.
37. Ibid., 19.276.
38. Ibid., 18.165.
39. Ibid., 18.297-301.

to his kingdom so that he ruled virtually the whole of the former territories of Herod the Great. He died in 43 (Acts 12:23).

2.2.6 Agrippa II, Bernice, Drusilla, and Felix

Agrippa II, son of Agrippa I, was brought up in Rome at the court of Claudius. He was made king of Chalcis on the death of his uncle, Herod of Chalcis, in 48, when he was about twenty; in 53 he was given, in place of Chalcis, the old territories of Philip together with Abilene, and in 54 Nero added part of Galilee and Peraea. He took the Roman side in the Jewish war and continued to rule these territories until about 92. However, "[Josephus] remarks that Agrippa II was hated by his subjects. They particularly begrudged his generosity to Berytus, where he transferred 'all' the art of his own kingdom."[40] He never married.

Bernice's first marriage was to a son of Alexander the Alabarch and her second, after his early death, was to her uncle Herod of Chalcis. After his death she lived with her brother, Agrippa II (who succeeded Herod as king of Chalcis), but, it is said because of allegations of incest,[41] she married Polemo, king of Cilicia. She left him to return to her brother, but again left his court in about 68 to live with Titus, the son of Vespasian, and appears to have continued that relationship on and off until Titus became emperor in 79. She may have hoped to marry him, or at least emulate his father's mistress, Caenis, a freed slave of Antonia the younger—after his wife's death: "Vespasian behaved with Caenis as though they were husband and wife . . . [she] grew tremendously wealthy by negotiating and conferring political and religious offices."[42]

Bernice was a formidable woman. In the year 68 as competing claimants for the imperial throne fought with one another, Agrippa II, returning hastily from Rome to Palestine, "arrived to find that [Bernice] had already in his absence pledged the support of his kingdom to the newly proclaimed emperor [Vespasian]."[43] Later:

> She risked her life in an attempt to keep Gessius Florus[44] from provoking the multitude [in Jerusalem], but was unsuccessful.

40. Paltiel, *Vassals and Rebels*, 300.

41. Josephus, *Ant* 20.145–46.

42. Cohick, *Earliest Christians*, 266. "[Caenis] remained his wife in all but name even when he became emperor" (Suetonius, *Twelve Caesars*, 282).

43. Jones, *Herods of Judaea*, 256.

44. Governor of Judaea—"a Greek from Asia Minor, whose oppressive rule showed nothing but hatred toward the Jewish population" (Stern, "Nero," 964).

When she attempted to pacify the rioters, they burned down her palace, forcing her to flee.⁴⁵

She seems to have been a worthy descendant of Salome Alexandra and of her great-grandmother, Salome the sister of Herod. After the death of Titus in 81 she "would have left Italy to return to her brother's kingdom."⁴⁶

Her sister, Drusilla, married Azizus, king of Emesa, whom she left to marry Felix, a freedman of Antonia. This second marriage did not please Agrippa II. "With . . . Felix, Agrippa's relations were for personal reasons strained—he could hardly be very cordial to the man who had abducted his sister."⁴⁷ There were other social and religious reasons to oppose the marriage. Felix was a freedman, a former slave, and Agrippa was of at least the sixth ruling generation of his family, and on the Hasmonean side traced his royal descent through ten generations from Mattathias.⁴⁸ Moreover, Felix was not Jewish: "[Agrippa I] insisted that gentiles who married into his family should accept circumcision,"⁴⁹ a rule continued by Agrippa II, who cancelled a marriage arranged by his father for Drusilla when the prospective husband refused to be circumcised and instead married her to Azizus, "who became a Jew."⁵⁰

Felix was brother to Pallas, a very powerful figure in the court of Claudius (and, for some years, of his successor, Nero), who was compelled to resign his office by Nero and was put to death in 62.⁵¹ Roman writers made plain their contempt for Felix. Suetonius, noting that he was a favorite of the emperor Claudius, sneered that "this Felix married three queens."⁵² Tacitus is more explicit:

---

45. Schalit, "Berenice," 602.

46. Kokkinos, *Herodian Dynasty*, 330.

47. Jones, *Herods of Judaea*, 231. As Drusilla was about fifteen at the time, "abducted" is not altogether inappropriate.

48. He and his sons were the heroes of I Maccabees and one of those sons, Simon Maccabeus, from whom Agrippa was descended, became leader of the Jewish people (1 Macc 14:35). 1 Maccabees was written around 100 BCE and was probably known to Agrippa II who bought a copy of one of the works of Josephus (see 2.2.8), so was interested in history, perhaps especially the history of his own family.

49. Jones, *Herods of Judaea*, 209.

50. Ibid., 219.

51. Syme, "Antonius Pallas," 117.

52. Suetonius, *Twelve Caesars*, 201.

Pallas' brother... Felix, who was the governor of Judaea, showed less moderation [in accumulating financial rewards]. Backed by vast influence, he believed himself free to commit any crime.[53]

Tacitus describes how Claudius protected him against accusers[54] but he was later recalled to Rome to answer charges and his subsequent history is unknown. The son of Felix and Drusilla died in 79 during the eruption of Vesuvius,[55] and, if then still alive, they may also have died at that time.

2.2.7 Salome and Aristobulus

Salome, the daughter of Herodias, first married Philip the tetrarch, her uncle on her father's side and great-uncle on her mother's side, and after his death married her first cousin, Aristobulus, the son of Herod of Chalcis.[56] "His queen was that Salome who as a girl had danced before Antipas and received as her reward the head of John the Baptist."[57] By Aristobulus she had three sons, Herod, Agrippa, and Aristobulus. That one of their sons was named Agrippa suggests that the hostility between Agrippa I and Antipas described in 2.2.5 was not inherited by Agrippa II, Aristobulus and Salome, who had close family ties, and, unlike Antipas, shared Hasmonean ancestry. Aristobulus was not appointed to succeed his father in Chalcis on his death in 48, but in 54 he was appointed king of Lesser Armenia, which he ruled until 71.[58] In 72 he was made king of "Chalcidene," that is, the territory of Chalcis, and took part in the invasion of Commagene in Asia Minor.[59] His new kingdom was probably the Chalcis in the Lebanese Beka'a valley.[60] This Chalcis had previously been ruled, not only by Herod the Great,[61] but also by Herod of Chalcis, father of Aristobulus and husband of Bernice, and then

53. Tacitus, *Ann*, 12.54.
54. Ibid., 12.54.
55. Josephus, *Ant* 20.144.
56. A son of Herod the Great, who later married Bernice—see 2.2.6.
57. Jones, *Herods of Judaea*, 260.
58. Differing, Tracey states that Aristobulus "had retrieved Chalcis, as king, after Agrippa II vacated it [in 53]. He... proved satisfactory, and was given Armenia Minor by Nero" (Tracey, "Syria," 248).
59. Josephus, *War* 7.226.
60. Although identified as a place of the same name (Chalcis ad Belum) in Northern Syria by Eliezer Paltiel (*Vassals and Rebels*, 253), the Lebanese Chalcis is preferred by Robyn Tracey ("Syria," 248, 252), Maurice Sartre (*L'Orient Romain*, 45) and Nikos Kokkinos, who addresses Paltiel's argument (Kokkinos, *Herodian Dynasty*, 312).
61. Tracey, "Syria," 247n61.

by Agrippa II, brother of Bernice and first cousin of both Aristobulus and Salome.

It is therefore possible, indeed probable, that Salome became queen of Chalcis in Lebanon.⁶² It was the only kingdom of Herod of Chalcis, then of his successor Agrippa II and then of Aristobulus, so each of them is likely to have made it a principal residence, and Bernice, after the death of her husband, Herod of Chalcis, may have continued to live there with her brother, his successor. Chalcis was close to the principal territories of Philip and then Agrippa I and was contiguous with Abilene,⁶³ albeit separated by the high mountains of the Anti-Lebanon. There was a trade route from Damascus through Abila, the capital of Abilene, and the Beka'a valley (Chalcis)⁶⁴ to the Roman colony of Berytus (Beirut).⁶⁵ Berytus was an important city for Agrippa I, Agrippa II, and Bernice,⁶⁶ all of whom enriched it with buildings and monuments. It seems probable that there would have been frequent communication between Abila and Berytus via Chalcis.

There would have been strong political reasons in favor of good relations between Agrippa II (as ruler of Abilene) and Aristobulus, as the territories were not only contiguous but would have faced similar problems. The region was mountainous, and in the time of Augustus the ruler of Chalcis (which then included Abilene) had been *"plus brigand que dynaste."*⁶⁷ Agrippa II and Aristobulus were successful in dealing with these problems:⁶⁸

> Dans la deuxième moitié du 1er siècle, l'œuvre de pacification et de mise en valeur était suffisamment avancée pour que Rome puisse prendre en charge elle-même l'administration de la région . . . L'annexion couronne le succès de la politique des Hérodiens.⁶⁹

---

62. Tracey claims that Salome's head appears on one of the coins of Chalcis ("Syria," 248n62).
63. Part of the territory of Agrippa II—see 2.2.6.
64. This route to Damascus was taken by Pompey (Josephus *Ant*, 14.40).
65. Millar, *Roman Near East*, 310, see also Isaac, *Limits of Empire*, 62.
66. Schwartz, *Agrippa I*, 132 including n101.
67. Sartre, *L'Orient Romain*, 18.
68. A similar situation had applied in Thrace, "an exceptionally difficult area to control," where the Romans left that task to members of local dynasties. "Once reasonable pacification had occurred, Rome was free to assume provincial control of the region [under Claudius], as it also had in Galatia" (Sullivan, *Near Eastern Royalty*, 323).
69. Sartre, *L'Orient Romain*, 18. Sartre may not have intended to include Aristobulus among the Hérodiens, but his territory was annexed at about the same time as that of Agrippa II.

As we have seen, Agrippa II, Aristobulus, and Salome also had close family connections. Salome was the niece of Agrippa I and Aristobulus was his nephew, so that each was first cousin to Agrippa II. Aristobulus and Bernice, the sister of Agrippa II, had a closer relationship: his father, Herod of Chalcis, had married Bernice who bore him two children. Aristobulus reigned until at least 87 "and it is possible that he did not die till A.D. 92, when his capital Chalcis initiated a new era to mark its transformation into a republic."[70] That is, he was ruler of Chalcis while Luke was writing Luke-Acts.

2.2.8 Philo and Josephus

Most of our information about the house of Herod comes from Philo (who may have been a source for Josephus) and Josephus. Both had links to members of that house. Philo was the brother of Alexander the Alabarch who lent a large sum to Agrippa I. Alexander's son, Philo's nephew, Marcus Julius Alexander, was the first husband of Bernice and another son (and nephew of Philo), Tiberius Julius Alexander, was procurator of Judaea from about 46/47 to 48/49.[71] Josephus had no familial relationship,[72] but sold copies of his works both to a "Herod" (who seems to have been the son of Aristobulus and Salome)[73] and to Agrippa II,[74] and named one of his own sons Agrippa.[75] Indeed, "Josephus was friendly with Agrippa and claims that Agrippa verified the accuracy of his historical accounts."[76] Even if this claim is exaggerated, these contacts suggest that Josephus had Herodian sources.[77]

---

70. Jones, *Herods of Judaea*, 260, so also Paltiel (*Vassals and Rebels*, 324). Both of these scholars place Aristobulus in Chalcis ad Belum, but this need not affect the dating.

71. Kokkinos, *Herodian Dynasty*, 198.

72. He was of Hasmonean blood (Josephus, *Life*, 3), but his descent was from the father-in-law of Salome Alexandra, remote from that of Agrippa.

73. Kokkinos, *Herodian Dynasty*, 313.

74. Josephus, *Apion* 1.51.

75. Josephus, *Life* 428.

76. Richardson, "Herod," 584.

77. Mason finds that Josephus had "outstanding sources for his accounts of the Herodian dynasty" (*New Testament*, 153).

2.3 LUKE'S ANTETEXT: MARK

2.3.1 Changes to Mark

Luke made substantial changes to Mark's account of Antipas. In this section we deal with the matters covered by Mark which Luke altered or omitted—Luke's new material will be considered in 2.4.

In his story of the execution of the Baptist, Mark first mentions "King Herod," that is, Antipas (Mark 6:14). Antipas was not a king (as we have seen, a cause of jealousy) and Luke corrects Mark in this, calling him "Herod the ruler" (Luke 9:7).[78] Mark (followed by Matthew)[79] makes Herodias "his brother Philip's wife" (Mark 6:17), but she was, according to Josephus, the wife of his brother Herod. Luke corrects Mark in this also, by saying only "his brother's wife," with no mention of Philip (Luke 3:19). Mark then describes what people are saying about Jesus, and adds: "But when Herod heard of it, he said, 'John, whom I beheaded, has been raised'" (Mark 6:16). Luke also alters this:

> Now Herod the ruler heard about all that had taken place, and he was perplexed, because it was said by some that John had been raised from the dead, by some that Elijah had appeared, and by others that one of the ancient prophets had arisen. Herod said, "John I beheaded; but who is this about whom I hear such things?" (Luke 9:7-9).

So, where Mark has Antipas say: "John . . . has been raised," Luke instead shows him simply asking who Jesus is, without supplying an answer. Mark's version seems implausible, as Antipas, like the other members of his family, was one "whose views on the after-life would probably have been more Hellenistic and Sadducaean";[80] he had been educated in Rome.[81] Moreover, "the great majority of the ancients . . . did not believe in resurrection."[82] Luke corrected Mark here also.

Luke totally omits Mark's story of the dance which led to the death of the Baptist (Mark 6:19-29). This may[83] have been because he had heard a

78. Also Matt 14:1.
79. Matt 14:3.
80. Hoehner, *Herod Antipas*, 189.
81. Josephus, *Ant* 17.20.
82. Wright, *Resurrection*, 82-83.

83. Luke omits most of a substantial section (6:14—8:26) of Mark, including this passage. Various explanations have been put forward for this, but that Luke decided to make a number of individual amendments, including this change, seems plausible. For example, the omission of Mark 7:1-22 may have been because it did not fit well with

different story, perhaps from the court of Salome (see 2.2.7) or that given by Josephus (see 2.2.4), or because he found the story incredible:[84]

> The picture in Mark's story of Herod as full of respect for John, but feeling morally bound to agree to honour a "blank cheque" offered to his/Herodias' daughter, strains credulity. The account in Josephus seems far more plausible.[85]

Luke, then, seems to have corrected Mark about a) the royal status of Antipas, b) the name of the first husband of Herodias, c) the allegation that Antipas thought Jesus was the Baptist raised from the dead and d) the story of the dancer. These corrections suggest that Luke had, in addition to Mark, at least one other source of information about the house of Herod.

Josephus suggests that "John is executed because Herod fears an insurrection."[86] There is co-textual evidence for the view that Luke was aware of this explanation—he describes how the Baptist told tax collectors and soldiers to do their duty (Luke 3:12-14).[87] The choice of these two professions, the mainstay of any state, and the specific instructions to them may have been intended to demonstrate that the Baptist was not a threat to the rule of Antipas. Luke does not give a reason for the execution of the Baptist, but, following Mark, tells us that he had been imprisoned "because of Herodias" (Luke 3:19). Antipas, for the reason given by Josephus (see 2.2.4), may, indeed, have been sensitive about his brother's wife; Luke suggests that Felix was also sensitive about his marriage.[88]

2.3.2 Luke's Herodian Source

Scholars have argued that the mention of Joanna, "the wife of Herod's steward Chuza" (Luke 8:3), and of Manaen, "a member of the court of Herod the ruler" (Acts 13:1), suggests that they may have been Lukan sources.[89] A further indication of a possible source may be drawn from Luke's unexplained

---

Luke's presentation of the Pharisees—see 4.5.

84. As a historian, he may have been aware of the similar story told of Xerxes (Herodotus, *Histories* 9.110-12).

85. Tuckett, "Mark," 898.

86. Ibid., 898.

87. We argue, in 3.3.1, that the soldiers (and therefore tax-collectors) whom the Lukan Baptist addressed were in the service of Antipas.

88. See 2.4.5.

89. E. g., Fitzmyer, *Luke I-IX*, 89.

mention of Abilene (Luke 3:1).[90] This was part of the territory of Agrippa II, having previously been a separate kingdom centered on Abila. It is unlikely that Agrippa followed the example of Philip and progressed around his territories administering justice and he may rarely have visited Abila, but he was a former ruler of Chalcis and a major patron of Berytus and in the course of his long reign probably visited that city often. There was, as we noted in 2.2.7, the possibility of frequent communication between Abila and Berytus along a trade route which passed through Chalcis, which in the time of Agrippa II was ruled by Aristobulus and his wife, Salome, whose very close family connections to Agrippa II and Bernice were described in 2.2.7. If Luke did have a source at Abila, he or she will have had contact with Chalcis and is likely to have heard the version of the death of the Baptist current at that court; Luke may have amended the story that he found in Mark in the light of this. It is possible that Luke mentioned Abilene, an obscure place unconnected with his story, because he envisaged his source as being among his potential readers.[91]

Two other possibilities in relation to Herodian sources for Luke have been identified in recent years. Richard Bauckham has argued that Joanna, mentioned in Luke 8:3, was the woman named by Paul as Junia (Romans 16:7) and to whom he sent greetings.[92] It is generally accepted that Paul wrote Romans shortly before he was sent to Rome, and if Paul sent greetings to her, it is likely that she was still in Rome when Paul (and Luke) arrived there. If so, Luke may have known her and obtained information about Antipas to whom her husband was steward.

It has also been argued that the centurion Julius (Acts 27:1) was in the service of Agrippa II (see 3.2.2). If so, the soldiers under his command will also have been in the service of Agrippa and Luke clearly had ample opportunity to get to know them, perhaps especially if our conjecture about Luke's age is correct.[93] One of these soldiers could have provided Luke with information, and, indeed, might have ended up in Abilene.[94]

---

90. "Why Luke singles out [this] tiny tetrarchy . . . is a mystery" (Fitzmyer, *Luke I-IX*, 458). For Bovon: "It is also possible that . . . he . . . has a particular interest in this region . . . At the time he wrote, it indeed still belonged to the Jewish king Agrippa II" (Bovon, *Luke 1*, 120).

91. Other details in Luke's narrative which may have been included with a particular element of his readership in mind are described in 1.6, 2.4.6 and 3.2.2.

92. Bauckham, *Gospel Women*, 109-202.

93. See 1.1.2.

94. If Julius himself ended up in Abilene he could appropriately be addressed as *kratiste*, a big fish in a small pond.

64 Luke's People

There is further evidence for a Herodian source for Luke[95] in the extensive non-Markan pericopes considered in 2.4, especially the story of the death of Agrippa I, as Schwartz considers that the accounts in Josephus and Luke are based on similar Jewish sources[96]—we have described in 2.2.8 the evidence for a Herodian source for Josephus. Each seems to have had a source of information close to the Herodian courts.

2.4 LUKE'S TWO-VOLUME WORK

2.4.1 Introduction

In considering the way in which Luke intends us to view the members of the house of Herod we need to bear in mind the story of Jesus's temptation in the wilderness. This story is told at the very beginning of Jesus's ministry and includes a description of the devil's power over the kingdoms of the world:

> Then the devil led him up and showed him in an instant all the kingdoms of the world. And the devil said to him, "To you I will give their glory and all this authority; for it has been given over to me, and I give it to anyone I please" (Luke 4:5–6).[97]

Mark's story of the temptation gives us no details, these come from Q, and Matthew is much less explicit (Matt 4:8–9); only the Lukan[98] devil claims that "this authority . . . has been given over to me." Not only is this claim uniquely Lukan, but Luke went on to describe in his narrative many men who possessed the "glory" and the "authority." The devil's claim warrants attention, and we believe that it is of great importance for understanding Luke's presentation of the powerful rulers who feature in both volumes. "In the first-century Mediterranean world, this claim can mean only one thing: The Roman emperor possesses authority because it has been given to him by the devil."[99] And so did the Herodian rulers, whether they obtained such authority at first- or second-hand. The relevance of the devil's claim to

---

95. The references to the wife of Chuza (Luke 8:3) and to Manaen (Acts 13:1) are of themselves evidence of a Herodian source.

96. Schwartz, *Agrippa I*, 146–49.

97. Paul describes the end-time, after Christ "has destroyed every ruler and every authority and power" (1 Cor 15:24). We discuss another parallel between Luke-Acts and 1 Corinthians in respect of prophecy (see 6.1.4.2, 6.1.4.3).

98. This is a Lukan addition to Q according to Fitzmyer (*Luke I–IX*, 507) and Gibson (*Temptations of Jesus*, 36–37).

99. Hays, "Liberation of Israel," 114.

Luke's own time can be understood in the light of the history of the house of Herod described in 2.2 and Luke's presentation of those to whom glory and authority had been given in both this and the following chapter.

2.4.2 Antipas and Philip

Luke's first references to the house of Herod are to Herod the Great (Luke 1:5), Antipas and Philip (Luke 3:1), primarily temporal markers, but the mention of Philip may be important in another way. It reminds us that the territories of Herod the Great were divided, and prepares us to understand why Jesus chose to go from the territories of Antipas to those of Philip, specifically to Bethsaida (Luke 9:10). At this point in the narrative we know that the Baptist had rebuked Antipas about Herodias and that Antipas had imprisoned him (Luke 3:19–20). His significance has been emphasized by first the baptism of Jesus (Luke 3:21–22), and then by the messengers from the Baptist and Jesus's praise of him (Luke 7:18–35). As we have seen in 2.3.1, Antipas now reappears in the narrative:

> Now Herod the ruler ... said, "John I beheaded; but who is this about whom I hear such things?" And he tried to see him (Luke 9:7–9).

In an example of analepsis, it is only at this point that Luke tells us that the Baptist had been killed. This information makes it clear that Antipas was not a disinterested observer, but a mortal threat to Jesus, who immediately (Luke 9:10) left his territories for a time. Mark, Luke's antetext, also describes a withdrawal by Jesus after informing us of the death of the Baptist, but he gives the reason as the need for a rest (Mark 6:31–32). Matthew, however, even more explicitly than Luke, has Jesus withdraw because of what Antipas had done (Matt 14:13), but both Mark and Matthew refer only to a deserted place: Luke specifies Bethsaida (Luke 9:10). He has earlier reminded us that Philip ruled a different territory, and we can deduce that he, and therefore the intended reader, knew that Bethsaida was part of that territory. As a result, the withdrawal to a separate jurisdiction is clearly seen as an immediate response to the threat from Antipas.[100] If Luke did not intend this, why mention Bethsaida when his antetext, Mark, did not?[101]

---

100. This is the more obvious if Luke used Matthew as a source.

101. Many scholars believe that "Luke has obviously derived the name from Mark 6:46" (Fitzmyer, *Luke I–IX*, 765). But why attribute his use of the name to a misreading of Mark, when there is an alternative explanation, that is, awareness of the separate jurisdiction?

We next see Pharisees warning Jesus that Antipas wants to kill him (Luke 13:31).[102] In view of the death of John and the withdrawal to Bethsaida this is not a surprise, either to Jesus or to us. Jesus responded by telling the Pharisees:

> Go and tell that fox for me, "Listen, I am casting out demons and performing cures today and tomorrow, and on the third day I finish my work. Yet today, tomorrow, and the next day I must be on my way, because it is impossible for a prophet to be killed outside of Jerusalem" (Luke 13:32–33).

In saying that he cast out demons he implicitly (for the intended reader) referred to the devil (the lord of the demons) who claimed, as we have seen, to have given rulers (including Antipas) their authority; defying Antipas, he did not again leave his territories except to go on his way to Jerusalem.[103] In considering what Jesus meant by his epithet of "fox" we should set aside connotations derived from Aesop (or Uncle Remus). Luke's intertextual image, which would have been recognized by his intended reader, is of the fox as destructive, vermin,[104] and comes from the Septuagint, and perhaps particularly from the Song of Songs:

> Catch us foxes,
> little ones that ruin vineyards (Song 2:15).[105]

The use of the metaphor of a vineyard for Israel is almost commonplace, and Luke has a long parable on this theme, which describes the murderous behavior of those to whom the vineyard had been entrusted (Luke 20:9–16). Luke himself tells us that the parable was directed against the chief priests (Luke 20:19), but it could also apply to Antipas, who, as the secular ruler of Galilee, had his own responsibilities for the vineyard.[106] His petty and destructive nature is shown when he personally joins with his soldiers in mocking Jesus in the next Herodian pericope, the trial:

---

102. This pericope is discussed further, in relation to the Pharisees, in 4.5.7.

103. He went through "the region between Samaria and Galilee" (17:11). The meaning of this is very unclear (see discussion in Fitzmyer, *Luke X–XXIV*, 1152–54). It may be that Luke wished to mention Samaria without having Jesus leave Galilee at this point.

104. Darr refers to "varmint," noting that: "Of all the connotations associated with foxes, *malicious destructiveness* stands out as most applicable to the Tetrarch" (Darr, *Character Building*, 144).

105. "Daughters of Jerusalem" (Luke 23:28) is the clearest allusion in Luke-Acts to the Song of Songs, where the phrase is used frequently (2:7; 3:5, 10; 5:8, 16; 8:4).

106. Antipas was also responsible for appointing the high priests, but Luke may not have known this. Haenchen, however, considers that he knew of the equivalent responsibility of Agrippa II (Haenchen, *Acts*, 674).

> And when [Pilate] learned that he was under Herod's jurisdiction, he sent him off to Herod, who was himself in Jerusalem at that time. When Herod saw Jesus, he was very glad, for he had been wanting to see him for a long time, because he had heard about him and was hoping to see him perform some sign.[107] He questioned him at some length, but Jesus gave him no answer. The chief priests and the scribes stood by, vehemently accusing him. Even Herod with his soldiers treated him with contempt and mocked him; then he put an elegant robe on him, and sent him back to Pilate. That same day Herod and Pilate became friends with each other; before this they had been enemies (Luke 23:7–12).

Part of the meaning of this passage can be understood by considering the last sentence: "That same day Herod and Pilate became friends with each other; before this they had been enemies" (Luke 23:12):

> It is transparently important for Luke that Herod and Pilate be seen as "friends" at the close of this scene, for this is a remark that seems otherwise out of place. In what sense have they become friends? The best commentary is provided in Acts, where it is said that Herod and Pilate "gathered together" in opposition against "your holy servant Jesus" (Acts 4:26–27). They are thus joined in their hostility against Jesus.[108]

The passage Green cites begins with a quotation from Psalm 2:2:

> The kings of the earth took their stand,
>
> and the rulers have gathered together
>
> against the Lord and against his Messiah.
>
> For in this city, in fact, both Herod and Pontius Pilate, with the Gentiles and the peoples of Israel, gathered together against your holy servant Jesus, whom you anointed (Acts 4:26–27).

The Jerusalem community see the psalm as describing the alliance between Pilate and Antipas, and at the end of this passage Luke tells us that the community was filled with the Holy Spirit (Acts 4:31), confirming their insight. Indeed, the quotation not only explains the alliance between Pilate and Antipas, but also, in uniting the kings and rulers of the earth against the

---

107. Luke makes it clear that looking for a sign from Jesus does not indicate any respect for him—see below.

108. Green, *Gospel of Luke*, 806.

Lord's anointed, can be seen as support for the devil's claim to have given those rulers their authority.[109]

Other co-textual references in the Gospel itself confirm the diabolical use of his authority by Antipas. To summarize Green,[110] we have seen Antipas as ruler of Galilee (Luke 3:1), imprisoning John (Luke 3:19–20), beheading John and trying to see Jesus (Luke 9:7–9), reported as trying to kill Jesus (Luke 13:31) and mocking him in the passage quoted above (Luke 23:7–12). Jesus recognized his malevolence, not only in his flight to Bethsaida and in his naming him as "that fox" (Luke 13:32), with its relation to the parable of the vineyard, but has also predicted both the mockery (Luke 18:32) and that the disciples would be brought before kings and governors (Luke 21:12–13). To all this should be added Jesus's own silence before Antipas (Luke 23:9)—he was not silent before Pilate (Luke 23:3).

Moreover, the naming of Antipas as "Herod"[111] links him closely with his father, Herod the Great, and perhaps with his brother, Archelaus. Agrippa I, the killer of James, is also called "Herod" (Acts 12:1–23), whereas that name is never applied by Luke to Agrippa II, who, as we see in 2.4.6, was not antagonistic to Paul. Luke makes it clear that Antipas is not only an enemy of Jesus but also misunderstands him:

> [To the portrait of Antipas described above] is now added his desire for a sign, an aspiration that was negatively evaluated in 11:16, 29–30. "Seeing" and "hearing" are often used in their metaphorical sense in the Third Gospel, and they operate on this level here, too, as Herod devotes his encounter with Jesus to sign-seeking and interrogation, and so fails to see and hear the revelation of Jesus' identity and status before God . . . Though Herod and the guards regard Jesus as little more than riffraff, they place on him the clothing that Luke and his readers will understand actually befits his station.[112]

Raymond Brown sees the co-text as confirming the antagonism of Antipas:

> A request to Jesus for a sign is seen by him as the mark of an evil generation (11:29) that should be refused. Requests for the marvelous (without the word "sign") constitute for Jesus a diabolic testing in 4:9–12 and a lack of faith in 4:23–24.[113]

---

109. A further intertextual reference for this passage is given in 2.4.4.
110. Green, *Gospel of Luke*, 803–4.
111. Herod was, of course, part of his official name.
112. Green, *Gospel of Luke*, 804, 806.
113. Brown, *Death of the Messiah*, 1:770.

The "elegant robe" in which Antipas clothed Jesus is a message which "indicated to Pilate that Antipas regarded Jesus' kingship with contempt and ridicule."[114] Pilate, indeed, tells us that Antipas did not find Jesus guilty (Luke 23:15), but we cannot read this as meaning he found him innocent—at this point Pilate himself has declared Jesus innocent (Luke 23:4) and Antipas must have been aware of this. Taken with the new friendship between Antipas and Pilate, and the conspiracy between them described in Acts, we should rather read this as meaning that Antipas was happy to let Pilate decide the issue,[115] and did not in any way seek to protect Jesus (who came from his own "vineyard"). Luke's presentation of Antipas continues to be extremely negative.

2.4.3 Archelaus

Before dealing with the members of the house of Herod described in Acts, we should consider Luke's possible references to another son of Herod the Great, Archelaus. One such reference is the census under Quirinius (Luke 2:2)[116] at the time of the birth of Jesus (Luke 2:1–2), as a census[117] was held at the time of the deposition of Archelaus and incorporation of Judaea as a Roman province and Quirinius was at that time governor of Syria. The primary purpose of the mention of the census by Luke may be a plot device to take Joseph and Mary to Bethlehem, but it will also remind the intended reader that another Herodian ruler was deposed by a Roman emperor for his cruelty (2.2.3), and serve as an introduction to the members of the family whom we meet later in Luke's narrative.

Peter Richardson argues that the parable of the ruler who went into a far country "to get royal power for himself" (Luke 19:11–27) is, insofar as it differs from the Q text preserved in Matthew,[118] a close description of the events (described in 2.2.3) following the death of Herod the Great. These led to the appointment of Archelaus as ruler of Judaea, although "Archelaus did

---

114. Hoehner, *Herod Antipas*, 243.

115. At this point Pilate still wanted to release Jesus.

116. Luke's mention of Quirinius may be because of his connection with the Caristanius family, as discussed in 1.6. Dating the birth of Jesus at this time raises severe chronological difficulties—see Brown, *Birth of the Messiah*, 547–56.

117. The census referred to by Gamaliel (Acts 5:37).

118. Or from Matthew if that Gospel was Luke's source.

not receive the 'kingdom' (he was made ethnarch)[119] . . . and he killed many *before* he left."[120]

2.4.4 Agrippa I

Agrippa I, like Antipas, is called Herod or King Herod (Acts 12:1) and he "had James, the brother of John, killed with the sword. After he saw that it pleased the Jews, he proceeded to arrest Peter" (Acts 12:2–3). Both Antipas[121] and Agrippa sought to please the Jews, and in 2.4.5 and 3.4.4 we shall see Felix and his successor as governor, Festus, described as having the same motivation (Acts 24:27; 25:9). But the apostles were not the only victims of Agrippa I, as he "laid violent hands upon some who belonged to the church" (Acts 12:1), and there is little doubt but that he planned to kill Peter, "intending to bring him out to the people after the Passover" (Acts 12:4). Peter was freed by divine intervention, but Herod did not recognize this and "examined the guards and ordered them to be put to death" (Acts 12:19). His bloodthirstiness was in the tradition of the rulers of the house of Herod, from Herod the Great through Archelaus and Antipas. "[Agrippa I] is presented as an evil ruler who not only persecutes the church but also is willing to accept divine honors and is punished for his hubris."[122]

Luke also tells us how Agrippa died, in a description broadly similar to that by Josephus,[123] but adding that he was eaten by worms (Acts 12:23).[124] This is the way that Josephus describes the death of Herod the Great, said to be "a judgement on him for his treatment of the professors (*sophistōn*)"[125]— we have argued in 2.3.2 that stories heard by Josephus about the house of

---

119. The difference between ethnarch and king is not very significant in the context of the parable. Both were titles of rulers and rulers were frequently called kings, even if they did not formally possess the title, for example Acts 12:1 (see 2.4.4) and Mark 6:14 (see 2.3.1). However, as we there argue, the difference was more important for Luke, a historian.

120. Richardson, *Herod: King of the Jews*, 300. Marshall also sees this resemblance (*Gospel of Luke*, 704).

121. In his mockery of Jesus reflecting the vehement hostility of the chief priests (Luke 23:10).

122. Tannehill, *Narrative Unity*, 2:157.

123. Josephus, *Ant* 19.343–50.

124. Such a death was also seen as a divine punishment by both Jews and Greeks— e.g., Herodotus, *Histories* 4.205. Barrett lists many other examples (Barrett, *Critical and Exegetical Commentary*, 1:591).

125. Josephus, *War* 1.656. *Sophistai* "is employed by Josephus as the equivalent of the Jewish 'Rabbi'" (LCL Jewish War, Books I–III, 306–7, note b, by Thackeray).

Herod could have been known to Luke. Such a death also has intertextual references, and these add rich resonances to the account of the death of Agrippa in the mind of the intended reader. The primary reference is perhaps the death of Antiochus IV Epiphanes, who was also eaten by worms (2 Macc 9:9).[126] Antiochus[127] "was the first Seleucid king to be designated *theos* ('god') on his coinage, a practice that probably increased Jewish opposition to him."[128] This trait in Antiochus is referred to in Daniel:

> He . . . will be exalted over every god and will speak strange things against the God of gods (Dan 11:36).

An adjacent passage may have been alluded to in describing the developing friendship between Pilate and Antipas (Luke 23:12): "And both kings—their hearts for evil and at one table—will speak lies" (Dan 11:27).[129] As Luke himself tells us (see 2.4.2), that friendship was foreseen in Psalm 2, but he may be alluding to both passages.[130]

2.4.5 Felix and Drusilla

Luke later tells us how Paul was brought to trial before Felix, who received an explanatory letter from the tribune in Jerusalem, and heard both Paul's accusers and Paul himself. Paul gave Felix a perfunctory *captatio*: "Knowing that for many years you have been a judge over this nation" (Acts 24:10), which contrasts sharply with the fulsome one from Tertullus—"three verses out of seven!—unusually broadly developed."[131] Felix, perfectly properly, adjourned the hearing until the tribune came down (Acts 24:22). However:

> Some days later when Felix came with his wife Drusilla, who was Jewish, he sent for Paul and heard him speak concerning

---

126. The king of Babylon who said, "I will be like the Most High" (Isa 14:14), is also punished by worms: "A worm will be your covering" (Isa 14:11). Here, however, ordinary burial is meant.

127. He had not only desecrated the temple (1 Macc 1:21–24) and "constructed an abomination of desolation on the altar" (1 Macc 1:54, similar Dan 11:31), but also "wherever there was found in someone's possession a book of the covenant, or if someone was conforming to the law, the judgment of the king put them to death" (1 Macc 1:57).

128. Harrington, "Antiochus," 69.

129. The clearest Lukan reference to Daniel is the name of Gabriel (Dan 9:21). For other references in the infancy narrative see Green, *Gospel of Luke*, 69n25.

130. Luke could combine very many Septuagintal references in a single passage—see, e.g., the citation from Ó Fearghail in 1.3.3.

131. Haenchen, *Acts*, 657.

faith in Christ Jesus. And as he discussed justice, self-control, and the coming judgment, Felix became frightened and said, "Go away for the present; when I have an opportunity, I will send for you." At the same time he hoped that money would be given him by Paul, and for that reason he used to send for him very often and converse with him. After two years had passed, Felix was succeeded by Porcius Festus; and since he wanted to grant the Jews a favor, Felix left Paul in prison (Acts 24:24–27).

Luke notes that Drusilla was Jewish, which reminds the intended reader that she was the sister of Agrippa II, and also suggests that she was the reason that Felix was "rather well informed about the Way" (Acts 24:22). Drusilla, unlike Bernice, is seen not at the public hearing but in the private meeting between Felix and Paul at which Felix became frightened (Acts 24:24–25):

> The adulterous marriage of Felix to Drusilla may be the background for Paul's remarks on such topics. The threesome mentioned would have been meant to remind Felix about his rapacity and greed, lust, and coming doom.[132]

His rapacity[133] is confirmed when, hoping for money from Paul, he kept him in prison and often conversed with him: "His hope for a bribe . . . fits in well with the black picture of Felix and his rapacity found in Tacitus and Josephus,"[134] a view of Felix that will have been known to the intended reader.[135] During this time in prison Paul evangelized Felix and his wife Drusilla but there is no indication that he was able to evangelize others, as he was to do later when in custody in Rome (Acts 28:30–31).

Felix left Paul in prison when he was recalled to Rome, although "Luke implies that [he] could have easily released Paul at this juncture but decided against doing so."[136] He did this because "he wanted to grant the Jews a favor" (24:27) but this was also an attempt to protect himself. Luke (and the intended reader) may have known the reason for his recall as told by Josephus:

---

132. Fitzmyer, *Acts*, 740. Haenchen has a similar view: "Felix's willingness to listen has its limits: the point at which the sermon touched upon his own conscience" (*Acts*, 662).

133. We shall see other people led astray by love of money in chapter 5.

134. Fitzmyer, *Acts*, 740.

135. Felix was a figure of political importance and personal notoriety who would have been remembered when Luke wrote, some 25 years after his recall.

136. Cassidy, *Society and Politics*, 106.

The leaders of the Jewish community of Caesarea went up to Rome to accuse Felix. He would undoubtedly have paid the penalty for his misdeeds against the Jews had not Nero yielded to the urgent entreaty of Felix's brother Pallas,[137] whom at that time he held in the highest honour.[138]

Although Tannehill argues that Luke's narrator "never supplies a clear explanation of Felix's inaction,"[139] the problem surely is that Luke supplies too many reasons. Felix a) is venal, b) wants to please the Jews, and c) is frightened by Paul's rebuke. Perhaps we should also consider a possible d), his desire to learn more about the Way, although if this existed it was soon overtaken by his rapacity and fear of the Jews. Felix is presented with less sympathy than almost all the other Roman officials discussed in chapter 3: "The self-interested actions of an unjust judge are obvious in the final verses of this scene."[140]

2.4.6 Agrippa II and Bernice

Turning to Agrippa II, we note that Luke does not call him "Herod," a first indication that he may differ from most of his Herodian predecessors, so named by Luke. Agrippa and Bernice came to Caesarea to welcome Festus on his arrival to replace Felix. He told them about Paul, and Agrippa asked to hear him, in so doing reminding us of Felix, and also of Antipas wanting to see (and hear) Jesus (Luke 9:9; 23:8–9). The following day Agrippa and Bernice came to the audience hall of the governor and Agrippa told Paul to "speak for yourself" (Acts 26:1).

Agrippa was believed to have had an incestuous relationship with his sister Bernice.[141] Luke will have heard these stories, although he may also have heard that there was no truth in them. In any event, the Lukan Paul treated Agrippa with great respect, addressing him with a full *captatio benevolentiae*, telling him that he was "especially familiar with all the customs and controversies of the Jews" (26:3) and using a number of honorific des-

---

137. Pallas himself was to be dismissed and executed by Nero (see 2.2.6).
138. Josephus, *Ant* 20.182.
139. Tannehill, *Narrative Unity*, 2:301.
140. Ibid., 303.
141. See 2.2.6. If such incest occurred, it was likely to have been in Chalcis (adjacent to Abilene), where Agrippa as king, is likely to have provided a home for his sister, who was the widow of his predecessor and whose father was dead. The fairly common practice of a new king marrying the widow of his predecessor may have contributed to the rumor.

ignations (Acts 26:2, 7, 13, 19, 26, 27). These compliments were lacking in Luke's report of Paul's speech before Felix—it is the narrator, not Paul, who tells us that Felix "was rather well informed about the Way" (Acts 24:22)—and Paul did not chide Agrippa about his alleged relationship with Bernice, a marked contrast to the rebuke which frightened Felix. Later, Agrippa and Bernice, with Festus and the others, agreed that Paul was innocent (Acts 26:31). Agrippa even said: "This man could have been set free if he had not appealed to the emperor" (Acts 26:32).

Apart from Agrippa's influence on Festus and on Paul's own fate, Luke tells us about his attitude to Christianity, shown in his response to a question of Paul's:

> "King Agrippa, do you believe the prophets? I know that you believe." Agrippa said to Paul, "Are you so quickly persuading me to become a Christian?" Paul replied, "Whether quickly or not, I pray to God that not only you but also all who are listening to me today might become such as I am—except for these chains" (Acts 26:27-29).

Paul's question is testing:

> Paul's rhetorical question is a real challenge: it asks a Herodian king to reach a conclusion that Paul, a Jew, considers obvious. Implicitly Paul is telling the king that what has happened . . . had already been foreseen by prophets in Israel, in whom he, as a Jewish king, should be believing.[142]

The meaning of Agrippa's response is not clear. Paul seems to have read it as meaning "with a little more time,"[143] alternatively it may involve some "witty interplay."[144] There is little doubt that Agrippa was being ironic; he was not converted. It may be that Luke was seeking to keep open the possibility of instructing Agrippa—he has already shown us the wife of Chuza and Manaen, important members of Herodian courts, become Christians (Luke 8:3; Acts 13:1). As we have seen, his stated objective in writing his two-volume work was "so that you [Theophilus] may know the truth concerning the things about which you have been instructed" (Luke 1:4), but the work was not directed to Theophilus alone, but to all his intended readers. His references to Abilene, to Joanna, Chuza and Manaen, and to the Italian and Augustan cohorts (see 3.2.2) may have been included to add interest for an audience in the Herodian courts. If so, he may have hoped

---

142. Fitzmyer, *Acts*, 764. So also Tannehill, *Narrative Unity*, 2:328.
143. Fitzmyer, *Acts*, 765.
144. Tannehill, *Narrative Unity*, 2:329.

indirectly to influence Agrippa, who was still living when Luke was writing Luke-Acts, and who, having been educated in Rome, is likely to have shared to some extent the ethos described in 3.4.4.

Bernice, like Agrippa himself, attended the hearing called so that Festus could have something to write to the emperor about the case (Acts 25:26–27), that is, as part of a group to help Festus in his judicial role.[145] That Bernice was part of such a body is totally consistent with the portrayal of her by Josephus,[146] and in Luke's narrative she, with Festus and Agrippa, is specifically identified as among those who "said to one another, 'This man is doing nothing to deserve death or imprisonment'" (Acts 26:31). Ivoni Richter Reimer finds that: "Neither Drusilla nor Bernice says a single word, nor do they decide anything. They probably exercise no influence on the events."[147] As regards Bernice, this is just wrong. She advised Festus with Agrippa and "the military tribunes and the prominent men of the city" (Acts 25:23), and is specifically named, with others, as declaring the innocence of Paul (Acts 26:30–32), so influencing the report which Festus would have sent to Rome.[148] There is, of course, no suggestion that she was at all convinced by Paul's message about the Way.

2.5 SUMMARY

In this chapter we have mainly used our tools of the historical context, Luke's changes to his Markan antetext and Luke's own co-text, to understand how Luke's intended audience would have read his portrayal of the rulers of the house of Herod. Luke has called Antipas and Agrippa I "Herod," told us how Antipas killed the Baptist and tried to kill Jesus, and how Agrippa I killed James. He has also, using intertextual allusions, reminded us that Agrippa I, like Herod the Great and Antiochus IV Epiphanes, died in a dramatic punishment by God. These men demonstrate that the kingdoms of the world had been given over to the authority of the devil. There is no ameliorating characteristic in Luke's portrayal; they are all evil men. Felix, a Roman official, although in Luke's narrative he did not kill anyone, was partial, venal, and self-serving, and Luke tells us of his connection with the house of Herod. Two other rulers referred to, Archelaus and Philip, are hardly described, although the territories of Philip provided a safe refuge

---

145. The advisory group, part of the Roman legal system, is described in the next chapter.

146. See 2.2.6.

147. Richter Reimer, *Women in Acts*, 250.

148. For the Roman judicial system, see 3.2.4.

for Jesus. The portrayal of Agrippa II provides a contrast to those of most of his predecessors. He listened to Paul, and, acting justly, concluded that he was innocent and so advised Festus. He was also interested in what Paul had to say about the Way, and, unlike Felix, was not corrupted by greed. As we suggested above, Luke may have hoped to evangelize Agrippa II through his contact in Abilene—we may take it that he shared the wish of Paul that all "might become such as I am" (Acts 26:29).

Luke also describes a number of women belonging to the House. He eliminates Mark's condemnation of Herodias, leaving only a reference to Antipas's own evil act in marrying his brother's wife. He also totally removes Mark's description of the dancer (Salome). Although Herodias and Drusilla are mentioned only in passing, Bernice is seen as a powerful and independent woman, who, like Agrippa II, listened to Paul and publicly stated his innocence. She shares in Luke's almost invariably positive presentation of women, discussed in chapters 6 and 7.

All of these men and women were rich,[149] most of them far, far, richer than almost any of the other characters in Luke's narrative. The men in the Gospel are presented as evil, as are Agrippa I and Felix in Acts. Later, Agrippa II and Bernice are presented much more sympathetically; we are even left to wonder if we are to take Agrippa seriously when he says: "Are you so quickly persuading me to become a Christian?" (Acts 26:28). Luke shows this extremely rich man, and Bernice, in a positive light. However, they do not become Christians, and Luke's intended readers are likely to have been aware that the Herodian women mentioned, Herodias, Drusilla, and Bernice, had all left their husbands for other men of greater wealth and higher social status. The narrator's viewpoint remains negative even for Agrippa II and Bernice.

---

149. Douglas Oakman has calculated that Herod the Great "was as wealthy as the wealthiest senators of the early empire" (Oakman, *Jesus and Economic Questions*, 70). His comparison, based on total income, is not altogether valid, as Herod, who was the ruler of a large territory, would have had to meet the costs of his administration and army out of his income. Nevertheless, he was richer than most senators and this was also true of Agrippa I (who ruled a territory broadly equivalent) and probably of Antipas and Agrippa II, although their territories and incomes were much smaller.

CHAPTER 3

The Roman Authorities

3.1 INTRODUCTION

In this chapter we consider Luke's presentation of the Roman authorities. We shall seek to demonstrate that Luke portrays Roman governors, part of the ruling elite of the Roman empire, as both corrupt and self-serving, and that even when one of them (Festus) is honest, the system he serves is itself corrupt, as would be expected of a system based upon the authority of the devil (Luke 4:6).[1] In contrast, soldiers, especially centurions, who were not part of that ruling elite, are seen positively, as generally are the municipal authorities, whose members were part of the local elites considered in chapter 5, although in their official capacity they were part of the system of Roman administration considered here.[2]

We again use our tools of context and co-text, making only limited use of intertext and antetext. In chapter 1 we argued that Luke, and, therefore, the intended reader, was familiar with the world of the Eastern empire in the first century, and that this would include the legal process in the courts of the Roman governors; thus Luke's intended readers had the background knowledge necessary to understand the proceedings. By carefully examining the words Luke wrote, the co-text, and taking full account of the context, we too can obtain a more comprehensive picture of what he understood to

---

1. "Luke tells his reader that the entirety of [the Roman imperial] system is under Satan's control. This is a crucial key to understanding Luke's portrayals of Roman officials" (Yamazaki-Ransom, *Roman Empire*, 97). See 2.4.1.

2. Tax collectors were also part of the Roman administration system, but those named, Levi (Luke 5:27) and Zacchaeus (Luke 19:2), were both Jewish, as were those baptized by the Baptist (Luke 3:12). Luke does not deal with tax collectors in their administrative role and they are considered in chapter 5.

have been the course of the trials before the governors. This, then, informs us about how his intended readers would see their characters, a procedure especially useful in regard to Festus. Section 3.2 describes elements of the context within which Luke wrote, in particular the Roman provincial administration, the army, and the legal system. We then consider Luke's presentation of the individuals concerned, making use of both context and co-text. 3.3 deals with soldiers, 3.4 with governors, and 3.5 with the municipal authorities. We summarize our findings in 3.6.

3.2 CONTEXT

3.2.1 The Provincial Administration of the Roman Empire

Rome governed the greater part of its empire through individuals with responsibility for the administration of specific provinces, who had various titles, but may be called governors. Some provinces, usually near the frontiers or for other reasons particularly sensitive, including Judaea, were ruled by governors who were "appointed and dismissed by the Emperor and stayed in office as long as he chose."[3] Such imperial provinces included both Syria, which was administered by a senatorial governor, that is, one who belonged to the highest echelon of Roman society, and Judaea, whose administrator was of equestrian, that is, lower, status, but still part of the empire's ruling elite:

> The Syrian governor was not just governor of a province and the commander of a large legionary force, but was generally regarded as the most distinguished governor in the Roman Empire, holding the highest charge . . . It is clear that these men quite overshadowed the equestrian governors ruling Judaea.[4]

The governors of Judaea were titled *praefectus* before the reign of Agrippa I and *procurator* thereafter.[5] They did not command any legionary force—for these they were dependent upon Syria—but did command a number of cohorts of auxiliary troops:

> Units raised from the gentile populations of Caesarea and Sebaste formed an important part of Herod's army, then (it seems

---

3. Millar, *Roman Near East*, 45.
4. Stern, "Province of Judaea," 314.
5. Millar, *Roman Near East*, 44, 61.

certain) of the army of the *praefecti*, then that of Agrippa I and finally that of the *procuratores*.⁶

Because the governors of Judaea had limited forces, each of them relied, in the last resort, on the forces of the governor of Syria, who, if necessary, could depose the governor of Judaea, as, in the end, happened to Pilate:⁷

> Pilate's relative strength as governor in comparison to that of his predecessors and successors was also due to the fact that down to 32 CE there was no governor of Syria . . . Only in 32 CE was a new legate appointed . . . In consequence of this . . . Pilate's actions were more restricted during the last years of his term than during his first five.⁸

Helen Bond argues that for Pilate this absence of the governor of Syria meant that "unlike his predecessors, he could not rely upon the immediate support of the legions in case of unrest."⁹ This point should not be overstated: in the event of serious problems it is unlikely that the absence of the Syrian governor would have prevented or long delayed the mobilisation of the legions, but his long-term absence undoubtedly will have lessened the constraints on Pilate's freedom of action.¹⁰

The governor of Judaea seems to have received an annual salary of 100,000 *sestercii*.¹¹ This was a substantial sum, but not so high as to prevent some governors from seeking to augment their income with bribes. Nevertheless, a salary of that magnitude, combined with the property qualification required for equestrian status (400,000 *sestercii*), meant that the governors of Judaea were wealthy by most standards, although not when compared with the Herodian rulers, or, indeed, the high priests (see 4.2.2).

The governors of other provinces encountered in Luke-Acts were not imperial appointees:

---

6. Ibid., 356.

7. Bond, *Pontius Pilate*, 73.

8. Stern, "Province of Judaea," 349–50. It is not that there was no governor of Syria, but rather that he was kept in Rome by Tiberias, and fulfilled his duties from there.

9. Bond, *Pontius Pilate*, 15.

10. However, it is not known in which year the trial of Jesus took place. Most commentators elect for either 31 (when the governor of Syria was in Rome) or 34 (when he was in Syria).

11. Stern, "Province of Judaea," 320.

> Macedonia, Achaia, and Asia . . . were senatorial provinces[12] . . . The governors who administered them were selected by the Roman senate and were themselves members of the senate . . . Since the power these governors exercised in the provinces was comparable to that of a consul in Rome, they were titled *proconsuls*. Their authority was supreme within the province's boundaries. However, in practice two factors significantly influenced their exercise of this authority. First, their term of office was only for one year. Secondly, another point of contrast with the governors of imperial provinces, they usually did not have a significant number of Roman troops or a large administrative staff directly under their control.[13]

For his year in office the "proconsul had the total power of administration, jurisdiction, and defence."[14] That these governors were senators meant that by ordinary standards they were already rich, for, as we have seen, the minimum property qualification for senatorial rank was one million *sestercii* and most were much richer.

3.2.2 The Roman Army

In this section we describe those elements of the Roman army relevant to Luke-Acts, including a description of their roles in that army. The Roman army comprised both legions and auxiliary forces and in Luke-Acts we are probably concerned only with auxiliary forces, which were of an inferior status.[15] Legions were commanded by a legate, of senatorial rank, assisted by six tribunes, one being of senatorial rank while the other five, generally equestrians, would usually have previously been prefect of an auxiliary cohort.[16] At a more junior level each legion had 60 centurions with a clear hierarchy of rank. The most senior was known as *primus pilus*, held office for a year and was then appointed to the equestrian order, perhaps going on to occupy other positions appropriate to his new status.[17] However, "the existence of a complicated hierarchy within the group of legionary centurions

---

12. As was Cyprus.
13. Cassidy, *Society and Politics*, 84.
14. Sherwin-White, *Roman Society*, 2.
15. Some scholars, e.g., Speidel, *Roman Army Studies*, 235, argue that regular forces could have served the Herodians.
16. Webster, *Roman Imperial Army*, 112–13.
17. Ibid., 114. As noted in 1.5.2, the annual salary of this office was 15,000 denarii, 60,000 sesterces.

is of less significance than the gap between all of them and the equestran officers of the Roman army"[18] as is shown by the use of the term *caligati*. "*Caliga*[19] was used for service in the lower ranks of the army"[20] and sharply distinguished those ranks from their superior officers.

Auxiliary units were organized on a similar basis, but were commanded by a member of the equestrian class.[21] Such a commander may have been at the beginning of his military career, hoping to go on to serve as a tribune in a legion, as described above. An auxiliary cohort also had centurions:

> Centurions in auxiliary cohorts at the time of Severus Alexander [222–235 CE] were *caligati*, as was everyone in the cohort except the tribune . . . Furthermore it seems a reasonable assumption that if auxiliary centurions were *caligati* at this time, they had always been.[22]

Some auxiliary units were recruited from Roman citizens and the name of the Italian cohort to which Cornelius belonged (Acts 10:1) suggests that it was originally such a unit. However, this could have changed by the time of Cornelius, the original members from Italy having been replaced by local recruits over a period of time. It was the norm for auxiliary recruits to be non-citizens, and from the time of Claudius, as part of the reward for service, soldiers in auxiliary units became Roman citizens on discharge after 25 years, receiving a bronze discharge diploma. Serving centurions in these auxiliary cohorts were usually Roman citizens, but may not have been so by birth—they may have been freedmen, or have purchased their citizenship. To sum up, the status of all the centurions mentioned by Luke was probably similar. They and their cohorts were at times in the service of the rulers of the house of Herod and at other times in that of the Roman governors, but their cohort continued its existence, and the centurions continued their employment[23] and each would have been a Roman citizen, by birth or otherwise. It is clear that both the centurion at Capernaum (Luke 7:2–10) and Cornelius (Acts 10) were economically comfortable, but they were of a very different status to the governors discussed in 3.4.

---

18. Isaac, *Near East*, 395.
19. Caligula, the nickname of the emperor Gaius, is closely related to this word.
20. Gilliam, *Roman Army Papers*, 44.
21. Webster, *Roman Imperial Army*, 146.
22. Gilliam, *Roman Army Papers*, 49.
23. Saddington, *Roman Auxiliary Forces*, 181; Roth, "Army and Economy," 377.

Luke mentions the Italian (Acts 10:1) and the Augustan (Acts 27:1) cohorts, both of which are named in extant inscriptions. There is a gravestone in Austria of an Arab soldier (from what is now Amman) of the Italian auxiliary cohort who died in 69–70 CE after seven years' service. When he was recruited the cohort could have been based in Judaea or in Syria.[24] Cornelius, a centurion of the Italian cohort, lived in Judaea, in Caesarea, but that does not mean that his cohort was based there.[25] Soldiers frequently retired elsewhere,[26] and centurions were often seconded away from their unit (for example, Julius, Acts 27:1). Caesarea was the headquarters of the army in Judaea and it is also possible that Cornelius "may have been seconded to headquarters duty."[27]

Speidel describes an inscription dating from 84 or 89 which names a centurion of the Augustan cohort who was clearly then in the service of Agrippa II, and notes a second similar inscription.[28] He sees Julius as a centurion in the same cohort, also in the service of Agrippa, and finds in this an explanation for an oddity in Acts. Luke tells us that, after the hearing before Festus and Agrippa, "*they* transferred Paul . . . to a centurion of the Augustan cohort" (Acts 27:1, emphasis added). Speidel plausibly argues that Agrippa's great pomp (Acts 25:23) will have included soldiers[29] and Julius, like the other centurions of the same cohort a generation later, was in the service of Agrippa.[30] If so, he must have been seconded by him for the task of conveying Paul to Rome, so that the use of "they," meaning both Festus and Agrippa, is appropriate, as Paul was the responsibility of Festus, but Julius was under orders of Agrippa.[31] If so, the name of the centurion Julius may have been significant to Luke's possible contact in Abilene, also in the service of Agrippa II, some 25 years later.[32]

---

24. Speidel, *Roman Army Studies*, 226–27.

25. Ibid., 229.

26. "All the [discharge] diplomas that refer to units stationed in Syria were found outside of that province, generally in the place to which the soldier retired" (Pollard, *Soldiers, Cities, and Civilians*, 120).

27. Speidel, *Roman Army Studies*, 228.

28. Ibid., 229.

29. Ibid., 231.

30. Agrippa's territories did not change during this period, so there is no reason to suppose the Augustan cohort subsequently transferred to his service.

31. Speidel, *Roman Army Studies*, 231. Barrett suggests that "they" means the officials of Festus (Barrett, *Critical and Exegetical Commentary*, 1:1181), similarly Fitzmyer, *Acts*, 769. But elsewhere Luke uses "he" in similar instances (e. g. Acts 12:1). If Speidel is correct about the inscription his interpretation is more plausible.

32. If the Augustan cohort was in the service of Agrippa, this would have been known by his retainers.

There will have been continuity in the personnel responsible for the administration of Abilene from the time of Agrippa I, ending in 44, to that of Agrippa II, beginning in 53, and probably in the administration of Galilee between the time of Antipas (ending in 39) and that of Agrippa II in the same place (beginning in 54). There may also have been some continuity between the court of Antipas and that of Aristobulus in Chalcis, at least among the personal servants of Salome. Stories told about earlier rulers could have provided information to Luke's Herodian sources.

The tribune, Claudius Lysias, had acquired Roman citizenship for a large sum of money (Acts 22:28), and his name suggests that he received his citizenship during the reign of Claudius or that of Nero.[33] A legate in charge of an auxiliary cohort would normally have been of equestrian status, which could be obtained by a provincial:

> It is possible that he had worked his way up through the ranks and the centurionate of the auxiliary army of Syria, and bought his way into the citizenship—and equestrian status and a military tribunate too—with his personal savings.[34]

However, this seems implausible—it would have required an extremely profitable army career. An alternative explanation may be that:

> In the auxiliary units the commanders under the Julio-Claudian emperors were generally the tribal nobility to whom the soldiers looked as their natural leaders.[35]

There were probably a number of auxiliary units in the area, especially from Ituraea,[36] to which this might have applied, and Lysias could have been such a tribal leader and acquired his citizenship before he took up his post. His wealth ensured that equestrian status which would have been essential for his military career.

These auxiliary soldiers, whether Roman citizens or not, would have been predominantly gentiles:

---

33. Paul was probably arrested around 59. Claudius reigned 41–54 CE. The name could have derived from Nero (54–68), also formally named Claudius.

34. Sherwin-White, *Roman Society*, 155–56.

35. Goodman and Sherwood, *Roman World*, 155–56.

36. Cheesman lists cohorts identified from inscriptions, including, in Syria, five "Chalcidenorum" and one "Flavia Chalcidenorum" (Cheesman, *Auxilia*, 181). Spaul partially disagrees, finding only three from Chalcis, which he takes to be Chalcis in the Lebanon (Spaul, *Cohors*, 422), and therefore confirms they are Ituraean, but also identifies either eight or ten others described as from Ituraea (437).

> Roman army life revolved extensively round the ruler-cult, the consecrated standards and the *auguria*; this . . . more particularly in Judaea during the first century of the current era, made Jews as reluctant to enlist as it made the authorities reluctant to accept them.[37]

An auxiliary unit in Herodian service would not have been subject to the same ruler-cult requirements as a Roman unit: Luke tells us that soldiers went to listen to the Baptist. However, we know that Herod recruited his army from the gentile cities of Caesarea and Sebaste and Josephus tells us that the troops of Agrippa I, like the gentile cities of Caesarea and Sebaste from which they came, rejoiced at his death.[38] Herodian troops were predominantly gentiles.

3.2.3 The Municipal Authorities

Setting aside Jerusalem, dealt with in chapter 4, the municipal authorities whom we meet in Acts were mainly in the senatorial provinces of Achaia and Asia. As we have noted, the governors in those provinces did not have large military or administrative staffs and local officials will have been responsible for the routine maintenance of law and order in their own areas on their own authority without reference to the governor. They would, of course, always have had to bear in mind that the governor could intervene whenever he wished, and had the sole right to inflict capital punishment (which may be why the Jews in Corinth brought Paul before the tribunal of Gallio—Acts 18:12–17). Local officials would also have to be especially careful in dealing with Roman citizens, or, indeed anybody with wealth, power, or influence, and be respectful of the governor in the cities which provided his base, including Corinth, capital of Achaia, and Ephesus, capital of Asia. Such authorities will all have been members of the local elite. We consider the local elites in chapter 5, and in this chapter confine ourselves to those actions carried out in the course of their role as magistrates.

3.2.4 The Roman Judicial System

The majority of the Roman officials presented in both the Gospel and Acts are seen performing duties relating to the Roman judicial system. To

---

37. Applebaum, "Legal Status," 459.
38. Josephus, *Ant* 19.357–58.

understand them we need to understand something of that system, which has been described by A. N. Sherwin-White. In Rome itself:

> The major offences against persons, society, and the government, were defined by a number of detailed statutes—*leges publicae*—concerning, for example, adultery, forgery, murder, bribery, and treason. The whole system was known as the *ordo iudiciorum publicorum* ... [However,] the offences of the common man, such as burglary and robbery, were not covered by the *ordo*. Essentially the *ordo* dealt with the offences of high society and the governing personnel. The crimes of the common man were left to the summary jurisdiction at Rome of the annual magistrates.[39]

In the provinces, the "offences of the common man" were also *extra ordinem*, but there the *ordo* applied only to Roman citizens, that is, non-citizens were subject to the jurisdiction of the local governor even in those matters which in Rome were dealt with by the *ordo*: "A provincial *peregrinus* had no claim to be tried by the rules of the *ordo*."[40] Indeed the power (*exercitio*) of the governor was almost unlimited:

> The extent of the governor's power over the ordinary provincial subject, or *peregrinus homo*, is best seen from the only law that limited it, the extortion law ... A proconsul could be as harsh and arbitrary as he liked, so long as he did not take money or property, "things," *res*, from a provincial, even with the provincial's consent. Then, and only then, did a suit for extortion lie, down to A.D. 11 ... It is probable that henceforth extreme cruelty, or *saevitia* as the sources call it, could be brought as a charge against a governor, even if not accompanied by financial extortion. But this remedy still remained only the remedy of the well-to-do, the *potentes*.[41]

As we have seen, governors in senatorial provinces did not have large administrative staffs. This meant that:

> The governor left a great deal of minor jurisdiction to the local municipal courts. His special concern was with matters affecting public order. These were largely but not solely the capital crimes of the Roman *ordo*. But since the traditions of provincial government were established long before the *ordo* was completed,

---

39. Sherwin-White, *Roman Society*, 13–14.
40. Ibid., 15.
41. Ibid., 3.

provincial jurisdiction was based on the *imperium* and the free exercise of the governor's judgment.[42]

The governor "might follow local custom if he liked, and . . . he was also free to adopt the rules of the *ordo* where this was appropriate. There was no compulsion to do so."[43] He generally followed the basic principles of Roman law:

> The characteristics of the later jurisdiction *extra ordinem* were three in number. First, there is the free formulation of charges and penalties . . . second is the insistence on a proper formal act of accusation by the interested party. Third, cases are heard by the holder of *imperium* in person on his tribunal, and assisted by his advisory cabinet or *consilium* of friends and officials.[44]

We clearly see this in operation in the trial before Festus. Serious, if vague, charges were brought by the Jews from Jerusalem (Acts 25:7), and Festus heard them in person (Acts 25:6) and "conferred with his council" (Acts 25:12). The composition of the council (*consilium*) is illustrated by the "military tribunes and the prominent men of the city" (Acts 25:23) who attended the subsequent hearing before Festus and Agrippa.

The situation of Roman citizens differed from that of *peregrini*:

> The *lex Iulia de vi* protected the Roman citizen who invoked the ancient right of *provocatio*, from summary punishment, execution or torture without trial, from private or public arrest, and from actual trial by magistrates outside Italy.[45]

As a result "the Roman citizen was protected throughout the Roman empire from the capital jurisdiction and violent *coercitio* of provincial governors."[46] An appeal to Caesar under these provisions was not, as is sometimes understood, an appeal against conviction or sentence. It was an election to have the whole question determined in the first instance in Rome, and appropriate documentation would be sent for that purpose.

---

42. Ibid., 14–15.
43. Ibid., 15.
44. Ibid., 17.
45. Ibid., 58. Peter Garnsey sees a similar right in the "little used if not virtually obsolete prerogative . . . (*reiectio Romam*)" (Garnsey, *Social Status*, 76).
46. Sherwin-White, *Roman Society*, 59.

3.3 SOLDIERS OF THE ROMAN ARMY IN LUKE-ACTS

3.3.1 Common Soldiers

Luke first mentions soldiers in describing the ministry of John the Baptist—these soldiers were in the service of Antipas; as we have seen, the auxiliary forces which had served Herod the Great went on to serve not only his sons, but also the Roman governors. The units in Peraea, a likely region for the Baptist's ministry, would have moved from the service of Herod the Great to that of Antipas, to that of the Roman prefects, to that of Agrippa I and then to that of the Roman procurators; their duties will have been similar during the whole of this period. Moreover, the instructions which the Baptist gave to the soldiers of Antipas were equally applicable to the soldiers we meet later in the Gospel and in Acts (who might have been the same individuals): "Do not extort money from anyone by threats or false accusation,[47] and be satisfied with your wages" (Luke 3:14). The prohibition of extortion is similar to the restriction imposed on Roman governors described above,[48] and contrasts with the rapacity of Felix (Acts 24:26). We should note that Luke's Baptist does not regard soldiering (or tax-collecting) as an occupation to be shunned; for him it is an acceptable way to earn a living, even though, then as now, a soldier's duties included the obeying of orders requiring the coercion of others, for Luke from those to whom the devil had given their authority. Indeed, the exemplary obedience expected of soldiers is confirmed co-textually in the message to Jesus from the centurion at Capernaum (Luke 7:8).

Luke first introduces Roman soldiers (auxiliaries) when they taunt Jesus as "king of the Jews" (Luke 23:36-38), picking up the mocking inscription over the cross (Mark 15:26). However, the "sour wine," *ochos*, they offered him (Luke 23:36) was "the ordinary wine used by soldiers,"[49] and intertextually "is implicitly a desirable drink in Num 6:3 and Ruth 2:14."[50] This suggests kindness[51] and the soldiers' mockery of Jesus is much milder than that in Luke's antetext (Mark 15:16-20).[52] The soldiers indeed crucify Jesus, obeying orders, but Luke does not tell us of any additional cruelty, and omits

---

47. For oppression of civilians by soldiers, see Campbell, *Emperor and Roman Army*, 246-54.

48. See 3.2.4.

49. Fitzmyer, *Luke X-XXIV*, 1505.

50. Brown, *Death of the Messiah*, 2:1063.

51. In Mark the wine is not offered by a soldier (Mark 15:36). In Matthew it is mixed with gall and Jesus cannot drink it (Matt 27:34).

52. Or in Matthew (Matt 27:27-31).

mention of the scourging,[53] which was "part of the sentence of crucifixion."[54] This omission is surprising as the Lukan Jesus (following the antetext) had predicted that he would be flogged (Luke 18:33), but by the omission Luke softens the soldiers' part in the crucifixion as far as possible—their actions as described by Luke could not be considered to be *saevitia*, extreme cruelty.

In Acts, the first soldier we meet served Cornelius, was described as "devout" (Acts 10:7) and was sent to lead the mission to Peter. His mission was successful and he presumably was one of those on whom the Spirit fell in the house of Cornelius (Acts 10:44). Later in Acts soldiers again did what they were told to do—they rescued Paul from the mob in Jerusalem (Acts 21:32), and then, on the order of the tribune, arrested Paul (Acts 21:33), and continued to protect him from the mob by carrying him to the barracks (Acts 21:35). They were also ready, at the instruction of the tribune, "to flog him to find out the reason for [the] outcry against him" (Acts 22:24). The tribune was prepared to flog a *peregrinus* involved in a disturbance, "the man who had provoked it,"[55] but Paul escaped this because he was a Roman citizen. There is no suggestion that, for a *peregrinus*, the tribune would, in ordering a flogging, have acted beyond his authority or in any way improperly. If a tribune could order such a flogging for such a reason, we should hesitate before condemning Pilate for offering to flog Jesus, also a *peregrinus*. He, and his superiors, would have seen such an action as appropriate, although such actions remind us (and perhaps Luke's intended reader) of the devil's claim to have bestowed their authority upon them.

Later, at the tribune's instructions, the soldiers again rescued Paul (Acts 23:10), and protected him as he was sent to Felix, and Paul was then kept in custody, presumably by soldiers.[56] On the way to Rome, soldiers saved Paul by cutting the ropes of the boat in which the sailors intended to desert the ship (Acts 27:32). As the danger continued, the soldiers planned to kill Paul and the other prisoners to ensure that they could not escape, but the centurion prevented them (Acts 27:42–43). Luke has already told us that the consequences of letting prisoners escape were dire: we have seen Agrippa I kill the guards who let Peter escape (Acts 12:19), and the gaoler at Philippi was "about to kill himself, since he supposed that the prisoners had escaped" (Acts 16:27). So the soldiers had reason to be fearful. These

---

53. "After sentence had been passed, the condemned person was scourged, the scourging being of such severe nature that loss of blood and frequently a general weakening... took place" (Winter, *Trial of Jesus*, 95).

54. Brown, *Death of the Messiah*, 1:851.

55. Barrett, *Critical and Exegetical Commentary*, 2:1046.

56. The jailer at Philippi was not, as far as we can tell, a soldier as Paul was imprisoned by local magistrates, who, unlike Felix, would not have soldiers at their command.

previous co-textual episodes, together with the action of the centurion in stopping the planned killing, reduce the impact of the soldiers' plan on the reader. However, the centurion stopped the soldiers because he was wishing to save Paul (Acts 27:43). The implication is that if it had not been for his regard for Paul he would have accepted, perhaps ordered, the killing of the prisoners—Luke shows us that soldiers regarded such killing of prisoners as preferable to letting them escape. Nevertheless, the centurion and soldiers successfully brought Paul to Rome where soldiers guarded him while he lived by himself (Acts 28:16) and continued his mission (Acts 28:30–31):

> The odyssey of Paul and the Christian message to Rome is the great climax of Luke's apologetic statement. Luke has presented the imperial army working in concert with Roman law and the providence of God to insure the preservation and expansion of the gospel message.[57]

3.3.2 Centurions

The first centurion we meet is at Capernaum, in a Q passage. Luke tells us that the centurion provided the synagogue at Capernaum—he had means and used them—and his friends in the Jewish community sought out Jesus on his behalf (Luke 7:3). Luke, following his Q antetext,[58] emphasizes this centurion's faith—he knew that Jesus did not even have to "come under my roof" (Luke 7:6) to heal his servant. Luke includes an intervention by the Jewish elders,[59] missing from Matthew, which praises the centurion because he built their synagogue. This may be a Lukan addition—the centurion at Caesarea was also "well spoken of" (Acts 10:22)—and both were generous with their resources.

The centurion at the crucifixion comes from Luke's Markan antetext (Mark 15:39), but is amended by Luke. His centurion, like Mark's, did not prevent the taunting of Jesus by those under his command, but after his death: "When [he] saw what had taken place, he praised God and said, 'Certainly this man was innocent'" (Luke 23:47).[60] The fact that, like the man

---

57. Walaskay, *We Came to Rome*, 60.

58. This may not come from Q, which has few miracle stories, but the strong verbal parallels suggest a written source used by both Matthew (Matt 8:5–13) and Luke (or Luke's use of Matthew). The Johannine version (John 4:46–53) differs.

59. The Jewish elders are further discussed in 5.2.5.

60. This seems more plausible than the Markan (and Matthean, Matt 27:54) version, seeing him as God's son.

with faith at Capernaum, he was a centurion co-textually prepares us for the first Roman convert in Acts, Cornelius, also a centurion (Acts 10:1).

Cornelius was living in Caesarea, the Roman headquarters for Judaea. He is described as "a devout man who feared God . . . [and] gave alms generously to the people" (Acts 10:2). He was, Luke tells us, the first leader of a gentile community to be converted, bringing his friends, relatives, and household with him (Acts 10:24; 11:14). His actions led to the endorsement of the gentile mission, and were also the occasion for the dramatic justification of commensality in Peter's vision. There are clear parallels with the centurion at Capernaum, not least in the generosity of both with their resources, but the importance of Cornelius is emphasized by repetition as the story of how he sent for Peter is told four times[61] at greater or lesser length.

There are other references to centurions in the story of Paul's arrest,[62] but they are not clearly differentiated from the ordinary soldiers whom they led—all we know of them is that they did their duty, which included saving Paul from a mob (Acts 21:32), from flogging (Acts 22:25–26), and from assassination (Acts 23:17). For the final journey to Rome, Paul, with some other prisoners, was in the charge of Julius, a centurion of the Augustan cohort (Acts 27:1). He treated Paul kindly at Sidon, and "allowed him to go to his friends to be cared for" (Acts 27:3). Later in the voyage Julius first followed Paul's advice and saved the ship, and then, as we have seen, saved Paul from the soldiers so that all came safely ashore in Malta. Julius is not further mentioned, but presumably he brought Paul to Rome and handed him over to the authorities there. We learn little further about the Roman authorities' treatment of Paul, except that he was able to teach "without hindrance" (Acts 28:31) for two years, in marked contrast to his two years in Caesarea, when he was unable to do so. Julius, who, as the representative of Festus and his employer Agrippa[63] will have advised the authorities in Rome, would be seen by the intended reader as having had some responsibility for this.

3.3.3 A Senior Officer

The only senior officer mentioned by Luke is Claudius Lysias, whose army position is described in 3.2.2. He was the tribune in Jerusalem who commanded the cohort of auxiliary troops in the service of Felix. He rescued Paul from the mob, and ordered him to be examined by flogging (Acts 22:24), but on being told that Paul was a Roman citizen, "he was afraid"

---

61. Acts 10:1–8, 22, 30–33; 11:13–14.
62. Acts 21:32; 22:25–26; 23:17, 23.
63. Agrippa had said to Festus: "This man could have been set free" (Acts 26:32).

(Acts 22:29). Then, hearing of the conspiracy to kill Paul, he arranged for him to be escorted in safety, by 470 soldiers,[64] to the governor at Caesarea. He also wrote a letter setting out the circumstances:

> Claudius Lysias to his Excellency the governor Felix, greetings. This man was seized by the Jews and was about to be killed by them, but when I had learned that he was a Roman citizen, I came with the guard and rescued him. Since I wanted to know the charge for which they accused him, I had him brought to their council. I found that he was accused concerning questions of their law, but was charged with nothing deserving death or imprisonment. When I was informed that there would be a plot against the man, I sent him to you at once, ordering his accusers also to state before you what they have against him (Acts 23:26–30).

Lysias tried to protect himself from the consequences of his errors, but this should not surprise us—"he would, wouldn't he?"[65] His statement that: "When I had learned that he was a Roman citizen, I came with the guard and rescued him" (Acts 23:27) is misleading. As we know, he rescued Paul first (Acts 21:32–33), then learned that he was a Roman citizen (Acts 22:26–27). But, in his defense, it could be pointed out that he again rescued Paul after he knew that he was a Roman citizen (Acts 23:10), so that, formally, his statement is true.[66] To cite another modern instance: "It contains a misleading impression, not a lie. It was being economical with the truth."[67] In his letter Lysias did not say anything that jeopardized Paul's position. Indeed, he not only said that "he was charged with nothing deserving death or imprisonment" (Acts 23:29), but also told of the plot against him. Cassidy is surely right when he finds that:

> Lysias is sending the governor a prisoner who is not only a Roman citizen, but a highly articulate one; and, to the degree possible, he wishes the "prisoner" as well as the governor to have a positive estimation of the way he has handled the matter.[68]

---

64. Acts 23:23. The significance of this large number of soldiers is addressed in 3.4.4.

65. Rice Davies, *ODQ*, 626.

66. Ben Witherington, taking this view, finds that at Acts 21:33 Lysias did not rescue Paul from the mob: the rescue was the result of his successful attempt "to prevent a full-scale riot and restore order" (Witherington, *Acts*, 657). As a result, at Acts 22:10, "we might properly speak of the tribune rescuing Paul, unlike the case in 21:37" (693).

67. Armstrong, *ODQ*, 25.

68. Cassidy, *Society and Politics*, 100.

3.4 ROMAN GOVERNORS

3.4.1 Introduction

The governors concerned in the major trials of Jesus and Paul were Pilate, Felix, and Festus, all governors of Judaea. Paul was also brought before a governor of a senatorial province, Gallio, and in addition met the senatorial governor of Cyprus, Sergius Paulus. We shall first consider the three governors of Judaea, then Gallio, then Sergius Paulus. We have given most attention to Festus—although scholars have re-evaluated Festus in recent years, his role is still misunderstood and our contextual and co-textual analysis clarifies Luke's narrative.

3.4.2 Pilate

Even before the trial of Jesus we are given an insight into Pilate's character when, in an episode unique to Luke, we learn from "some present . . . about the Galileans whose blood Pilate had mingled with their sacrifices" (Luke 13:1). This story demonstrates a streak of viciousness and cruelty in Pilate.

In comparing Pilate with Felix and Festus, we need to bear in mind the difference in status between the Lukan Jesus and the Lukan Paul, a Roman citizen. Jesus was not a Roman citizen, nor was he a member of the local elite, merely an ordinary provincial, a *peregrinus*. As we saw in 3.2.4, there were no specific laws applying to *peregrini*, and a *peregrinus* could properly be flogged for little reason. They were subject to the power of the governor and, for a governor, administering a flogging was not a major matter.

The charge before Pilate is Lukan: "We found this man perverting our nation, forbidding us to pay taxes to the emperor, and saying that he himself is the Messiah, a king" (Luke 23:2). "Perverting" is *diastrephonta*, which can mean to pervert or to mislead.[69] Misleading would have been of little official interest to Pilate but perverting, that is, the crimes specified in the Lukan charge (urging people not to pay taxes, and to acknowledge a king not appointed by the emperor) were appropriately brought before the Roman forum. This charge of perverting the people, *diastrephō*, has strong intertextual resonances. It was the allegation against Moses and Aaron (Exod 5:4) and against Elijah (1 Kgs 18:17), in both cases by the civil authority (Pharaoh and Ahab, respectively).[70] These intertextual references suggest

---

69. BDAG, 237.

70. The well-known stories of the Exodus and of Elijah are of great importance to Luke; Moses and Elijah are the two men whom Peter identified as being with Jesus at the transfiguration (Luke 9:33).

(or confirm) to the intended reader that the charge was an attempt to thwart one who was acting to further God's purposes.

Jesus, invited by Pilate to claim the kingship, declined, and Pilate found that there was: "No basis for an accusation against this man" (Luke 23:4). But the Jews were insistent and expanded the charge to include "[stirring] up the people . . . from Galilee where he began" (Luke 23:5). Pilate grasped at an excuse to send Jesus off to Herod. After Herod sent him back, Pilate, without further examination, in another passage not found in the Markan antetext,[71] for the second time proclaimed that Jesus was not guilty of the charges against him, and decided to flog and release him (Luke 23:16). There is no doubt that Pilate had the authority to flog any trouble-maker, whether guilty or not, and, indeed this would be expected of him, a routine exercise of imperial power. The proposed flogging does not suggest that Jesus was guilty of anything more than being a focus of trouble, like Paul (Acts 22:24). Faced with a continuing demand for a death sentence, Pilate, a third time, declared that Jesus was innocent of the charges, and said again that he would flog him and release him (Luke 23:22). Where the Markan Pilate gave only one, somewhat ambiguous, declaration of Jesus's innocence (Mark 15:14),[72] the Lukan Pilate gave three, much more explicit, declarations.

But then Luke tells us three times that Pilate condemned Jesus at the demand of "them"; "*their* voices prevailed" (Luke 23:23); "*their* demand should be granted" (Luke 23:24); "he handed Jesus over as *they* wished" (Luke 23:25)—emphases added. Three times he declared Jesus innocent, three times we are told that he condemned him as they required. Who were they? Jesus was brought before Pilate by "the assembly . . . as a body" (Luke 23:1), the assembly being "the elders of the people, both chief priests and scribes" (Luke 22:66). The first response to Pilate's declaration of innocence comes from "the chief priests and the crowds" (Luke 23:4), the second from "the chief priests, the leaders, and the people" (Luke 23:13) and the third from "they" (Luke 23:23), clearly referring to the same group. That the chief priests are a more commanding voice than the mob is confirmed by Paul's appearances before Felix (Acts 24:1) and Festus (Acts 25:2), and also by the rescue of Paul from the mob (who were without the support of the chief priests) by Claudius Lysias (Acts 21:32).

These extended repetitions indicate that both Pilate's declaration of the innocence of Jesus and his surrender to the demands of the group of leaders are very important to understanding the narrative. He is totally ruled by the

---

71. Or in Matthew.

72. The Matthean Pilate never declared Jesus innocent although his wife did (Matt 27:19). His declaration: "I am innocent of this man's blood" (Matt 27:25) may imply the innocence of Jesus, but it does not state it.

high priests and their supporters. Luke further emphasizes Pilate's craven surrender, when, without mention of the justification given in his antetext (Mark 15:6),[73] he tells how he released Barabbas as soon as the mob asked him to do so (Luke 23:25):

> Not only does he allow a man to be crucified whom both he and Herod have found innocent, but he releases a political prisoner simply because the crowd asks for it. In the governor's court injustice has triumphed over justice.[74]

It is clear that despite having the ability to weigh evidence and come to the right conclusion, in releasing Barabbas he not only had no commitment to justice, he did not even do his duty by the emperor; he released a dangerous man and was content to allow an innocent man to be crucified. His actions indicate that his exercise of authority is lacking in both honesty towards his employer and in justice and can be described as diabolical in nature.

Pilate's personal responsibility for the death of Jesus is co-textually confirmed specifically by only one of the references to the crucifixion in Acts; that is, in the prayer of the Jerusalem community (Acts 4:24–30), which attributed the execution of Jesus to "both Herod and Pontius Pilate, with the gentiles and the peoples of Israel" (Acts 4:27).[75] Elsewhere, Paul, in a speech in the synagogue in Pisidian Antioch (Acts 13:27–28), merely mentioned him and a number of references omit any mention of Pilate's guilt;[76] these are all in speeches addressed to the Jerusalem Jews. The speakers, in the tradition of the prophets, are concerned to persuade their audience to repent and use rhetoric appropriate to that purpose. The references cited above which do mention Pilate are in a prayer to God, and in an address to diaspora Jews to whom Paul imputes no culpability. In these there is no call to repentance and no rhetorical allocation of responsibility; they are a more reliable guide to the views of the narrator. We shall deal further with Luke's portrayal of the Jerusalem authorities in chapter 4.

3.4.3 Felix

We have discussed Felix in the previous chapter (2.4.5), but some further points relating to the trial before him should be made here. Paul fared better

---

73. Also found in Matt 27:15.
74. Bond, *Pontius Pilate*, 159.
75. See 2.4.2.
76. Acts 2:23; 3:13; 4:10; 7:52.

than Jesus before the courts, partly because he was a Roman citizen, but also because Claudius Lysias had sent him from Jerusalem to Caesarea, where the pressure from the Jewish leaders was not so great. They did not there have a mob of supporters so found it advisable to be represented by an advocate, Tertullus, who spelt out the charge against Paul:

> We have, in fact, found this man a pestilent fellow, an agitator among all the Jews throughout the world, and a ringleader of the sect of the Nazarenes. He even tried to profane the temple, and so we seized him (Acts 24:5–6).

This was a charge which would require evidence to support it, but there was none—the Jews from Asia who had made the original allegation about the temple were not present. Moreover, as we saw in 3.3.3, Lysias had told Felix that:" I found that he was accused concerning questions of their law, but was charged with nothing deserving death or imprisonment" (Acts 23:29). But trying to profane the temple was a charge which would both warrant the intervention of the governor and deserve, at the least, imprisonment, being "a serious breach of a Jewish religious law which the Romans were pledged to uphold."[77] Lysias in his letter ignores the accusation of the mob (Acts 21:28), which does refer to profaning the temple, and reports only on the accusation before the council (Acts 23:29), and when the mob's accusation (profaning the temple) is picked up by Tertullus as the reason Paul was seized (Acts 24:7), Felix was surprised. He, quite properly, decided to await oral evidence from Lysias, but this never came, and Luke gives us Felix's true motive for continuing to keep Paul in custody—"he hoped that money would be given him by Paul" (Acts 24:26).[78] Links between the devil and money are discussed in 5.4.2, and Felix, like Pilate, acted in a manner to be expected of one to whom the devil had given authority.

3.4.4 Festus

Haenchen found that: "Festus is an honourable man, thoroughly imbued with the fundamental principles of Roman constitutional law and, therefore, painfully correct,"[79] but more recent commentators are hard on him. Tannehill, considering the review of the case given to Agrippa, finds that

---

77. Alexander, "Acts," 1057. The penalty was death, as is shown by extant inscriptions (Fitzmyer, *Acts*, 698), but this would not be binding upon a governor.

78. That Lysias would not have traveled from Jerusalem to Caesarea during a period of two years is hardly plausible.

79. Haenchen, *Acts*, 674.

"Festus is unmistakeably portrayed presenting a summary that is decidedly biased in his own self-interest,"[80] and also that "Festus, like Felix, is not committed to justice but seeks to please the powerful."[81] Witherington finds that his review of Paul's case for Agrippa shows him to be "not only self-serving but also a novice,"[82] and is also unsure about what Festus intended in suggesting a transfer to Jerusalem: "Paul . . . appears to have read something else between the lines."[83] C. K. Barrett is also deeply suspicious of him, saying: "Festus does not [at 25:20], *as he does, or may do, or appears to do*, in 25:9, say that he himself would preside over a hearing in Jerusalem."[84] He also does not understand why the Jews should want a transfer to Jerusalem:

> No doubt (according to Luke) they would have liked best to conduct the trial on their own, but a trial in Jerusalem with the Procurator in the chair would have been better than nothing, though it is hard to see what they would have gained by thus transferring a Roman trial from Caesarea to Jerusalem unless some form of the plot (v. 3) and an appeal to violence were in mind.[85]

This argument is not at all convincing. Festus clearly says that the Jerusalem hearing will be "before me" (Acts 25:9), and Barrett's doubts are baseless. Luke has told us about the plot (Acts 25:3) so that we know that killing Paul is what the chief priests and leaders have in mind. Moreover, a trial in Jerusalem would be very different from one in Caesarea, as we have seen Pilate coerced into crucifying a man he had three times declared innocent. Indeed, Paul would have been even more vulnerable as, after the arrest of Stephen, the Jerusalem crowd was consistently hostile to the infant church. It is not possible here to deal in detail with the views of other scholars, so we set out our understanding of Paul's appearance before Festus, including the proposed transfer to Jerusalem (Acts 25:9), an understanding based on both the context, that is, the way in which the Roman legal system functioned, and the co-text, a careful analysis of Luke's narrative. Both aspects would have been understood by the intended reader.

---

80. Tannehill, *Narrative Unity*, 2:309, citing Cassidy (*Society and Politics*, 111), with whom he agrees.
81. Cassidy, *Society and Politics*, 307.
82. Witherington, *Acts*, 729.
83. Ibid., 722.
84. Barrett, *Critical and Exegetical Commentary*, 2:1140, emphasis added.
85. Ibid., 1127.

The Romans kept detailed court records[86] and the letter of Lysias, together with other information about the trial before Felix, was available to Festus; that letter had been read by Felix[87] in Paul's presence (Acts 23:33-34). The ancients read aloud[88] so Paul was aware of the evidence of Lysias, and also knew that it was known to Festus, which explains his statement: "I have done no wrong to the Jews, as you very well know" (Acts 25:10). The charge before Festus was the same as that before Felix quoted above; it had never been dropped. It was of being a political agitator, as Paul clarifies by his denial: "I have in no way committed an offense against the law of the Jews, or against the temple, or against the emperor" (Acts 25:8).

The chief priests and leaders had previously "requested, as a favor to them against Paul, to have him transferred to Jerusalem" (Acts 25:3). "Transferred" is *metapempsētai*, which is an ordinary verb, used nine times in Acts, and its primary meaning is "to summon." It does not imply in any way that they wanted the trial to be before the Sanhedrin—indeed, we know that they had little interest in the trial because we have been told that they planned to kill Paul before he reached Jerusalem. Rather, the chief priests, in Jerusalem, asked Festus, in Jerusalem, to summon Paul to Jerusalem and there hear the case. This was confirmed when Festus told Agrippa that they had asked him for "a sentence, *katadikēn*, against [Paul]" (Acts 25:15), that is, condemnation by him. Festus could hold the trial in Jerusalem as readily as in Caesarea, and could start it in one place and finish it in another—as we saw in 3.2.4 the powers of a governor had few formal limitations.

When Paul appeared before him in Caesarea, Festus, "wishing to do the Jews a favor," (Acts 25:9) asked Paul if he wanted a trial in Jerusalem (Acts 25:9) as the chief priests had requested. Luke gives us some other possible reasons for the proposal. First, Festus did not understand the charges brought against Paul in his court: "When the accusers stood up, they did not charge him with any of the crimes that I was expecting" (Acts 25:18). He was expecting the political charges set out in his papers, as formulated by Tertullus. Without Tertullus, a professional advocate, the Jews seem to have reverted to the religious charges (Acts 25:19) referred to by Lysias (Acts 23:29), closer to their real grievance. Nevertheless, the charges raised by Tertullus were on file and could not be ignored by Festus. They had to be resolved by conviction or dismissal of the charges.

86. "Over 250 extant papyri of official court proceedings . . . similar to those recorded in Acts 24ff have been published to date" (Winter, "Official Proceedings," 306).

87. "Certified copies of official documents relating to judicial proceedings were available to a defendant" (ibid., 308).

88. "[He] probably [read] out loud, as was the almost universal practice in antiquity" (Witherington, *Acts*, 701—see Achtemeier, "Omne Verbum Sonat," 15-17).

Second, the relevant witnesses, "some Jews from Asia" (Acts 24:19), were not present, so the prosecutors were unable to prove their case (Acts 25:7). But this was because Festus had summoned to Caesarea only "those of you who have the authority" (Acts 25:5), so that the failure to provide witnesses at this stage could not justly be used to acquit Paul. As a third reason, Festus "was at a loss how to investigate these questions" (Acts 25:20), and the available *consilium* in Caesarea ("the military tribunes and the prominent men of the city" (Acts 25:23) would not have been competent to advise, as they were predominantly, perhaps exclusively, gentiles. Festus could well have thought that it was advisable to use a *consilium* in Jerusalem, as Sherwin-White suggests.[89] So, Festus had good reasons for wanting to hold the trial in Jerusalem, and could have so decided. But he did not—he asked Paul if he wanted his trial in Jerusalem (Acts 25:9). This is a strong indication that Festus wanted a fair trial.

The view that Festus intended to transfer Paul for a Jewish trial is based on Paul's speech in response to that suggestion:

> I am appealing to the emperor's tribunal; this is where, *hou*, I should be tried . . . if there is nothing to their charges against me, no one can turn me over, *charisasthai*, to them. I appeal to the emperor (Acts 25:10–11).

However, the text does not support such a view. The first problematic word in the passage is "where," *hou*, "a locative adverb."[90] Apart from this instance, it is used in Luke-Acts thirteen times[91] always referring to an identifiable location. Indeed, in the New Testament it is used in a figurative sense only in the Pauline corpus. So, although it is possible that it is meant figuratively (in the Roman court), it is much more likely to mean in Caesarea.

The second problematic word is "turn over," *charisasthai*. "The two meanings usually assigned to this verb, 'show kindness to' and 'graciously bestow' can hardly be separated."[92] Here, it has to be interpreted co-textually, in the light of the use of the related word *charis* of the Jewish leaders by the narrator (Acts 25:3) and the use of the same verb by Festus (Acts 25:16). As we saw above, when the leaders in Jerusalem asked Festus for a favor, *charis*, they were asking him to hold *his* trial in Jerusalem. Festus himself

---

89. Sherwin-White, *Roman Society*, 67.

90. Balz, "Hou," 539. To put it more fully: "The genitive relative pronoun without an antecedent functions like a locative adverb" (Culy and Parsons, *Acts*, 12).

91. Luke 4:16, 17; 10:1; 23:53; 24:28; Acts 1:13; 2:2; 7:29; 12:12; 16:13; 20:8; 25:10; 28:14.

92. Moulton and Milligan, *Vocabulary of the Greek Testament*, 684.

used the verb to explain how he refused the request by the chief priests and elders who asked for a condemnation in *his* Roman court. Paul's use of *charisasthai* is very similar and should be interpreted in the same way, referring to the action of the Roman tribunal. That is, if Paul is not guilty (there is nothing to the charges against me) no one (no Roman tribunal) can turn me over to them.

Paul was aware of the first plot against him, and also of what had happened in Jerusalem to Jesus, to Stephen, and to James. He also knew that, but for Lysias, he could very well, on the evidence of false witnesses, have been legally executed by the Sanhedrin for violating the temple. He probably feared a further plot, and Luke has prepared the intended reader for this by telling of precisely such a plot earlier in the chapter. Paul's use of *charisasthai* is perfectly compatible with the view that he understood Festus to want to move his tribunal to Jerusalem, and that he was extremely anxious that this should not happen. He therefore appealed to the emperor, removing the issue from the jurisdiction of Festus. But this does not necessarily mean that Paul thought Festus dishonest. He would not have forgotten the plot but Luke has made it clear that he also had his own reasons for wanting to go to Rome (Acts 19:21; 23:11).

There are three further criticisms of the conduct of Festus. First, scholars accuse him of a self-serving summary of events for Agrippa (see Acts 25:24–27). However, a procurator had a duty to impress a ruler like Agrippa with both the power and the justice of the Roman empire, and presenting himself as favorably as possible to important provincials was part of that duty. The case differs from the self-serving account by Lysias, described above, which was given to his superior officer, and so in no way could be seen as part of his duty.

Second, Festus said that Paul had "appealed to be kept in custody for the decision of his Imperial Majesty" (Acts 25:21), and it has been argued[93] that he misrepresented Paul as there is no mention of custody in Paul's speech. But this is naive. Paul (and the intended reader) could not have expected that making an appeal to the emperor on a capital charge (Acts 24:6; 25:11, 24) would have led to his being freed to make his own way to Rome, and Luke would not have to labor this.

Thirdly, Festus did not release Paul although he is said to have found him innocent, as he told Agrippa and the assembled dignitaries (the council he consulted at Acts 25:12) that: "I found that he had done nothing deserving death" (Acts 25:25). But the trial was not over, the Jews had not presented their evidence, Festus had not reached a verdict. Fitzmyer's translation

---

93. E.g., Witherington, *Acts*, 729; Cassidy, *Society and Politics*, 111.

is better: "Yet I could not discover that he had done anything deserving death."[94] This is a "not proven" or "not yet proven" verdict, not a declaration of innocence—that came later when Luke tells us that:

> Then the king got up, and with him the governor and Bernice and those who had been seated with them; and as they were leaving, they said to one another, "This man is doing nothing to deserve death or imprisonment" (Acts 26:30–31).

Yet this in itself is not an unambiguous declaration of innocence. It refers to what Paul "is doing," not what he has done. Furthermore, Festus was free to politely avoid disagreement with Agrippa, knowing that his implied agreement had no legal significance. He did not respond when Agrippa said Paul could have been freed (Acts 26:32), and, indeed, could hardly have done so as the case had, at Paul's request, been transferred to the tribunal of Caesar himself.

So in these matters Festus acted in the way a Roman governor was expected to act, energetically and in accordance with the Roman legal ethos. However Luke identifies two failures. First Festus ignores the threat against Paul which Lysias took so seriously that he sent Paul from Jerusalem to Caesarea with an escort of 470 men (Acts 23:23) under two centurions. This information will have been on file. The very large number of soldiers needed to safeguard Paul shows both how seriously Lysias viewed the plot and, by contrast, the inexperience and naivety of Festus in ignoring it. He may have been confident of his ability to protect Paul, but Paul was not and the intended reader, knowing of the second plot, would have been of the same view. However, the main charge against Festus, as against both Pilate and Felix, was that each of them wanted to placate the Jews (Pilate, Luke 23:24; Felix, Acts 24:27; Festus, Acts 25:9):

> Bias enters the picture, and justice ceases to be blind when Festus succumbs to the desire to placate the Jewish elite and do them a favor in the Paul matter.[95]

But Romans (and Greeks) would have regarded this as not only natural, but also right and proper. Garnsey found that

> the formulary procedure of the civil law . . . demonstrates the wide variety of ways in which the procedure itself, and the magistrates and judges who administered it, denied equal protection

---

94. Fitzmyer, *Acts*, 752—similar GNMM and Phillips.
95. Witherington, *Acts*, 720.

and equal rights to those who were regarded as socially undesirable or simply inferior.[96]

The position was not very different in respect of criminal cases, where "the principal criterion of legal privilege ... was ... derived from power, style of life, and wealth."[97] Indeed, as we saw in 3.2.4, the very structure of Roman law differentiated between the powerful (subject to the law—the *ordo*) and the common people (dealt with at the discretion of the magistrate). Pilate, Felix and, potentially, Festus each allowed their desire to please the Jews to have a determining influence on the judicial process—they did not seek justice, but used the legal process to achieve their own ends, or in the case of Festus, the ends of the empire he served. That empire was not concerned to deliver impartial justice; it had been given its authority by the devil and used it in a fashion which reflected this.

When Paul appealed to Caesar, it appeared to lift a weight from Festus's mind.[98] He had wanted to please the Jews, or at least, not antagonize them, but was aware both of their hatred of Paul and the first plot against him which Lysias had employed 470 men to foil. Yet, like Pilate, he would not willingly have chosen to execute an innocent man. Now the fate of Paul was no longer his problem; instead he had merely to provide a report to the emperor setting out the case. Preparing this provided a good start to his relationship with Agrippa, so it is no wonder that he warmed to Paul. Even when he said that Paul was insane (Acts 26:24), his reference to his great learning lets us see the remark as a jovial comment on the strange beliefs of these provincials. Finally, he moved, in the seclusion of his gentile (and Herodian) *consilium*, from his previous verdict of not proven (Acts 25:25) to one of being able to appear to agree with Agrippa that Paul was innocent (Acts 6:31). The verdict could not, of course, be official, as Paul had appealed to Caesar and Festus had accepted that appeal (Acts 25:12).

The narrator's acceptance of gentiles is shown by the words of Peter:

> I truly understand that God shows no partiality, but in every nation anyone who fears him and does what is right is acceptable to him (Acts 10:34-35).

---

96. Garnsey, *Social Status*, 7.
97. Ibid., 279.
98. Sherwin-White's analysis (see 3.2.4) suggests that Festus had no choice but to permit the appeal. Garnsey disagrees about the applicability of the *Lex Julia* (Garnsey, "Lex Iulia," 185) but believes that Festus did have the power to permit Paul to appeal (Garnsey, *Social Status*, 76).

Such acceptance of gentiles was shown at the beginning of the Gospel in the words of Simeon, "a light for revelation to the Gentiles" (Luke 2:32) and by Jesus at Nazareth, speaking of Naaman and the widow of Zarapheth (Luke 4:25–27). What is right is described by the words of the Baptist to the soldiers (who were gentiles) in the service of those appointed by the emperor.

Luke may have had some understanding of the ethos of the Roman aristocracy, as he lived for some six or seven years in the Roman colony of Philippi, and, we argue, received his education there as a resident of the household of Lydia. We can get some understanding of that ethos from the letters of the younger Pliny. He was born around the year 53 and as his letters were edited for publication, they probably describe a somewhat idealized version of his virtues and those of his friends. But those virtues would be the ones to which the Roman elite aspired, and there are some parallels between Pliny's letters and Luke's writings, for example, the treatment of extortion. We have already mentioned the words of the Baptist to soldiers: "Do not extort money from anyone by threats or false accusation" (Luke 3:14), and the Roman legal requirement that governors should also avoid extortion. Pliny prosecuted a number of cases of extortion and taking of bribes, including the governor and deputy-governor of the province of Africa,[99] and his letters show a strong interest in a successful outcome to such cases, perhaps as part of his frequently shown repugnance for the excessive pursuit of money.

3.4.5 Gallio

There was one other trial of Paul before a governor in Acts, that before Gallio, the proconsul of Achaia. Gallio was the brother of Seneca, one of the richest senators of the time,[100] and he himself had been adopted as an adult into another senatorial family.[101] It is likely that he also was very rich. Paul was brought before his tribunal in Corinth, charged with "persuading people to worship God in ways that are contrary to the law" (Acts 18:13). This charge had force only because Corinth was a Roman city[102] but Gallio refused to hear the case and dismissed it, without even examining Paul or knowing that he was a Roman citizen. He also ignored the beating of Sosthenes, the official of the synagogue: "But Gallio paid no attention to any of

---

99. Pliny, *Letters* 2.11, 12.
100. Duncan-Jones, *Economy of the Roman Empire*, 343.
101. Momigliano and Griffin, "Annaeus Novatus," 95.
102. There was a similar charge at Philippi (Acts 16:21), another Roman city.

these things" (Acts 18:17). Whether Sosthenes was a Christian mobbed by Jews,[103] or a Jew mobbed by Jews,[104] or a Jew mobbed by Greeks[105] is difficult to determine. However, we think it most probable that the beating was at the hands of Jews, not gentiles, and Gallio ignored it as he did not see disputes within that community as a matter for his attention. As we saw above, "the governor left a great deal of minor jurisdiction to the local municipal courts."[106] Luke presents Gallio as doing the minimum required, with no interest in Jewish (or Christian) matters,[107] but, from the Roman perspective, his worst crime was indolence.

3.4.6 Sergius Paulus

Sergius Paulus was also a proconsul, in Cyprus. As noted in 1.6.3, he came from Pisidian Antioch, the place to which Saul (after changing his name to Paul) went on leaving Cyprus. He "summoned Barnabas and Saul and wanted to hear the word of God" (Acts 13:7), that is, like Cornelius, he took the initiative. When he saw Paul's mighty work, the blinding of Elymas, "he believed, for he was astonished at the teaching about the Lord" (Acts 13:12), that is, a Roman governor is shown as a believer.[108] The first soldier, the first centurion, and the first governor whom Luke presents to us in Acts all became Christian—this is a clear indication that being a Christian was in no way incompatible with service in the Roman army and administration.

However, Paulus may have been interpreted by the intended reader in a more nuanced fashion. Pisidian Antioch would have been known in Luke's time as the home of three senators, this Sergius Paulus, his son, and Caristanius Fronto. The influence of Sergius Paulus, including his power of patronage in his home town, had been great enough to lead to Paul's name-change and dash to Antioch. There his initial reception was good, but Paul was eventually rejected by the Antiochene elite despite the initial patronage of Paulus, whose conversion may have faltered, for Luke was aware that

---

103. Sherwin-White, *Roman Society*, 104.

104. Fitzmyer, *Acts*, 631.

105. Haenchen, *Acts*, 541.

106. Sherwin-White, *Roman Society*, 14.

107. Some of the writings of Gallio's brother, Seneca, express anti-Jewish sentiments (Haacker, "Gallio," 902).

108. As noted in 1.6.3, secular scholars doubt that Sergius Paulus was governor of Cyprus, and also doubt that he became a Christian. He may have been a deputy or other associate of the actual governor, and as for not being a Christian, Luke has given reasons why people fall away from the faith (see below) and also tells us that it is difficult for a rich man (as Paulus was) to be saved (Luke 18:24–25).

belief may not endure, as shown in the parable of the sower (Luke 8:4–15), and, to cite just one example, in the treachery of Judas.

3.5 MUNICIPAL AUTHORITIES

Although Paul was harassed in a number of places, there were only a few where magistrates, formal representatives of municipal authorities, were said to be involved. When we consider them co-textually there is a clear trajectory in Luke's presentation. We first see that in Iconium "an attempt was made by both Gentiles and Jews, with their rulers, to mistreat [Paul and Barnabas] and to stone them" (Acts 14:5). They escape by fleeing. The use of the term "rulers," *archon*, indicates magistrates,[109] although no mention is made of judicial process and in a Greek city the use of stoning suggests not a legal punishment but a mob attempt at lynching.[110] It reminds the intended reader of the stoning, also without legal process, of Stephen (Acts 7:58).

Later, at Philippi:

> But when her owners saw that their hope of making money was gone, they seized Paul and Silas and dragged them into the marketplace before the authorities. When they had brought [Paul and Silas] before the magistrates, they said, "These men are disturbing our city; they are Jews and are advocating customs that are not lawful for us as Romans to adopt or observe." The crowd joined in attacking them, and the magistrates had them stripped of their clothing and ordered them to be beaten with rods. After they had given them a severe flogging, they threw them into prison and ordered the jailer to keep them securely . . . When morning came, the magistrates sent the police, saying, "Let those men go." And the jailer reported the message to Paul, saying, "The magistrates sent word to let you go; therefore come out now and go in peace." But Paul replied, "They have beaten us in public, uncondemned, men who are Roman citizens, and have thrown us into prison; and now are they going to discharge us in secret? Certainly not! Let them come and take us out themselves." The police reported these words to the magistrates, and they were afraid when they heard that they were Roman citizens; so they came and apologized to them. And they took them out and asked them to leave the city. After leaving the prison they went to Lydia's home; and when they had seen and

---

109. As in Luke 12:58. See also 5.2.1.

110. Stoning is a form of capital punishment, obsolete in Greek cities in Luke's day and, in any event, beyond the power of local magistrates.

encouraged the brothers and sisters there, they departed (Acts 16:19–23, 35–40).

Philippi was a Roman, not a Greek, city[111] and the magistrates acted in a more formal manner, although they may not have allowed the accused to defend themselves. Paul, for whatever reason, like Silas, did not initially disclose his Roman citizenship. The following morning the magistrates sought to release them, presumably because the flogging already administered seemed an adequate punishment for their actions. Paul then disclosing their Roman citizenship, they gained a clear advantage over the magistrates, who humbled themselves and apologized, and *asked*, not ordered, Paul and Silas to leave the city. They did so, but, in a deliberate snub to the magistrates, first went to Lydia's home. At Philippi the magistrates acted as magistrates, but did so without due process and as a result were humiliated.

Then, in Thessalonica:

> But the Jews became jealous, and with the help of some ruffians in the marketplaces they formed a mob and set the city in an uproar. While they were searching for Paul and Silas to bring them out to the assembly, they attacked Jason's house. When they could not find them, they dragged Jason and some believers before the city authorities, shouting, "These people who have been turning the world upside down have come here also, and Jason has entertained them as guests. They are all acting contrary to the decrees of the emperor, saying that there is another king named Jesus." The people and the city officials were disturbed when they heard this, and after they had taken bail from Jason and the others, they let them go (Acts 17:5–9).

Thessalonica was a Greek city, larger and more important than Philippi. The accusations by the mob were heard by the magistrates, but they did not take any action other than obtaining a bond[112] from Jason, a supporter of Paul and Silas. They appear to be acting with a concern for public order, but without punishing Paul and Silas. It may be that we are to understand that they were aware of their status as Roman citizens—the story of the recent events at Philippi had reached Thessalonica. It seems that Paul and Silas were notorious.

---

111. A city Luke knew well—see 1.1.2.

112. "Bail" used in NRSV normally means a guarantee that the accused will appear before the court—it is not quite appropriate here. Jason "is giving security for the good behaviour of his guests" (Barrett, *Critical and Exegetical Commentary*, 2:816, citing Sherwin-White, *Roman Society*, 95).

Finally, in Ephesus, as in Philippi, a mob raised by commercial interests[113] attacked Paul in the theatre, a place of assembly. Those leading the mob were merchants deriving their business from the temple of Artemis, a very important aspect of the public and commercial life of Ephesus. Although magistrates were not said to be involved, a single official, the "town clerk," undoubtedly a magistrate acting in an official capacity, succeeded in quieting and dismissing the mob, telling them to bring charges before the courts or the governor if they wanted to take the matter further (Acts 19:28–41). He acted appropriately and competently, restoring order but not interfering with the activities of either Paul or the disciples.

Luke's depiction of the magistrates moves from attempted stoning (death), to flogging, to a bond, to no action: the effect of this trajectory is to leave the reader with a more positive view of the authorities, especially as there were exceptions to the hostility and indifference described above, although not among those acting in a judicial capacity. In Philippi the gaoler and his whole family were baptized (Acts 16:33). In Athens Dionysius the Areopagite may have been seen by the intended reader as among the magistrates—he believed (Acts 17:34). In Ephesus "some officials of the province of Asia . . . were friendly to [Paul]" (Acts 19:31). On Malta, in the last such reference, Publius, the leading man of the island, "received [Paul and his companions] and entertained [them] hospitably for three days" (Acts 28:7).

However, we should not forget that the authorities frequently failed in their duty to protect Paul and his colleagues in going about their lawful business. There were other plots or riots, with no recorded action by the local authorities to prevent them, in Damascus (Acts 9:23–24), Pisidian Antioch (Acts 13:50), Lystra (Acts 14:19), Beroea (Acts 17:13), and Greece (Acts 20:3).[114] But Luke does not emphasize these failures and does not intend us to form an unduly adverse view of the authorities in these places. The idea that they could protect foreigners from casual violence may derive from modern methods of reading which, as noted in 1.3.7.2, we should set aside. It is probable that Luke's intended reader would have had a more realistic and robust view of these incidents, as "with regard . . . to fire-fighting and policing, the ancient city seems to us to have done a good deal less than it might for its citizens,"[115] and, we may take it, even less for non-citizens.

It is also noteworthy that the Lukan Paul did not meet serious trouble, and usually met no trouble, in the provincial capitals of Antioch on the

---

113. Led by Demetrius—see 5.4.2.

114. This failure was noted by Steve Walton in "State They Were In," a paper presented to the Acts seminar of the British New Testament Society and subsequently published.

115. Reynolds, "Cities," 34.

Orontes (Acts 13:1–3; 14:26–28; 15:30–39), Paphos (13:6–12), Corinth (18:1–11),[116] Ephesus (19:1–20) and, indeed, Caesarea (21:8–14), where Paul's troubles were due to the activities of the Jerusalem Jews and had nothing to do with the municipal authorities.[117] The greater the Roman presence, the safer Paul was.

3.6 SUMMARY

Luke gives a generally favorable description of ordinary soldiers in Acts which accords well with the Baptist's acceptance of the role of the soldier and he omits the cruelty of the soldiers at the Markan crucifixion. Favorable, too, is his description of centurions and, in the end, of the municipal authorities who become notably less hostile as we follow Paul on his journey to Rome, and do not trouble Paul in the centres of imperial authority. Claudias Lysias, although he sent a self-serving account of events to Felix, is also shown as doing his duty—he protected Paul and declared him innocent of any offence deserving death. But few of these men accepted the Christian message.

The governors are shown less favorably. Pilate crucified an innocent man not because to do so served the empire, but as a result of pressure by the chief priests, whom Felix and Festus also tried to placate. Felix, not only partial but also venal, clearly acted unjustly and Festus risked the triumph of injustice. Festus, like Lysias, is shown to have described his actions in a way which presented those actions in the best possible light, but he was talking to Agrippa II, a client king, and this was what was expected of Roman officials in such circumstances. From the Roman point of view, Lysias (for the most part), Festus, and indeed, Gallio, were doing their duty.

However, Luke has a different perspective, learnt from the Septuagint.[118] Justice must be impartial and answer to God, not the emperor.[119] Pilate, Felix and Festus were partial, as, probably, was Gallio. They had little interest in justice for its own sake. With (perhaps) the sole exception of Sergius Paulus, who believed, the intended reader sees that even the best of the senior Roman officials were serving a kingdom whose authority came from

---

116. There was trouble in "Greece" (20:2), which is usually taken to refer to Corinth, because of Paul's letters to that city, but Luke does not say this.

117. Like Paul, Philip had no problems in Caesarea (Acts 8:40; 21:8).

118. E. g, "Keep judgment; do righteousness" (Isa 56:1). Luke cites an adjacent verse (56:7, in Luke 19:46) and the Ethiopian eunuch was reading Isa 53:7–8 when Philip met him (Acts 8:32–33).

119. "Justice [is] granted the king by God for the purpose of judging the people rightly, especially the poor and lowly" (Bacote, "Justice," 415).

the devil, and Luke's narrative shows the consequences of this. Nevertheless, centurions and soldiers are presented sympathetically and Luke tells us that the Roman authorities brought Paul to Rome where he was able to proclaim the kingdom of God and teach "about the Lord Jesus Christ with all boldness and without hindrance" (Acts 28:31). In this the actions of the Roman authorities served the purposes of God.

CHAPTER 4

The Jewish Authorities

4.1 INTRODUCTION

This chapter considers the Jewish authorities including the chief priests and the Pharisees. In 4.2 we describe certain aspects of the context of Luke's work, including a summary of social conditions in Galilee and Judaea, and of the key character groups which feature in Luke's narrative. We also consider possible links between the Jews of Luke's own time and the time of Jesus, and then go on to discuss the dynamics of honor/shame in Palestinian society, important in understanding the relationship between Jesus and the Pharisees.

In the light of that context—but see 4.2.1.1—and drawing on intertext and especially co-text, 4.3 considers Luke's use of various terms (Pharisees, scribes, etc.) to describe these religious and secular authorities. We conclude that the use of these terms in the Gospel can best be understood by examining just two groups of characters, the chief priests and their allies (the elders and temple functionaries) on the one hand and the Pharisees and their associates (the scribes[1] and teachers of the law) on the other. In 4.4 we briefly examine Luke's presentation of the chief priests, and in 4.5, in greater detail, his presentation of the Pharisees. Our findings are summarized in 4.6.

---

1. Some scribes are associated with the chief priests—see 4.2.3 and 4.3.

4.2 CONTEXT

4.2.1 Galilee

4.2.1.1 Introduction

There has been much disagreement between scholars about social and economic conditions in Galilee in our period, including such matters as the extent to which there was a monetary economy (see 4.2.1.2), the existence of a Galilean ruling elite (4.2.1.3), the attitude towards Jerusalem and the temple (4.2.1.4), and the extent of the use of the Greek language (4.2.1.5). We attempt to summarize and partially synthesize these views with some additional emphases which are important for our purposes. However, we need to bear in mind that whereas we can be fairly sure that Luke[2] (and, therefore, his intended reader) was aware of the social background of the Eastern empire in such places as Greece and Asia, we can have no such confidence about his knowledge of the very different social situation in Galilee and Jerusalem, the setting of the whole of the Gospel and the first part of Acts.[3] Accordingly, in this chapter we make less use of context although remembering that it forms the background against which Luke's antetext was shaped and can, therefore, be helpful in interpreting Luke's narrative. Against that background we use our interpretative tools, in particular co-text and antetext.

4.2.1.2 Social and Economic Conditions

Richard Horsley has provided generally convincing descriptions of economic and social conditions in Galilee, although his use of epigraphs about mountains[4] from Fernand Braudel is worrying. Galilee[5] features hills, not mountains, and differs greatly from the mountains of the Mediterranean which Braudel described:

> High, wide, never-ending mountains . . . impressive and demanding presences: some because of their height, others because of their density or their deep, enclosed, inaccessible

---

2. The reliable narrator tells us of his travels in these places.

3. "[Luke's] knowledge of [Palestinian] geography and customs seems inadequate" (Fitzmyer, *Luke I–IX*, 35).

4. Horsley, *Galilee*, 19; Horsley, *Archaeology, History, and Society*, 15, 88. He does not give references—they are to Braudel, *Mediterranean*, 33, 34 and 33, 38.

5. Described by Freyne, *Galilee from Alexander the Great*, 9–15.

valleys. They turn towards the sea impressive and forbidding countenances.[6]

The Sea of Galilee is not a sea, Luke never calls it such, and it is very different from the Mediterranean, Braudel's "sea." It is a lake, some "twelve miles long by five miles wide at its broadest point,"[7] and to the west the plain, centered on Tiberias, is relatively low-lying, and separated by ranges of hills and narrow valleys from another plain running west from Sepphoris—these regions together are known as Lower Galilee. To the north are the higher hills of Upper Galilee, which does not feature specifically in Luke's work.

Galilee has been seen as a monetary economy. Ze'ev Safrai argues that "during the Roman period the economy of Judaea [including Galilee] was for the most part an open one and dependent both on internal and external trade."[8] A similar view on a more limited scale was taken by Douglas Edwards:

> Villages mentioned in [the canonical gospel] tradition were near (Capernaum, Bethsaida) or connected to (Nazareth, Caesarea Philippi, region of Tyre and Sidon) urban areas and linked to a vibrant regional market network.[9]

But Horsley has a different view:

> Far from the village being a market economy, it appears that most village communities as well as their constituent households were relatively self-sufficient.[10]

Although we agree with Horsley in regard to the greater part of Galilee, where villages were built on hills away from the main roads and the cities,[11] we would see the area around the Lake as different. Both Capernaum and Bethsaida (Julias) were fishing villages (on the north coast of the sea) and fish have to be sold. Some could be sold fresh (and perhaps also be dried or salted) locally, but much of the catch was probably sent to Tarichaeae

---

6. Braudel, *Mediterranean*, 26. Braudel lists his mountains—the nearest to Galilee are those of Lebanon.
7. Freyne, *Galilee from Alexander the Great*, 14.
8. Safrai, *Economy of Roman Palestine*, 429.
9. Edwards, "Socio-Economic and Cultural Ethos," 72.
10. Horsley, *Archaeology, History, and Society*.
11. Freyne, *Galilee from Alexander the Great*, 12–13.

(Magdala),[12] a major center for the processing of fish[13] towards the middle of the Lake, some six miles from both Capernaum and Bethsaida. A little further south was the city of Tiberias, also a market for fish which was mainly eaten by the better-off,[14] although no doubt fishermen, despite being poor, also ate it. Brine, probably a watered form of the fish-based condiment garum, was eaten by the poor as a sauce with their barley bread.

A boat of the period recently excavated was designed for a crew of five,[15] and the size in itself suggests a substantial catch which would need marketing. Fish was subject to taxation[16] (a general sales tax, tolls, and specific taxes, including a license fee permitting fishing on the Lake) and, if it was to be preserved, also needed salt—the market in salt was a Roman monopoly.[17] The taxes, including the license fees, were collected by tax collectors[18] like Levi.[19] There was a substantial amount of transport traffic on the lake[20] as "the development of the fishing industry is . . . dependent upon . . . trade and transportation networks."[21]

Both fishing and transport were activities requiring the use of coinage. Safrai reports that almost half of a quantity of coins found at Migdal (Magdala/Tarichaeae), were from Syrian cities,[22] suggesting a widely based trade. Even local commerce, for example, the sale of fish to the processors

12. The introduction of fish-processing at Tarichaeae is dated to Ptolemaic times and there is evidence from Egypt that fish "preservation and marketing . . . was controlled by a large-scale enterprise, either a royal concern or one managed by the holder of a gift estate . . . The king or holder of the estate made a large amount of profit, whereas the fishermen made very little" (Freyne, *Galilee from Alexander the Great*, 174). If Tarichaeae was like this at its foundation by Palestine's Egyptian rulers, it was probably so during the time of Jesus.

13. The name Tarichaeae indicates this: "Processed Fishville" (Hanson and Oakman, *Palestine in the Time of Jesus*, 110).

14. Hamel, *Poverty and Charity*, 25. "Fish held a place of honor on the Palestinian table . . . the typical Sabbath dish" (Broshi, *Bread, Wine*, 134).

15. Hanson and Oakman, *Palestine in the Time of Jesus*, 110—cf. Mark 1.20. They describe the fishing industry, 106–10.

16. "Cash-based facets of the economy were more easily and cheaply taxable" (Hamel, *Poverty and Charity*, 143).

17. The importance of taxes on fishing as a source of revenue is exemplified by Herodotus, who, listing the revenues of all the provinces of the empire of Darius, named only a single specific source: "Egypt . . . paid 700 talents, in addition to the money from the fish in Lake Moeris" (*Hist* 3.91).

18. Hanson and Oakman, *Palestine in the Time of Jesus*, 106.

19. Called while beside the Sea in the antetext, Mark 2:13–14.

20. Safrai, *Economy of Roman Palestine*, 290–91.

21. Ibid., 164.

22. Ibid., 399. He does not give the date.

and the materials used by the fishermen, "flax for nets, cut-stone for anchors, wood for boat-building and repairs, baskets for transporting,"[23] would have required cash, also needed to pay taxes.[24] The processors themselves also used various materials and the products (dried or salted fish and fish sauces) had to be transported to markets.[25] The fishermen and tax-collectors described in the Gospel are to be understood against this background.

4.2.1.3 A Galilean Ruling Elite?

The cities, Sepphoris and Tiberias, had some of the attributes of a *polis* (although they did not control the surrounding rural areas)[26] and acted as centers for the collection of taxes for Antipas, who ruled Galilee without serious incident for over forty years. There were rich elites in the cities, but, except for the extraction of rent and taxes, they seem to have had little connection with the villages where the bulk of the population lived, and the cities and their elites were much hated. We describe in section 4.2.2 the process of acquisition of land by the urban elites of Judaea; it is probable that a similar process took place in Galilee, but perhaps at a slower rate, as there is little evidence of social banditry there. The social distance between these urban elites and the general population is perhaps the reason why the urban elite of Galilee do not feature in either Luke's narrative[27] or his antetext.

4.2.1.4 Attitudes towards Jerusalem and the Temple

Horsley believes that the Galilean population was mainly descended from the ancient tribes of the Northern kingdom who were never deported,[28] whereas Freyne finds that "by the first century CE the successors of . . .. Hasmonean settlers constituted the bulk of Galilean Jews."[29] Perhaps as a consequence of his views, Horsley finds that "Galileans tended to resist the demands of the Temple authorities and official interpretations of the

---

23. Hanson and Oakman, *Palestine in the Time of Jesus*, 107.

24. For contemporary taxes on fishing in Egypt see Wallace, *Taxation in Egypt*, 219–22, and for capitation taxes on fishermen, 212, retail sales taxes, 209 and the farming of fishery taxes, 289.

25. Hanson and Oakman, *Palestine in the Time of Jesus*, 107.

26. As noted in 1.5.4.5.

27. The only possible reference would seem to be the rich man in the Lazarus parable (Luke 16:19–31)—see 5.3.1.

28. Horsley, *Galilee*, 26–27, 45.

29. Freyne, *Jesus*, 82.

Torah."[30] On the other hand, Freyne claims that "there was a strong attachment to the mother-city, its temple and customs, among Galilean Jews of Jesus' day"[31] and describes "the much older and deeper loyalties to Jerusalem and its cult center [than to the Herodian cities of Lower Galilee]."[32] Freyne's view is more generally accepted:

> The people recognized Jerusalem as their center and as the center of Jewish government; those who lived in Jerusalem and who were educated were considered to be the ruling class, even by Galileans.[33]

Luke implies that a great many people went from Galilee to Jerusalem for the Passover (Luke 2:44), and the views of Freyne and Saldarini are consonant with this.

4.2.1.5 *The Use of Greek*

Scholars agree that Aramaic was the main language in Galilee but differ on the extent to which Greek was used, Freyne arguing that "Greek was certainly widely used even among the lower, uneducated classes,"[34] whereas Horsley finds that: "If we consider separately the sites close to Tiberias, there is much less of an indication that Greek was an everyday language in the rest of Lower Galilee."[35] For both, Greek was widely used in the area around the Sea of Galilee, which includes most of the places identified by Luke.

4.2.2 Jerusalem and the Chief Priests

Apart from Caesarea, Judaea had only one significant city, Jerusalem, the site of the temple which was the center of the cult. "The striking characteristic of most Jewish leaders before Herod is in fact the origin of their authority not in wealth but in a religious function, usually that of priest."[36] But after Herod was appointed as king by the Romans, he destroyed the old

---

30. Horsley, "Pharisees and Jesus," 134.
31. Freyne, *Jesus*, 82.
32. Freyne, "Urban-Jewish Relations," 85.
33. Saldarini, *Pharisees, Scribes*, 104.
34. Freyne, *Galilee from Alexander the Great*, 144.
35. Horsley, *Archaeology, History, and Society*, 171.
36. Goodman, *Ruling Class of Judaea*, 37.

Hasmonaean ruling class in Judaea, and it was replaced by appointees, first of Herod and then of the Romans.

> Herod systematically undermined the reputation of the high priesthood through appointing men of insignificant families and dissolving the principle of hereditary succession.[37]

These new men (high priests) and their families may have been given estates by Herod but subsequently their wealth derived from the temple. After the deposition of Archelaus:

> The Roman governor [following the example of Herod] appointed a High Priest from a family probably never previously honoured with the post . . . His family was to dominate the high priesthood in the next sixty years.[38]

The new elite of Jerusalem were almost wholly dependent upon the temple or the governor—there was no independent landed class of substance. Nevertheless, these families were rich: "Archaeologists have unearthed in Jerusalem private houses of great size and luxurious appointments."[39] Martin Goodman has argued that "the Temple's funds . . . were specifically kept under the close supervision . . . of the procurator"[40] but Magen Broshi has estimated that a "minimalistic computation" of the annual yield of the half-shekel levy was one million denarii,[41] to which must be added the substantial gifts to the temple "both from Jewish pilgrims and from gentile visitors from outside Palestine."[42] It is difficult to see such massive sums being safe under the "close supervision" of a procurator, a post which, as we noted in 3.2.1, received a salary of 25,000 denarii a year.[43] The temptation would surely have been too great even for someone less avaricious than Felix. These flows of money will undoubtedly have provided wealth for the elite, which was used to acquire land, usually through loans on which the peasant was expected to default,[44] and the loss of their land by the peasants led to social banditry, or a flight to the city, Jerusalem.[45] Between the death

37. Schaper, "Pharisees," 418.
38. Goodman, *Ruling Class of Judaea*, 44.
39. Ibid., 55.
40. Ibid., 112.
41. Broshi, *Bread, Wine*, 194.
42. Goodman, *Ruling Class of Judaea*, 52.
43. "When Pilate used some of this money to build an aquaduct for Jerusalem, a rebellion followed" (Gabba, "Social, Economic, and Political History," 137).
44. Goodman, *Ruling Class of Judaea*, 56–58. See also ibid., 108.
45. Ibid., 62–65.

of Herod and the outbreak of the war the population of Jerusalem approximately doubled[46] and during this time, "the increasingly difficult situation . . . forced the eminent priestly families and the leading Pharisaic scribes to cooperate."[47]

The lack of an independent elite is illustrated by the position of tax-collectors, who "in other provinces of the Roman empire . . . were among the most respected members of society" but were despised in Palestine as lacking "any of the criteria for status generally accepted by Jews, such as good birth or wisdom through knowledge of Torah."[48] The tax collectors were entrepreneurial, their income depended upon their own actions, and they were also despised because their trade provided the opportunity to lie to increase their income,[49] confirmed in Luke's Gospel by the words of the Baptist (Luke 3:13) and the story of Zacchaeus (Luke 19:8), and also by the adverse references to them by the Pharisees.

The Sanhedrin in Jerusalem was perhaps a governing council,[50] but Martin Goodman finds no evidence for this in our period[51] and suggests that:

> The Sanhedrin was not a regular political council at all . . . it met only at the request of the High Priest as his advisory body, and . . . its influence was only as great as that of the sum total of its members.[52]

The high priest and his immediate associates were known as the chief, or high, priests. There was only one high priest at any one time, but the plural was often used and Jeremias sees this as referring to "the permanent chief priests of the Temple, who by virtue of their office had seats and votes in the Sanhedrin where they formed a well defined group"[53]—a description of its composition broadly compatible with Goodman's view of the Sanhe-

---

46. Broshi, *Bread, Wine*, 118, 120.
47. Schaper, "Pharisees," 423.
48. Goodman, *Ruling Class of Judaea*, 131–32.
49. Wills, "Methodological Reflections," 260 and nn24–25. The temptation to lie or cheat was later seen as a reason to regard any trade as despicable—see Jeremias, *Jerusalem*, 303–6, and 310–12, which refer to tax-collectors.
50. The traditional view—see Schürer, *History of the Jewish People*, 199–226; more recently Gabba, "Social, Economic, and Political History," 135.
51. Josephus tells us that it was an autonomous council in the time of Hyrcanus, but that Herod executed almost all its members on becoming king (Josephus, *Ant* 14.175).
52. Goodman, *Ruling Class of Judaea*, 114.
53. Jeremias, *Jerusalem*, 179.

drin. As well as the priestly class, the Sanhedrin included the "elders," who were "Judaean aristocrats";[54] such a one was Joseph of Arimathea.[55]

4.2.3 The Scribes

"Scribe" was a term familiar to Luke as it was used in the whole of the Greek speaking world. The functions of those to whom the term was applied will have differed from place to place, but always required literacy. In Palestine they were also concerned with the interpretation of Torah, and, being literate, they were probably routinely involved in relations with the ruling authorities.

> The socially lowest type of scribe would have been the village scribe who was little more than a copyist who knew how to draw up letters and legal documents. The village scribe might also have been a low level administrator reporting to the authorities, keeping records and carrying on communication between the government and people . . .
>
> Most scribes . . . were middle level officials. They were the agents of the central government and probably served in various bureaucratic posts. Their position gave them some power and influence, but they were subordinate to and dependent on the priests and leading families in Jerusalem and Herod Antipas in Galilee . . .
>
> The highest level of scribe may have come from or joined the governing class . . . those at the center of the government . . . would have achieved great influence and some power.[56]

It was perhaps such high-level scribes whose employment by the temple was described by Josephus; on several occasions he adds temple, or government, scribes to his recapitulation of Israel's histories,[57] and he also mentions a scribe of the council killed during the siege of Jerusalem.[58] Such officials[59] would have benefited from the resources of the temple: "The scribes employed at the Temple . . . had a regular income," but most of the

---

54. Schaper, "Pharisees," 414. He sees the Sanhedrin as a governing council, but Goodman's advisory council would also include such men. "Aristocrats" may be misleading—they were rich but probably without respected ancestry.

55. See 4.4.4.

56. Saldarini, *Pharisees, Scribes*, 274–75.

57. Josephus, *Ant* 7.319, 364; 11.248, 250, 287.

58. Josephus, *War* 5.532.

59. All cited Saldarini, "Scribes," 1014. See also his *Pharisees, Scribes*, 261–64.

scribes belonged to "the poorer classes."⁶⁰ Luke, as we see in 4.3.2, shows scribes affiliated to both of his main character groups (the chief priests and the Pharisees) and this may reflect the differing classes of scribes described by Saldarini and Jeremias.

4.2.4 The Pharisees

For Saldarini, the "Pharisees function as rich and powerful patrons of the peasants within the village society and as brokers for the peasants in their relations with the outside world,"⁶¹ and for Horsley they were "representatives of the Temple who pressed [Galilean villagers] mercilessly to pay their tithes and squeezed them to the limits of their subsistence."⁶² But these views suggest that Pharisees and scribes fulfilled very similar functions⁶³ and there seems no need for such a conflation—the Pharisees were essentially a religious organization although some, perhaps many, Pharisees may have been scribes by occupation. "It is most likely that Pharisees were bound together by certain beliefs and practices . . . and by endeavors to influence social change."⁶⁴ Their leaders Hillel and Shammai "gathered modest groups of enthusiastic followers who strove to convince other Jews to join them and sought influence and power over social policy."⁶⁵ In this they faced opposition as, "expertise in the interpretation of the Law could always be challenged by experts working in a different tradition,"⁶⁶ such as the Sadducees, or indeed, Jesus. From the time of Herod "Pharisaism . . . acquiesced in Roman overlordship and Herodian rule. Political quietism was the price the Pharisees paid in return for survival and official toleration":⁶⁷

> It is possible that the officials and retainers of Herod Antipas supported and encouraged the Pharisees . . . [whose] emphasis on tithing and practices which promoted Jewish identity could be used to promote loyalty to a Jewish king.⁶⁸

---

60. Jeremias, *Jerusalem*, 115.
61. Saldarini, *Pharisees, Scribes*, 176.
62. Horsley, "Pharisees and Jesus," 142.
63. So, ibid., 119–22.
64. Saldarini, *Pharisees, Scribes*.
65. Ibid., 289.
66. Goodman, *Ruling Class of Judaea*, 132.
67. Schaper, "Pharisees," 422.
68. Saldarini, *Pharisees, Scribes*, 296.

The Pharisees generally were not wealthy and it is likely that they were a cross-section of all but the poorest elements of Jewish society. "The Pharisaic communities were mostly composed of petty commoners, men of the people,"[69] and: "Most of [the Pharisees] did not have hereditary ties to positions of power."[70] Nevertheless, Pharisees had to have "sufficient leisure to embark upon the task of scriptural exegesis and legal decision-making,"[71] although this was not necessarily true of all their followers. Luke presents them as interpreters of the law on the basis of their understanding of Scripture, as we see in 4.5.

4.2.5 The Priests

Ordinary priests were not at all wealthy: "The majority of [ordinary priests] lived in great poverty,"[72] and, according to Josephus, some died of starvation, during both the governorship of Felix and that of Albanus, because their share of the temple tithes was plundered by the chief priests.[73] As we noted in 4.2.2, the high priests after Herod were distinguished only by wealth, and: "There were thousands of other priests whose birth was just as impressive as theirs but who were excluded from power because they were poor."[74] But there are different views with regard to connections between priests and Pharisees. Jeremias argues that the Pharisaic movement grew up among the priesthood[75] and says that "we know that a large number of priests were Pharisees."[76] E. P. Sanders rejects the evidence put forward by Jeremias, finding only that "a few priests and Levites were Pharisees,"[77] and notes that "in Josephus, the Pharisees are lay [non-priestly] interpreters of the law."[78] He points out that priests were necessarily literate, and were forbidden from working on the land, and plausibly suggests that many priests

---

69. Jeremias, *Jerusalem*, 259.
70. Saldarini, *Pharisees, Scribes*, 282.
71. Schaper, "Pharisees," 405.
72. Jeremias, *Jerusalem*, 108.
73. Josephus, *Ant* 20.181, 206–7.
74. Goodman, *Ruling Class of Judaea*, 119.
75. Jeremias, *Jerusalem*, 265.
76. Ibid., 256.
77. Sanders, *Judaism*, 412.
78. Sanders, *Jesus and Judaism*, 188.

(and Levites) made their living as scribes.[79] Possible implications of these opposing views for the understanding of Acts 6:7[80] are discussed in 4.5.10.

4.2.6 The Jews in Luke's Own Time

By the time Luke began to write his two-volume work:

> Jerusalem and the temple were destroyed and Judaism lost its traditional center and any vestige of priestly self-government... Those Jewish groups that survived the wars cherished the biblical tradition and continued to live in the traditional way in both Palestinian villages and Diaspora cities.
>
> ...
>
> A new group of scholars, fervently devoted to the Jewish way of life, emerged... Their teachings and customs were strongly influenced by the prewar Pharisaic way of life, with its stress on maintaining for themselves the ritual purity proper to priests in the temple, tithing food according to biblical law and later custom, and strictly observing Sabbaths and festivals.[81]

It seems that "the later way of life and historical views of the rabbis are very probably related to the phenomenon of Pharisaism, but not simply an extension of it,"[82] although "evidence is not abundant."[83] Nevertheless, the later rabbis adopted the Pharisees as their predecessors,[84] and this process may have begun in Luke's time, ten to twenty years after the destruction of the Temple. Luke portrays Pharisaism as widespread in Palestine (Luke 5:17), and also implies that it was long established in Tarsus (Acts 23:6; 21:39) and had reached Antioch (Acts 15:1, 5). Thus he may well have believed (or known) that some diaspora Jews[85] were linked to the Pharisees.[86] The rabbis began the reconstruction of Judaism at Yavneh in about 80, and

---

79. Sanders, *Judaism*, 181–82.
80. "A great many of the priests became obedient to the faith" (Acts 6:7).
81. Saldarini, "Jewish Responses," 409–10, 419.
82. Saldarini, *Pharisees, Scribes*, 201.
83. Ibid., 8.
84. Ibid., 214.

85. Our evaluation of Luke's autobiographical material suggests that he was himself a diaspora Jew: he was "especially familiar with the Jewish sub-culture [of the countries bordering the sea in the eastern portion of the Empire]" (Witherington, *Acts*, 54).

86. "The principle figure... Yohanan ben Zakkai [is] described in rabbinical writings as Hillel's leading disciple" (Neusner, *Judaism in the Beginning*, 89).

probably had little influence on the diaspora until well after Luke had completed his work.

4.2.7 Honor/Shame and Challenge/Response

Recent approaches to the understanding of the New Testament, drawing upon social science and anthropology, have tried to analyze the way that certain Mediterranean types of social interaction are reflected in the narrative. One of the most important of these is the honor/shame dynamic, which we find helpful in understanding the way in which Luke presents the Pharisees.

Honor/shame and challenge/response are described by Bruce Malina. He finds that honor, "a claim to worth *and* the social acknowledgement of that worth"[87] was one of the most important social elements of life in the society described in the New Testament, and acquiring or defending it was a constant preoccupation. Indeed, in New Testament times we see "a society that looks on all social interactions outside the family or substitute family (circle of friends, in-group) as a contest for honor":[88]

> In biblical times honor meant everything, including survival . . . Honor can be *ascribed* or *acquired*. Ascribed honor derives from birth . . . Acquired honor, by contrast, is the result of skill in the never-ending game of challenge and response. Not only must one win to gain it; one must do so in public because the whole community must acknowledge the gain . . . Since honor is a limited good, if one person wins honor, someone else loses . . . The game of challenge and response is deadly serious and can literally be a matter of life and death.[89]

"The interaction over honor, the challenge-response game, *can take place only between social equals*,"[90] and "it falls to the bystanders to decide whether or not the challenged person successfully defended his . . . honor."[91] It worked as follows:

> The game of challenge-riposte is a central phenomenon [of the competition for honor] and is always played in public. It consists of a challenge (almost any word, gesture, or action) that

---

87. Malina, *New Testament World*, 31.
88. Ibid., 36.
89. Malina and Rohrbaugh, *Social Science Commentary*, 310.
90. Malina, *New Testament World*, 35.
91. DeSilva, *Honor, Patronage*, 29.

seeks to undermine the honor of another person and a response that answers in equal measure or ups the ante and thereby challenges in return. Both positive (gifts, compliments) and negative (insults, dares) challenges must be answered to avoid a serious loss of face.[92]

It is not necessary to accept these scholars' understanding of the overriding importance of challenge and response. It was not shared by the Lukan Jesus: he rarely made such challenges, except in response to the Pharisees (we discuss the way in which the Pharisees challenged Jesus in 4.5.2). In the parable of the Pharisee and the tax collector (addressed to Pharisees, see 4.5.8), Jesus said that "all who exalt themselves will be humbled, but all who humble themselves will be exalted" (Luke 18:14) and he later rebuked the disciples who disputed among themselves about which one of them was to be regarded as the greatest (Luke 22:24–27). He also on several other occasions rebuked those who sought honor (e.g., Luke 11:43; 20:46). The views of the Lukan narrator are aligned with those of the Lukan Jesus, including his attitude to challenge and response, so that he does not expect the intended reader to take the game at the Pharisees' own valuation. Nevertheless, it was a pervasive feature of life in the times which Luke described and was both important to the Lukan Pharisees and comprehensible to his intended readers.

4.3 LUKE'S CHARACTER GROUPS

4.3.1 Introduction

Luke uses a number of different terms to describe elements of the Jewish religious leadership, the most important being the chief or high priests and the Pharisees. The terms which he uses are derived from his antetext, but he often changes them. Luke, as we suggested in 4.2.1, may have had little knowledge of conditions in Galilee and Judaea, and his changes to his antetext, therefore, may have been due to his attempts to make sense of the story rather than to independent sources of information. In his narrative the term "priests" does not usually refer to the religious leadership—ordinary priests served in the temple when it was their turn to do so and drew a share of the offerings, but derived no other benefit from their position, and, as we have seen, were frequently poor. Another term, "elders," is usually used of leaders (probably secular) of the Jews in Jerusalem but it is also used of leaders of the local Jewish community in Capernaum (Luke 7:3), and in Acts of

---

92. Malina and Rohrbaugh, *Social Science Commentary*, 306–7.

leaders of the Christian community.[93] However, Luke's usage does not lead to any risk of confusion for the intended reader—in this section we consider only the Jerusalem elders.

4.3.2 Links between Groups

Especially in the Gospel, Luke very frequently links two or more terms together, for example, "Pharisees and teachers of the law" (Luke 5:17). He frequently refers to the two main groups, the chief priests and the Pharisees, and almost all of the other terms which he uses are consistently associated with one of these groups. Only the scribes are associated with both.

The links in the Gospel may be summarized as follows:

1. Lawyers are almost always associated with Pharisees: 5:17 ("Pharisees and teachers of the law"), Luke 7:30 ("the Pharisees and the lawyers"), Luke 11:45 (a lawyer says "Teacher, when you [insult the Pharisees] you insult us too"), Luke 14:3 ("the lawyers and Pharisees"). In Acts, Gamaliel is described as "a Pharisee in the council [and] a teacher of the law" (Acts 5:34). Paul, described as a Pharisee (Acts 26:5), says he was "brought up in [Jerusalem] at the feet of Gamaliel, educated strictly according to our ancestral law" (Acts 22:3). There are two exceptions. First, the teachers who listened to Jesus in the temple in the infancy narrative (Luke 2:46). These teachers do not fit readily into any of the categories, and as the infancy narrative differs in many ways from the remainder of the Gospel, we have excluded them from our analysis. The other exception was a single lawyer who tested Jesus (Luke 10:25, discussed below).

2. Pharisees and scribes are often associated: Luke 5:21 ("the scribes and the Pharisees"), Luke 5:30 ("the Pharisees and their scribes"), Luke 6:7 ("the scribes and the Pharisees"), Luke 11:53 ("the scribes and the Pharisees"), Luke 15:2 ("the Pharisees and the scribes"), Luke 20:39 ("some of the scribes answered, 'Teacher, you have spoken well'")—opposing the Sadducees), Acts 23:9 ("certain scribes of the Pharisees' group," also opposing the Sadducees).

3. Scribes are more often associated with the chief priests and/or the elders: Luke 9:22 ("the Son of Man must . . . be rejected by the elders, chief priests, and scribes"), Luke 19:47 ("The chief priests, the scribes, and the leaders of the people"), Luke 20:1 ("the chief priests and the scribes

---

93. Acts 11:30; 14:23; 15:2, 4, 6, 22, 23; 16:4; 20:17; 21:18. It is also used in Acts, in the same way as in the Gospel, of the leaders of the Jews in Jerusalem (Acts 23:14; 24:1).

came with the elders"), Luke 20:19 ("the scribes and chief priests"), Luke 22:2 ("the chief priests and the scribes"), Luke 22:66 ("the assembly of the elders of the people, both chief priests and scribes"), Luke 23:10 ("the chief priests and the scribes"), Acts 4:5 ("their rulers, elders and scribes"), Acts 6:12 ("the elders and the scribes"). Some scribes may be associated with the Sadducees (Luke 20:39), who themselves are associated with the chief priests (Acts 4:1;[94] 5:17; 23:6–9). In this category we would also put the denunciation of the scribes (Luke 20:46–47); and will argue that these scribes are closely associated with the Temple cult.[95]

4. The elders are associated with the chief priests in passages listed above[96] and elsewhere: Luke 22:52 ("the chief priests, the officers of the temple police, and the elders"), Acts 4:23 ("the chief priests and the elders"), Acts 22:5 ("the high priest and the whole council of elders"), Acts 22:30 ("the chief priests and the entire council"), Acts 23:14 ("the chief priests and elders"), Acts 24:1 ("the high priest Ananias . . . with some elders and an attorney"), Acts 25:15 ("the chief priests and the elders of the Jews").

Luke tells us that "*some* of the scribes answered, 'Teacher, you have spoken well'" (Luke 20:39, emphasis added). The scribes are not a homogeneous group; as we have seen, some are associated with the Pharisees and some with the chief priests, but in almost all the references in both Gospel and Acts Luke is explicit about which group the scribes are associated with. Apart from the denunciation of the scribes, there is only this one exception, when, in the question about the resurrection, "some of the scribes" approved of Jesus's answer (Luke 20:39). But they, unlike the Sadducees, believed in the resurrection and Luke later tells us, at Acts 23:8, that this was a characteristic of the Pharisees. So this co-textual evidence shows that these scribes were also associated with the Pharisees. In so distinguishing the two groups of scribes Luke ensured that the Pharisees were seen as distinct from the chief priests, as we argue in 4.5.

Although the lawyers and teachers of the law (who appear to be identical to lawyers) may be a different group from the scribes, it is not, in practice, possible to distinguish between them. "Pharisees and teachers of the law" listened to Jesus (Luke 5:17), while "the scribes and the Pharisees" reacted to what he said (Luke 5:21) and after the woes to the Pharisees and

---

94. "Priests," NRSV. The references to "the captain of the temple" (4:1) and to "the high priestly family" (4:5) suggest that chief priests are meant here.

95. See 4.4.2.

96. Including "the leaders of the people" (Luke 19:47).

lawyers (Luke 11:42–52) it was "the scribes and the Pharisees" who reacted (Luke 11:53). As described above, the lawyers are always explicitly associated with the Pharisees except when a lawyer asked Jesus what he must do to inherit eternal life (Luke 10:25).[97] That he asked such a question suggests that he was a Pharisee, as belief in the after-life was one of the features which distinguished them from the Sadducees. After Jesus responded, he asked his further question wanting "to justify himself," *dikaiōsai heauton* (Luke 10:29). The co-textual evidence indicates that the phrase "justify himself" is a further sign that this lawyer was a Pharisee. The parable of the Pharisee going to pray was told to "some who trusted in themselves that they were righteous," *pepoithotas eph' heautois hoti eisin dikaioi* (Luke 18:9), whom we, with most scholars, take to be Pharisees. A similar phrase is used in the question of paying taxes to Caesar, spies "who pretended to be honest," *hypokrinomenous*[98] *heautous dikaious* (Luke 20:20),[99] that is, spies of the chief priests who, the repetition of *dikaios* suggests, perhaps pretended to be Pharisees. Luke here amends his antetext, Mark, to ensure that this question, to which the wrong answer could mean death,[100] was asked not by Pharisees but by spies.

Jesus himself distinguished between Pharisees and lawyers in that the woes to the Pharisees (Luke 11:42–44) differed in important ways from the woes to the lawyers (Luke 11:46–52), but most of the differences do not seem to be significant for our purposes;[101] indeed, as we have seen, the reaction of those present confirmed the links between the Pharisees and the lawyers. As a result, "the reader . . . assumes that Jesus' ensuing criticisms of the lawyers also reflect poorly on the Pharisees."[102]

We therefore see Luke as presenting us with two major character groups, the high priests with their allies (the chief priests) and the Pharisees, with their associates, while the scribes, each time they are referred to, are linked with one or other of these groups. In the following sections we shall examine more closely Luke's presentation of these character groups,

---

97. In the nearest parallels the question about the resurrection is asked by one of those opposed to the Sadducees and impressed by what Jesus has said to them. For Mark he is "one of the scribes" (Mark 12:28) and for Matthew one of the Pharisees (Matt 22:35).

98. This word and its cognates are discussed in 4.5.6.

99. Mark has Pharisees and Herodians (Mark 12:13), as has Matthew (Matt 22:15–16).

100. Compare the charges against Jesus and Paul, discussed in 3.4.2 and 3.4.4.

101. See 4.5.4.

102. Darr, *Character Building*, 104.

beginning with the chief priests whose stark depiction helps us to understand the more nuanced presentation of the Pharisees.

4.4 THE CHIEF PRIESTS

4.4.1 Introduction

The murderous intentions of the chief priests and their allies are co-textually made very explicit, being foretold by Jesus (Luke 9:22) and described by the narrator from their first appearance: "The chief priests, the scribes, and the leaders of the people kept looking for a way to kill him" (Luke 19:47).[103] So the intended reader knows what is in their minds when Luke tells us that the chief priests, the scribes and the elders asked by what authority Jesus taught (Luke 20:1–2). He responded with a counter-question about the Baptist, and went on to tell the parable of the vineyard. As a result:

> When the scribes and chief priests realized that he had told this parable against them, they wanted to lay hands on him, *epibalein ep' auton tas cheiras*, at that very hour, but they feared the people (Luke 20:19).

In the Septuagint, used of people[104] *epibalein tas cheiras* usually means destroy or kill;[105] the exceptions are all blessings,[106] and it is clear that that is not what is intended here. They wanted to kill Jesus, who is now being pursued to the death by a single homogeneous group. They tried to trap him with the question about paying taxes (Luke 20:20–22). He evaded the trap and "they became silent" (Luke 20:26).

4.4.2 The Denunciation of the Scribes

Luke then describes the denunciation of the scribes by Jesus:[107]

> In the hearing of all the people he said to the disciples, "Beware of the scribes, who like to walk around in long robes, and love to be greeted with respect in the marketplaces, and to have the best seats in the synagogues and places of honor at banquets.

---

103. See also Luke 20:19; 22:2; 23:2, 18, 21, 23; 24:20.
104. It is also used of objects—cf. Luke 9:62.
105. Gen 22:12; Exod 7:4; 2 Sam 18:12; Esth A:13; 6:2; Ps LXX 80:15; Isa 5:25; 11:14.
106. Gen 46:4; 48:14, 17.
107. Closely following Mark 12:38–40.

They devour widows' houses and for the sake of appearance, *prophasei*, say long prayers. They will receive the greater condemnation" (Luke 20:45-47).

H. Fleddermann argues that the word translated pretense,[108] *prophasei*, can mean pretext,[109] and that a better translation is:

> Who devour the houses of the widows and for a pretext say long prayers—these will receive a more severe condemnation. [That is] the long prayers are the pretext for devouring the houses of the widows.[110]

Explaining the pretext, he points out that: "In the context . . . the long prayers must be a reference to the cult. The scribes are draining the widows' resources by the temple costs."[111] He links the passage to the cleansing of the temple, where the Lukan Jesus said: "My house shall be a house of prayer; but you have made it a den of robbers" (Luke 19:45-46),[112] and finds that "what Jesus is opposed to is the buying and selling itself; the buying and selling is called robbery."[113]

Here we disagree[114] as the buying and selling is not done by the scribes and there is a better, intertextual, explanation. A den of robbers is not where the robbers normally do their robbing; they go out from the den to do that.[115] The phrase "den of robbers" is a quotation from Jeremiah, who, addressing those who "oppress guest, and orphan and widow" (Jer 7:6), says (NRSV):[116]

> Will you steal, murder, [etc.] . . . and *then* come and stand before me in this house? . . . Has this house, which is called by my

---

108. "Pretense" in RSV, on which Fleddermann comments. "Sake of appearance" in NRSV in both Mark and Luke.

109. Confirmed in relation to this passage by BDAG, 889.

110. Fleddermann, "Warning about the Scribes." Although Fleddermann addressed the Gospel of Mark, the application to Luke differs little.

111. Ibid., 65.

112. Described in Mark (11:15-17), whose wording of the saying of Jesus is closely followed by Luke.

113. Ibid., 63.

114. Although the acts of the high priests in taking by force the ordinary priests' share of the temple sacrifices described in 4.2.2 could fairly be described as robbery, there is no indication that it was to this that the Lukan Jesus referred.

115. The Greek (*spēlaion*) has the same connotation—its primary meaning is "cave" (Balz and Schneider, "Spēlaion," 264).

116. The thrust of the verbose Septuagint text is similar.

name, become a den of robbers[117] in your sight? (Jer 7:9–11, emphasis added).

Luke's robbers, like those of Jeremiah, do not rob in the temple, they are not the sellers (Luke 19:45). They are those denounced by Jesus, whose base is the temple, but who go outside the temple to rob, to devour widows' houses on the pretext of long prayers, that is, the temple scribes persuading the poor to give to the temple funds. Immediately after praising the generosity of the widow of the two small coins (whose house is devoured), although not commending her action,[118] Jesus predicts the destruction of the temple:[119]

> When some were speaking about the temple, how it was adorned with beautiful stones and gifts dedicated to God, he said, "As for these things that you see, the days will come when not one stone will be left upon another; all will be thrown down" (Luke 21:5–6).

Although the scribes are said to seek "the best seats in the synagogues," a description earlier applied to the Pharisees (Luke 11:43), the close connection with the temple in both the immediate co-text and the Jeremiah reference mean that the intended reader will understand that these scribes are associated with the chief priests. Like the Pharisees they want to be honored by the people, but the fault for which they are condemned, very different from the faults of the Pharisees and teachers of the law (see 4.5.4), is devouring the houses of widows.

4.4.3 Hostility and Murder

From this point on Luke continues to show us the murderous intentions of the leaders towards Jesus—we see them seeking to kill him[120] and succeeding in doing so,[121] and, unlike the people, they showed no sign of remorse. After the crucifixion the disciples at Emmaus said: "Our chief priests and leaders handed him over to be condemned to death and crucified him" (Luke 24:20), making them the principals in the killing, although in Acts Peter acknowledged that they, like the crowd, "acted in ignorance" (Acts

---

117. *Spēlaion lēistōn* in both Jeremiah and Luke.
118. Argued in Wright, "Widow's Mites."
119. These passages are also consecutive in the antetext (Mark 12:38—13:2).
120. Luke 22:2–5, 47–53, 66–71; 23:1–5, 10, 13–25.
121. Luke 23:35; 24:20.

3:17). Later the chief priests and their allies were hostile to the apostles:[122] "They were enraged and wanted to kill them" (Acts 5:33). Their antagonism soon turned on Stephen, who was brought before the council on false charges (Acts 6:11–14). After listening to his speech, they, that is, the council, without legal process, "dragged him out of the city and began to stone him" (Acts 7:58). It was presumably also the council which was responsible, again without due process, for the "severe persecution [which, that day] began against the church in Jerusalem" (Acts 8:1), and it was the high priest who authorized Saul to go and arrest those "who belonged to the Way, men or women . . . [and] bring them bound to Jerusalem" (Acts 9:1–2). Although the responsibility for this is said by Ananias to be "authority from the chief priests" (Acts 9:14), a view confirmed by the synagogues in Damascus (Acts 9:21), there is no contradiction. Luke does not wish to distinguish between the high priest and his close colleagues.[123] So the high priests and their allies plotted against the first Christians and, in part by deceiving the people by the use of false witnesses (cf. Mark 14:56), killed Stephen and persecuted the infant church (Acts 8:1–3), topping this with complicity in the killing of James and the arrest of Peter by Agrippa I (Acts 12:2–3).

The Jewish leaders appear again in an extended series of scenes, beginning on Paul's return to Jerusalem and discussed, in relation to the Roman authorities, in 3.4.4. The attack on Paul, like that on Stephen, was started by the crowd, not the high priests and their allies, and it was only on the following day that the chief priests and the Sanhedrin became involved, when Lysias brought Paul before them: "Then the high priest Ananias ordered those standing near him to strike him on the mouth" (Acts 23:2). Paul's subsequent speech ended in uproar and he was again rescued by Lysias. The following morning more than forty Jews "joined in a conspiracy and bound themselves by an oath neither to eat nor drink until they had killed Paul" (Acts 23:12–13), and their plot was approved by the chief priests and the elders (Acts 23:14). The conspiracy was foiled and Paul was taken to Caesarea (Acts 23:16–33). The high priest and "some elders" (Acts 24:1) followed and accused him before the governor, Felix, and then his successor, Festus (Acts 25:2, 7); they promoted a second plot to kill him (Acts 25:3) which was also unsuccessful. Paul escaped by appealing to Rome, whither Festus sent him (see 3.4.4).

---

122. Acts 4:3, 5–7, 16–17, 21; 5:17–18.

123. Paul attributes this authority to "the high priest and the whole council of elders" (Acts 22:5).

4.4.4 Joseph of Arimathea

Before leaving the chief priests and their allies we should consider the one individual among them who differed in that he did not oppose Jesus. "Now there was a good and righteous man named Joseph, who, though a member of the council, had not agreed to their plan and action" (Luke 23:50–51). More light is cast on Luke's presentation of Joseph if we examine the changes he has made to his Markan antetext, which read: "Joseph of Arimathea, a respected member of the council, *euschēmōn bouleutēs*, who was also himself waiting expectantly for the kingdom of God" (Mark 15:43). Now, "when Joseph of Arimathea . . . is described as *euschēmōn* . . . the papyri make it clear that this means a wealthy landowner,"[124] a reading confirmed by the word's definition "of honourable position."[125] Luke does not use *euschēmōn*, does not describe Joseph as wealthy, but rather calls him "good and righteous."[126] "Righteous," *dikaios*, was used of Zachariah and Elizabeth (Luke 1:6) and of Simeon (Luke 2:25) at the beginning of the Gospel, and they were not rich. Luke does not make Joseph poor, but does not mention his wealth, and describes only his positive moral qualities, including generosity with his resources (in his burial of Jesus) and his actions make the intended reader see him as one of the followers of Jesus.[127]

4.4.5 Summary

The chief priests and their allies were unremittingly and murderously hostile to first Jesus and then the infant church. Luke does not give us any explicit reason for this. The parable of the vineyard, told against the scribes and chief priests (Luke 20:19), was not the explanation, for it followed on from the murderous hostility (Luke 19:47) and cannot be the cause of it; rather their hostility was the cause of Jesus's denunciation. Luke may have intended the reader to understand that the chief priests and elders, wielding authority in Jerusalem, had, like the Herodian rulers and the Roman governors discussed in chapters 2 and 3, derived that authority from the devil and acted accordingly. But a more plausible interpretation is that Luke

---

124. Jeremias, *Jerusalem*, 96. Matthew may agree, for he changes Mark's description to *plousios*, rich (Matt 27:57).

125. Moulton and Milligan, *Vocabulary of the Greek Testament*, 266. Cf. Acts 13:50; 17:12.

126. Fiedler ("*Euschēmōn*," 86) suggests that Luke thought that *euschēmōn* meant good and righteous.

127. Matthew states this explicitly (Matt 27:57).

saw their rejection and crucifixion of Jesus, accepted and supported by the Jerusalem crowd, as being responsible for the second destruction of the city and the temple, just as the actions of rulers and people had led to the first destruction.

Joseph of Arimathea was an exception. Like Agrippa II (2.4.6) and Sergius Paulus (3.4.6), he did not show hostility to Jesus or the church. But Joseph was not one of the chief priests—he came from the town of Arimathea, not Jerusalem, so he was, it seems, one of the elders, the secular members of the Sanhedrin. It is unlikely that he was a Pharisee—the narrator describes him as *dikaios* (Luke 23:50), a word which has just been applied to Jesus (Luke 23:47), and was never applied to the Pharisees except by themselves (Luke 10:29) or ironically (Luke 16:15; 18:9; 20:20).

4.5 THE PHARISEES

4.5.1 Introduction

> The Pharisees are the observers *par excellence* of God's will as manifested in Jesus and others. Nevertheless, they continually fail to recognize it. They therefore embody the theme of "seeing but not seeing, and hearing but not hearing."[128]

We agree with the main thrust of Darr's study of the Lukan Pharisees, which he summarized in a later work, describing: "Their obtuseness as a primary trait . . . and their didactic function as a paradigm of many of the story's anti-values."[129] But Darr did not contrast the Pharisees with the chief priests, nor did he consider Acts, and he has therefore underestimated or overlooked various positive aspects of Luke's presentation.[130] In what follows we mainly examine those aspects which differentiate the Pharisees from the chief priests; we do not stress their obtuseness,[131] which resulted in an inability to accept Jesus, but we should not forget that in the Gospel it was their primary characteristic.

---

128. Darr, *Character Building*, 126.

129. Darr, "Irenic or Ironic," 131.

130. Darr also took a different approach in that: "For the sake of clarity, we work with a first-time reader, that is, one who has not read Luke-Acts and formulated opinions about it previously" (*Character Building*, 28). Our reasons for assuming the intended reader would read and re-read Luke-Acts are given in 1.3.4.

131. This is well described by Darr.

4.5.2 Challenge and Response

The Pharisees (who, as we have seen, can be regarded as including the lawyers, and also the scribes until the narrative reaches Jerusalem) play the game of challenge and response[132] at length.[133] Time and again the Pharisees challenge Jesus, and, indeed, he, in response, challenges them, but, regardless of who makes the challenge, Jesus always triumphs. We shall examine both the various passages in the game and also the reaction of the Pharisees and of Jesus to the successive outcomes. In describing these incidents Luke has on several occasions altered his antetext Mark, sometimes including or excluding Pharisees in a particular interchange, always ensuring that the contrast between them and the chief priests is preserved.

Luke first presents five challenges, consecutively and almost seamlessly. The first was the cure of the paralyzed man (Luke 5:17–26), where Luke changes the antetext to include Pharisees among the challengers.[134] Up to this point Luke has told us nothing of the Pharisees, but now we hear, and hear only from Luke, that the Pharisees and teachers of the law "had come from every village of Galilee and Judea and from Jerusalem"[135] (Luke 5:17). That they came from the whole of the Jewish homeland ensures that Luke's readers understand that the Pharisees in his narrative are representatives of all Pharisees. They "began to question, *dialogizesthai*," (Luke 5:21),[136] each other about his claim to forgive sins and, speaking to one another, accused him of blasphemy. He knew what they were saying and answered the challenge with the cure; as a result, they, as part of the crowd, "glorified God and were filled with awe" (Luke 5:26).[137] Luke begins to develop the Pharisees as a character group who respond to Jesus in specific ways, and their response to this mighty work of Jesus suggests that they might be capable of accepting his message—there is never any similar response on the part of the chief priests.

---

132. Described in 4.2.7.

133. Gowler discusses challenge and response between Jesus and the Pharisees (Gowler, *Host, Guest*, 16–17).

134. Luke has added the Pharisees to the scribes in his Markan antetext (Mark 2:6). Matthew also has only scribes (Matt 9:3).

135. Luke has added this to the antetext (Mark 2:1–12).

136. This refers back to Simeon's oracle which tells that Jesus is to be "a sign that will be opposed so that the inner thoughts (*dialogismoi*) of many will be revealed" (2:34–35—Darr, *Character Building*, 84).

137. This response is very similar to that in Mark (Mark 2:12) and Matthew (Matt 9:8).

In the second challenge, at Levi's banquet (Luke 5:29–32), the Pharisees and their scribes[138] complained, *egongyzon*,[139] to the disciples about eating and drinking with tax-collectors and sinners (Luke 5:30). Jesus, although not himself addressed, dealt with the complaint, gaining more honor, and in his reply said that he had come "to call not the righteous, *dikaious*, but sinners to repentance" (Luke 5:32). The Pharisees were gradually being made aware that Jesus had a view of God's demands which was very different from theirs.

The next challenge (Luke 5:33–39), an immediate[140] riposte to Jesus's victory on the question about eating with tax-collectors, was made by "they" (Luke 5:33), clearly, in a clarification of his antetext, meaning the Pharisees and their scribes.[141] It was a complaint to Jesus about the disciples, comparing them unfavorably to the disciples both of John and of the Pharisees themselves, saying they ate and drank rather than fasted. Jesus answered them with the parable about new wine and old wine-skins, and a proverb (included by neither Mark nor Matthew): "And no one after drinking old wine desires new wine, but says, 'The old is good'" (Luke 5:39). Here we have, in a phrase from Jesus himself, the first indication that the Pharisees, or perhaps only some of them, may reject Jesus.

The fourth challenge (Luke 6:1–5), the plucking of grain by the disciples, again follows immediately in the narrative but is separated in observed time, "one Sabbath," in both Mark (Mark 2:23) and Luke (Luke 6:1). *Some* of the Pharisees[142] made the challenge (another indication that the Pharisees were not monolithic in their response to Jesus).[143] Jesus triumphed, and Luke immediately takes his narrative to the fifth challenge (Luke 6:6–11) by

---

138. Mark attributes this challenge to the scribes of the Pharisees (Mark 2:16) and Matthew to the Pharisees (Matt 9:11).

139. For resonances of this word-group see 7.2.4.1.

140. NRSV "then," *hoi de*, "To mark the continuation of a narrative" (BDF §251). Mark's link, "*kai*," (Mark 2:18) has no such implication. Matthew's "*tote*" (Matt 9:14) is nearer in meaning to Luke but his questioners differ.

141. Mark attributes this challenge to "they" (Mark 2:18), apparently meaning the disciples of both John and the Pharisees (NRSV has "people") and Matthew attributes it to the disciples of John (Matt 9:14).

142. Mark (2:24) and Matthew (12:2), like Luke, portray Pharisees as the opponents but, unlike Luke, do not indicate any potential breach in their unanimity.

143. "The reader's inclination to build the group consistently ... militate[s] against readers making facile distinctions among Pharisees in Luke's story. The text would have to be much more explicit and emphatic in its differentiations for the audience to distinguish among ... Pharisees" (Darr, *Character Building*, 94). But Luke's intended readers, our focus, would understand his presentation. This would be clearer when listening to the text being read aloud.

the scribes and Pharisees[144] "on another sabbath," the story of the man with the withered hand. This time there was no overt challenge, Luke explaining that they were watching Jesus "to see whether he would cure on the sabbath, so that they might find an accusation against him" (Luke 6:7).[145] But Jesus "knew what they were thinking" (Luke 6:8), responded and again gained honor: "I ask you, is it lawful to do good or to do harm on the sabbath, to save life or to destroy it?," and he healed the man (Luke 6:9–10).

4.5.3 The Fury of the Pharisees

After this "they were filled with fury, *anoias,* and discussed with one another what they might do, *poiēsaien,* to Jesus" (Luke 6:11). "The optative mood projects the sense of possible action. No clear plan of opposition is certain."[146] Luke here differs from Mark and Matthew, who have virtually identical responses: "The Pharisees went out and immediately conspired with the Herodians against him, how to destroy, *apolesōsin,* him" (Mark 3:6), and "The Pharisees went out and conspired against him, how to destroy, *apolesōsin,* him" (Matt 12:14). To understand Luke's version we must examine it closely, both intertextually and co-textually.

First, their "fury,"[147] *anoia,* should be treated with caution.[148] "Fury" is the standard translation,[149] but the word does not normally mean fury—it means "absurdity, lack of understanding,"[150] "without understanding,"[151] or "want of understanding, folly."[152] Mason translates it as "filled with incomprehension."[153] Nevertheless, the dictionaries cited all give anger as the meaning in this passage, without stating their reasons,[154] which are probably similar to that given by Tannehill:

144. Mark (Mark 3:2) and Matthew (Matt 12:10) both have "they," both probably meaning Pharisees.

145. "At no time in the narrative of Luke do the Pharisees challenge Jesus publicly about one of his own actions. Thus they only offer an indirect and corporate affront to the honor of Jesus" (Gowler, *Host, Guest,* 17).

146. Ibid., 212–13.

147. "Fierce passion . . . [especially] wild anger, frenzied rage" (*OED,* s.v. "anoia").

148. Neither Mark nor Matthew has an equivalent phrase.

149. NRSV, RSV (fury), NJB, JB, NIV (furious), GNMM (rage), NEB (anger), Rieu (infuriated).

150. Balz, "Anoia," 105.

151. BDAG, 84.

152. Thayer, *Greek-English Lexicon,* 48.

153. Mason, *Josephus, Judea,* 344.

154. "*Anoia* . . . often means no more than 'folly.' But Plato . . . distinguished two

It is not clear whether this describes their reaction to this healing or is a general comment on the imperceptiveness which they have shown since 5:17 and continue to show in discussing what they might do to Jesus. In the former case, it probably refers to an extreme anger and frustration which makes them act like they were deranged.[155]

But we should consider whether fury is, indeed, what Luke means, or whether, as Tannehill also suggests, it is their imperceptiveness.[156] The latter reading is supported by the thirteen instances of *anoia* in the Septuagint,[157] Luke's intertext, which clearly relate to folly, not fury. Tannehill also argued that: "The choice of the word *anoia* . . . may prepare readers for a later manifestation of a fateful "ignorance (*agnoia*)" which will lead to Jesus' death (Acts 3:17; cf.13:27),"[158] but *agnoia* is attributed to the people of Jerusalem, not the Pharisees who are not associated with the death of Jesus,[159] and *anoia* is not the same word as *agnoia*. Nevertheless, ignorance or folly or imperceptiveness would be nearer to Luke's intentions. He changed his Markan antetext to exclude the murderous hostility there described. There is no obvious reason to read *anoia* as fury.

We should also look at the rest of the phrase, where they discussed what they might do, *poiēsaien*, to him. *Poieō* is a word with many meanings, it "can refer to every kind of action,"[160] and to understand what the Lukan Pharisees meant we need to look at what follows in the narrative, what the scribes and Pharisees actually did or tried to do to Jesus—see 4.5.7. As we shall see, they do not subsequently do anything demonstrating fury against Jesus.

---

kinds of it: *mania* ('madness, fury') and *amathia* ('ignorance'). The former meaning suits the Lucan context better; it expresses the hardness of the hearts of Jesus' critics" (Fitzmyer, *Luke I-IX*, 611). But this begs the question—we do not see the actions of the Lukan Pharisees as demonstrating hardness of heart.

155. Tannehill, *Narrative Unity*, 1:176.

156. As for the dictionaries cited and for Mason.

157. Job 33:23; Ps LXX 21:2; Prov 14:8; 22:15; Eccl 11:10; Wis 15:18; 19:3; 2 Macc 4:6, 40; 14:5; 15:33; 3 Macc 3:16, 20.

158. Tannehill, *Narrative Unity*, 1:176.

159. *Anoia* is also linked to *aphrōn*, fool, used of the Pharisees by Jesus (Luke 11:40). "Almost synonymous with *aphrosynē* and *aphrōn* are *agnoia*, *agnōsia*, *anoia* and *anoētos*, among others" (Zeller, "Aphrosynē," 184).

160. Radl, "Poieō," 124.

4.5.4 Jesus Rebukes the Pharisees

The next mention of the Pharisees, peculiar to Luke, sees the narrator tell us that "by refusing to be baptized by [the Baptist], the Pharisees and the lawyers rejected God's purpose for themselves" (Luke 7:30).[161] Jesus then confirms this assessment, but does it rather obliquely. He rebukes "the people of this generation" (Luke 7:31) who said that Jesus was a glutton and a drunkard (Luke 7:34), and although this meant the Pharisees, who had earlier implied this of Jesus (Luke 5:30, 33),[162] he does not name them. Jesus, in meeting the first five challenges, had treated his opponents gently, not rebuking them but answering their questions. Here, for the first time, he does rebuke them, but in a way that does not challenge their honor, does not shame them publicly.

Luke tells us of an immediate response: "One of the Pharisees [Simon] asked Jesus to eat with him" (Luke 7:36), leading to Luke's anointing story.[163] After the sinful woman had anointed Jesus, Simon "said to himself, 'If this man were a prophet, he would have known who and what kind of woman this is who is touching him—that she is a sinner'"(Luke 7:39). Jesus read the thoughts of Simon, accepted them as a challenge, and made a successful riposte, telling him the parable of the two debtors, and asking him a question. Simon gave the correct response, leading to a further speech by Jesus:

> Do you see this woman? I entered your house; you gave me no water for my feet, but she has bathed my feet with her tears and dried them with her hair. You gave me no kiss, but from the time I came in she has not stopped kissing my feet. You did not anoint my head with oil, but she has anointed my feet with ointment (Luke 7:44–46).

This rebuke by Jesus could be regarded as a challenge, intended to increase the honor of Jesus while reducing that of Simon, but it is better seen as an attempt by Jesus to bring Simon to repentance, to change his pattern of behavior. Simon's show of hospitality is revealed as inadequate; although he had asked Jesus to eat with him he had shown none of the courtesies listed by Jesus. But Simon did respond correctly to the questioning of Jesus, he is not totally blind like the chief priests.

---

161. The Matthean Jesus tells the chief priests and elders (Matt 21:23) that they did not believe John (Matt 21:32).

162. Specifically, they accused his disciples.

163. Neither Mark (Mark 14:3–9) nor Matthew (Matt 26:6–13) includes Pharisees in the anointing story.

We are not told how Simon responded to Jesus' persuasive speech. Simon is left "on a threshold," and we can imagine either that he rejects what Jesus has said or that he begins to understand and agree.[164]

This is a further hint that some Pharisees, perhaps including Simon, will both hear and understand Jesus. Indeed, Jesus's forgiveness of the woman's sins does not arouse the usual Pharisaic response, rejection—instead "those who were at the table with him began to say among themselves, 'Who is this who even forgives sins?'" (Luke 7:49).[165] They seem, like the first Pharisees we saw at Luke 5:26, to have been more open to Jesus.

We next see the Pharisees and their associates in another challenge, when a lawyer[166] asked Jesus: "What must I do to inherit eternal life?" (Luke 10:25). Jesus then responded to another question from the lawyer with the parable of the good Samaritan:

> And [Jesus] said to him, "You have given the right answer; do this, and you will live." But wanting to justify himself, [the lawyer] asked Jesus, "And who is my neighbor?" . . . [Jesus, after the parable, said] "Which of these three, do you think, was a neighbor to the man who fell into the hands of the robbers?" He said, "The one who showed him mercy." Jesus said to him, "Go and do likewise" (Luke 10:28-29, 36-37).

We are not told how the lawyer reacted to this. Like Simon earlier, he was left "on a threshold." Luke gives us clues, but they do not all point in the same direction. The lawyer asked his question "to test Jesus" (Luke 10:25), and later, "wanting to justify himself," he asked another question (Luke 10:29). However, he correctly answered the two counter-questions put to him by Jesus, who told him first that: "You have given the right answer; do this, and you will live" (Luke 10:28), and later: "Go and do likewise" (Luke 10:37). We are to make up our own minds about the lawyer's reaction, but Jesus did not in any way suggest that he shared the faults of his colleagues, described shortly thereafter. This is another hint that some lawyers and Pharisees will come to understand and follow Jesus.

At the next appearance of the scribes and Pharisees, Jesus's attitude was very different. For the second time a Pharisee invited Jesus to dine with

---

164. Tannehill, "Should We Love Simon," 432.
165. The Pharisees are still obtuse; Jesus does not here forgive the woman's sins—see 7.4.3.
166. We argue in 4.3.2 that the lawyer was a Pharisee.

him and "was amazed to see that [Jesus] did not first wash, *ebaptisthē*,[167] before dinner" (Luke 11:38). In response Jesus, in a passage mainly derived from Q,[168] bitterly attacked the Pharisees, and, after an intervention by a lawyer, turned on the lawyers too:

> Now you Pharisees clean the outside of the cup and of the dish, but inside you are full of greed and wickedness . . . you tithe mint and rue and herbs of all kinds, and neglect justice and the love of God . . . Woe to you Pharisees! For you love to have the seat of honor in the synagogues and to be greeted with respect in the marketplaces. Woe to you! For you are like unmarked graves . . . Woe also to you lawyers! For you load people with burdens hard to bear,[169] and you yourselves do not lift a finger to ease them . . . Woe to you lawyers! For you have taken away the key of knowledge; you did not enter yourselves, and you hindered those who were entering (Luke 11:39–52).

Jesus told the Pharisees that they were "full of greed, *harpagēs*, and wickedness, *ponērias*" (Luke 11:39), where Matthew has greed and *akrasias*, self-indulgence (Matt 23:25)—the co-text can help us to understand Luke's meaning. The *ponēros* word-group is used a further four times in chapter 11 as follows (emphases added). The first instance is addressed to the disciples: "If you then, who are *evil*, know how to give good gifts to your children" (Luke 11:13). The next refers to demons: "Then it goes and brings seven other spirits more *evil*[170] than itself . . . and the last state of that person is worse than the first" (Luke 11:26). The third is addressed to the crowd: "This generation is an *evil* generation" (Luke 11:29). So is the fourth: "If [your eye] is *not healthy*, *ponēros*, your body is full of darkness" (Luke 11:34). With one of these epithets addressed to the disciples and two to the crowd, *ponēros* here may not be more condemnatory than Matthew's self-indulgence. Jesus saw that the Pharisees needed to repent, but they were not beyond redemp-

---

167. "The one who criticizes Jesus' failure to 'baptize' himself . . . before the supper has not himself been baptized with the baptism that really counts, that unto repentance (7:30)" (Darr, *Character Building*, 104).

168. The attack in Matthew (Matt 23:1–36) is much harsher, especially as it is included in an address to the crowds. In the Lukan version only the host, a Pharisee, and his guests are present. They are criticized but not publicly shamed. The importance of making a challenge in public is described in 4.2.7.

169. Richard Horsley sees the "heavy burdens" (Luke 11:46) as the financial ones of tithes (Luke 11:39) and taxes (Horsley, "Pharisees and Jesus," 142). This is dependent on his reading of the historical Pharisees (described in 4.2.4); in our view the accusation about not easing burdens fits better with other, legalistic, kinds of burden imposed by the lawyers.

170. *Ponēros* is also used of evil spirits at Luke 7:21; 8:2; Acts 19:12, 13, 15, 16.

tion, and[171] he told them how to repent: "Give for alms those things that are within" (Luke 11:41).[172]

Although this passage could clearly diminish the honor of Pharisees and lawyers, it took place in private, not in public, and so should not be seen as part of the game of challenge and response. Jesus is again calling the Pharisees to repentance, using a different and more aggressive method, perhaps because his earlier, gentler, attempts had failed.

4.5.5 The Hostility of the Pharisees

Whatever the reason for Jesus's condemnation of them, the response of the scribes and Pharisees was not surprising:[173]

> When he went outside, the scribes and the Pharisees began to be very hostile toward him and to cross-examine him about many things, lying in wait for him, to catch him in something he might say (Luke 11:53-54).

Those present in this episode, including the Pharisee who expected Jesus to wash before eating (Luke 11:38) and the lawyer who said that Jesus had insulted him too (Luke 11:45), were not left "on a threshold" like the individual lawyer and Simon the Pharisee whom we discussed in 4.5.4, but were among those who "began to be very hostile toward [Jesus]" (Luke 11:53). This "hostility"[174] of the Pharisees is solely Lukan but the translation "very hostile" (*deinōs enechein*) is dubious, as *TDNT* has "pursue, press upon" as the meaning of the active form of *enechō*,[175] and BDAG has "have a grudge against," although it gives "be very hostile" for this passage,[176] because of the use of the adjective *deinos*, "an extremely negative point on a scale relating to values."[177] But it is not clear why *deinōs* turns *enechein* into "very hostile" instead of something more like "having a terrible grudge."[178]

---

171. Differing from Matthew.

172. He also called them: "You fools, *aphrones*" (Luke 11:40). In the Septuagint *aphrōn* is used of "one who refuses to acknowledge dependence on God" (Zeller, "Aphrosynē," 185). This recalls the earlier use of *anoia*.

173. Matthew does not tell us of any reaction.

174. "Of, pertaining to, or characteristic of an enemy; pertaining to or engaged in actual hostilities" (*OED*, s.v. "hostile").

175. Hanse, "Echō," 828.

176. Balz, "Anoia," 105.

177. BDAG, 215.

178. Mason translates it as "bear a serious grudge" (Mason, *Josephus, Judea*, 347).

Other translations come closer to the *TDNT* meaning. NJB and JB have "began a furious attack on him," clearly a metaphorical phrase. RSV has "press him hard," NEB "assail him fiercely," NIV "oppose him fiercely," GNMM "criticize him bitterly," and Rieu, "gave vent to their animosity." The only use of the active form of the verb[179] in the Septuagint is Gen 49:23,[180] where the meaning is given by L&S as "press upon, be urgent against,"[181] a meaning they also apply to this Lukan passage. The adverb is a strong intensifier, but it does not introduce hostility when it is not already present in the verb.

Doubt about the appropriateness of "hostility" is increased when we examine the rest of the passage. What they began to do was "to cross-examine, *apostomatizein*, him about many things" (Luke 11:53). *Apostomatizō* does not appear elsewhere in the New Testament, nor does it occur in the Septuagint. The word is generally used in master-pupil relationships:[182] "the [verb] is to be seen against the background of the activity of the teacher who questions a student,"[183] an interpretation similar to "question closely, interrogate, quiz,"[184] or the "press him hard" of RSV and the equivalent in the other translations listed above. They were "lying in wait," *enedreuontes*; the aim here is "to catch him, *thēreusai*, in something he might say."[185] *Thēreuō* is used only by Luke in the New Testament; in the Septuagint its primary meaning is the catching of animals, although it is also often used metaphorically. But Luke's meaning is clear—the scribes and Pharisees will continue their attempts to defeat Jesus at the game of challenge and response.[186]

4.5.6 Hypocrisy

As we saw above, Jesus told the disciples: "Beware of the yeast of the Pharisees, that is, their hypocrisy, *hypokrisis*" (Luke 12:1). The phrase about yeast

---

179. The only other occurrence of *enechō* in the New Testament is in the passive, as are three of the four references in the Septuagint, where the meaning is "to be caught in . . . entangled in" (Lust et al., *Greek-English Lexicon*, 1:152).

180. "Would have it in for him" (Gen 49:23).

181. L&S, 479. Similarly "to be vehemently against" (Lust et al., *Greek-English Lexicon*, 1:152).

182. L&S, 200.

183. Schneider, "Apostamizō," 146.

184. BDAG, 122.

185. The enemies of Jeremiah similarly listened to him to entrap him (Jer 18:18), using the word *logizomai*. Luke uses this word with a different meaning (Luke 22:37, Acts 19:27).

186. Darr reads this as the Pharisees beginning to plot against Jesus (Darr, *Character Building*, 106). But if so, where is the plot?

is in both Mark (Mark 8:15) and Matthew (Matt 16:6, 11), but only Luke mentions hypocrisy, and he has situated the saying differently. We question the translation "hypocrisy," which means:

> The assuming of a false appearance of virtue or goodness, with dissimulation of real character or inclinations, esp. in respect of religious life or beliefs; hence in general sense, dissimulation, pretence, sham.[187]

In the Septuagint there are several instances in the story of Eleazar in 2 and 4 Maccabees where words of the *hypokrisis* group are used of pretense[188] but elsewhere they have a different meaning: "The *hypokritēs* is the ungodly man, the ungodly man is the *hypokritēs*."[189] The story is similar in Jewish secular literature—Josephus uses the word group to mean pretense but others do not:

> In more or less the whole literature of Dispersion Judaism . . . the *hypokritēs* is bad as such and *hypokrisis* is a form of wrongdoing. In this respect there is no question of presenting a righteous appearance so that the true face of evil is disguised. Hence the translation "hypocrisy" is hardly apt. What is meant is the "deception" which characterises evil as apostasy against God or opposition to Him.[190]

Nevertheless, the story of Eleazar was popular, as is shown by the two surviving versions,[191] and the use of this word-group for hypocrisy, in the OED sense, became common, and it was so used by Josephus and Mark.[192] However, the question is, was it so used by Luke? He does not use it often. Where these terms are used in his Markan source, he omits or changes them,[193] and in Q passages, whereas Matthew uses these words seven times in the sermon on the mount,[194] Luke does not use them in the sermon on

---

187. *OED*, s.v. "hypocrisy."

188. 2 Macc 5:25; 6:21, 24, 25; 4 Macc 6:15, 17.

189. Wilckens, "Hypokrinomai," 564.

190. Ibid., 565. BDAG, differing, has pretense as the primary meaning for this word-group (1038).

191. In 2 & 4 Macc.

192. 12:15 and possibly 7:6, introducing an Isaiah quotation.

193. Mark 7:6, Luke omits the passage; Mark 12:15, Luke changes to "*panourgian,* craftiness."

194. 23:13, 15, 23, 25, 27, 28, 29. "In virtually each of the seven sayings in Matthew 23 Jesus pointed up the Pharisees' inconsistency between different types of behavior" (Marshall, "Who Is a Hypocrite?," 142). Clearly, if Matthew was Luke's written source, his dislike for the word group in this context is confirmed.

the plain¹⁹⁵—we do not know whether Luke omitted these words or Matthew added them.

Luke uses the verb, *hypokrinomai*, meaning to pretend or play-act¹⁹⁶ once about the spies of the chief priests (Luke 20:20). He uses *hypokritēs* three times (Luke 6:42; Luke 12:56; Luke 13:15) but on none of these occasions does the word mean hypocrite as the *OED* defines it—there is no element of dissimulation.¹⁹⁷ The instance mentioned above, his only use of *hypokrisis* (Luke 12:1), is more problematic:

> Beware of the yeast of the Pharisees, that is, their hypocrisy, *hypokrisis*. Nothing is covered up that will not be uncovered, and nothing secret that will not become known. Therefore whatever you have said in the dark will be heard in the light, and what you have whispered behind closed doors will be proclaimed from the housetops (Luke 12:1–3).

The explanation in verses 2 and 3 is about the uncovering of what was secret, which could refer to hypocrisy in the *OED* sense, but it may also refer to leaven (yeast in NRSV): "'Leaven' in the Bible is frequently used as a symbol for a hidden but pervasive corrupting influence (1 Cor 5:6–8)."¹⁹⁸ Jesus himself has just told us that the influence of the Pharisees is corrupting and hidden—they are like unmarked graves which pollute (Luke 11:44), but because they are full of corruption, not because they are deceitful—there is no indication of that in the woes. Jesus was much harder on the lawyers, but he again made no suggestion of dissimulation. So there is no need to imply pretense in this passage—*hypokrisis* is understandable as the normal usage by both Luke and the Septuagint, inconsistency signifying godlessness, which is, like the yeast, corrupting.

The next appearance of the Pharisees is the story of the crippled woman (Luke 13:10–17). Jesus was criticized, because he had cured on the Sabbath, by the leader of the synagogue, who, like the Pharisees and their associates, was indignant (Luke 13:14), although he did not express his indignation to Jesus directly, but rather to the crowd. Jesus responded by calling his opponents *hypokritai* (Luke 13:15) and demonstrating their

---

195. Matthew also uses *hypokritēs* (Matt 24:51)—Luke uses *apistōs*, unfaithful (12:46).

196. Its original meaning (Giesen, "Hypokrisis," 403).

197. Marshall agrees that at Luke 6:42 "the basic problem is inconsistency and self-deception" (Marshall, "Who Is a Hypocrite?," 137), and also so reads 12:56 (138) and 13:15 (139). It is difficult to find translations which do not use "hypocrites" in these instances, but NLT has "You fools" and *The Message* has "frauds" at 12:56 and at 13:15.

198. Franklin, "Luke," 944.

godlessness in opposing God's great work of healing. He shows that they objected to the cure, while caring for their ox or donkey, but there is no suggestion of secrecy or dissimulation. Nevertheless, "all his opponents were put to shame; and the entire crowd was rejoicing" (Luke 13:17). The use of "all" associates the leader of the synagogue with the Pharisees whose godlessness and attitude to Jesus he shared.

4.5.7 What the Pharisees Did to Jesus

After the rebuke to the ruler of the synagogue, in a uniquely Lukan passage, the Pharisees warned Jesus against Herod (Luke 13:31). Their action, benevolent in purpose, should be regarded as another phase of the honor game, what Malina and Rohrbaugh call a "positive challenge." Jesus responded by turning the challenge against them, by giving them a message for Herod, thus associating them with him, to their shame. In warning Jesus they had again demonstrated their obtuseness: "Even if the Pharisees have the best of intentions, they do not understand that Jesus as a prophet *must* suffer and die,"[199] as Jesus himself makes clear (Luke 13:33). They yet again failed to understand Jesus and his mission.

Immediately after this, in another passage unique to Luke, another Pharisee, indeed one of their leaders, asked him to eat a meal on the sabbath, the third such invitation. "They were watching him closely, *paratēroumenoi*" (Luke 14:1).[200] "They" were Pharisees in the house of their leader. Here Jesus issued the challenge about a man with dropsy: "Is it lawful to cure people on the sabbath, or not?" (Luke 14:3) and they were unable to respond: "But they were silent" (Luke 14:4). Jesus then healed the man and told, first the assembled company, and afterwards the host specifically, how to act and how to give a banquet. Jesus is again calling them to repentance.

One of the guests responded by saying: "Blessed is anyone who will eat bread in the kingdom of God" (Luke 14:15). To demonstrate how badly the guest had misread the situation Jesus told the parable of the great dinner specifically to that guest, ending with the host in the parable saying: "For I tell you, none of those who were invited will taste my dinner" (Luke 14:24), a much harsher comment than the Matthean parallel.[201] This was condem-

---

199. Gowler, *Host, Guest*, 240–41.

200. A variant on "lying in wait" in 11:54, while repeating a word previously used of the Pharisees (6:7) and which we shall see again used of the chief priests (20:20) and the Damascus Jews (Acts 9:24). The Damascus Jews were linked to the chief priests (Acts 9:2).

201. Matthew has: "Many are called but few are chosen" (Matt 22:14).

natory, an even stronger rebuke than the woes, but it needs to be taken in conjunction with the whole preceding story of the sabbath meal. Jesus has given advice to both host and guests, and the parable was intended to show what would happen if the Pharisees ignored Jesus's teaching. But Jesus was still calling them to repentance.

The next episode shows us the Pharisees and the scribes "grumbling, *diegongyzon*"[202] and saying: "This fellow welcomes sinners and eats with them" (Luke 15:2). Jesus responded with the parables of the lost sheep, the lost coin and the prodigal son, and the story of the prodigal son included a warning, probably clearer to Luke's first readers than to those of today. Kenneth Bailey[203] has convincingly argued that the elder son has offended his father to almost the same degree as the younger son, and that the form of the parable, which he calls a parabolic ballad, imposes an expectation on the reader/listener which is not fulfilled. The expected final verse of the ballad, telling how the elder son repents and joins in the celebration, is missing.[204] The elder son does not join the celebration, rather he slanders and disowns his younger brother, saying: "When this son of yours comes back, who has devoured your property with prostitutes" (Luke 15:30). We note that he says "your son" not "my brother" and the accusation about prostitutes, as a casual term of denigration, is not to be believed by the intended reader. The view that the elder brother represents the Pharisees, that "[his] attitude is now understood in terms of [the grumbling Pharisees and scribes],"[205] is fully justified. Nevertheless, "the father's attitude towards his older son does not change in spite of the latter's objections to his younger brother";[206] the Pharisees are not rejected.

4.5.8 Lovers of Money

Immediately following is the parable of the dishonest steward, linked to a theme relating to possessions which runs throughout the chapter. Wealth is a master, not a servant, and: "You cannot serve God and wealth" (Luke 16:13). Immediately, "the Pharisees, who were lovers of money, heard all this, and they ridiculed him" (Luke 16:14), another challenge. Love of money has not been an obvious characteristic of the Pharisees as we have so far seen them, although Jesus had told them that they were "full of greed" (Luke

---

202. The Septuagintal usage of this word and its cognates is discussed in 7.2.4.1.
203. Bailey, *Poet and Peasant*, 158–206.
204. Ibid., 203.
205. Fitzmyer, *Luke X–XXIV*, 1085.
206. Brawley, "God of Promises," 284.

11:39), but the charge is here made explicit. They are told that: "God knows your hearts" (Luke 16:15). As Halvor Moxnes has said:

> The accusations in 16:14–15 represent the harshest criticism . . . so far . . . They are accused of worshipping not God, but mammon. Their wealth has become an idol that holds a demonic rule over them. They are bound in slavery to an idol.[207]

Luke almost immediately goes on to describe the evil effect of wealth, telling the parable of the rich man and Lazarus (Luke 16:19–31). This rich man had done nothing whatsoever to help the poor man at his gate, "even in Hades he thinks of Lazarus as there to look after *his* wants, while in his lifetime he had never spared a thought for Lazarus's wants."[208]

Jesus had earlier described the fundamental faults of the Pharisees. They neglected justice and the love of God and sought human respect: "You love to have the seat of honor in the synagogues and to be greeted with respect in the marketplaces" (Luke 11:43). Luke's long sequence of honor/shame challenges has already confirmed this fault, but wealth is an effective means of obtaining this respect (see Jas 2:1–4), which is why the Pharisees love money. Such love of money differs from avarice: "Money, goods, and any sort of wealth are really a means to honor, and any other use of wealth is considered foolish. The acquisitive and grasping rich are greedy fools!"[209] The Pharisees are guilty not of this, but of pursuing honor. It is the narrator, not Jesus, who calls them lovers of money, and this epithet may be intended to clarify the connection between the Pharisees and some of the opponents of the apostles in Acts, also lovers of money and of honor.[210] But "lovers of money" are not the same as robbers. The Pharisees do not devour the houses of widows and are not subject to the same condemnation as the temple scribes (see 4.4.2).

At the Pharisees' next appearance (Luke 17:20) Jesus had just healed ten lepers, and the Pharisees asked when the kingdom of God was coming. NRSV separates the episodes, Luke 17:20 beginning: "Once," but there is no such separation in the Greek (and most other translations[211] do not have any equivalent), so that the question follows on directly from the healing of the lepers:

207. Moxnes, *Economy of the Kingdom*, 148. The connection between wealth and idolatry is discussed in 5.4.2.
208. Marshall, *Gospel of Luke*, 637.
209. Malina, *New Testament World*, 38.
210. See 5.4.2.1.
211. E.g., RSV, NJB, JB, NEB, *The Message*, and Rieu. NIV also has "once," Phillips has "later."

After this display of God's miraculous power [the healing of the lepers] the Pharisees ask when the kingdom of God was coming. The evidence could not be more clear—the Isaianic proclamation of release is being fulfilled before their eyes—and the Pharisees do not recognize it (cf. 10:8–12; 11:20).[212]

Later, Jesus told the parable of the Pharisee and the tax collector "to some who trusted in themselves that they were righteous, *pepoithotas eph' heautois hoti eisin dikaioi*, and regarded others with contempt" (Luke 18:9). The "contempt" reminds us of the elder brother, and, although not specifically so identified, there can be no doubt that these people were Pharisees.[213] Turning to the parable, the Pharisee could say: "I fast twice a week; I give a tenth of all my income" (Luke 18:12), but his prayer did not justify him because he gloried that "I am not like other people: thieves, *harpages*, rogues, adulterers, or even like this tax collector" (Luke 18:11).[214] Gowler points out that in this parable, the Pharisee uses five first person verbs (consolidated to four in NRSV), underlining his trust in himself.[215] In contrast, the tax collector uses "not one first person singular verb."[216] The Pharisee had only one recorded fault, but it was a crucial one: he, like those to whom the parable was addressed, trusted in himself that he was righteous and regarded others with contempt. After the parable, Jesus told his audience, the Pharisees, that: "All who exalt themselves will be humbled, but all who humble themselves will be exalted" (Luke 18:14).

In the final appearance of the Pharisees in the Gospel, we see them make another challenge, complaining about the enthusiasm of the disciples, and saying: "Teacher, order your disciples to stop" (Luke 19:39), but Jesus dismisses their complaints, saying: "If these were silent, the stones would shout out" (Luke 19:40). They remain, to use Darr's description, obtuse. From this point on we see that the opposition to Jesus is no longer from the Pharisees and scribes but is now specifically attributed to "the chief priests, the scribes, and the leaders of the people [who] kept looking for a way to kill him" (Luke 19:47).

We saw above that the Pharisees discussed what they might do to Jesus. We can now understand this discussion, the meaning of "what they

---

212. Gowler, *Host, Guest*, 265.

213. See the discussion of a similar phrase at Luke 10:29 in 4.3.2.

214. "The reader knows that the Pharisees are precisely *harpages* and neglectors of justice, for Jesus has already condemned them as such (see 11:39, 42)" (Darr, *Character Building*, 114).

215. The similar verbal egocentricity of Martha is discussed in 7.5.1.1.

216. Gowler, *Host, Guest*, 267–68, including n186.

might do, *poieō*"²¹⁷ in the light of what the Pharisees actually did or tried to do to Jesus. What they did was ask him to dinner, no less than three times. They warned him about Herod's plot to kill him. They also continued to try to defeat him in the game of challenge and response, that is, to demonstrate to the bystanders, but also to Jesus himself, that he was wrong and that their understanding was the clearer. They failed, but they were never violent, they showed no sign of murderous rage and Luke has amended his antetext to eliminate any suggestion that the Pharisees were involved in plots against Jesus. He very clearly distinguishes them from the chief priests and their allies, and in the Gospel he never shows them as active in Jerusalem. They, therefore, do not share in the actions of the chief priests, described in 4.4, which led to the destruction of the city and the temple.

There are similarities between the presentation of the Pharisees and those of some of the Herodian and Roman authorities discussed in chapters 2 and 3. Although most of the Herodian and Roman authorities were evil, without redeeming features, there were exceptions in Agrippa II and Festus. Both seem to have been open-minded about Paul, as the Pharisees are open-minded about Jesus and although they are not converted the intended reader has some sympathy for them.

4.5.9 Gamaliel

In Acts we meet Gamaliel who was a Pharisee. He was obeyed when he ordered the apostles to be put out of the room, emphasizing his authority; he advised the council to "keep away from these men and let them alone" (Acts 5:38), and the council were convinced by him. Gamaliel was "respected by all the people." We should bear in mind that this means that he was "greeted with respect in the marketplaces" (Acts 5:34) which is not a positive sign— cf. Luke 11:43 and see 4.4.2.²¹⁸ He has not recognized the coming of the kingdom of God and, indeed, he was the teacher of Saul (Acts 22:3) who was later involved in the killing of Stephen (Acts 8:1) and then "was ravaging the church" (Acts 8:3). However, like the Pharisees in the Gospel, he himself displays no murderous intention towards Jesus or the Christians (and Saul, as we have seen,²¹⁹ was acting under the direction of the chief priests). In the Gospel we saw the Pharisees try to save Jesus from Herod who was trying to kill him, in Acts Gamaliel saves the lives of the apostles. Moreover, his

---

217. See 4.5.7.

218. Darr sees the portrait of Gamaliel as ironic for a number of reasons (Darr, "Irenic or Ironic?," 125–39).

219. See 4.4.3.

words, his willingness to address the idea that "this undertaking [may be] of God" (Acts 5:38–39), suggest that perhaps he might eventually have been capable of recognizing the coming of the kingdom of God, like Saul, his pupil, the Pharisaic Christians in Acts (see 4.5.10) and some of the Pharisees we saw in the Gospel.

4.5.10 Pharisaic Christians

We saw in 4.2.5 that Jeremias claimed that many priests were Pharisees, but that Sanders, in our view more plausibly, suggested that few were Pharisees, but many were scribes. We suggested in chapter 1 that Luke had little knowledge of Palestine, but he did know that priests regularly came to the city to serve at the temple (Luke 1:8). He also tells us that "a great many of the priests became obedient to the faith" (Acts 6:7). The meaning of this is unclear, but the unremitting hostility of the chief priests in both Gospel and Acts, described in 4.4, makes it unlikely that Jerusalem priests were meant. As we saw in 4.3.2, Luke associated scribes, outside Jerusalem, with Pharisees. If he thought (with Jeremias) that many priests were Pharisees, or (with Sanders) that many were scribes, he may have meant that many Pharisees (or associated scribes, outside Jerusalem) were converted.[220] This would be the first fulfillment of the many indications described above, hinting that Pharisees might come to respond to Jesus.

But later Luke is more specific, indeed he tells us that some Pharisees became Christians, describing an attempt to impose Mosaic law upon the gentiles, causing "no small dissension and debate" (Acts 15:2), first in Antioch and then in Jerusalem (Acts 15:5).[221] It is clear that, even though these Pharisees were at odds with Paul, they were not in any way associated with the chief priests and the enemies of the church. Moreover, after the failure of their attempt to insist upon circumcision, they, included in the phrase "with the consent of the whole church" (Acts 15:22), accepted the ruling against them by James.[222] Luke has on other occasions described Christians who misunderstood aspects of the good news, including Simon Magus, whose response to correction was ambiguous (Acts 8:24),[223] but also Apollos who

---

220. Fitzmyer suggests the priests may have included Essenes (*Acts*, 351), but Luke shows no other signs of interest in Essenes, whereas his interest in Pharisees is evident.

221. In Acts 15:5 he makes it clear that Pharisaic Christians are responsible, but those who first raised the matter (Acts 15:2), sharing the views of the Pharisees, should be included among them.

222. Darr finds that: "We do not know exactly how the decision sits with them" (Darr, *Character Building*, 191n26). But we do.

223. His response is discussed in 5.4.2.1.

accepted instruction from Priscilla and Aquila and went on to preach the Gospel in Achaia (Acts 18:26-28). The Pharisaic Christians, too, accepted instruction from James, Peter and the council.

Later, brought before the Sanhedrin in Jerusalem, Paul cunningly provoked a disagreement between the Pharisees and Sadducees, so that: "Certain scribes of the Pharisees' group stood up and contended, 'We find nothing wrong with this man. What if a spirit or an angel has spoken to him?'" (Acts 23:9). The high priestly element of the Sanhedrin was extremely hostile to Paul, as is conveyed to the reader by the preceding hostility of the crowds who cried out against him (Acts 22:22-23), clearly shared by the high priest who told his servants to strike Paul (who had hardly begun to speak) in the mouth (Acts 23:2) and also evidenced by the violent dissension during which the Pharisees supported Paul (Acts 23:7-10). The murderous hostility of the Jewish leaders is then confirmed by the conspiracy to kill him (Acts 23:12-15). But it was the violent dissension caused by the support of the Pharisees, themselves members of the Sanhedrin, which led to the rescue of Paul by the Roman commander, Claudius Lysias (Acts 23:10).

Luke again distinguishes the Pharisees from the rest of the Jerusalem leadership and shows them as preventing violence. Paul himself confirmed that he was "a Pharisee, a son of Pharisees" (Acts 23:6), and claimed that: "I have . . . lived as a Pharisee" (Acts 26:5). Paul was taught by Gamaliel, a fact of which he was clearly proud, claiming to be "educated strictly according to our ancestral law" (Acts 22:3). For Luke, Paul was the ideal of a Pharisee, who having lived strictly as a Jew, became a Christian and an exemplary apostle, fully accepting the message of Jesus.

4.5.11 To Sum Up

The role that this group, the Pharisees, play in the Gospel narrative is as opponents of Jesus:

> Jesus' teachings, authority, and person all become clearer when they are contrasted with those of the Pharisees. Because of his victories in the verbal contests with the Pharisees, Jesus gains honor and confirms his stature as God's beloved son.[224]

Luke has amended Mark[225] so that he clearly shows that, although the Pharisees were obtuse, their objectives differed markedly from the murderous intentions of the chief priests and their allies. Jesus said that: "The Son

---

224. Gowler, *Host, Guest*, 179.
225. And perhaps Matthew.

of Man must . . . be rejected by the elders, chief priests, and scribes, and be killed" (Luke 9:22). Luke has taken this saying from Mark 8:31, and (as in Mark)[226] the Pharisees are notable by their absence. Luke shows us the Pharisees as seeking to serve God, but, because of their love of money and status, not knowing how to do this, so that they were, in effect, godless and their godlessness corrupted the people by contagion, like leaven or unmarked graves. However, except for Saul, who acted on the instructions of the chief priests, they were never violent and three times acted to try to prevent violence: they warned Jesus about Herod, Gamaliel advised the Sanhedrin to leave the apostles alone, and later the Pharisees sided with Paul before the Sanhedrin leading to his rescue by the Romans.

The Pharisees in the Gospel did not accept Jesus's message, they were sure that they were right and he was wrong, but believed that it was possible to convince the bystanders and Jesus himself of his error, and to that end they used the game of challenge and response. Jesus attempted to persuade them, and, failing, rebuked them sharply, but he never stopped his attempts to bring them to repentance. Simon and the lawyer came to be "on a threshold," and some Pharisees acknowledged the mighty deeds of Jesus, while others continued to listen to what he said and offered him hospitality. Gamaliel was one of those who rejected Jesus, but he was willing to address the idea that the new movement might be of God, so that the intended reader thinks that he too might come to respond. Later in Acts we meet Pharisaic Christians so Jesus (or the apostles) succeeded with at least some of the Pharisees, and Luke tells us that Paul, the protagonist of the second half of Acts, was a Pharisee. This is confirmation both that the Pharisees were called by Jesus, and that they could, and did, become his followers. Jesus did not come to call the righteous (Luke 5:32), but Luke shows that he did call those who thought themselves righteous, the Pharisees, and some responded to his call.[227]

4.6 SUMMARY

There is no single character group representing the Jewish authorities. Rather, there are two main groups, and one individual, Joseph of Arimathea, whom the intended reader sees as a follower of Jesus. The Pharisees and their associates comprise a complex character group, which develops during Luke's two-volume narrative in an organic way, with the seeds of their final

---

226. And Matt 16:21.

227. Mason also sees the presentation of the Pharisees as developing in the course of Luke-Acts (Mason, *Joseph, Judea*, 343–50, 362–63).

appearance as Christians seen on their first appearance, when they "glorified God" (Luke 5:26). They were sure that they were right, and righteous, and most were not convinced by Jesus's attempts to bring them to a truer understanding, so they tried and tried again to bring him to their way of thinking. They always failed, but some were, at least in part, receptive to his teaching and, after the death of Jesus, one of their number, Gamaliel, was able to consider whether the new movement might be of God. Some of the Pharisees became Christians, and, although initially resistant to the development of the gentile mission, accepted the ruling by James (Acts 15:22). And the main focus of the second half of Acts, Paul, a Pharisee, became an exemplary apostle.[228]

The second group are less complex and do not evolve. The chief priests and their allies sought to destroy first Jesus and then the apostles, as had been foretold by Jesus long before. They succeeded in killing Jesus, but God defeated them by raising him from the dead. Nevertheless, they continued their unremitting and murderous hostility, now directed against the infant church and the apostles. Their actions led to the destruction of the temple and the city. The chief priests and their allies did not survive, whereas the Pharisees did, some becoming Christians in Greek cities, while others were coming to terms with the destruction, leading to the new development in Judaism at Jamnia. We understand that Luke hoped that, like Agrippa and perhaps Festus, they "might become such as I am" (Acts 26:29).

---

228. The difference between our view and that of Darr is exemplified here. For Darr "the strongly unfavorable impressions [of the Pharisees] gained in the gospel cast a cynical and ironic shadow over the Gamaliel story and all the other references to the Pharisees in Luke's second volume" (Darr, *Character Building*, 43). But we see the story of Paul and the acceptance of the decision of the Jerusalem council by the Pharisaic Christians as illuminating the hints of acceptance of Jesus in the Pharisaic responses in the Gospel.

CHAPTER 5

The Male Local Elites and Non-Elite

5.1 INTRODUCTION

In chapter 1 we described the general social and economic situation in the Roman empire of the first century. The house of Herod, the Roman authorities and the Jewish authorities were discussed in subsequent chapters and we now turn to the remaining male[1] individuals in Luke's narrative, members of other local elites, excluding Jerusalem which, for Luke, was primarily of religious significance, and the non-elite. Women will be discussed separately in chapters 6 and 7. We again use the tools of context, intertext, co-text and antetext and begin by examining further the particular social and economic background of the cities in which the narrative is set—that of Galilee and Jerusalem is described in 4.2.1 and 4.2.2.

In the second half of Acts Luke describes the progress of the Pauline mission. To help us to understand him we can draw on the work of scholars who over the last few decades have attempted to define the social and economic status of the first Christians (for and among whom Luke wrote) as revealed by the authentic Pauline letters. The predominant view has changed, from that associated with Adolf Deissman which argued that they were mainly poor or slaves, to a view that they included some people of high status.[2]

---

1. This chapter discusses some groups of women who are presented as associated with groups of men.

2. The development of the debate has been summarized by Bengt Holmberg (*Sociology and the New Testament*, 28–76) and Steven Friesen ("Poverty in Pauline Studies," 324–37). Friesen argues that Deissman has been misunderstood, and that he meant that Paul's assemblies "contained a cross-section of society. Only members of the ruling elite were not present" (ibid., 326).

More recently Gerd Theissen argued that the leaders of Paul's Corinthian community belonged to the upper classes, meaning those who were wise, powerful or of noble birth,[3] whereas Wayne Meeks found that there were people of several social strata but no members of the elite (except, perhaps, for Erastus) and also that "there is no specific evidence of people who are destitute."[4] C. S. De Vos adds Gaius as another member of the local elite and, like Meeks, sees some other members of the communities as "modestly wealthy."[5] A similar view, but with very limited numbers of those with such wealth, is taken by Friesen.[6] On the other hand, Justin Meggitt argues that "the Pauline communities . . . *shared fully in the bleak material existence . . . of the non-élite inhabitants of the empire*."[7] We do not share Meggitt's view that the lot of all the non-elite was so bleak,[8] and prefer an intermediate view (which seems close to Friesen's interpretation of Deissman):

> Some members of the Pauline communities were possibly relatively prosperous and perhaps belonged to the group of the rich of their city. Nonetheless, they lack the decisive signs of status of the upper stratum.[9]

However, this is a literary study and we are concerned with how the status of the individuals whom Luke described would have been understood by his intended readers; they will have known the social and economic make-up of their own communities. The ruling elite formed a very small part[10] of the population of the Roman empire, but Luke's cast of characters, as we have seen in chapters 2 through 4, includes men of very high status and wealth. In this chapter we shall endeavor to understand how Luke's intended readers would have understood the status of the remaining male characters in his narrative. We shall argue that some were clearly members of local elites, and that some were those whom we have called *penētes*, with some resources which they could deploy. For example, the man and woman in the parables of the lost sheep and the lost coin (Luke 15:3–10) were not

---

3. Theissen, *Social Setting of Pauline Christianity*, 57, 95.
4. Meeks, *First Urban Christians*, 73.
5. De Vos, *Church and Community Conflicts*, 202.
6. Friesen, "Poverty in Pauline Studies," 357–58.
7. Meggitt, *Paul, Poverty and Survival*, 153. These differing views may be in part a matter of terminology. There would be circumstances such that a man whom Theissen would have described as upper class could be described by Meggitt as non-elite.
8. See 1.5.4.
9. Stegemann and Stegemann, *Jesus Movement*, 296.
10. About 1%—see 1.5.2.

of the elite but had resources in sheep and coins[11]—they clearly belonged to the *penētes*.

The most common signs in the narrative indicating that a character has resources are the ability to travel, to have a household or to provide hospitality (see below), but there may be other indications. Some sell property, some have slaves. Each individual in the narrative needs to be considered in the light of all the available information. We should note that Luke never uses *penēs*, perhaps because in the Septuagint "synonymous and parallel use of *ptōchos* and *penēs* abounds [in the psalms]. In other words, the two terms are interchangeable."[12] Moreover, he only uses *ptōchos* of one character in his narrative—the woman of the two small coins (Luke 21:3), of whom he also uses the word *penichros* (Luke 21:2), related to *penēs*.[13] Nevertheless, the use of these categories, distinguishing between, on the one hand, people working for a living, wage-earners or self-employed, not of the elite but with some resources, and on the other hand those without any resources, seems valid. Luke and his intended readers will have been well aware of the distinction.

The idea that the ability to travel, to have a household or offer hospitality is a sign of some wealth was put forward by Theissen[14] and has been rejected by, for example, Meggitt,[15] who was concerned to show that they are not signs which identify the elite: in this he is right. Nevertheless, these signs can serve to distinguish those we have called the *penētes* from the *ptōchoi*. A home, however small, even a fraction of a room, can offer shelter to guests, but the homeless cannot. Those with some food can share it, but those without any cannot.[16] Travelers can walk to their destinations, but it is a great deal more difficult for those with neither money nor food.[17] Local communities may have helped to meet the travel costs of missionaries whom they sent out, as Luke suggests in respect of Paul's journey to

11. Schottroff describes the ten coins as "at best a minimal emergency fund for a few weeks survival" (Schottroff, *Lydia's Impatient Sisters*, 96), but she has these resources. The destitute did not.

12. Roth, *Blind, Lame, and Poor*, 116n80.

13. His antetext, Mark, in the equivalent phrases uses *ptōchos* twice (Mark 12:42, 43). Matthew omits the passage.

14. Theissen, *Social Setting of Pauline Christianity*, 83–94. Also, with some reservations, the view of Meeks (*First Urban Christians*, 57).

15. Meggitt, *Paul, Poverty and Survival*, 133–35.

16. A reader will assume that those able to share what they have are not destitute as they do have something to share.

17. Luke describes how the needs of Jesus and his companions were met (Luke 8:3); that he finds it necessary to do so is an indication of the difficulty of travel without resources.

Caesarea and Tarsus (Acts 9:30), his return to Antioch (Acts 11:26) and his journey to Jerusalem with Barnabas (Acts 11:30). However we, and the intended reader, would still consider the ability to travel to be an indication of having some resources, even if derived from a sponsoring community. In Luke-Acts travel is particularly important as an indicator of resources. "A crucial factor in each of the episodes in Acts 16–21 is Paul's encounter with numerous foreigners, who like himself have moved into urban centers."[18] A great many of Luke's characters have traveled.[19]

People like those described in Luke's narrative will not primarily have thought of themselves as *penētes*; they will have seen other determining characteristics as more important. For example, the distinctions between slave[20] and free and between citizen and *metic* (a non-citizen) or foreigner were of great weight, and in Roman cities[21] freeborn and freedman could often be distinguished by their very names.[22] Such distinctions were permanent or semi-permanent, whereas the economic status, whether *penēs* or *ptōchos*, of an individual could be temporary. Moreover, as inscriptions analyzed by Sandra Joshel show, the occupation of individuals (slave or free) was very important to them,[23] as was their status in the various bodies (trade or religious associations, burial clubs, etc.) to which they belonged.[24] She was investigating matters in Rome, but the importance of a person's occupation would not have been very different in the East.

However (except for the soldiers and Pharisees discussed in earlier chapters), Luke does not often give us information which would help us to understand how one of his characters would have seen their status. He rarely identifies whether someone is slave or free[25] or, except for soldiers and tax-collectors, gives their occupation.[26] He does tell us about two Roman

---

18. White, "Urban Development," 38.

19. Including Jesus and the disciples, the apostolic missionaries and all those from a city other than that in which Luke places them.

20. A slave would not be classed among the *penētes* but could have some resources—see 1.5.4.4.

21. In Acts, Pisidian Antioch, Lystra, Troas, Philippi, Corinth, and Rome itself.

22. For example, perhaps, Lydia—see 7.3.4. In Greek cities the distinction was also important but was incorporated into that between citizen and *metic*—see 1.5.4.4.

23. Joshel, *Work, Identity, and Legal Status*, 169.

24. Ibid., 113–22.

25. Luke does not tell us about this aspect of the status of either the Ethiopian eunuch or Felix.

26. He also identifies the occupation of some of the disciples of Jesus, of Paul, Lydia, Aquila and Priscilla, of Simon the tanner, of the jailer at Philippi, of several magicians, and of the Ephesian silversmiths.

citizens, Paul and Silas, and we understand that there are two others,[27] but the distinctions[28] that seem important to Luke, about which he often gives us information, are Jew or gentile, healthy or ill, and sometimes the holding of leading positions in church or synagogue. The latter is also an indication of economic status, as the destitute will not have held such posts.

In his narrative Luke features only one man who can be identified as probably a slave (the Ethiopian eunuch),[29] although there are others mentioned in passing as part of a group, such as the slaves of Cornelius (Acts 10:7) and probably some members of other households, for example, that of the jailer at Philippi (Acts 16:31–34).[30] It has been argued that the jailer himself would have been understood to be a public slave; this may be the case but it is by no means certain, and we treat him as one of the *penētes*. Luke does not tell us that Felix was a freedman, but his status was well-known and the intended reader will have been aware of it—he was a member of the ruling elite and is discussed in 2.4.5. Luke describes many individuals who were ill or possessed—these are to be seen as among the *ptōchoi*.[31]

In this chapter we analyze most of Luke's remaining male characters, almost all of whom can be seen as being (a) local elite, (b) *penētes*, or (c) *ptōchoi*. This is a more detailed analysis than that of Meggitt,[32] who treats all below the elites as a single stratum, but is less detailed than the four categories used by Friesen.[33] But both of these scholars were attempting a historical analysis of the Pauline communities; our purpose is to analyze characters in a literary text, and the nature of the task is different. We are not concerned with evaluating the balance of probabilities about real people, the task of a historian, but with how the information provided about Lukan characters or character groups was to be interpreted by the intended reader whose concepts of social class, like Luke's own, were those of the first century. Luke does not provide much information, leaving the intended reader to fill in the gaps using both the social background shared with Luke and the clues provided in the narrative. Such also is the aim of this study.

---

27. John Mark and his mother—see 5.4.3.

28. Other than those reflected in the structure of this study, that is, male or female and having elite or non-elite status.

29. The test is whether the intended reader would so have seen him.

30. The slave of the centurion at Capernaum, whose principal role is his need for healing, is among those discussed in 5.5.2. Luke's presentation of slaves is discussed in 7.5.2.

31. See 1.5.4.4.

32. Meggitt, *Paul, Poverty and Survival*, 50.

33. Friesen, "Poverty in Pauline Studies," 347.

In 5.2 we consider members of local elites and in 5.3 those men mentioned in the Gospel who were of the non-elite, but who had some resources. In 5.4 we consider similar men featured in Acts, and in 5.5 men who were to be seen as destitute, usually those who were sick or possessed. We discussed the municipal authorities, who belonged to the local elites, in chapter 3, where we also considered centurions and other soldiers who were *penētes*. So, too, were the Pharisees considered in chapter 4—Lukan Pharisees were able to travel[34] and had sufficient leisure to study the law.[35] Our findings are summarized in 5.6.

5.2 THE LOCAL ELITES

5.2.1 The Local Elites in the Gospel

In the Gospel the only man outside Jerusalem belonging to a local elite is the rich ruler, *archōn*, in a story (Luke 18:18) closely based on the antetext, Mark,[36] but Luke provides additional information about the character. Elsewhere he often uses *archōn* of associates of the chief priests[37] but this man is not so connected. He was "very rich," *plousios sphodra*,[38] and the combination of "very rich" and "ruler," in the context described in chapter 1, tells us specifically what was only implied in the antetext, that he belonged to the local elite of his town. He asked Jesus:

> "Good Teacher, what must I do to inherit eternal life?" Jesus said ... "There is still one thing lacking. Sell all that you own and distribute the money to the poor, and you will have treasure in heaven; then come, follow me" (18:18–19, 22).

This ruler is told to sell and distribute all that he owns, something which clearly is not required of Levi,[39] Zacchaeus[40] or Ananias[41] and probably

---

34. E.g., Luke 5:17; Acts 15:1 (relating to Pharisees—see 4.5.10).

35. See 4.2.4.

36. Luke has amended his antetext's *eis*, one (Mark 10:17), translated "a man" in NRSV. Matthew also has *eis*, translated "someone" (Matt 19:16), but later calls him a "young man" (Matt 19:20).

37. Luke 23:13, 35; 24:20; Acts 3:17; 4:5, 8, 26. Stephen also uses it three times of Moses (Acts 7:27, 35 *bis*).

38. Mark tells us he "had many possessions," *echōn ktēmata polla* (Mark 10:22), as does Matthew (19:22).

39. See 5.3.2.

40. See 5.3.3.

41. See 5.4.2.1.

not of Barnabas who "sold *a* field" (Acts 4:37, emphasis added). At the end of the story, whereas the Markan man "went away grieving" (Mark 10:22),[42] the Lukan ruler did indeed become "sad" but was not said to go away (Luke 18:23). The Lukan Jesus then, closely following the Markan antetext (Mark 10:25),[43] went on to say that "it is easier for a camel to go through the eye of a needle than for someone who is rich to enter the kingdom of God" (Luke 18:25), although "what is impossible for mortals is possible for God" (Luke 18:27). Considering this co-text, we are left unsure, as we are not in Mark,[44] as to whether the ruler did as Jesus asked. He did not do so immediately, as at the end of the story Peter told Jesus: "We have left our homes and followed you" (Luke 18:28), "emphasizing the contrast with the ruler"[45] as the "we," *hēmeis*, is stressed. The rich elite, this rich ruler, could enter the kingdom of God, but what *he* had to do was explicit. Wealth is to be *used*, specifically in almsgiving as is confirmed almost immediately by the uniquely Lukan story of Zacchaeus (Luke 19:1–10). Indeed: "In 19:1–10 a rich man will actually be transformed."[46]

There are other passages which can shed light upon the rich ruler and the requirement to give away all his possessions. The first is when Jesus said:

> So therefore, none of you can become my disciple if you do not give up all your possessions, *pasin tois eautou hyparchousin* (Luke 14:33).

The translation is deceptive as "possessions" are not always material possessions. The same Greek word is used of the money-loving Pharisees, who "possess" a form of idol, the love of money (Luke 16:14), and of Stephen (Acts 7:55) who "possessed" the Holy Spirit. It is clear from the immediate co-text (Luke 14:26–32, in which there is no reference to material possessions)[47] that the "possessions" of which Jesus speaks primarily, perhaps exclusively, refer to non-material things which could prevent a person from becoming a disciple, for example, family or even life itself (Luke 14:26). Of course, as the story of the rich ruler tells us, material things can also do so. The remainder of the passage makes it clear that the cost (not the material cost) of discipleship will be substantial and should be carefully assessed.

The other passage is:

---

42. As in Matt 19:22.
43. As Matt 19:24.
44. Nor Matt 19:22.
45. Tannehill, *Narrative Unity*, 1:120.
46. Ibid., 187.
47. Other than as metaphor.

Sell your possessions, *hyparchonta*, and give alms. Make purses for yourselves that do not wear out, an unfailing treasure in heaven, where no thief comes near and no moth destroys. For where your treasure is, there your heart will be also (Luke 12:33–34).

Here the mention of alms shows that material possessions, which can be sold, are meant, but there is no mention of "all" one's possessions. The injunction, addressed to the disciples, calls on them to act like Levi, Zacchaeus, Barnabas, and Ananias, and to use their possessions to further the kingdom of God (specifically, to give alms). They are not required to give all away, but to ensure that their treasure is not in possessions but in heaven. Total renunciation applies only to the rich ruler, and it is not clear whether this applies to all rich rulers, or to this specific man.

5.2.2 The Local Elites in Acts

In Acts Luke identifies only one individual who certainly belonged to a local elite, Publius in Malta, who was "the leading man of the island . . . received us and entertained us hospitably for three days" (Acts 28:7). Fitzmyer sees "us" as "the 276 mentioned in 27:37,"[48] but even if it were only the centurion, Paul and a few others, he provided significant hospitality. Paul cured his father and the rest of the people on the island who had diseases. As a result: "They bestowed many honors on us, and when we were about to sail, they put on board all the provisions we needed" (Acts 28:10). Publius was hospitable, but did not become a Christian; indeed, Luke does not tell us of any evangelization in Malta.

Two other individuals should probably be considered as belonging to a local elite. One was a Christian prophet and teacher, "Manaen a member of the court of Herod the ruler" (Acts 13:1). The Greek is *syntrophos* which refers to the custom of the Herodian court whereby, "as in Hellenistic royal houses . . . the sons of leading families were educated with the princes."[49] Luke's description explains this man's status. The other was Dionysius the Areopagite (Acts 17:34). Although the exact meaning of Areopagite is not certain, the description is intended to convey meaning and he probably was "a member of the prestigious Athenian council which held its sessions at or near the Areopagus."[50] He, like Manaen, became a Christian. The status

---

48. Fitzmyer, *Acts*, 783.
49. Jeremias, *Jerusalem*, 88.
50. *EDB*, s.v. "Areopagite."

of the Athenians (other than Dionysius) who heard Paul is unclear—they "would spend their time in nothing but telling or hearing something new" (Acts 17:21), which suggests that they had a great deal of leisure, but this does not necessarily make them part of the elite—their economic status is uncertain, but they were surely not destitute. Their response was mixed: "Some scoffed; but others said, 'We will hear you again about this'" (Acts 17:32). As we shall see, this mixed response was, for Luke, typical of the local elites.

In addition to the above, Luke tells us of a number of groups of men who seem to have belonged to local elites.[51] In Thessalonica and Beroea converts included, respectively, "a great many of the devout Greeks and not a few of the leading women" (Acts 17:4) and "not a few Greek women and men of high standing" (Acts 17:12). The men in Beroea, and probably those in Thessalonica,[52] belonged to local elites, as did the women. Luke also tells us that "some officials of the province of Asia [the Asiarchs] . . . were friendly to [Paul]" (Acts 19:31)—there is little doubt that they belonged to a local elite.[53] But other members of such elites were hostile.

We noted in 1.6 that Sergius Paulus came from Pisidian Antioch. There are three indications that this link may have meant something to Luke, and therefore to his intended reader: first, Saul's change of name to Paul, of which Luke tells us (Acts 13:9) immediately after describing his meeting with Sergius Paulus (Acts 13:7), secondly that, also after that meeting, Paul immediately set out on a journey from Cyprus to Pisidian Antioch (Acts 13:13–14), and thirdly, the mention of Quirinius (Luke 2:2), between whom and one of the leading families of Antioch (the Caristanius family) there were, as we described in that section, ties of patronage. These ties dated from almost a hundred years before Luke wrote, but as we saw in 2.2.2, such ties could continue for several generations; those between the rulers of Rome and the House of Herod had, by the time Luke wrote, extended for well over 100 years.

After his arrival in Pisidian Antioch, Paul made a major speech to the synagogue. In this, for the first time in Acts, he twice specifically addressed god-fearers[54] (Acts 13:16, 26). We are then told, in a third reference, that "many Jews and devout converts to Judaism [god-fearers] followed Paul and

---

51. Women of the local elites are discussed in 7.5.2.

52. Being associated with the "leading women."

53. Identified Asiarchs of the period were Roman citizens of important local families active as benefactors (Kearsley, "Asiarchs," 496).

54. For "god-fearers," "proselytes," and similar terms, see Barrett, *Critical and Exegetical Commentary*, 1:629–31; Levinskaya, *Diaspora Setting*, 19–126, esp. 120–26; and Fitzmyer, *Acts*, 449–50, with a full bibliography.

Barnabas" (Acts 13:43), and then there is a mention of "devout women of high standing" (Acts 13:50), a fourth allusion. We have previously seen that repetition, especially when Luke tells us something three or four times, is likely to be significant. If the Sergius Paulus connection has any relevance it is likely to be linked to this four-fold reference to god-fearers, the fourth specifically to those of high status. That is, there were god-fearers among the family or connections of Sergius Paulus.

However, "the Jews incited the devout women of high standing[55] and the leading men of the city,[56] and stirred up persecution against Paul and Barnabas" (Acts 13:50) and drove them from the city and its territory. The Paulus connection was not enough to protect them and, indeed, the opposition came from the elite.[57] There were few families of "high standing" in Pisidian Antioch but by Luke's time at least three[58] were of, or maritally connected to, senatorial status. These families, knowing their sons had a career to make in the imperial service and regarding Christianity as a potential hindrance to this endeavor,[59] may have been among those who opposed Paul and drove him out of the city.[60] Caristanius Fronto and the second of the Sergii Pauli were alive (and Caristanius in high office) when Luke wrote, and other members of the families or their retainers would also have been living. This may be why Luke was not explicit about the opposition to Paul—we have previously noted his favorable presentation of Agrippa II, also alive when he wrote,[61] and his extremely condemnatory presentation of the Jerusalem chief priests, who had all already perished with the destruction of the city and the temple.[62] Anxious that all should "become such as I am" (Acts 26:29), Luke did not speak ill of the living.

---

55. See Levinskaya, *Diaspora Setting*, 122–24, for the god-fearing status of these women.

56. These gentile "leading men" may have been magistrates but are not described as such, so were not discussed in chapter 3.

57. Discussed further in 7.5.2.

58. The Sergii Pauli, the Caristanii and the Calpurnia Pauli—see 1.6.

59. Progress in the imperial service "usually entailed priestly appointments in imperial and local religious orders" (Hubbard, *Christianity in the Greco-Roman World*, 153).

60. An inscription was erected in Antioch at about the time of Paul's first visit by one Caristanius Fronto, probably the father of our Caristanius. It is discussed in relation to Paul's rejection by Robert Mowery who concludes: "It is possible that C. Caristanius Fronto Casianius Iullus was one of the leading men who played a role in this event [the rejection]" (Mowery, "Paul and Caristanius," 242).

61. See 2.4.6.

62. See 4.4.

Members of this local elite who opposed Paul were associated with the senatorial rulers of the empire, and the only other members of a local elite to oppose him were in Iconium (Acts 14:5), the city to which Paul went on leaving Antioch; it was about a hundred miles away along the main road, the Via Sebaste, leading to Antioch on the Orontes. This is significant, being near enough to be influenced by the senatorial families of the rich and powerful colony of Antioch. Iconium differed from Antioch in many ways—it was not a Roman colony, but an ancient, although not rich, city which will have retained much of its character (Phrygian, not Greek) under Roman rule.[63]

Luke shows this mission in Pisidian Antioch as the scene of Paul's first major missionary speech, the first announcement by Paul and Barnabas that "we are now turning to the Gentiles" (Acts 13:46), and also the place where god-fearers first rejected the Christian message.[64] Paul successfully returned to the city (Acts 14:21–23), confirming some success for his mission, although this may not have included any members of the local elite—the implication is that all such rejected him. Indeed, the saying that: "It is through many persecutions that we must enter the kingdom of God" (Acts 14:22) may imply that the violence which had driven Paul and Barnabas from the city was a continuing problem for the local converts to whom it was addressed.

The significance of the Sergius Paulus connection is not generally accepted—many scholars have been happy with a purely temporal significance for the mention of Quirinius and see as coincidence that the change of name by Paul and his journey to Pisidian Antioch took place immediately after his meeting with Sergius Paulus. It may be so.[65] There is, however, no doubt that Pisidian Antioch was a city where the members of the local elite were very rich, and it was there that Paul, after some initial success, was rejected by them. It is upon this rejection that our conclusions about the local elite are based.

As we have seen in our description in chapter 1, these local elites were among the substantial property owners who governed the empire, largely in their own interests, but their scope was local, and they had much less status and power than the ruling elites discussed in chapters 2 and 3. Nevertheless, they differed greatly in status from those men discussed in the next two

---

63. It became a Roman colony under Hadrian—this does not imply Roman settlement—"the title colony . . . became a privilege increasingly sought out by *municipia* as the highest grade of civic dignity" (Sherwin-White et al., "Colonization, Roman," 364).

64. For the view that the rejection was caused by the Jewish response to a successful Christian mission, see Levinskaya, *Diaspora Setting*, 124–26.

65. The linking of the Sergii Pauli to Pisidian Antioch is relatively recent—see 1.6.

sections, the *penētes*. Their response to the apostles also fell between the almost unanimous rejection of Jesus and the apostles by the ruling elites and the acceptance of their message by most of the *penētes*, discussed below. A few members of the local elites were responsive and some were friendly, but many others were not, and some were hostile. But some of the most hostile, who drove Paul from their city, Antioch of Pisidia, were closely allied to, even part of, the senatorial elite.

5.3 THE PENĒTES IN THE GOSPEL

5.3.1 Men in the Parables

In the Gospel we see a number of men outside the elites who possessed some economic resources, but nearly all of these clearly had to work for a living. There are two exceptions mentioned in parables, the rich fool and the rich man in the story of Lazarus. The rich fool said: "I will say to my soul, Soul, you have ample goods laid up for many years; relax, eat, drink, be merry" (Luke 12:19). He is a landowner—not necessarily rich (he may have worked his land in the past), he did not intend to work in the future, and having to work was the distinguishing mark of the *penētes*. His foolishness lay not in his riches, but in his decision to "relax, eat, drink, be merry." That was not the proper use of riches. They are to be used "toward God" (Luke 12:21), that is, in alms giving (Luke 12:33).

The other rich man "was dressed in purple and fine linen and . . . feasted sumptuously every day" (Luke 16.19). As Luke has already told us: "Those who put on fine clothing and live in luxury are in royal palaces" (Luke 7:25). This rich man was to be taken as a member of the elite, a rich Herodian or chief priest, or perhaps a very wealthy resident of the cities of Tiberias or Sepphoris, described in 4.2.1.3. He is condemned, as are his five brothers (Luke 16:28–31), whom we also must take to be rich.

In other parables Luke shows us men who did (or did not do) what is right, who were not rich but had resources; they were *penētes*. The good Samaritan obviously was not rich—he traveled without servants—but he was able to give funds to the inn-keeper (Luke 10:35). In the story of the prodigal son, the elder brother "was in the field" (Luke 15:25), that is, he was working, so the family was not of the ruling elite. Indeed, for this man the prospect of "a young goat so that I might celebrate with my friends" (Luke 15:29) was an unfulfilled ambition. He, like his father and brother, was no aristocrat (perhaps the family had a similar landholding to the rich fool), and they were significantly poorer than the rich man of the Lazarus story.

In a number of other parables[66] there is a leading character who is a ruler or a landlord, but he represents God, reacting to the good or bad deeds of his servants. So, in Luke's parables the elite (the rich man in the Lazarus story) and the idle rich are condemned, but the *penētes* are more often praised.[67]

5.3.2 The Call of the First Disciples

In the Gospel Luke introduces a number of men who can be seen from the co-text to be *penētes*.[68] The Baptist's message of repentance was addressed to all those with goods to spare: "Whoever has two coats must share with anyone who has none" (Luke 3:11). This call was not confined to the elite—not many of them would have been among the crowds[69] who went into the desert to hear the Baptist—and it clearly referred to those we consider here, including specifically the soldiers (Luke 3:14) whom we discussed in 3.3.1 and the tax-collectors (Luke 3:12) who were also part of the non-elite, the *penētes*.

We described the economic situation around the Sea of Galilee in 4.2.1, and Luke's Galilean characters are to be understood against this background. Shortly after the beginning of the Galilean ministry, Luke, following his Markan antetext, tells us of the call of the disciples. Simon Peter was a fisherman, he had a boat, had one or more people, who are not named, in the boat with him (Luke 5:9) and was in partnership with James and John, who had another boat (Luke 5:10).[70] Although the attribution of the boat to Simon Peter is by a simple genitive, which may or may not indicate ownership, Luke departs from his antetext to make it clear that Peter was in charge—he personally decided to let down the nets (Luke 5:5).[71] Luke also does not tell us precisely who followed Jesus—he merely says "they followed him" (Luke 5:11).[72] There is no indication of what then happened to the

---

66. E.g., the watchful slaves (Luke 12:35–40), the faithful slave (Luke 12:41–48), the owner of the house (Luke 13:25–30), the great dinner (Luke 14:16–24), the dishonest manager (Luke 16:1–13), the pounds (Luke 19:11–27), and the wicked tenants (Luke 20:9–16).

67. The elder brother is not praised—see 4.5.7.

68. Including Zachariah and Joseph.

69. Luke 3:7, 10, 15, 18.

70. We described the fishing industry in Galilee in 4.2.1.2.

71. Mark (1:16–20), followed by Matthew (4:18–20), tells us that Simon Peter and Andrew were fishermen, which could mean that they were day laborers employed by a boat owner, like the hired men in Mark 1:20.

72. Mark names Simon, Andrew, James, and John (Mark 1:16, 19).

catch of fish, the boats and the business, nor, indeed, to Peter's wife.[73] But it is clear that, for Luke, those who followed Jesus were fishermen on their own account, not day-laborers, and therefore *penētes*.

Levi, the tax collector (*telōnēs*), was called by Jesus from his place at the tax booth to be a disciple (Luke 5:27). The nature of Levi's business has been misunderstood. Fitzmyer tells us that "Levi is depicted as an agent at work for a chief toll-collector."[74] The dictionaries have a different view, which we prefer as it fits better with the description both of Levi's banquet and of Zacchaeus (Luke 19:1–10):

> *Telōnēs* denotes a person who purchases from the state the rights to official taxes and dues . . . and who collects these from the people who owe them . . . the analogy with neighboring Egypt suggests that in Palestine . . . the Hellenistic system of small tax collectors was maintained till the end of the first century [CE].[75]

That Levi himself was at the booth confirms his status as one of the *penētes*; he was not a wealthy tax-farmer. He "left everything" (Luke 5:28) to follow Jesus, but there is no agreement as to precisely what this means. The Greek is *kai katalipōn panta anastas*, literally abandoning everything and rising, and the participles are aorist, indicating a single point of time. Marshall comments that this "can hardly mean that he simply left his office there and then without some formal settling of his business,"[76] but we see it as meaning precisely this. Levi, like the fishermen, abandoned everything on his table (a Lukan addition to the antetext) and immediately began to follow Jesus.[77]

Levi was responsible for (and profited from) the collection of the taxes on fishing described in 4.2.1.2, the sales tax and the tolls on goods imported from the adjacent territory ruled by Philip. After he had become a disciple, Levi "gave a great banquet for [Jesus] in his house" (Luke 5:29). Luke here follows his antetext (Mark 2:15),[78] but emphasizes the extent of Levi's hospitality by introducing the term "banquet," *dochēn*. The fact that as a follower of Jesus, he gave such a banquet tells us that for Luke hospitality was important and also that there was no incompatibility between being a dis-

---

73. The reference to Peter's wife in 1 Cor 9:5 is discussed in 7.6.1.

74. Fitzmyer (*Luke I–IX*, 590), so also Marshall (*Gospel of Luke*, 219) and Green (*Gospel of Luke*, 179).

75. Merkel, "Telōnēs," 349.

76. Marshall, *Gospel of Luke*, 219.

77. Green (*Gospel of Luke*, 246) so reads it, noting the tension when a disciple gives a "banquet."

78. Also Matthew 9:10 (calling the tax collector Matthew).

ciple and giving a great banquet. It also confirms that Levi, after "[leaving] everything" retained the power to dispose of his property, for he could not have given the banquet without resources, and the term "banquet" suggests that they were considerable.

5.3.3 Other Penētes in the Gospel

Jesus spoke about the rich in the sermon on the plain, where, after the blessings on the poor,[79] he continued:

> But woe to you who are rich,
> for you have received your consolation.
> Woe to you who are full now,
> for you will be hungry.
> Woe to you who are laughing now,
> for you will mourn and weep.
> Woe to you when all speak well of you, for that is what their ancestors did to the false prophets (Luke 6:24–26).

Jesus described a series of reversals, but who did he have in mind? Co-textually, the Magnificat helps us to understand this, as there the rich, who are sent away empty (Luke 1:53), are paralleled with the proud and the powerful on thrones (Luke 1:51–52), that is, the figures in Luke's narrative whom we discussed in chapters 2, 3, and 4, the ruling elites who were extremely wealthy. The woes apply to them. It is difficult to imagine that these woes were intended to apply to Levi, whom we have met, to Zacchaeus, Jairus, or the centurion at Capernaum, but they surely also apply to the rich fool and the rich man in the story of Lazarus. The fourth woe, to those of whom all speak well, was addressed to the Pharisees who were not wealthy, but wished all to speak well of them, sought for what was "prized by human beings" (Luke 16:14), that is, "respect in the marketplaces" (Luke 11:43; 20:46).[80]

The Jewish elders (unique to Luke) who interceded with Jesus for the centurion at Capernaum (Luke 7:3–5) would also have been *penētes*. Their intercession on behalf of a gentile differentiates them from the crowds at Nazareth, who were infuriated by Jesus's references to the widow of Zarephath and Naaman the leper, and from the Jews who attacked Paul after his missions to gentiles.[81] They intercede with Jesus, and it is clear that they

---

79. Considered in 5.4 and 5.5.
80. See 4.5.8.
81. Mission to gentiles, Acts 13:44; trouble Acts 13:45; also, Acts 13:48, 50; 14:1, 2,

believe that Jesus can effect a cure. The story is not about them, but they demonstrate faith in Jesus.

The other named male characters who had means and were not considered in previous chapters are Jairus and Zacchaeus.[82] Jairus was a leader of the synagogue (Luke 8:41), a man of some position like the elders described above, and he believed in Jesus. So did Zacchaeus, who was "rich" (Luke 19:2), but not of the elite as he was a tax-collector,[83] an occupation which was despised in Judaea[84] as is co-textually confirmed by the bystanders (Luke 19:7). He also "climbed a sycamore tree to see [Jesus]" (Luke 19:4), which suggests that he was not conscious of his dignity in the way that might be expected of a member of the elite. Jesus told him: "I must stay at your house today" (Luke 19:5). Delighted by this recognition he welcomed Jesus and responded:

> "Look, half of my possessions, Lord, I will give to the poor; and if I have defrauded anyone of anything, I will pay back four times as much." Then Jesus said to him, "Today salvation has come to this house, because he too is a son of Abraham. For the Son of Man came to seek out and to save the lost" (Luke 19:8–10).

It is possible for one who is rich to enter the kingdom of God (Luke 18:27). Wealth is to be used, and Zacchaeus has shown how it is to be used.[85] Jesus's acceptance led to repentance, demonstrated by almsgiving and restitution. "When Zacchaeus restores his ill-gotten gains . . . this follows his acceptance by Jesus and does not precede it."[86] Zacchaeus is not only one of the *penētes*, he is a tax-collector and therefore a sinner, and not just in the Pharisaic sense[87]—he has defrauded people.

We have earlier discussed other *penētes* in the Gospel, the centurions and soldiers in 3.3 and the Pharisees in 4.5. The centurions are presented favorably. The soldiers (and one centurion) crucified Jesus, but were carrying out their orders—Luke has softened the picture presented in his Markan antetext, eliminating the cruelty and most of the mocking depicted there. The Pharisees are also treated more favorably than in the antetext, in no way seen as murderous, but Luke still shows them as resistant to Jesus; they

8–18, 19; 17:4, 5, 12, 13; 18:8, 12; 21:29, 28.

82. Judas, who ended up with resources, is considered in 5.4.2.

83. In Jericho, near the border between Judaea and Antipas's other territory, Peraea.

84. See 4.2.2.

85. Like Levi, he retained the use of his resources.

86. Marshall, *Gospel of Luke*, 681.

87. The meaning of "sinner" for the Pharisees and for Jesus is discussed in 7.4.

misunderstood him due to their obtuseness and, in their desire for "respect in the marketplaces," continually sought to defeat him in the game of challenge and response.[88] In the Gospel, although there are a number of signs that some listened to Jesus, none of them is shown to have responded to him, but in Acts we see that some did do so and became his followers.

5.4 THE PENĒTES IN ACTS

5.4.1 Introduction

In Acts we again meet a number of characters who belonged to the *penētes*. We have already discussed the centurions, soldiers and Pharisees. Here we first consider, in 5.4.2, those who rejected the message of the apostles. We see that they all have a common characteristic; they are associated with money, and also with the devil, magic or false gods, but, as we demonstrate co-textually (5.4.2.1) and confirm intertextually (5.4.2.3), these themselves are linked. We go on to consider, in 5.4.3, those who accepted that message.

5.4.2 Those Who Rejected the Message of the Apostles

5.4.2.1 *The Co-Text: Money, the Devil, Magic, and False Gods*

There were a number of men among the *penētes* who rejected the message of the apostles: Judas, Ananias, Simon Magus, Bar-Jesus, the owners of the slave-girl, the Jewish exorcists, with whom we shall consider the book-burning magicians, and Demetrius. Of these, the first three and the book-burning magicians had been followers of Jesus before they fell away.

First, Judas. Whereas the Markan antetext gives no reason other than money for Judas's betrayal of Jesus (Mark 14:10–11),[89] Luke's Gospel confirms that they "agreed to give him money" (Luke 22:5), but further tells us that "Satan entered into [him]" (Luke 22:3), linking Satan and money in evil-doing. Acts then confirms money as a motivating factor (Acts 1:18).

Ananias, too, was destroyed by the love of money. As he was entitled to do, he kept back some of the proceeds of property which he had sold, but then he lied about it. Peter asked him:

> Why has Satan filled your heart to lie to the Holy Spirit and to keep back part of the proceeds of the land? While it remained

---

88. See 4.5.2.
89. Matthew (26:14–16) follows Mark closely.

unsold, did it not remain your own? And after it was sold, were not the proceeds at your disposal? How is it that you have contrived this deed in your heart? You did not lie to us but to God! (Acts 5:3-4).

Again, Satan and money were linked, and a Christian who had received the Holy Spirit (Acts 4:31) was destroyed by them. We are not told why Judas and Ananias coveted money, but it seems to be implicit that some of those discussed later in this section, like the Pharisees discussed in 4.5.8, were concerned with money as a means to status.[90] It is likely that we are intended to believe the same of Judas and of Ananias—in his case status amongst the Christians seems to be the motive.

Simon Magus had successfully practiced magic in the city of Samaria (Acts 8:9), and his name suggests that, if he was not a Samaritan, he was a Jew.[91] He was greatly impressed by Stephen, was baptized, and then received the Holy Spirit from Peter (Acts 8:17). He then tried to use money to buy the power to give the Spirit to others. Money and magic are linked and Klauck is surely correct in attributing Simon's lapsing to his desire for greater success in his profession:

> Like almost all his professional colleagues, he practised only for a fee. If he is now willing to invest a large sum, he does so in hope of even higher earnings in the future: this new power of the Spirit will help him to offer a wider spectrum of services and so win new clients.[92]

Peter condemned him, and told him to: "Repent . . . of this wickedness of yours" (Acts 8:22). Simon did so, or so his words in response, "Pray for me to the Lord, that nothing of what you have said may happen to me" (Acts 8:24) imply, and "Luke's story of [Simon] ends on a favorable note."[93] Like Zacchaeus, he repented, although we are not told what he then did with whatever resources he had.

Bar-Jesus was also a magician, in Cyprus; he was "with the pro-consul, Sergius Paulus" (Acts 13:7), which probably means that he was employed by him as an adviser or astrologer.[94] He "tried to turn the proconsul away from the faith" (Acts 13:8), perhaps hoping to preserve his own influence

---

90. This is explicit for Demetrius—see below.

91. This is not certain. Simon was also a Greek name, used by Aristophanes (cited Thiede, *Cosmopolitan World of Jesus*, 68, 140nn33–34).

92. Klauck, *Magic and Paganism*, 20–21.

93. Fitzmyer, *Acts*, 407.

94. Klauck, *Magic and Paganism*, 51.

with him, which must have been a source of profit as well as status. Luke describes him as "a Jewish false prophet" (Acts 13:6)—he was not a Christian. Paul called him "son of the devil" (Acts 13:10), so the devil and magic are linked and money is implicitly involved, in that he derived his living from his association with Sergius Paulus.

In Philippi the owners of the slave girl with a spirit of divination, *pneuma pythōna*, had made a great deal of money from her fortune-telling (Acts 16:16) and the description of the spirit, *pythōna*, indicates that it was connected to Apollo, a pagan, and therefore a false god. After the spirit was exorcised by Paul, they "saw that their hope of making money was gone" (Acts 16:19). Money was very explicitly the reason why they brought Paul and Silas before the magistrates, although they did not bring charges relating to their financial loss, but used a false pretext. They were like Bar-Jesus in that their monetary loss led them to try to turn the people of Philippi "away from the faith," saying: "These men . . . are advocating customs that are not lawful for us as Romans to adopt or observe" (Acts 16:20–21). As Philippi was a Roman city this accusation made sense, but their real motive was the money they had lost, linked to their worship of the false god, Apollo.

The next incident, at Ephesus, again deals with Jewish wonder-workers:

> Then some itinerant Jewish exorcists tried to use the name of the Lord Jesus over those who had evil spirits, saying, "I adjure you by the Jesus whom Paul proclaims." Seven sons of a Jewish high priest named Sceva were doing this. But the evil spirit said to them in reply, "Jesus I know, and Paul I know; but who are you?" Then the man with the evil spirit leaped on them, mastered them all, and so overpowered them that they fled out of the house naked and wounded (Acts 19:13–16).

It is clear that the "itinerant Jewish exorcists" made their living, that is, got money, from their profession. But there was never a high priest called Sceva and "this is a 'stage name' of the seven."[95] They may not even have been Jewish. The seven exorcists contrast with the seven demons (Luke 8:2; 11:26), but "the reversal of the customary situation, seven against one rather than one against seven, does not help these seven exorcists at all."[96] In fact, the main point of the story is not the sons of Sceva, although their downfall is amusing and tells the reader that the power of Jesus's name cannot be used by unbelievers. Following their discomfiture:

---

95. Ibid., 100.
96. Ibid.

The Male Local Elites and Non-Elite 171

> When this became known to all residents of Ephesus, both Jews and Greeks, everyone was awestruck; and the name of the Lord Jesus was praised. Also many of *those who became believers* confessed and disclosed their practices. A number of those who practiced magic collected their books and burned them publicly; when the value of these books was calculated, it was found to come to fifty thousand silver coins. So the word of the Lord grew mightily and prevailed (Acts 19:17–20, emphasis added).

Here money, a great deal of money, is closely linked to magic.[97] However, the translation "those who became believers" is questioned by a number of commentators:

> The perfect participle in the Greek text indicates that [those who became believers] have been members of the Christian community for some time already; they are not Jews and Greeks who enter the community only now, under the impact of these recent events.[98]

These believers either "suddenly [realised] that they had not been fully open when they became Christians, and now [wanted] to put things right [or had] lapsed into magical practices, and now [wished] to put an end to these by means of an unreserved confession."[99] The first possibility, not being open about their activities, recalls Ananias, and the second, lapsing in pursuit of money, recalls Simon Magus. For both possibilities, it was the lure of magic which corrupted them. Repenting, they "disclosed their practices" (Acts 19:18): "As the potency of spells resides largely in their secrecy, their disclosure would be regarded as rendering them powerless."[100] They also burnt their very valuable books:

> The only appropriate expression of readiness to renounce one's possessions and follow Jesus is the destruction of these

---

97. This took place at Ephesus where the cult of Artemis was of very great importance—see 1.5.4.5, so the practice of magic and the large sum of money involved is understandable. "Artemis was . . . worshipped because of her lordship over supernatural powers" (Trebilco, "Asia," 317).

98. Klauck, *Magic and Paganism*, 101. This understanding of the Greek is shared by Haenchen, *Acts*, 567; Barrett, *Critical and Exegetical Commentary*, 2:912; Witherington, *Acts*, 582; and Fitzmyer, *Acts*, 651 ("who had become believers").

99. Klauck, *Magic and Paganism*, 101.

100. "The public and communal nature of such an act seems to be an important part of the repudiation of the contents of the books concerned" (Trebilco, "Asia," 315). So also Bruce, *Acts*, 359.

> corrupting wares—not an action such as selling the books and giving the proceeds to the poor.[101]

The value of the books burnt is a way of emphasizing that these believers would not, like Judas, Ananias and Simon Magus, be led astray by money, for what are fifty thousand silver coins to those who believe in Jesus? That they specifically eschewed magic tells us that they were not like Simon Magus, Bar-Jesus or the sons of Sceva, or, indeed, Demetrius, the next man to reject the teaching of the apostles. They, like the itinerant Jewish exorcists, were clearly not of the elite, but had resources. They are among the *penētes*.

Also in Ephesus, Demetrius was explicitly led to oppose Paul by money, telling the artisans: "Men, you know that we get our wealth from this business" (Acts 19:25). He had obtained his wealth by selling silver shrines of Artemis, and the initial members of the mob he brought together were "the artisans [and] workers of the same trade" (Acts 19:24–25). The service of the false god, Artemis, is both similar to the practice of magic and linked to money. Demetrius told the artisans, correctly, that Paul taught that "gods made with hands are not gods" (Acts 19:26), concluding that all who depended on the Artemis cult were threatened by Paul. But he did not use only economic arguments—his final appeal was not to economic matters, but to the majesty of Artemis herself, which brought status to those who worked in her service:

> And there is danger not only that this trade of ours may come into disrepute but also that the temple of the great goddess Artemis will be scorned, and she will be deprived of her majesty that brought all Asia and the world to worship her (Acts 19:27).

5.4.2.2 A Co-Textual Perspective

Luke in the Gospel co-textually provides another link between the devil, money and status. At the end of the temptation narrative the devil "departed from [Jesus] until an opportune time" (Luke 4:13). He reappears, as we have seen, when we are explicitly told that he "entered into Judas" (Luke 22:3). But there is also a clear sign of his presence in the desire for status demonstrated later in the chapter in an important passage.

> A dispute also arose among them as to which one of them was to be regarded as the greatest. But he said to them, "The kings of the Gentiles lord it over them; and those in authority over them

---

101. Klauck, *Magic and Paganism*, 102.

are called benefactors. But not so with you; rather the greatest among you must become like the youngest, and the leader like one who serves. For who is greater, the one who is at the table or the one who serves? Is it not the one at the table? But I am among you as one who serves. You are those who have stood by me in my trials; and I confer on you, just as my Father has conferred on me, a kingdom, so that you may eat and drink at my table in my kingdom, and you will sit on thrones judging the twelve tribes of Israel.

Simon, Simon, listen! Satan has demanded to sift all of you like wheat, but I have prayed for you that your own faith may not fail; and you, when once you have turned back, strengthen your brothers" (Luke 22:24–32).

Although NRSV, like most modern translations, has a major section break when Jesus addresses Simon, this may not be appropriate. "Luke signals no break in Jesus' instruction."[102] Luke Timothy Johnson has no break in his translation,[103] and explains the devil's demand:

> The statement shows that they are in a period of "testing" (*peirasmos*) just like that experienced by Jesus at the beginning of his ministry (4:1–13); for the disciples, this is the "season" (*kairos*) Satan was waiting for (Luke 4:13). He has sifted out Judas by entering his heart (22:3); will he succeed with the rest?[104]

Luke is not explicit about the way in which the devil was to test the apostles, but we see it beginning in the dispute about "which one of them was to be regarded as the greatest" (Luke 22:24). In Luke's antetext (Mark 10:35–45)[105] the dispute was with James and John and their mother.[106] Luke both extends it to cover all of the apostles, and also moves it to a much more significant part of his narrative, the last supper, shortly after the foretelling of the betrayal by Judas (Luke 22:21–23), into whom the devil entered (Luke 22:3). The devil entered Judas by the desire for money, and tries to enter the others by the desire for status. We have seen how money and status are

---

102. "This is indicated by the use of the second-person plural pronoun (v 31 NRSV: 'all of you') and the narrator's introduction to vv 35–38 ('he said to *them*')" (Green, *Gospel of Luke*, 771).

103. Johnson, *Gospel of Luke*, 343.

104. Ibid., 346.

105. And Matthew (20:20–28).

106. The omission of this discreditable reference to a woman chimes with Luke's general approach.

linked, both earlier in this section and in the description of the Pharisees in 4.5.8.

5.4.2.3 An Intertextual Perspective

These individuals or groups are all led astray by money, to which are linked either the devil, magic or false gods. But the dictionaries make it clear that these are all connected. False gods are linked to demons or magic,[107] and "the [Septuagint] takes for granted . . . that *daimonion* is a contemptuous term for heathen gods."[108] Moreover, "demons, and finally Satan, lie behind all paganism, and especially behind magic"[109] and "in popular Greek belief the *daimōn* is a being . . . placated, controlled or at least held off by magical means."[110] *Magos*, a magician, originally meant a "member of the Persian priestly caste,"[111] that is, a priest of a false god, and "more generally the possessor and user of supernatural knowledge and ability."[112] In the Septuagint (Dan 2:2–4) it means "the possessor of the religious and magical arts of Babylonian mediators between the higher powers and men."[113] So the Septuagintal intertext tells us that the devil, magic and false gods are linked, and Luke, co-textually, links each of them to that desire for money and status which led the Pharisees astray.

5.4.2.4 Summary

All of these people sought money, but, except for Judas and Ananias, both of whom were destroyed after the devil entered into them (Luke 22:3; Acts 5:3), they were also involved in magic or the service of pagan gods. Magic, pagan gods and the devil are all closely associated with money, and taken together they represent a strong reminder that: "You cannot serve God and wealth" (Luke 16:13). In the second half of Acts the worship of false gods is a recurrent theme,[114] and for these men it is linked to money. Some years

---

107. Cf. Deut 32:16–17; 2 Kgs 23:24; Bar 4:7; 1 Cor 10:20; Rev 9:20.
108. Foerster, "Daimōn," 12. "What pagans sacrifice [to idols], they sacrifice to demons" (1 Cor 10:20).
109. Foerster, "Diaballō," 80.
110. Foerster, "Daimōn," 8.
111. Delling, "Magos," 356.
112. Ibid., 357.
113. Ibid., 358.
114. Worship of false gods is referred to when Peter tells Cornelius "I am only a mortal" (Acts 10:26, cf. Acts 14:15), in connection with the death of Agrippa (Acts

before a disciple of Paul had written of "Greed (which is idolatry)" (Col 3:5)[115] and Luke holds a similar view.[116] Perhaps more significantly, Judas, Ananias, Simon Magus and the book-burning magicians of Ephesus were all followers of Jesus who fell away from the faith in trying to serve God and wealth. But corruption by money and magic is not necessarily final. The book-burners certainly, and Simon Magus probably, rejected both money and magic and returned to the Way.

In Acts the narrative sequence of lovers of money and followers of magic or false gods has a similar role to that of the Pharisees in the Gospel. Both groups opposed the good news and by their opposition demonstrated that Jesus or the apostles spoke with the authentic voice of the one true God. Both groups were lovers of money and status, but also worshipped false gods. The Pharisees thought that they worshipped the one true God, but as Jesus made clear, they distorted the meaning of that worship, and were effectively godless, *hypokritai*, worshippers of mammon, which includes both money and that which money can buy, honor or status. Jesus three times specifically rebuked those who sought such respect.[117]

5.4.3 Those Who Accepted the Message of the Apostles

One of the most striking features of the presentation of the rich (and of the poor) in the early part of Acts is the sharing of property (Acts 2:44-46; 4:32-37; 6:1). These passages show those Christians who owned property using it for almsgiving, following the instructions of Jesus in the Gospel. One of these was Barnabas (Acts 4:37), who went on to recruit Paul to assist him in the mission to the gentiles outside Palestine. No others are identified by name[118]—the sharing of property was regarded as a matter of course—but we find that, as in the Gospel stories of Levi and Zacchaeus:

> This sharing of property presupposes that possessions were *not* disposed of . . . Whenever there is need of money for the poor

---

12:20-23), in the worship of Paul and Barnabas in Lystra (Acts 14:11-18), in the prohibition of food sacrificed to idols (Acts 15:29; 21:25), in the debate between Paul and the philosophers in Athens (Acts 17:18-32), and in the story of the viper in Malta (Acts 28:3-6).

115. Eph 5:5 includes a similar concept.
116. See 4.5.8.
117. Luke 18:14; 20:46; 22:26-27.
118. Ananias and Sapphira who pretended to do so are discussed in 5.4.2.1 (Ananias) and 7.5.1.1 (Sapphira).

of the congregation, one of the property-owners sells his piece of land or valuables, and the proceeds are given to the needy.[119]

The next individual we meet who accepts the message does not fall neatly into the formal categories of the Roman empire, and, indeed, came from beyond the boundaries of that empire. The Ethiopian eunuch was rich and powerful, "in charge of [the] entire treasury" (Acts 8:27) of Candace,[120] queen of the Ethiopians, but was probably a slave; that he was a eunuch tells the intended reader that he had certainly been a slave in the past. Those in charge of the "treasury" of the Roman emperors were freedmen, former slaves, but Luke's Greek-speaking intended readers lived in a culture which was less inclined to free slaves. They may not have expected a potentate, from what to them would have seemed the barbarian ends of the earth, to give freedom so readily, especially to a eunuch.

He was returning home after going to Jerusalem to worship and was proactive in the events leading to his conversion. At his request, Philip explained scripture and the good news about Jesus to him; he then asked for baptism, and, after Philip had baptized him, he "went on his way rejoicing" (Acts 8:39). Although he had been to Jerusalem, he was a gentile, but, like "the queen of the South"[121] (which could be a definition of his mistress Candace) he was on the fringes of Judaism, as were the Samaritans whom Philip had converted earlier. The intertext is helpful—he was reading Isaiah 53:7–8, and if, after Philip's departure, he had read a little further "he would have found the following promise":[122]

> To the eunuchs who keep my sabbaths, who choose the things that please me and hold fast my covenant, I will give in my house and within my walls a monument and a name better than sons and daughters . . . these I will bring to my holy mountain, and make them joyful in my house of prayer; their burnt offerings and their sacrifices will be accepted on my altar; for my house shall be called a house of prayer for all peoples (Isa 56:4–7).[123]

Luke had already quoted part of this passage (Isa 56:7, in Luke 19:45), and it may have provided some aspects of the story of the eunuch.[124]

---

119. Haenchen, *Acts*, 192.
120. Candace is a title, like Pharaoh.
121. Luke 11:31.
122. Klauck, *Magic and Paganism*, 27.
123. Translation Klauck, *Magic and Paganism*, 27.
124. This is not to suggest Luke invented the story—he tells us that he stayed in the house of Philip (Acts 21:8)—see 7.5.1.3.

Philip's action was inspired (Acts 8:26) and the Spirit endorses it (Acts 8:39-40) by taking him to the gentile city of Azotus to continue his work of evangelization.

In the next chapter Luke tells us how Peter stayed for some time in Joppa,[125] in the house of Simon the tanner (Acts 9:43)—that his occupation is given makes it clear that he was not of the elite. The house was by the seaside (Acts 10:6), had a roof on which Peter prayed (Acts 10:9), and a gate (Acts 10:17), and the household included someone to prepare food when Peter was hungry—he did not have to wait to eat with the rest of the household (Acts 10:10). It was also large enough to give lodging, at Peter's request, to the three men sent to him by Cornelius (Acts 10:23). It is clear that Simon had significant resources although he worked for a living, that is, he was of the *penētes*, and although we are given information about him only incidentally, he is presented very favorably—he provided generous hospitality to Peter and allowed him to invite three men, gentiles, to be guests in his house. Simon was a Jew, and to receive gentiles in his home at the request of another was no small matter. That he was a tanner is significant in that the trade was repugnant to Jews because of the stench produced by the tanning process,[126] and the stench would have ensured that it was also looked down on by gentiles.

Other *penētes* in Acts are described very briefly. Jason and others, in Thessalonica, were able to provide bail (Acts 17:9), so had funds. Aquila (Acts 18:2, 18, 26) was a tent-maker, as was his wife, Priscilla, and they traveled from Rome to Corinth to Ephesus. They were in such a way of business that Paul was able to work with them (Acts 18:3) and they had sufficient leisure to explain the Way of God to Apollos more accurately (Acts 18:26). Apollos himself was a native of Alexandria, "an eloquent man, well versed in the scriptures" (Acts 18:24), so did not come from a deprived background; he was also mobile, traveling to Ephesus (Acts 18:24) and then to Achaia (Acts 18:27). On the basis we described in 5.1, we can say that each was of the *penētes* and all were Christians.

After the early scenes in Jerusalem we are not told what those with resources did with their wealth, but the repeated emphasis on the sharing of goods in Jerusalem implies that subsequent converts acted in a similar way; we are to understand that, as described in the Gospel and Acts 2 and 4, they used their possessions for the benefit of those in need. On occasion

---

125. The cities visited by Philip, the city of Samaria (Acts 8:4), Azotus, and Caesarea (Acts 8:40) were gentile, those visited by Peter, Lydda (Acts 9:32) and Joppa (Acts 9:36-39), were Jewish.

126. Jeramias, *Jerusalem*, 308.

this is made explicit through the provision of hospitality. For example,[127] in Corinth first Aquila and Priscilla (Acts 18:3) and then Titius Justus (Acts 18:7) were able to offer hospitality to Paul. Then, on the way to Jerusalem, they stayed with "Mnason of Cyprus, an early disciple" (Acts 21:16). It is not clear how many were with Paul at this point, but seven other companions on this journey had previously been named (Acts 20:4). There is no indication that any of them had left him, and one of them, Trophimus, was still with him after they arrived in Jerusalem (Acts 21:29). Also, some disciples from Caesarea went with "us" to Jerusalem (Acts 21:16)—this is one of the passages where Luke uses "we."[128] So a co-textual analysis tells us that the group staying with Mnason could have numbered as many as a dozen. Hospitality for such a number was no small matter and implies significant resources, even if shared between several households.

The missionaries themselves are also shown as having resources. Paul and Silas were Roman citizens (Acts 16:37) as was, in all probability, John Mark,[129] about whom we are told that his mother (also probably to be read as a Roman citizen) had a substantial house (Acts 12:12–13).[130] Citizenship certainly indicated status, as is evident from the reactions when Paul claimed it for himself. Luke shows Paul as reluctant to reveal his Roman citizenship—he and Silas accepted being beaten publicly in Philippi (Acts 16:22–24) although they could have avoided this by disclosing their status. In Jerusalem Paul told Claudius Lysias the tribune that he was a citizen of Tarsus (Acts 21:39), and did not mention Rome until he had to do so to avoid being flogged (Acts 22:25). Luke clearly shows that the missionaries would not have boasted of their citizenship, and such reluctance confirms that they did not seek status. Paul himself worked with his hands but he paid the costs of four men in Jerusalem under a vow (Acts 21:23–24) and traveled extensively. Barnabas sold property for the benefit of the community (Acts 4:36–37), Philip was able to give hospitality to Paul and his companions in Caesarea (Acts 21:8), and other hospitality is both explicit and implicit. These men had resources, but there is no indication that any of them be-

---

127. Further examples of hospitality are described below.

128. The ability to travel suggests that all of these were *penētes*, but it is possible that such missions were funded by the local churches or by Paul.

129. Among Jews of the diaspora "Mark occurs with fair frequency, not as a name on its own, but only as the praenomen of Jews who had acquired the Roman citizenship" (Williams, "Palestinian Jewish Personal Names," 105).

130. We know it was a substantial house because the text mentions an "outer gate" (Acts 12:13). The Western text omits this, making the house (which belongs to a woman) smaller, which is part of the "anti-feminist" tendency of that version discussed in 7.6.6.

longed to the elites. They not only accepted but lived and promulgated the Christian message.

5.5 THE DESTITUTE AND THE SICK

5.5.1 Introduction

In the first century, as described in 1.5.4.4, most of those (other than the elite) who became sick rapidly lost any resources they might have had, and we may therefore assume that, unless there is evidence to the contrary, those who were ill, that is, who suffered from illness or possession, should be included among the destitute.[131] Indeed, some of the sick are specifically said to be beggars or without resources.[132] In both Gospel and Acts the sick were cured, tangible signs of the good news for the poor, the destitute. Indeed, the way in which the destitute are to be regarded is made clear at a very early stage of the Gospel in Mary's canticle:

> He has shown strength with his arm;
> he has scattered the proud in the thoughts of their hearts.
> He has brought down the powerful from their thrones,
> and lifted up the lowly;
> he has filled the hungry with good things,
> and sent the rich away empty (Luke 1:51–53).

This is Septuagintal language, and reflects God's concern for the poor, which is described by the Baptist (3:11), and again at Nazareth, when Jesus read from Isaiah, also part of the intertext:

> The Spirit of the Lord is upon me,
> because he has anointed me
> to bring good news to the poor.
> He has sent me to proclaim release to the captives
> and recovery of sight to the blind,
> to let the oppressed go free,
> to proclaim the year of the Lord's favor (Luke 4:18–19).

God's concern and benevolent action for the poor is again shown in the Beatitudes, a Q passage where Luke's concern for those actually destitute, specifically the poor (cf. 4:18) and hungry (cf. 1:53), emphatically distinguishes his version from the Matthean parallel (5:3–12):

---

131. "Those who are harassed by evil spirits are understood by Jesus to overlap those who are designated as 'the poor' (*ptōchoi*)" (Klutz, *Exorcism Stories*, 118).

132. Luke 8:27, 43; 18:35; Acts 3:2.

> Blessed are you who are poor, *ptōchoi*,
> for yours is the kingdom of God.
> Blessed are you who are hungry now,
> for you will be filled.
> Blessed are you who weep now,
> for you will laugh (Luke 6:20–21).

We see it yet again in Jesus's message to the Baptist:

> Go and tell John what you have seen and heard: the blind receive their sight, the lame walk, the lepers are cleansed, the deaf hear, the dead are raised, the poor, *ptōchoi*, have good news brought to them (Luke 7:22).

These passages are all towards the beginning of the Gospel, setting the tone for the whole of the two-volume work, but there are later references to alms giving.[133] In Acts concern for the poor is expressed in the passages about the community of goods,[134] and also when Paul told the elders of Ephesus that:

> You know for yourselves that I worked with my own hands to support myself and my companions. In all this I have given you an example that by such work we must support the weak (Acts 20:34–35).[135]

5.5.2 The Destitute as a Character Type

S. John Roth has argued that, in the Septuagint:

> The captive, the shattered, the blind, the deaf-mute, the lame, lepers, the maimed, the dead, and the poor ... have no personality. They are anonymous. They do not act upon others; rather, they are acted upon in the course of human events. Correspondingly, they are at the mercy of others. Importantly, however, these types routinely attract the sympathy of the [Septuagint] reader.[136]

---

133. E.g., Luke 11:41; 12:33; 19:8, and see below.

134. Discussed in 5.4.3 and 5.5.4.

135. "In Acts 20:35 the participle *asthenountes* designates *the economically weak, the poor*" (Zmijewski, "Asthenēs," 171).

136. Roth, *Blind, Lame, and Poor*, 140.

He sees these types fulfilling a similar function in the Gospel, where, in a given episode, "the blind, poor, or lame 'character' has no personality, or authority, or virtue as the case may be in that episode."[137] Roth does not argue that these individuals have no power to act, but rather that their action as described is no more than a function required by their illness, perhaps to request healing, or to offer praise when it is received:

> They display neither piety nor impiety, neither moral character nor immoral character. As character types, they conform to their [Septuagint] stereotype: they are typically anonymous, powerless, vulnerable, and a-responsible.[138]

He finds that in the Septuagint these characters do not only elicit the reader's sympathy:

> Those so afflicted are in some way also the promised beneficiaries of God's protection, God's saving action, or God's intrusion into human affairs to reverse this fate. This is to be a cause of joy for all God's people . . . In the end, the [Septuagint] presents these characters as character types who are standard, conventional recipients of God's favor . . . because their future is ultimately secured by God, and indeed, by God alone.[139]

In the Gospel Roth sees God's saving action for the destitute, those without resources, as also recipients of God's favor delivered through Jesus:

> Jesus' benefactions toward the blind, the lame, the poor, and the others characterize Jesus scripturally for Luke's intended audience. The fact that Jesus saves these character types as only God or God's agent in the [Septuagint] can do confirms his status as God or God's agent. In other words, his saving acts toward the blind, the lame, the poor, and so on characterize Jesus as God's unique eschatological agent of salvation.[140]

This interpretation nearly always fits the Gospel narrative, but there are exceptions, and understanding why there are exceptions is of importance for our argument. Roth confined his examination to passages using specific Greek words, but we have also considered individuals in the narrative

---

137. Ibid., 144. Using a socio-stylistic approach, Klutz takes a similar view of the man with the unclean spirit (Luke 4:33–37) noting that: "Not once . . . is this man portrayed as an agent of a material action" (Klutz, *Exorcism Stories*, 42).

138. Roth, *Blind, Lame, and Poor*, 215.

139. Ibid., 141.

140. Ibid., 215. Klutz's socio-stylistic approach reaches a similar conclusion ((Klutz, *Exorcism Stories*, 150).

whom we interpret as destitute, whatever words are used to describe their situation. In addition to identified individuals, a great many are healed but only mentioned in summaries—these, of course, all follow the pattern,[141] they are cured and may praise God, but do not display any other individual characteristics.

We regard the following individual characters who are cured in the Gospel as conforming to Roth's stereotype, that is, their only actions are functions of their illness or of its cure:

> The man with the unclean spirit (Luke 4:33–35), a leper (Luke 5:12–14), a paralytic and his supporters (Luke 5:18–26), a man with a withered hand (Luke 6:6–11), the centurion's slave (Luke 7:2–10), the widow's son at Nain and his mother (Luke 7:11–16), the daughter of Jairus and her parents (Luke 8:41–56), a boy with a demon and his father (Luke 9:37–43), a mute demon (Luke 11:14), a crippled woman (Luke 13:10–13), a man with dropsy (Luke 14:1–6), nine out of ten lepers (Luke 17:11–19), a blind beggar[142] (Luke 18:35–43).

The inclusion of the blind beggar in our list above may need explanation as after the cure the beggar "followed him, glorifying God; and all the people, when they saw it, praised God" (Luke 18:43). But Luke is drawing on Mark: "Immediately he regained his sight and followed him *on the way*" (Mark 10:52, emphasis added). "Followed," *ēkolouthei,* means 'follow . . . in the literal secular sense' and also "bears the [figurative] sense of *follow as a disciple.*"[143] It is probable that Mark meant the term figuratively,[144] but Luke, as explained below, alters the sense so that "follow" has its literal meaning.

He had done the same in the introduction to the Last Supper, where Mark has: "Go into the city, and a man carrying a jar of water will meet you; follow him" (Mark 14:13). Luke here also avoids any ambiguity about "follow":

> It is instructive how Luke can, even where he retains the Markan *akoloutheō,* alter the sense of a statement . . . In Luke 22:10 the secular "following" (behind the one who carries the water) is distinguished from the special use of *akolouthein* in connection with being a disciple of Jesus by the addition of the words *eis tēn oikian* [into the house].[145]

141. We shall discuss those who do not fit the stereotype in 5.5.3 and 5.5.4.
142. See below.
143. Schneider, "Akoloutheō," 49.
144. Ibid., 51; Völkel, "Hodos," 492.
145. Schneider, "Akoloutheō," 51. "A man carrying a jar of water will meet you;

Similarly for the blind beggar in Luke 18:43, if Mark there meant the figurative sense,[146] Luke changed Mark's meaning. Luke used "the way," *hodos*, for the Christian teaching as a whole so, whether Mark used *hodos* in a literal sense or not, if Luke had used the Markan phrase, it would have been understood by the intended reader in a figurative way. He changed Mark, so the blind man followed "glorifying God." This is a phrase used several times by Luke in the Gospel, and never indicating discipleship.[147] Luke's use of it here indicates that his blind man did not become a disciple and so conformed to the stereotype.

So, Roth's explanation seems correct, but in the Septuagint God's people are also required to help the destitute.[148] This theme is found in the Gospel, for instance, in the instruction of the Baptist (Luke 3:11), Jesus's advice as to whom to ask to dinner (Luke 14:12–14) and the story of the rich ruler (Luke 18:22), all emphasizing the need to care for those in need. It is also found in Acts—see 5.5.4.

5.5.3 Those Who Do Not Fit the Stereotype in the Gospel

The following, for one reason or another, do not fit the stereotype: Simon's mother-in-law (Luke 4:38–39), Mary Magdalene and the women who had been cured (Luke 8:2–3), the Gerasene demoniac (Luke 8:38–39), the woman with a hemorrhage (Luke 8:43–48), the tenth leper (Luke 17:15–19). Three of the five who do not fit are women, and as we shall seek to demonstrate in chapters 6 and 7, Luke usually presents women as active in promoting God's purposes, and these women are examples of this,[149] discussed further in chapter 7. They have a special role as women which results in action, so they are not "powerless, vulnerable and a-responsible."

The other two are the Gerasene demoniac and the tenth leper, both foreigners, a gentile and a Samaritan. After the exorcism[150] the demoniac sought to become a disciple, like Mary Magdalene. He was not allowed to follow Jesus (Luke 8:39), probably because he was a gentile, but in words

follow him into the house he enters" (22:10).

146. He may not.

147. Luke 2:20; 5:25, 26; 7:16.

148. As, for example, in the references to widows and orphans listed in appendix II.

149. Even the crippled woman "stood up straight and began praising God" (Luke 13:13). She conforms to the stereotype, but she *did* praise God, which is not said of all those cured.

150. His actions before the exorcism are to be attributed to the demon, signs of his need for healing.

close to the Markan antetext (Mark 5:20) he proclaimed "throughout the city how much Jesus had done for him" Luke 8:39). We see a variant on this theme in the uniquely Lukan story of the ten lepers. All were cured, but only one, a Samaritan, returned to thank Jesus, who noted the failure of the others:

> "Was none of them found to return and give praise to God except this foreigner?" Then he said to him, "Get up and go on your way; your faith has made you well" (Luke 17:18–19).

The nine do not share in this second healing, a response to the Samaritan's expression of faith. The gentile demoniac and the Samaritan leper, like the women, fulfill a second role in the narrative in addition to that required by their illness. The demoniac bore witness to Jesus before his gentile neighbors and the Samaritan leper is contrasted with the other nine, Jewish, who do not even, as Jesus notes, fulfill the Septuagintal stereotype by giving thanks and praise to God. Both are foreigners and their role as foreigners leads to the actions described. Their stories remind us that Jesus shocked the people of Nazareth when he spoke about the widow of Zarephath and Naaman the Syrian, so that they "were filled with rage" (Luke 4:26–28). Luke is showing us in the Gospel that gentiles are not excluded, preparing the way for the story of the gentile mission in Acts.

5.5.4 Those Who Do Not Fit the Stereotype in Acts

Turning to Acts, Roth finds that there:

> The function of [these groups] is to assist in characterizing the apostles as prophets who announce Jesus' resurrection from the dead and display the power of God's Spirit and Jesus' name through miraculous deeds.[151]

This is true up to a point, but it does not adequately deal with the sharing of goods in Jerusalem. In Acts most of those in need of healing conform to the stereotype,[152] they were not active, did not even ask for healing or praise God, and the women who did more, Tabitha (Acts 9:36–42) and perhaps the slave-girl with the spirit of divination (Acts 16:16–18),[153] fulfill an active role

---

151. Roth, *Blind, Lame, and Poor*, 211.

152. Aeneas (Acts 9:33–34), the crippled man (Acts 14:8–10), Eutychus (Acts 20:9–12) and the father of Publius (Acts 28:8).

153. See 7.5.2. It is questionable whether the actions of the slave-girl are to be regarded as her own or those of the spirit of divination. It is also unclear whether her exorcism is to be regarded as a cure.

as women, like those in the Gospel. But the man lame from birth did not conform; he initially reacted to his cure stereotypically, when "he stood and began to walk" (Acts 3:8), but he did more than this. He "entered the temple with them" (Acts 3:8), "clung to Peter and John" (Acts 3:11), and went with them before the Council (Acts 4:9, 14). He was not just "acted upon." He is shown as breaking the Septuagintal stereotype.

This is also the case for the poor who are mentioned in the summary description of life in the early church, when the proceeds from the sale of possessions were given "to all, as any had need" (Acts 2:45) and the recipients "broke bread at home and ate their food with glad and generous hearts" (Acts 2:46). We are not told a great deal about what these formerly destitute people did, but the fact that they did anything other than request help and give thanks is significant. In this they do not fit Roth's pattern and the explanation is to be found in the story of the community of goods in Jerusalem, when, as a result of the actions of those with property, "there was not a needy person among them" (Acts 4:34). There was now no-one among them who was poor, who conformed to the stereotype, who needed the special intervention of God, because their needs had been met by God's agents, the first members of the church. They had changed, were no longer destitute, and their response to healing changed also, as seen in the story of the man lame from birth. He became a believer and shared in the community of goods which Luke immediately describes in the narrative. After the death of Stephen, the Christians were driven out of Jerusalem and the community of goods was no more, but in the later stages of Acts we find signs of community in the offering and acceptance of hospitality and the sending of alms to Jerusalem.

5.5.5 Penēs and Ptōchos

In the Psalms *penēs* and *ptōchos* are, as we have seen, synonymous interchangeable terms, used in parallel,[154] and Luke may, to some extent, have agreed, regarding the poor (*ptōchoi*), to whom good news is to be brought, as including all the non-elite, *penētes* as well as *ptōchoi*. Many scholars have seen the widows in Acts 6:1 and Acts 9:39 as dependent on the support of the apostles and Tabitha respectively. We do not see these widows as dependent (see 7.2 and 7.2.4.3), indeed, we see both groups as active in charitable works. They do not share the characteristics of the *ptōchoi*.

---

154. As described in Roth, *Blind, Lame, and Poor*. This was, as we have seen in 1.5.4.6, the view of the elites.

However, if there are no *ptōchoi* in Acts, this may be because Luke regarded the need to work for a living as an important criterion distinguishing those who were likely to promote the proclamation of the good news. This could be attributed to the general rule that people without resources can do little, but there is an alternative interpretation, following the grain of the narrative. There are no needy Christians in Acts, which suggests that Luke saw the sharing of goods continuing in each Christian community, so there was, indeed, not a needy person among them and all were able to play their part in bringing about the kingdom of God.

5.6 SUMMARY

We see a clear distinction between Luke's portrayal of the ruling elites, discussed in chapters 2 through 4, and that of both the local elites and the non-elite whom we have considered in this chapter. The ruling elites were almost all opposed to Jesus or the early church, often murderously so, but the local elites are presented in a less one-sided fashion and there is no indication that, like the Herodian and Roman authorities, they have been given their authority by the devil. In the Gospel we are not told the final reaction of the rich ruler; he was left "on a threshold." In Acts some local elite groups accepted Paul's message, while others, at least some of them closely linked to the Roman ruling elite, rejected it, and some were friendly to Paul, even if they were not converted. Indeed, some members of the local elites did become Christians, including both men and women in Thessalonica and Beroea, Dionysius the Areopagite and Manaen, a prophet and teacher.

There is an even stronger contrast with the ruling elite when we consider the *penētes*, especially in the Gospel. There, they are receptive to Jesus, and even the Pharisees listen to him and offer him hospitality. Peter and his partners and Levi become disciples. Zacchaeus gives half his wealth to the poor, while one centurion, generous with his resources, is praised by Jesus for his faith and another centurion praises Jesus. In Acts we also find many men belonging to the *penētes* who are receptive to the message of the apostles, including some Pharisees and another centurion, also generous in almsgiving, but we also find a number who are not. Those of the *penētes* who rejected the Gospel are all corrupted by money, and are also led astray by the devil, magic or false gods, three demonic forces which are linked with each other and co-textually, always, with money. But after the sons of Sceva are overpowered by the evil spirit, a substantial number of former magicians give up their magical practices, disclose their secrets and destroy their extremely valuable books. Luke tells us that it is possible, even for those who make money from magic, to repent and receive the good news.

Luke's treatment of the destitute, and of the sick who so often are destitute, usually follows the Septuagintal pattern described by Roth, that is, they are acted upon but do not themselves act upon others. They are not agentic, so that Luke's description of their actions is restricted to requesting healing and offering praise after they are cured, and some, like nine of the lepers, fail even to do that. There are exceptions, in particular women and foreigners who fill more than one role in Luke's narrative. The other exceptions, in Acts, are the man lame from birth and the poor of the Jerusalem community. The man lame from birth joined the community and, like other formerly destitute people, he was able to benefit from the sharing of property, so that in that community there were no needy, no *ptōchoi*. The Septuagintal stereotype no longer applied and all were able to play their part in the bringing about of the kingdom.

CHAPTER 6

Women in the Introduction to the Gospel

6.1 INTRODUCTION

In this and in the following chapter we seek to understand the way in which Luke presents women in his two-volume work, and demonstrate that they are presented in similar ways in each volume. In both Gospel and Acts those women described in any detail are usually shown as active in promoting God's purposes. Some were prophets; most of them provided personal service, *diakonia*, or witness.

The roles of most of these women in Luke's narrative have been the subject of much discussion by feminist scholars. Our view of Luke's presentation of women differs radically from that of many of these writers, and we see the reason for this as arising from their acceptance of traditional patriarchal interpretations of Luke's narrative which color their work even when not overtly addressed. We show these interpretations to be at best insecure, and identify two other matters, apparently not previously considered, which cast a new light on Luke's presentation of women. It will be helpful to deal with these before proceeding with our detailed analysis of the female characters in Luke's text. They are:

(i) Erroneous Patriarchal Interpretations

1. Luke required Judas to be replaced by a man—6.1.2.
2. Widows are a symbol of destitution in the Septuagint—6.1.3.

3. Prophecy consists of oracular utterances and Luke does not describe prophecies by women—6.1.4.

(ii) New Insights

1. Lydia is an important character—6.1.5.
2. In Luke-Acts women are always autonomous—6.1.6.

Additionally, Luke's presentation of Anna (Luke 2:36-38) has, we believe, been misunderstood and we pay particular attention to this in 6.3 below.

To help in our understanding of Luke's presentation of women we give, in 6.1.1, a brief summary of their role in the first century. Then, in 6.1.2 through 6.1.6, we set out our view of the misunderstandings described above. Personal service, *diakonia*, is an important factor in understanding women in Luke-Acts, and is discussed briefly in 6.1.7.[1] Then, in 6.2, we provide an overview of the women in Luke-Acts, in 6.3 we discuss Anna and in 6.4 Mary and Elizabeth, again using the tools of context, co-text, intertext, and antetext. The presentation of these women, who feature in the introduction to the Gospel, is a key to understanding the other identified women whom we consider in chapter 7. In 7.6 we examine the context of the Christian churches around the late first century in order to show that our understanding of Luke's presentation of women is historically plausible.

6.1.1 The Role of Women in the First Century

In the first century the roles of men and women were accepted as being clearly differentiated, that of men being public and that of women private and domestic. This separation is most clearly seen in the ruling elite, who had the necessary resources and leisure to achieve such differentiation. Men of that elite were involved in politics and the management of their estates and women in domestic affairs and child rearing.[2] Such a separation was not at all possible for the destitute, the *ptōchoi*, and was difficult for the *penētes*, for whom it was probably little more than an aspiration as their limited resources obliged them to be flexible in fulfilling their desired, that is, socially stereotyped, gender roles. But even among the rich there were exceptions, with some women active in public life.

---

1. And in more detail in 7.3.1.
2. Stegemann and Stegemann, *Jesus Movement*, 364-69.

Much of the evidence for such exceptions is in regard to office-holding and liturgies (that is, gifts to one's city), described in inscriptions throughout the Greek world. However, Riet van Bremen finds that women usually gave the gifts and held the offices commemorated in these inscriptions as representatives of their families, in order to enhance the family's reputation. Moreover, the decision by all-male civic bodies that a woman should "take on an office or liturgy" was made by "the fathers, and husbands, and brothers of our women."[3] Other, literary, evidence from the period relates to the women of the imperial household, who undoubtedly exercised a great deal of power. Perhaps because of disapproval of women exercising such power, there was a pattern in the literature of the ancient world of showing women with political influence as leading a "dissolute life."[4] We see examples of this pattern in the allegations of incest against Bernice which we discussed in 2.2.6 and 2.4.6, and it may also be seen in the Markan portrayals of Herodias and Salome (Mark 6:17–28).[5]

Mireille Corbier finds that the lack of male heirs of the Julio-Claudians led to marriages, divorces, and adoptions for dynastic reasons, largely driven by the male emperors.[6] Elsewhere, she has described the objectives of the marriage and inheritance strategy of the Roman elite as the desire for "biological reproduction, the transmission and increase of the family property, and the diversification and growth of their symbolic capital."[7] Such a desire can explain the imperial marriages and adoptions, and the third objective, the diversification and growth of symbolic capital, has strong resonances with the reasons of family reputation identified by van Bremen for the office-holding and liturgies of women in the Greek East. Indeed, objectives of this kind form a large part of the pursuit of status of the elites described in chapter 1. However, most of the women who feature in Luke-Acts do not pursue status, either for themselves or for their families—their importance derives from their pursuit of God's purposes.

Some women who were not of the elite may have belonged to families with resources such that their women were not obliged to work outside the home, and this in itself would have added to their familial symbolic capital. However, the majority of women among the *penētes* will have had to work in

---

3. Bremen, *Limits of Participation*, 301.

4. Stegemann and Stegemann, *Jesus Movement*, 367.

5. The view that Mary Magdalene was a prostitute, for which there is no evidence in the canonical texts, also reflects this pattern. That she was named in all four Gospels suggests that she was an important figure in the early church.

6. Corbier, "Male Power and Legitimacy," 191–92.

7. "Family Behavior," 190.

some way, and this would be the case for all women among the *ptōchoi*—this is discussed further in 7.2.2.

6.1.2 The Selection of Matthias

6.1.2.1 *The Text*

> *According to Luke* the position of Judas can be taken by "one of the men (*anēr*) who have accompanied us during all the time that the Lord Jesus went in and out among us beginning from the baptism of John until the day when he was taken up."[8]

Many scholars read the Matthias passage in this way[9] leading to a presumption that Luke was opposed to women's leadership[10] in the churches, and recently Turid Karlsen Seim, found that Luke's use of *diakon* terms was such that:

> The actions of women are by way of Jesus' placing himself in the same role in 22:27, converted to an ideal to be followed by the new leadership of the people of God. This is, however, a leadership from which women are excluded because maleness is stated as an explicit criterion for eligibility.[11]

But before accepting such a conclusion we should consider in detail Luke's words, set out below (with emphasis added):

> In those days *Peter* stood up among the believers (together the crowd numbered about one hundred twenty persons) and said, "Friends, *the scripture had to be fulfilled, which the Holy Spirit through David foretold* concerning Judas, who became a guide for those who arrested Jesus—for he was numbered among us and was allotted his share in this ministry . . . For it is written in the book of Psalms,
> 'Let his homestead become desolate,
> and let there be no one to live in it';
> and
> 'Let another take his position of overseer, *Tēn episcopēn autou labetō heteros*.'

---

8. Schüssler Fiorenza, *Discipleship of Equals*, 114, emphasis added.

9. A similar view is expressed by, for example, Schaberg, "Luke," 281, 291; Seim, "Luke," 744; Osiek and Balch, *Families in the New Testament World*, 141; and D'Angelo, "Anēr Question," 50.

10. E.g., Gench, *Back to the Well*, 95.

11. Seim, "Feminist Criticism," 70.

> So one of the men, *andrōn*, who have *accompanied us during all the time that the Lord Jesus went in and out among us, beginning from the baptism of John until the day when he was taken up from us*—one of these must become a witness with us to his resurrection." So they proposed two, Joseph called Barsabbas, who was also known as Justus, and Matthias. Then they prayed and said, "Lord, you know everyone's heart. Show us which one of these two you have chosen to take the place in this ministry and apostleship from which Judas turned aside to go to his own place." And they cast lots for them, and the lot fell on Matthias; and he was added to the eleven apostles (Acts 1:15–26).

6.1.2.2 *The Speaker*

The first point to note is that it was not Luke (the narrator) who spoke the words Schüssler Fiorenza cites, but Peter, a character in Luke's narrative. Some scholars do note or imply that the words were said by Peter, but regard them as authoritative,[12] although it is not clear why at this point Peter should be so regarded. As in judging the reliability of statements in any narrative, we must consider the speaker and assess his or her own reliability, considering especially the evidence of the period shortly before the speech[13] and the speech itself. So, what had Peter most recently said?

> Woman, I do not know him (Luke 22:57).

> Man, I am not! (Luke 22:58).

> Man, I do not know what you are talking about! (Luke 22:60).

This triple denial of Jesus is emphatically not evidence of a reliable character. We should also look at the last thing Peter did.

> But Peter got up and ran to the tomb; stooping and looking in, he saw the linen cloths by themselves; then he *went home*, amazed at what had happened (Luke 24:12, emphasis added).

Peter "went home." We can contrast this with the immediate responses of Luke's other witnesses:

---

12. "Replenishing their number to twelve is a clear priority in the opening of Acts" (Philips, *Paul, His Letters, and Acts*, 139n34).

13. Earlier actions by Peter, noted below, are not inconsistent with those we cite here.

> Returning from the tomb, they told all this to the eleven and to all the rest. Now it was Mary Magdalene, Joanna, Mary the mother of James, and the other women with them who told this to the apostles (Luke 24:9–10).

and

> That same hour [the two at Emmaus] got up and returned to Jerusalem; and they found the eleven and their companions gathered together. They were saying, "The Lord has risen indeed, and he has appeared to Simon!" Then they told what had happened on the road, and how he had been made known to them in the breaking of the bread (Luke 24:33–35).

That he went home was another failure on Peter's part. The story of the two disciples at Emmaus tells us that it was the testimony of the women (Luke 24:23) and of other disciples who told what they saw (Luke 24:24) which had prepared them for the recognition of Jesus in the breaking of bread. Then, after they had recognized Jesus, they said to each other: "'Were not our hearts burning within us?' [and] that same hour they got up and returned to Jerusalem" (Luke 24:32–33) to tell what had happened. Their reference to "their hearts burning" indicates that they were influenced by the Spirit and they rushed to impart the good news. But Peter, despite having been previously told that he was to "strengthen his brothers," failed to take any action—he told no one what he had seen, his action was only known to the omniscient narrator, who recounts it for a purpose.

6.1.2.3 The Commands of Jesus

We might then ask if Peter had been given instructions. He, and the others, had indeed.

> And see, I am sending upon you what my Father promised; so *stay here in the city until you have been clothed with power from on high* (Luke 24:49, emphasis added).

> While staying with them, *he ordered them not to leave Jerusalem, but to wait there for the promise of the Father.* "This," he said, "is what you have heard from me; for John baptized with water, but you will be baptized with the Holy Spirit not many days from now" (Acts 1:4–5, emphasis added).

So Peter had been told, and told twice, to wait for the Spirit, the promise of the Father, and, in a third reminder of those instructions, had also been told that: "You will receive power when the Holy Spirit has come upon you" (Acts 1:8). Peter had, very emphatically, been told to wait. But he did not wait until he had received power, did not obey the threefold commands of Jesus.[14]

6.1.2.4 Appearance of the Risen Jesus to Peter?

Luke is understood to have told us that the risen Jesus subsequently appeared to Peter (Luke 24:34), but the disciple concerned is there called Simon, not Peter. This is at best ambiguous as Simon the Zealot is one of the named disciples at Acts 1:13 (and Luke 6:15), so may be the person referred to. But Jesus changed Simon's name to Peter (Luke 6:14) and thereafter, in both Gospel and Acts, the narrator always refers to him as "Peter" or "Simon Peter," as does Jesus except for one occasion when he addresses him very personally and emphatically: "Simon, Simon, listen!" (Luke 22:31).[15] Immediately before the Matthias passage Luke lists the eleven, beginning with "Peter" and ending with "Simon the Zealot and Judas son of James" (Acts 1:13). It is difficult to see how a skilled writer could have called a man "Simon" in an important passage at the end of the Gospel and then called the same man "Peter," without explanation, in an important passage at the beginning of Acts.

Nevertheless, the traditional reading takes "Simon" to be Peter,[16] and to show the fulfillment of a prediction made by Jesus about Peter:

> Simon, Simon, listen! Satan has demanded to sift all of you like wheat, but I have prayed for you that your own faith may not fail; and you, when once you have turned back, strengthen your brothers (Luke 22:31–32)."

This view is taken by many commentators,[17] for example:

> Simon is to be understood as Simon Peter . . . This appearance to Simon makes him the first official witness of the resurrection . . . [It] is the basis on which he will reinforce his brothers . . . it

---

14. This does not necessarily mean deliberate disobedience. He, like the other disciples, often misunderstood Jesus. But the omniscient narrator does not.

15. James calls him "Simeon" (Acts 15:14).

16. Fitzmyer (and other commentators) are influenced by Paul's mention of an appearance to Cephas, that is, Peter (1 Cor 15:5), but we are concerned with understanding what Luke actually wrote.

17. Recently Tannehill, *Narrative Unity*, 1:279, 292–93; Johnson, *Gospel of Luke*, 397; Green, *Gospel of Luke*, 850–51; Mullins, *Luke*, 515; and Bovon, *Luke 3*, 376.

is the grace given by the risen Christ to the one who will play the leading role in the Christian community depicted in Luke's second volume.[18]

This assumes that Luke says "Simon" when he means "Peter." But the first appearance Luke describes was to characters who do not otherwise feature in the Gospel, on their way to Emmaus, his second,[19] on the face of it, to a named but minor member of the twelve and his third to all the disciples gathered together (Luke 24:36–53). Is not this plausible, or even probable? We should note that Luke omits the prominence his antetext Mark gives to Peter in his story of the empty tomb (Mark 16:7).[20] To read "Simon" as "Simon (Peter)" is to restore the Petrine emphasis which Luke omitted, without textual justification; it may be seen as an example of a patriarchal interpretation against the grain of the text[21] which should not be accepted without clear evidence, which is lacking. The commentators noted above, like Fitzmyer, see this as a sign that Peter has "turned back," and taken up his position as leader of the disciples. But Luke gives a spectacular description of Pentecost, which seems much more plausible as the occasion for Peter's "turning." Whether the Lukan Jesus made an individual appearance to Simon Peter or not, Luke tells us of no instructions, and there is no other indication that, at that time, he "turned back."

6.1.2.5 *The Reason for the Speech*

Why did Peter want to fill the place left vacant by Judas? Luke gives us an explanation in the words of Jesus, who said:

> You are those who have stood by me in my trials; and I confer on you, just as my Father has conferred on me, a kingdom, so that you may eat and drink at my table in my kingdom, and you will sit on thrones judging the twelve tribes of Israel (Luke 22:28–30).

Jesus's words followed on a dispute about "which one of them was to be regarded as the greatest" (Luke 22:24).[22] We can fill in the gap about motive

---

18. Fitzmyer, *Luke X–XXIV*, 1569.

19. Described by Lukan characters, not the narrator.

20. "But go, tell his disciples and Peter that he is going ahead of you to Galilee" (Mark 16:7).

21. There is another example in 6.1.5.2.

22. Matthew places the reference to twelve thrones much earlier in Galilee (Matt 19:28). Luke puts the saying here with the effect of explaining the motives for Peter's action.

in Luke's narrative by imagining the Lukan Peter, anxious to be regarded as the greatest, perhaps worried that Jesus had made an individual appearance to Simon and not to him, and conscious of the fact that eleven people cannot fill twelve thrones, acting to resolve the issue.[23] Luke has earlier given us examples of his tendency to act first and think later, and of his ambition.[24]

We may here see Satan continuing to sift Peter and the others, as he had done at the Last Supper (Luke 22:24), on the Mount of Olives (Luke 22:45), on several occasions during the passion, and on their being told of the resurrection (Luke 24:11). On this occasion the testing, to which Peter again succumbs, is in regard to the desire for status, which, as we saw in 4.5.8 and 5.4.2, leads to the downfall of many characters in Luke-Acts. Indeed, Jesus had specifically warned his disciples: "Beware the yeast of the Pharisees" (Luke 12:1), a warning which followed close upon his long description of their faults, concluding with:

> Woe to you Pharisees! For you love to have the seat of honor in the synagogues and to be greeted with respect in the marketplaces (Luke 11:43).

The disciples had previously argued about who was the greatest (Luke 9:46); this second such dispute (Luke 22:24) shows that they, including Peter, had not heeded his warning.

6.1.2.6 *The Pretext*

We should also look at the reasons Peter gives in the Matthias passage, in particular that: "The scripture had to be fulfilled, which the Holy Spirit through David foretold concerning Judas." Peter then goes on, so he says, to cite that scripture, including: "Let another take his position of overseer." This is a quotation from a psalm of David,[25] 108 in the Septuagint, 109 in standard bibles. In this psalm David asks for God's help against those who

---

23. "The desire to make up the number of the Twelve was presumably related to the fact that Jesus intended them to be leaders of a restored Israel" (Peterson, *Acts*, 126).

24. E. g., the making of three dwellings for Jesus, Moses and Elijah "not knowing what he said" (Luke 9:33), and his self-promoting claim that: "We have left our homes and followed you" (Luke 18:28), when, as we have noted in 5.2.1, the "we" is emphasized. He also took part in both of the disputes about "which one of them was to be regarded as the greatest" (Luke 9:46; 22:24).

25. Omitted from the Roman breviary "because of [its] imprecatory character" (*Divine Office*, 1:lxi).

curse him, and almost half[26] of the psalm is taken up with the curses of those enemies, directed at David, beginning:

> "Appoint a sinner against him;
> and let a slanderer stand on his right.
> When he is tried, may he come out condemned,
> and let his prayer be counted as sin.
> Let his days become few,
> And may another seize his position, *tēn episcopēn autou laboi heteros*.
> Let his sons become orphans,
> and his wife a widow (Ps 108: 6–9).

It is a phrase used by the enemy in cursing David, "may another seize his position," that the Lukan Peter cites. It is absurd to use it in this way and call it fulfillment of Scripture foretold by David. Peter may have been "uneducated and ordinary" (Acts 4:13) but Luke was not. He understood the implication of what he was imputing to Peter.

6.1.2.7 The Criteria

Peter describes the necessary criteria for selecting the replacement for Judas—he is to be male, but also one who had accompanied Jesus from "the baptism of John" to "the day he was taken up from us." Yet:

> Matthias does not fall away in apostasy, but he does fall into oblivion, never seen again after Acts 1; likewise, nine of the remaining eleven apostles receive their last mention in 1:13. (Only Peter and John appear again.) In their places we encounter new witnesses such as Stephen, Philip, Barnabas, James, and, of course, Paul.[27]

Not one of these meets the criteria set out by Peter.[28] He believed that he knew the way forward, but Luke, with the omniscience of the narrator, knows better. The Spirit chooses the witnesses, and their previous history is not important.

---

26. Vv. 6–19, 14 verses out of 31. Although there is some room for argument about who utters the curses in this psalm, NETS, NRSV, and NJB, among others, attribute them to David's adversary.

27. Spencer, *Journeying Through Acts*, 40.

28. James was in Galilee but was not a disciple "from the baptism of John" (see Luke 8:19).

6.1.2.8 The Sequel

These things in themselves would seem to be enough to show that Peter, at this point, remains the uncomprehending and ambitious individual seen earlier, so that we understand his motive and realize that he is unreliable and that no weight is to be given to his words. But we can also look at what happens immediately after the Matthias episode.

> When the day of Pentecost had come, they were all together in one place. And suddenly from heaven there came a sound like the rush of a violent wind, and it filled the entire house where they were sitting. Divided tongues, as of fire, appeared among them, and a tongue rested on each of them. All of them were filled with the Holy Spirit and began to speak in other languages, as the Spirit gave them ability (Acts 2:1–4).

This is the "story of the outpouring of the Spirit on the apostles as the preliminary for Peter's proclamation in Jerusalem,"[29] and is the fulfillment of the promises of Jesus described above. Luke describes how the coming of the Holy Spirit changes all those present and implies, as he describes no other occasion, that it was at this point that Peter "turned back" and was able to strengthen his brothers and sisters. Indeed, Peter is a changed man after the coming of the Holy Spirit as he fearlessly leads the apostles in evangelization (Acts 2:14—4:22).

We see that Matthias plays no special part in subsequent events, but indeed, Luke shows us the Spirit descending upon "all of them" (Acts 2:4), that is, the 120 (Acts 1:15), and then Stephen (Acts 6:10), Philip (Acts 8:26–29), Saul (Acts 9:4–18) and, implicitly, those scattered from Jerusalem who proclaimed the word (Acts 8:4; 11:19–21). It is these people who take Luke's story forward. Finally, in yet a further aid to our understanding of this passage, when another of the original twelve, James, the brother of John, is killed by King Herod (Acts 12:1–3), neither the Spirit nor Luke shows interest in filling the alleged vacancy.

6.1.2.9 Summary

All in all, Luke could hardly have made it clearer that Peter, in the selection of Matthias, was making a personal attempt to safeguard the position of the remainder of the twelve, and, therefore, of his own leadership. He failed to understand what Jesus meant when he referred to "my kingdom" or when

---

29. Fitzmyer, *Acts*, 232.

he said that he was "among you as one who serves" (Luke 22:27). The spirit-filled activity of the post-Pentecostal Peter cannot be used to give spurious retrospective authority to what he said or did before Pentecost. We conclude that Luke did not think it necessary to replace Judas, and that maleness is of little consequence.

6.1.3 Widows in the Septuagint

6.1.3.1 *Septuagintal Usage*

> Widows in Jewish tradition were, of course, representatives of the most destitute and needy members of society for whom the Law made explicit provision through the obligations of care that fell on the rest of the Israelites.[30]

Many feminist scholars also see widows as symbolizing the destitute, for example:

> Mention widows in a biblical context and immediately what comes to the mind of most people is the classic image of poor, helpless women, without social status and with no resources of their own.[31]

However, this is overstated—in the Septuagint widows, when mentioned on their own, are *never* symbols of destitution and are only regarded as destitute and passive in two stylized contexts, punishment and when associated with orphans. The term for "widow" in Hebrew had a specific meaning:

> The Hebrew substantive *almanah*, usually translated "widow," often does not simply denote a woman whose husband is dead, but rather a once-married woman who has no means of financial support, and is therefore in need of special legal protection. Many widows would fall into such a classification because of their husbands' death, but others who could rely on the support of a new husband (by levirate marriage or otherwise), an adult son, or a father-in-law, would not. Thus, the *almanot* as a class in Israelite society in biblical times were often considered as comprising not merely women whose husbands had died but rather

---

30. Rius-Camps and Read-Heimerdinger, *Acts in Codex Bezae*, 2:19–20. A similar view is taken by Laffey, "Ruth," 555, and Elder, "Judith," 458.

31. Reid, "Power of the Widows," 73. Similar views are expressed by Seim, "Luke," 757, and Spencer, *Journeying through Acts*, 75.

once-married women who no longer had any means of financial support. Such being the case, many famous biblical widows (e.g., Ruth, Orpah, and Naomi (Ruth 1–4); Abigail (I Sam. 25); Bath-Sheba (II Sam. 11) . . . are never referred to as *almanot* [and] there is doubt as to whether they were regarded as such. All of them must have had some means of financial support.[32]

This definition in itself suggests that women whose husbands had died and were left with no means of financial support were exceptional. But *chēra*, the Greek equivalent to *almanah*, does not have the same connotations, as it is, for example, applied to Judith, a woman of great wealth. It is used almost seventy times in the Septuagint, and cognates, *chēreia*, *chēreuein*, and *chēreusis*, take the total to near eighty, listed in Appendix II.

In about 25% of instances these words are used, often in conjunction with either orphans or childlessness, to describe the punishment that will befall those who oppose God, sometimes applied to Israel, more often to its enemies,[33] for example, being used in such a way by the enemies of David in Psalm 108 cited in 6.1.2.6. Essentially, these examples are about the death of the men concerned. If there is a reference to the poverty of the widow and children, it is part of the hyperbole of the curse.

A further 40% also refer to widows and orphans[34] linked together as passive objects of the benevolence of others, or of God, a stereotype very similar to that identified by Roth and discussed in 5.5.2. Although the orphans are not usually explicitly shown as children of the widows, they are described in parallel, and have strong resonances with the women and children referred to in the curses described above. Widows so associated with orphans do represent destitution, that is, dependence on others in the Septuagint, but it does not follow that this is true of all widows. A woman who does not have to look after a child can work and may be little poorer than a man with an equivalent lack of resources, especially if the man has dependents. But a woman who has to care for a fatherless child,[35] especially more than one child, will not only have greater needs but will find it much more difficult to find suitable work. It is not surprising that the Septuagint sees such women as dependent on others or upon God.

---

32. Cohen, "Widow—Biblical Period," 487–88.

33. These instances refer to men, for example: "Let their wives become childless and widowed" (Jer 18:21).

34. In the Septuagint "orphans" means children without a father.

35. It may be that, in this context, "orphan" refers to a child too young to earn his or her own living, perhaps under ten.

6.1.3.2 Individual Widows

But on most other occasions (about 20%) when these words are used they refer to five individual women. The women are (i) Tamar,[36] (ii) the wise woman of Tekoa, (iii) the widow of Zarephath, (iv) Judith and (v) the unnamed mother of the seven brothers whose martyrdom is described in 2 and 4 Maccabees.

1. Tamar tricked her father-in-law, Judah, into siring children for her, to continue the name of her dead husband (Gen 38). There is no suggestion that she was in any economic need, as she returned to the house of her father (Gen 38:11)—as we saw in 6.1.3.1, women who could rely on male support were not regarded as in need.

2. The wise woman pretended to be a widow in order to persuade David to forgive his son, Absalom, who had killed his brother (2 Sam 14). She pretended her own son had killed his brother and asked mercy for him of the king. There is no suggestion of economic hardship—the wise woman's pretense is that her concern, like that of Tamar, was "to establish for my husband . . . [a] name on the face of the earth" (2 Kgdms 14:7). When the king pardoned her son she asked him to do the same for his own son.

3. The widow of Zarephath fed Elijah during a famine (1 Kgs 17). She was not destitute in the ordinary sense; she had an upper room where Elijah was lodging and in which he restored one of the woman's children to life (17:13–23). It was because of the famine that she told Elijah that:

   > There is only a handful of meal in the jar and a little oil in the jug, and behold, I am now gathering two sticks, and I shall go in and make [the cake] for myself and my children, and we shall eat and die (3 Kgdms 17:12).

   It is relevant that, in the Septuagint, she has children, whereas in the standard bible she has one child, her son (1 Kgs 17:12), that is, in the Septuagint she is associated with "orphans"—see the discussion of Luke's reference to her in 7.2.4.3.

4. Judith saved her people by killing Holofernes (Jdt 13–14). She is discussed further below (6.3.7.5), but we may note here that "her husband had left her gold and silver and male and female servants and

---

36. Another Tamar, the daughter of David, is also mentioned as having to live as a widow, that is, celibately.

cattle and fields, and she remained over them" (Jdt 8:7). She was very far from destitute.

5. The mother of the seven brothers encouraged her sons to accept death by torture rather than eat swine's flesh, and was then killed herself (2 Macc 7; 4 Macc 8–18). There are no clear indications as to her economic status, but some of her sons were married (4 Macc 16:9), so, as marriage requires resources, they, and she, are to be understood as not destitute.

These women were not passive, far from it, nor were any of them destitute in the ordinary meaning of the term. Indeed, the only one in economic need, the widow of Zarephath, had orphaned children, so is covered by the standard stereotype. Apart from these named women, there are only two references to widows in the Septuagint with implications for economic status,[37] in Proverbs, about God's protection, and in the Wisdom of Solomon, where the impious plan evil deeds:

> The Lord tears down the homes of the insolent,
> But he established the border of the widow (Prov 15:25).

and

> Let us oppress the righteous poor man, *penēta*;
> Let us not spare the widow (Wis 2:10).

The Proverbs reference clearly indicates that the property of the widow will be protected, so the widow has property. In the Wisdom passage there is no explicit reference to the economic status of the widow, but she is closely associated with the poor man, one of the *penētes*, who, as we saw in 1.5.4.1, are not destitute.[38] Moreover, although the impious oppress the righteous man for sport in Wisdom 2:12–20, the widow reference is part of a section (2:6–11) which focuses on the good things enjoyed by the impious, for example, "costly wine and perfumes" (2:7). There is an implication, as very often in the Septuagint, that the luxuries of the rich are paid for by despoiling the poor, taking from them what little they have. In conclusion, we find that widows, unless associated explicitly with orphans, are not symbols of destitution in the Septuagint, so that the economic context of each reference in Luke-Acts must be considered on its merits—these references are among those listed in 6.2 and are discussed in 6.3 and chapter 7. We find that Luke

---

37. Other references include two relating to the qualification required to marry a priest, two identifying men as the son of a widow, and several with no implication as to economic status.

38. In Proverbs as in Psalms *penētes* may not have the same connotations—see 5.1.

rarely saw widows as destitute, and, indeed, saw them as agentic, like the named widows described above.

6.1.4 Prophecy

6.1.4.1 Prophets Identified in Luke-Acts

Many feminist scholars seem to consider that the gift of prophecy is shown by the utterance of oracles, also a fairly widely held view among other scholars. Apparently because of this understanding of prophecy, many take the view that Luke demonstrates a patriarchal ideology because he does not tell us of any prophetic words spoken by women.

> The prophetic activity of both men and women is a sign of the Spirit at work in the church (Acts 2:17–18)) but in telling his story of the church, Luke almost completely ignores women's prophetic ministry.[39]

But this is to misunderstand the meaning of prophecy for Luke. The importance of the prophetic function, especially for women, is demonstrated at the beginning of both Gospel and Acts. In the Gospel we see the prophecies in the form of the oracles of both Mary and Elizabeth, Anna is named as a prophet, and in Acts, Peter quoted Joel:

> Your sons and your daughters shall prophesy . . .
> Even upon my slaves, both men and women,
> In those days I will pour out my Spirit;
> And they shall prophesy (Acts 2:17–18).

Thus, the scene is set for us to meet women prophets, but throughout the remainder of the two-volume work there appear to be none except for the unmarried daughters of Philip (21:9), whose work of prophecy is not described. Mary Rose D'Angelo explains why this is so for the Gospel:

> In the ministry of Jesus the mentions of the spirit and of prophecy disappear almost entirely after the sermon in the synagogue at Nazareth; the spirit is wholly identified with the activity of Jesus.[40]

However, this does not explain the apparent absence of women prophets in Acts, where "prophets who are specifically mentioned and sometimes

---

39. O'Day, "Acts," 308. Similarly, Schaberg, "Luke," 275, 291; Seim, *Double Message*, 255; Martin, "Acts," 786–87; D'Angelo, "(Re)Presentations of Women," 186.

40. "Redactional View," 452.

named . . . illustrate the activity of the Spirit in the time of the Church."[41] But Luke tells us co-textually that prophecy and witness are linked: "*All the prophets testify* about [Jesus] that everyone who believes in him receives forgiveness of sins through his name" (Acts 10:43—emphasis added). This link is also evident in the prophet Anna, who gave witness when she spoke about the child (Luke 2:38) and in the Baptist, "a prophet . . . and more than a prophet" (Luke 7:26) who himself spoke at length about Jesus (Luke 3:16–17). Prophecy for Luke often means testimony about Jesus.

To understand prophecy in Acts we should consider those who are there named as prophets. These included Agabus and others[42] (Acts 11:27–28), Barnabas, Saul and three other named men at Antioch (Acts 13:1), Judas and Silas (Acts 15:32), about twelve disciples at Ephesus (Acts 19:7) and Agabus again (Acts 21:10–11). These are men, but also identified are the four daughters of Philip (Acts 21:9). The actions of some of these prophets are described.

Agabus predicts a severe famine, and later predicts Paul's arrest and imprisonment. Judas and Silas, in the verse where they are named as prophets, "said much to encourage, *parekalesan*,[43] and strengthen, *epestērizan*, the believers" (Acts 15:32). Of the others, Barnabas is called "son of encouragement, *huios parakleseōs*" (Acts 4:36). Paul and Barnabas "strengthened, *epistērizontes*, the souls of the disciples and encouraged, *parakalountes*, them to continue in the faith" (Acts 14.22). Paul and Silas "encouraged, *parekalesan*, the brothers and sisters" (Acts 16:40) and Paul encouraged, *parakalesas*, the disciples (Acts 20:1).[44] The actions of Judas, Silas, Barnabas and Paul are more fully reported than those of Agabus, and Barnabas and Paul, in particular, are much more important characters in the narrative. It is in what they do, rather than what Agabus does, that we find the most important indications about Luke's understanding of the meaning of prophecy; encouragement is a major element as is strengthening. The only one of these prophets who utters an oracle is Agabus,[45] and, most of the identified male prophets, like the daughters of Philip, never speak. There may be another oracle in Tyre where "the disciples . . . told Paul [through the Spirit] not to go on to Jerusalem" (Acts 21:4).[46] It is not clear whether this is an oracle, a

---

41. Schnider, "Prophētēs," 186.

42. Who may have included women.

43. "Encourage," *parakalōn* (NRSV exhortations), is used of the Baptist (Luke 3.18), also a prophet.

44. Further examples in 6.1.4.3.

45. Although not named as a prophet, Stephen also utters an oracle (Acts 7:56).

46. The meaning of this passage is unclear as it seems to contradict the Spirit's message to Paul (Acts 20:22–23). See 6.1.4.4 and discussions by Tannehill, "Cornelius and

prophecy or something different, but it is not necessary to suppose that the disciples concerned were all male: women are mentioned in Acts 21:5.

6.1.4.2 Prophecy in 1 Corinthians

Prophecy figures substantially in chapter 14 of Paul's first letter to the Corinthians and Paul there makes it clear that women are expected to prophesy (1 Cor 11:5). We should bear in mind that not only did the Lukan narrator claim to have been a companion of Paul's, but Paul had evangelized personally most, if not all, of the areas outside Palestine about which Luke wrote, so that Paul's letters can help us to understand Luke's intention,[47] even if, as most scholars believe, he had no knowledge of them.

That this is the case as regards the meaning of "prophecy" is confirmed by very strong links between the description of prophecy in Acts and that in 1 Corinthians 14. In that chapter Paul wrote that: "Those who prophesy speak to other people for their upbuilding and encouragement, *paraklēsin*,[48] and consolation" (1 Cor 14:3) and: "For you can all prophesy one by one, so that all may learn, *manthanōsin*, and all be encouraged, *parakalōntai*" (1 Cor 14:31). He also seems to mean prophecy when he says "I would rather speak five words with my mind, in order to instruct others" (1 Cor 14:18) and throughout he tells us that the purpose of prophecy is the building up of the church (1 Cor 14:3, 4, 5, 12, 17, 26). John Barclay explains how Paul understands prophecy:

> "Prophecy" is never defined, but seems to constitute speech which instructs, encourages, consoles, or challenges its hearers (vv. 3, 24–5, 31).[49]

This can be compared with Acts (see 6.1.4.1) where we described the frequent use of *parakaleō*. Luke does not use *manthaneō*, learn, used by Paul (above), but he frequently shows the converse, teaching, in the testimony

---

Tabitha," 263–64; Barrett, *Critical and Exegetical Commentary*, 2:990–91; and Witherington, *Acts*, 630–31.

47. Brodie ("Tracing the Gospels," 110–16) sees 1 Cor as a source for Luke-Acts, and Goulder also argues that Luke was familiar with 1 Corinthians (Goulder, *Luke*, 132–41).

48. "*Paraklēsis* is equally applicable to the unfolding of theological issues implicit in the gospel" (Gillespie, *First Theologians*, 147, drawing on 1 Thessalonians).

49. Barclay, "1 Corinthians," 1129. For a similar, but fuller, description see Gillespie, *First Theologians*, 197.

about Jesus (including that by prophets, the Baptist and Anna)[50] described in both Gospel and Acts.

6.1.4.3 Prophecy in Acts

David Hill finds that the meaning of prophecy in Acts differs from that elsewhere in the New Testament and that the description of the actions of Paul and Barnabas offers insight: "There they strengthened the souls of the disciples and encouraged them to continue in the faith" (Acts 14.22). He summarizes prophecy in Acts:

> Under the direct and immediate inspiration of the Spirit, the prophet exhorts and strengthens the Christian community by pastoral guidance and instruction, and through the power of the Spirit he witnessed to the character of his living Lord, who is himself the Prophet of the End-time.[51]

We have seen the way in which Paul understood prophecy in the first letter to the Corinthians, which was written in Ephesus about the mid-50s, not long before Paul's final journey to Jerusalem (and Luke's second voyage) in 57. Therefore, when Luke was with Paul on that voyage, Paul's understanding of prophecy had only recently been articulated and may have been included, implicitly or explicitly, in his addresses to fellow-Christians on that voyage at which Luke was present.[52] So the Lukan Paul spoke at Troas (Acts 20:7–12), where the disciples "were not a little comforted" and to the elders of Ephesus (Acts 20:18–38), where he described how he testified, *diamartyromenos* (Acts 18:21), *diamartyretai* (Acts 18:23), *diamartyrasthai* (Acts 18:24), and built up, *oikodomēsai* (Acts 18:32). Building up (exhorting and strengthening as Hill put it) was Paul's main purpose in these meetings with the congregations he had founded and at which Luke was present. So, we find, in agreement with Hill, that for Luke prophecy primarily related to exhortation (that is, encouragement) and strengthening of the church by pastoral guidance and instruction,[53] a meaning similar to that found by Barclay in 1 Corinthians. This is not conveyed in direct speech or oracles, by either the men or the women in Acts, rather, he shows it in progress.

---

50. See 6.1.4.1.

51. Hill, *New Testament Prophecy*, 109. Hill also compares prophecy in Acts with the description in 1 Corinthians (ibid., 103).

52. Or in discussions heard by Luke but not included in Acts.

53. Paul's understanding has been said to be that: "Prophecy . . . mediates the gospel to the church in intelligible speech" (Gillespie, *First Theologians*, 126).

Women in the Introduction to the Gospel 207

However, as we noted above, prophecy in Acts does include testimony about Jesus and we see this in a number of the speeches included in Luke's text, and in the instruction of Apollos by Priscilla and Aquila (Acts 18:26).

6.1.4.4 Oracles in Acts

However, Luke's understanding of prophecy as oracle also merits attention. We noted above that there were two, perhaps three, instances of prophecy as oracle in Acts. First, Agabus "stood up and predicted by the Spirit that there would be a severe famine over all the world; and this took place during the reign of Claudius" (Acts 11:28). Luke knew as well as we do that this was an exaggeration—the famine did not affect the whole world—but hyperbole is a recognized rhetorical technique much used by Luke.

It is not clear whether the next occurrence is an oracle or not.

> At Tyre . . . we looked up the disciples and stayed there for seven days. Through the Spirit they told Paul not to go on to Jerusalem (Acts 21:3-4).

This may be the description of an oracle which Paul ignores. Barrett regards this as "unthinkable" and finds that Luke "failed adequately to express [his meaning]," which was similar to the prophecy of Agabus[54] (Acts 21:10-11).[55] But, for us, postulating a Lukan failure to express his meaning is "unthinkable,"[56] and we prefer Fitzmyer's explanation:

> He, however, is not deterred by the message given him by these Tyrian Christians, who know about his coming troubles from "the Spirit." He has already been said to be traveling to Jerusalem under the Spirit's impulse (20:22), and so he is depicted as being willing to suffer for the gospel (20:24).[57]

That is to say, the Tyrian Christians receive a valid communication from the Spirit, but misinterpret it, a reading which acquits Luke of failure and is compatible with his next description of an oracle which also involved Agabus:

> He came to us and took Paul's belt, bound his own feet and hands with it, and said, "Thus says the Holy Spirit, 'This is the

---

54. See below.
55. Barrett, *Critical and Exegetical Commentary*, 2:990.
56. Luke, of course, could have failed to express his meaning but to assume he did so in any particular instance is likely to lead to misinterpretation.
57. Fitzmyer, *Acts*, 688.

way the Jews in Jerusalem will bind the man who owns this belt and will hand him over to the Gentiles'" (Acts 21:11).

Luke later describes what happens to Paul in Jerusalem and it is clear that Agabus's prophecy is wrong in every detail, surprising as Luke both recounts the prophecy (and tells us he was one of those who heard it) and later describes the outcome at some length; the Jews did not bind Paul and did not hand him over to the gentiles. The oracle gets it wrong, presumably because, like the Tyrians, Agabus misunderstands or cannot communicate the heavenly message.

This failure to get a prophecy right seems to apply even to Jesus. He said:

> See, we are going up to Jerusalem, and everything that is written about the Son of Man by the prophets will be accomplished. For he will be handed over to the Gentiles; and he will be mocked and insulted and spat upon. *After they have flogged him*, they will kill him, and on the third day he will rise again (Luke 18:31–33, emphasis added).

But Luke describes these events, and does not show us Jesus being flogged.[58] However, we do not see this as a prophetic failure. Jesus was flogged, it was a standard part of the penalty of crucifixion;[59] Luke does not mention it for the rhetorical reasons described in 3.3.1. But authentic prophetic inspirations are misunderstood by the Tyrians and wrongly communicated by Agabus. Luke did not rate the reliability of oracles highly, and in this he is like many of his secular contemporaries.[60]

6.1.5 Lydia

6.1.5.1 Heavenly Interventions

Little attention has been given to Lydia, either by feminists or by mainstream scholars; she is seen as "Paul's Cosmopolitan Hostess," the title of a

---

58. See 3.3.1.
59. See Winter, *Trial of Jesus*, 95, noted in 3.3.1.
60. The story of Croesus and the oracle at Delphi was well known. Croesus asked if he should go to war with Persia. The oracle replied that if he attacked the Persians he would destroy a mighty empire, so he went to war, but the empire destroyed was his own (Herodotus, *Histories* 1.50–86). The vast amounts of gold and silver described as given by Croesus to the oracle (1.50–52) have resonances with Luke's treatment of idols and money as discussed in 5.4.2.

Women in the Introduction to the Gospel 209

recent book by Richard Ascough.[61] But Luke's presentation of Lydia begins before she herself is introduced, as he tells us that Paul, with Silas, was told to change his plans:

> They went through the region of Phrygia and Galatia, having been forbidden by the Holy Spirit to speak the word in Asia. When they had come opposite Mysia, they attempted to go into Bithynia, but the Spirit of Jesus did not allow them; so, passing by Mysia, they went down to Troas. During the night Paul had a vision: there stood a man of Macedonia pleading with him and saying, "Come over to Macedonia and help us." When he had seen the vision, we immediately tried to cross over to Macedonia, being convinced that God had called us to proclaim the good news to them. We set sail from Troas and took a straight course to Samothrace, the following day to Neapolis,[62] and from there to Philippi, which is a leading city of the district of Macedonia and a Roman colony (Acts 16:6–12).

After three direct heavenly interventions, by the Holy Spirit (Acts 16:6), by the Spirit of Jesus (Acts 16:7) and by a vision seen as sent by God (Acts 16:9), Paul went direct to Philippi, picking up Luke on the way in Troas. After a few days there they spoke to women who had gathered "where we supposed, *enomizomen*, there was a place of prayer, *proseuchēn*" (Acts 16:13). Among them was Lydia, and: "The Lord opened her heart to listen eagerly to what was said by Paul" (Acts 16:14). This is the fourth direct heavenly intervention, and we see the four as linked and the conversion of Lydia as an important part of God's purpose in Luke's narrative.

6.1.5.2 The Place of Prayer

Luke may put further emphasis on the importance of Lydia. As we saw above, Luke (in NRSV) uses *nomizō*, to suppose (that there was a place of prayer), but:

> Except in Acts 16:13, where a positive narrative character makes a correct assumption, *nomizō* in Luke-Acts always is used of a false assumption, which in some instances is criticized in direct discourse by the opponent . . . and is elsewhere related as an *erroneous assumption*.[63]

---

61. Ascough, *Lydia, Paul's Cosmopolitan Hostess*. A similar view is taken by O'Day, "Acts," 310.
62. Neapolis is the port of Philippi, some 10 miles away.
63. Schenk, "Nomizō," 470.

The word occurs with this sense nine times in Luke-Acts, three times in Matthew,[64] and if all the other usages are in relation to false assumptions, perhaps, *contra* Schenk, that is also the case here.

If it is a false assumption, then Lydia and her companions were not at a place of prayer, *proseuchē*.[65] If *nomizō* is used in its ordinary sense, so is *proseuchē*, and Paul and his companions thought that there was a synagogue by the river, but were mistaken. There was no synagogue or place of prayer, but they met a number of women who had gathered by the river. Lydia was probably a god-fearer (Acts 16:14),[66] and if the other women were also god-fearers, they may have gathered for a religious purpose. However, it could have been a social event or, as Lydia's trade (a dealer in purple cloth) may have involved substantial use of water,[67] the other women may have been co-workers, and, indeed, Luke gives no indication that they were god-fearers. Paul spoke to the women and, as we have seen, Lydia responded very positively—we are told nothing of the other women.

The *proseuchē* is mentioned again:

> One day, as we were going to the place of prayer, *proseuchē*, we met a slave-girl who had a spirit of divination and brought her owners a great deal of money by fortune-telling (Acts 16:16).

"One day" is absent from the Greek, "*egeneto de*," and other translations omit any temporal reference, for example, "It happened that" (NASB) or "As we were going to" (ESV). This lack of a temporal marker is seen as ambiguity:

> If the reader is to understand this as a flashback to the Sabbath walk related in v. 13, the narrator has not been clear, but if, on the other hand, it relates a subsequent trip to the place of prayer, clarity is equally lacking.[68]

However, the ambiguity is caused by the understanding that Luke uses *nomizō* in an unusual way, to mean correct understanding. In its ordinary meaning their understanding was incorrect, there was no *proseuchē* by the

---

64. Mt 5:17; 10:34; 20:10; Lk 2:44; 3:23; Acts 7:25; 8:20; 14:19, 27; 17:29; 21:29; also 1 Cor 7:26, 36; 1 Tim 6:5. The Matthean and 1 Timothy usages also convey falsity. The Corinthian usages do not convey falsity, but do convey uncertainty.

65. "[*Proseuchē*] is nearly always equivalent to *synagōgē* in the sense of a cultic place" (BDAG, 878).

66. "The words do not necessarily mean more than that she feared God; she was a devout woman" (Barrett, *Critical and Exegetical Commentary*, 2:783).

67. If she dyed the cloth.

68. Pervo, *Acts*, 404.

river, and the text should be read as a flashback, "as we were going to the (supposed) place of prayer." In this reading, Luke has used prolepsis, placing the meeting with Lydia, not in its chronological sequence after the first meeting with the slave-girl, but before, and he has done this to emphasize the importance[69] of the encounter. The traditional interpretation of *nomizō* as meaning a correct understanding, by eliminating the emphasis given to Lydia by Luke's use of prolepsis, may be another example of a reading against the grain of the text to promote a patriarchal ideology and explain why this interpretation is, as Pervo says "not . . . clear."

6.1.5.3 The Importance of Lydia

When we are told that: "The Lord opened her heart," we should appreciate that this was a rare honor in Acts, the only other individuals on whom the Lord is said to have so worked being Stephen (Acts 7:55, the Holy Spirit), Philip (Acts 8:39, the Spirit of the Lord), Saul (Acts 9:5–6, Jesus), Ananias (Acts 9:10–16, the Lord) and Peter (Acts 10:13, a voice). Stephen, Philip, Saul and Peter are the main characters in Acts, driving nearly all of the narrative. The function of Ananias in Acts 9 is clearly totally related to the conversion of Saul, so what is the function of Lydia, whose importance is emphasized by a sequence over nine verses of four separate direct heavenly interventions? Having Paul stay in her home during his time in Philippi would not seem to warrant such narrative emphasis, and the belief that this was because Lydia was the first convert in Europe assigns to the geographical entity of Europe a significance which would have seemed strange to Luke and his contemporaries.[70] If we remember that Paul, Silas and Luke arrived in Philippi (Acts 16:12) and stayed at Lydia's home (Acts 16:15), and that Paul and Silas left Philippi (Acts 16:40), we can see the divine purpose as directed towards Luke's own stay under Lydia's roof until he left Philippi

---

69. The Bezan text differs, "as we were going to prayer" (Rius-Camps and Read-Heimerdinger, *Acts in Codex Bezae* 3, 262), which removes the prolepsis. If our understanding of the standard text is correct, the alteration in Codex Bezae may be part of the tendency in the Western texts of Acts (including Bezae) to reduce the importance of women—see 7.6.6.

70. See Dunn, *Beginning from Jerusalem*, 669n42. Alexander argues that: "To a world-view centred on Jerusalem . . . [Paul's] crossing of the Bosporus marks a breaking out of the known world" (Alexander, *Ancient Literary Context*, 80). Perhaps, but did Luke have such a world-view? "For the narrator of Acts . . . sea travel is a matter of consuming interest . . . [he] is perfectly at home on the sea" (ibid., 84). And the sea was the Aegean—Phillipi was on one side, Troas the other, both sides were Greek-speaking parts of the Roman empire and before that of the Macedonian.

with Paul some six or seven years later (Acts 20:6).[71] Luke was self-effacing, but there is no reason to suppose he did not think his work important. Lydia is discussed further in 7.3.4.

6.1.6 Autonomy of Women

In Luke-Acts *all* women are shown as autonomous in that no-one at all, whether man or woman, in either the Gospel or Acts tells a woman to do, or not do, anything. Moreover, Luke omits three instances (two specific, one more subtle) in his Markan antetext when a woman is told to do something. Mark shows us Herodias telling her daughter to ask Antipas for the head of the Baptist (Mark 6:24). Luke omits the passage. And in Mark the young man at the tomb tells the women: "But go, tell his disciples and Peter that he is going ahead of you to Galilee; there you will see him, just as he told you" (Mark 16:7). Again, Luke omits it.[72]

The third, more subtle, amendment to Mark is in the story of the woman with the hemorrhage. In both Mark and Luke, Jesus, knowing power has gone forth from him, asked: "Who touched my clothes?" (Mark 5:30), or "Who touched me"? (Luke 8:45). In both versions the word "Who?" *Tis?* is masculine, that is, generic, with no indication as to gender. In Mark Jesus does not say anything further, but: "He looked all around to see who had done it" (Mark 5:32). Here "who, *tēn*," is feminine. Jesus knows that he has been touched by a woman. This meaning is rarely brought out by modern English translations, although it is explicit in older versions like AV[73] and Douay. In interpreting this passage we can imagine that the actions of Jesus made this clear, perhaps by looking at the women in the crowd to identify who it was who had touched him, which could be seen as putting pressure on the woman to reveal herself when asked to do so by the man who had cured her. This would have been brought out more clearly when the text was read aloud.

But in the Lukan equivalent Jesus does speak—he says: "Someone touched me" (Luke 8:46), and the "Someone," *Tis*, is again the generic masculine pronoun, giving no indication as to gender, nor is gender indicated elsewhere. He puts no pressure on the woman and although, as in Mark, she identifies herself, this is not because of perceived pressure from Jesus, but because "she could not remain hidden." Her daily toil, to acquire, and

---

71. Luke's autobiographical material is discussed in 1.1.2.

72. He also does not have the Matthean equivalents, when first an angel (Matt 28:7) and then the risen Jesus (Matt 28:10) instructed the women in a similar way.

73. "He looked round about to see her that had done this thing."

dispose of, rags of cloth could not have been kept secret, so her condition, and therefore its cure, would necessarily have been known to her family and associates. In sum, Luke removes the Markan suggestion that Jesus, knowing that it was a woman who had been cured, was indicating that she should identify herself.

There are some instances where Jesus appears to give a command, such as when he tells the daughter of Jairus: "Child, get up" (Luke 8:54). But this is not really a command—he is telling the child that she is no longer dead and can live her life. There is confirmation of this reading of such "commands" when Jesus tells ten lepers: "Go and show yourselves to the priests" (Luke 17:14).[74] But one of them, a Samaritan, did not do this but "turned back, praising God with a loud voice [and] prostrated himself at Jesus' feet and thanked him" (Luke 17:15–16). Jesus then commends him, indicating that this had been the right thing to do (Luke 17:17–19), despite the apparent disobedience. Another possible exception is where Jesus tells the women of Jerusalem: "Do not weep for me, but weep for yourselves and for your children" (Luke 23:28). But this is not a command—he does not tell the women not to weep—they are right to weep, and Jesus's prophecy confirms the rightness of their action. So Jesus never tells an individual woman, or a discrete group of women, what to do.

But too much should not be made of this point. As part of a mixed group Jesus does tell women what to do, for example, as disciples, as members of the crowd, or when they are instructed together with men, like the wife of Jairus (Luke 8:56). But he never does so to women by themselves or only with other women. We see this as a deliberate choice on Luke's part—that the pre-Resurrection Jesus issues no instructions to women in either Mark or Matthew may not be of great significance as their narratives include few women and there is, therefore, little opportunity for them to show Jesus telling a woman what to do. Luke has ample opportunity, but does not avail of it.

Although no one in Luke-Acts tells a woman to do anything, there is no lack of examples of women giving instruction to men. Elizabeth insists on the name to be given to her child (Luke 1:57–63), implicitly Mary does the same (Luke 2:21), as it was to her alone that the angel had spoken, saying "you will name him Jesus" (Luke 1:31).[75] Later, Jesus "was obedient to [his parents]" (Luke 2:51). Again, Martha asks Jesus to "Tell [Mary] then to help me" (Luke 10:40);[76] the woman suffering from hemorrhages "touched the

---

74. Discussed in 5.5.3.
75. In Matthew's story, Joseph names the child (Matt 1:25).
76. See 7.5.1.1.

fringe of his clothes" (Luke 8:44), so that he should heal her; and in a parable a woman continually calls on an unjust judge for justice (Luke 18:2–8). In Acts Lydia prevailed upon Paul and his companions (Acts 16:15) and Priscilla (and Aquila) "took [Apollos] aside and explained the Way of God to him more accurately" (Acts 18:26). Such an imbalance in the presentation of gender relationships is hardly unintended.

6.1.7 Diakonia—Personal Loving Service

In Luke-Acts a number of women offer personal loving service, *diakonia*, sometimes referred to by that term, but more often by a description of the service given. This word has a special meaning:

> The word group is distinct from other terms that are related in meaning in that it "has the special quality of indicating very personally the service rendered to another."[77]

Indeed, "In *diakoneō* there is a stronger approximation to the concept of a service of love."[78] It was this form of service that Jesus had in mind when he said:

> For who is greater, the one who is at the table or the one who serves? Is it not the one at the table? But I am among you as one who serves, *diakonōn* (Luke 22:27).

It is fairly generally accepted that the words of the Lukan Jesus at Nazareth, at the beginning of his ministry, are programmatic, that is, they show how Jesus is going to act. In a similar way, at the end of his ministry, the Lukan Jesus sums up its message in these words about service.[79] This is especially important in understanding Luke's presentation of women. *Diakonia* is discussed further in 7.3.

---

77. Weiser, "Diakoneō," 302, citing Beyer, "Diakoneō," 81.
78. Beyer, "Diakoneō," 81.
79. See Seim, "Feminist Criticism," 69–70, discussed in 6.1.2.1.

6.2 OVERVIEW OF THE WOMEN IN LUKE-ACTS

6.2.1 Introduction

Carla Ricci[80] has listed the women mentioned in the Gospel and Ivoni Richter Reimer[81] has prepared a similar list of the women in Acts. We have adapted and summarized the lists as follows, annotating them with the function or functions of each individual or group of women, and, where we later discuss their role at any length, we give references to the appropriate section. We have used the following categories:

D *Diakonia*: the provision of personal service, in the Gospel usually to Jesus;

P Prophet: including providers of instruction, encouragement and consolation;

R Responsive: showing a willingness to respond to the message of Jesus (or the covenant), but where the nature of the response is not described;

W Witness: the provision of witness or testimony about Jesus, a specific form of prophecy. We include under this category those who praised God after being cured;[82]

U Unresponsive: unwilling to respond to the message of Jesus (or the covenant).

6.2.2 Women in the Gospel

The women in the Gospel may be listed as follows:

Elizabeth (Luke 1:5–25, 40–45, 57–66) **P, D**—see 6.4 below;

Mary, the mother of Jesus (Luke 1:26–56; 2:5–7, 16–19, 21–35, 39–51; 8:19–21; also Acts 1:14)[83] **P, D**—6.4;

Anna the prophet (Luke 2:36–38) **P, W**—6.3;

Herodias (Luke 3:19) **U**—7.5.2;

Peter's mother-in-law (Luke 4:38–39) **D**;

The widow of Nain (Luke 7:12–15) **R**—7.2.4.3;

The woman who anointed Jesus (Luke 7:36–50) **D**—7.4;

---

80. Ricci, *Mary Magdalene*, 63.

81. Richter Reimer, *Women in Acts*, xxv–xxvi.

82. We argued in 5.5.2 that this was a stereotyped response, but, nevertheless, it was a response.

83. Ricci's list did not cover Acts.

Some women: Mary Magdalene, Joanna, Susanna and many others (Luke 8:2-3—Mary Magdalene, Joanna, Mary the mother of James and "other women with them" also at Luke 23:55; 24:10) **D, W**—7.3.2;

The woman suffering from a hemorrhage (Luke 8:43-48) **W**—7.4;

Jairus's daughter and his wife[84] (Luke 8:41-42, 49-56) **R**;

Martha and Mary (Luke 10:38-42), Martha **D**, Mary **R**—7.5.1;

The woman who said: "Blessed is the womb" (Luke 11:27-28) **W**;

The woman who was bent over (Luke 13:11-13) **W**;

The widow at the temple (Luke 21:2-4) **R**;

The servant girl at the house of the high priest (Luke 22:56-57) **U**—7.5.2;

The women who beat their breasts (Luke 23:27-31) **R**.

6.2.3 Women in Acts

The women in Acts may be listed as follows:

Women at the beginning of the church (Acts 1:14) **R**;

Quotation from Joel (Acts 2:17-18) **P**—6.2.4;

Sapphira (Acts 5:1-11) **R**—7.5.1;

Women in the growing church (Acts 5:14) **R**;

Hellenist widows (Acts 6:1) **D**—7.2;

Unnamed women persecuted by Saul (Acts 8:3) **R**;

Unnamed women converted by Philip (Acts 8:12) **R**;

Candace (Acts 8:27) **U**—6.2.4;

Unnamed women persecuted in Damascus (Acts 9:2) **R**;

Tabitha and the widows (Acts 9:36-41) **D**—7.2.4.3;

Mary, the mother of John Mark, and Rhoda (Acts 12:12-17) **D**;

Women "of high standing" in Antioch stirred up against Paul and Silas (Acts 13:50) **U**—7.5.2;

The mother of Timothy (Acts 16:1) **R**;

Lydia and other women (Acts 16:13-15) **D**—7.3.4;

The slave with the Pythian spirit (Acts 16:16-18) **U**—7.5.2;

---

84. Ricci omits the wife of Jairus.

Leading women in Thessalonica converted (Acts 17:4) **R**;

Women "of high standing" in Beroea converted (Acts 17:12) **R**;

Damaris in Athens (Acts 17:34) **R**;

Priscilla (Acts 18:2–3, 18–19, 24–28) **D, W**—7.4;

Women and children at Tyre (Acts 21:5–6) **R**;

Women prophets at Caesarea (Acts 21:9) **P**—7.5.1.3;

Paul's recollection of persecution (Acts 22:4) **R**;

Paul's sister (Acts 23:16)—6.2.4;

Drusilla (Acts 24:24) **U**—7.5.2;

Bernice (Acts 25:13, 23; 26:30–31) **U**—7.5.2.

6.2.4 Women Excluded from the Lists

These women do not include those referred to by inclusion in masculine form plurals, although the use of "disciples" as including women is discussed in 7.3.2.1. Luke also uses *adelphoi*, which NRSV often translates as "brothers," yet BDAG tells us that "[the plural] can also mean *brothers and sisters*."[85] This dictionary also finds that "there is no doubt that in Lk 21:16 *adelphoi* = *brothers and sisters*."[86] If Luke uses it with that meaning at Luke 21:16, we should assume, unless there is reason to the contrary, that he does so elsewhere.[87] There is further antetextual support for such an assumption in Luke 8:19–21 where, for the same group of people whom Luke calls *adelphoi*, his antetext, Mark, has both *adelphoi* (Mark 3:31) and *adelphoi . . . kai . . . adelphai* (Mark 3:32). There is no reason to believe Luke excluded the sisters, so for Luke *adelphoi* is a term including both genders,[88] as in a number of modern European languages.[89]

Richter Reimer notes that: "We are struck by the fact that the majority of passages [in Acts] concerning women report that they were converted to

---

85. BDAG, 18, with over a dozen examples.

86. Ibid., 18. It is not clear why this particular instance is singled out.

87. IMGL has: "*adelphoi* brother and sister, like Lat. *fratres*."

88. This is not accepted by all scholars—Fitzmyer says that Luke's version of the story "[omits] the sisters completely" (*Luke I–IX*, 723), a view shared by Marshall (*Gospel of Luke*, 331–32).

89. The use of the masculine plural to include the feminine for nouns which vary for gender only in the ending is commonplace in languages derived from Latin (e.g., *hermanos* in Spanish, *fratelli* in Italian, both meaning siblings).

Christ."[90] This is also true of the Gospel, although use of the term "converted to Christ" is anachronistic there, and the equivalent is either faithfulness to the covenant of Israel or responsiveness to Jesus. Some of the women listed above are not truly characters in Luke's narrative; we can set aside those mentioned in the quotation from Joel, Candace, Timothy's mother and Paul's sister (who may have been dead), and Lydia's companions. The unresponsive women are few: in the Gospel Herodias and the servant at the house of the high priest, and in Acts, the noble women in Antioch, the slave with the spirit of divination, Drusilla and Bernice. We discuss all these women in 7.5.2.

6.3 ANNA

6.3.1 Introduction

Towards the end of his infancy narrative, Luke introduces Anna to us in the following words:

> There was also a prophet, Anna the daughter of Phanuel, of the tribe of Asher. She was of a great age, having lived with her husband seven years after her marriage, then as a widow to the age of eighty-four. She never left the temple but worshiped there with fasting and prayer night and day. At that moment she came, and began to praise God and to speak about the child to all who were looking for the redemption of Jerusalem (Luke 2:36–38).

It is a long passage, 82 words, 59 in Greek, and it is not at all clear why Luke has given us so much information about this woman, apparently ignoring what Darr calls "the strictures of narrative economy."[91] There have been a number of recent attempts to elucidate the passage[92] but in our view none of these scholars succeeds in explaining why Luke should have told us so much about a woman whose words are not even recorded. We shall use our tools of intertext and co-text to argue that the first part of the passage (Luke 2:36–37a) is a sequence of Septuagintal references similar to those identified by Ó Fearghail,[93] perhaps drawn from, or an epitome of, a

---

90. Richter Reimer, *Women in Acts*, xxvi.
91. Darr, *Character Building*, 61 (referring to the infancy narrative as a whole).
92. Elliott, "Anna's Age"; Wilcox, "Anna Bat Phanuel"; Bauckham, "Anna of the Tribe of Asher"; Eddy, "Contributing out of her Poverty"; and Thurston, "Who Was Anna?"
93. See 1.3.3.2.

florilegium[94] relating to women.[95] These references are of two kinds—some relate to the contrasting fidelity and infidelity[96] of the people of Israel as shown throughout salvation history in the Septuagint, but most of them refer to the role of women in that history, women both autonomous and agentic, who act decisively at crucial moments, on their own initiative, without reference to any man, to promote God's purposes.

We argue in 6.3.11 that the criteria set out in 1.3.3.2 for accepting Septuagintal references are met.[97] We have not attempted to find all references to "daughter"[98] or "widow,"[99] as these words are used very frequently in the Septuagint.[100] In the following sections we consider the Septuagintal references in the passage in the order of the NRSV text.

6.3.2 Prophet

The first word used by Luke to describe Anna is "prophet" in the feminine form, *prophētis*. This is used of four women in the Septuagint: Miriam (Exod 15:20), Deborah (Judg 4:4), Huldah (2 Kgs 22:14, and in the parallel passage 2 Chr 34:22) and the wife of Isaiah (Isa 8:3), in which instance the word seems to mean "prophet's wife,"[101] and whom we shall exclude from consideration.[102] Miriam and Deborah, women who acted decisively, will be discussed further in 6.3.7.2 and 6.3.7.3.

The story of Huldah is told in a very similar fashion in both 2 Kings and 2 Chronicles. The version in 2 Kings is particularly relevant, as the ending of that book is closely paralleled by the ending of Acts. Huldah warned

---

94. "An anthology of key scriptural texts arranged to support . . . [a] hermeneutic" (Alexander, "Acts," 1029, referring to Qumran).

95. Carolyn Osiek points out that women taught women, but we have little knowledge of the content of this kind of teaching (Osiek, "Women in House Churches," 313). It could have incorporated such a *florilegium*.

96. Although not strictly relevant to our argument, we elucidate these to show that each detail in the passage serves Luke's purposes.

97. We have considered only one of the two Septuagintal women called Anna/Hannah (see 6.3.3), but regard this as justified in view of Luke's reworking of Hannah's canticle (1 Sam 2:1–10) in the Magnificat (Luke 1:46–55).

98. We discuss "daughter of Phanuel" in 6.3.4.

99. The use of the term "widow" in the Septuagint is considered in 6.1.3.

100. Some possible associations of the term "widow" in this passage are discussed in 6.3.9.

101. *OED*, s.v. "prophetess."

102. The Babylonian Talmud lists seven women as prophets, Sarah, Miriam, Deborah, Hannah, Abigail, Huldah, and Esther (Wilcox, "Anna Bat Phanuel," 1574).

Josiah the king of Judah that his kingdom would be destroyed because of unfaithfulness (2 Kgs 22:16–17), but that the king himself, because he had repented, would die in peace (2 Kgs 22:19–20).[103] Josiah was the only member of his family in five generations who so repented. His father, Amon, his grand-father Manasseh,[104] his sons Jehoahaz[105] and Eliakim, who changed his name to Jehoiakim,[106] and his grandsons, Jehoiachin and Zedekiah,[107] did evil and did not repent. Huldah is at the center of a long history of evil kings of Judah, but was particularly associated with the one repentant and faithful king in this period, Josiah. This reference brings together the two themes of women and the unfaithfulness of Israel. Although we do not consider Huldah further, it should be noted that she, like the other women we consider, was both autonomous and agentic.

6.3.3 The Name of "Anna"

The prophet at Jesus's presentation in the temple (Luke 2:36) in English (and by us) is called "Anna" but in the Greek text she is called "Hannah." To add to the confusion, the mother of Samuel (1 Sam 1:2) in English and by us is called "Hannah," but in the Greek text of the Septuagint she is called "Anna." This demonstrates the similarity of the two names, but it may be that at the time Luke wrote his Gospel the names were seen as identical. Luke's language, Koine, like classical Greek, does not have a letter H, and its sound is indicated by a diacritical mark, rough breathing. Breathing marks did not come into use in any written work until some centuries after Luke wrote, and it is very difficult to determine whether or how "rough breathing" applied to semitic personal names in Luke's time. "The MS evidence . . . is deserving of little confidence in itself, and these witnesses are anything but agreed among themselves."[108] So the name Anna very strongly calls to mind Hannah, the mother of Samuel, who will also be considered in 6.3.7.4.

---

103. 2 Kgs tells us that, although his kingdom was destroyed, Josiah did not die in peace but was put to death (2 Kgs 23:29). The inaccurate prophecy by Huldah is similar to the inaccurate prophecies in Acts discussed in 6.1.4.4.

104. "Did what was evil in the sight of the Lord" (4 Kgdms 21:20; similar 2 Chr 33:22).

105. 2 Kgs 23:32; 2 Chr 36:2.

106. 2 Kgs 23:34, 37; 2 Chr 36:4–5.

107. 2 Kgs 24:9, 19; 2 Chr 36:9, 12.

108. Blass, *Grammar of New Testament Greek*, 16.

6.3.4 Daughter of Phanuel of the Tribe of Asher

Phanuel is a name in two genealogies,[109] and also the name of two towns, which are more significant. One of these features in the story of the oppression of Israel by the Midianites, and their subsequent destruction at the hand of Gideon. After his victory Gideon, with three hundred men, pursued the Midianites. He asked the town of Phanuel for bread for his men, was refused, and threatened vengeance (Judg 8:8–9). After his return from the battle, "he . . . broke down the tower of Phanouel, and killed the men of the city" (Judg 8:17).

The second town of that name is referred to after the death of Solomon, when, under Jeroboam, the northern tribes (including Asher) seceded from Judah. To ensure these tribes were also separated from the temple in Jerusalem, Jeroboam made two golden heifers for the people to worship, a clear and classic example of infidelity to the Lord (1 Kgs 12:26–33). In the immediately preceding verse we are told how Jeroboam founded the city of Phanuel (1 Kgs 12:25). Both towns of Phanuel, therefore, are places closely associated with Israel turning away from the Lord, and Phanuel is a reminder, if not a symbol, of infidelity. That his daughter, Anna, is notably faithful to the Lord is analogous to the contrast between the faithfulness of Josiah, and the evil deeds of his grandfather, father, sons and grandsons, described above.

The tribe of Asher also has significance for the theme of faithfulness and infidelity, deriving from the cleansing and repair of the temple by Hezekiah and the restoration of temple worship. After the work was completed and the temple restored, Hezekiah sent messengers to call all Israel to celebrate the Passover with the tribe of Judah in the temple at Jerusalem. Here the Septuagint differs significantly from standard bibles:

> And the couriers passed through city from city in Mount Ephraim and Manasse and as far as Zaboulon, and they were, as it were, as people deriding and mocking them. But the people of Aser and some of Manasse and of Zaboulon were moved to shame and came to Ierousalem (2 Chron 30:10–11).

This contrasts with NRSV: "Only a few from Asher, Manasseh and Zebulun" (2 Chr 30:11). In the Septuagint the whole tribe of Asher[110] demonstrated their faithfulness by coming to the temple to worship with Judah,

---

109. 1 Chr 4:4; 8:25 (in some versions).

110. *Contra*, OSB, a translation from the Septuagint used liturgically by the Orthodox churches, has "some from Asher, Manasseh and Zebulun." This is also the reading in standard bibles, following the Hebrew text.

an appropriate ancestry for Anna who "never left the temple, but worshiped there" (Luke 2:37). Moreover, Anna represents one faithful tribe, Asher, and Simeon may represent the other, Judah. Jerusalem was in the territory of Judah, and the intended reader may have assumed that Simeon, in Jerusalem, was of the tribe of Judah; there is apparent co-textual support in Luke's genealogy of Jesus, which includes "Simeon, son of Judah" (3:30).

6.3.5 Serah, Daughter of Asher

Apart from the theme of fidelity described earlier, Anna's tribe, Asher, may also be significant for the theme of the role of women. The names of the grand-children (and some great-grand-children) of Jacob are listed in a genealogy at Genesis 46, at the time when Jacob and his family went down into Egypt. Only two names out of some sixty-six in the Genesis genealogy are said to be women, one being Serah, Sara in the Septuagint, the daughter of Asher (Gen 46:17). This information about Serah is given twice more,[111] three times in all, which makes it especially significant for Luke. M. Wilcox[112] raises the parallel of Anna with Serah, the daughter of Asher, pointing out that Serah was an important figure in rabbinic literature and was also regarded as a prophet or sage. He acknowledges that all of the rabbinic references are much later than the time of Luke, and Brown finds that this "makes a parallel between Luke's Anna and Serah of uncertain value."[113]

However, as for Anna and Hannah, we again see similar, indeed identical, names.[114] In the Septuagint the daughter of Asher was called Sara at Genesis 46:17 and Numbers 26:30,[115] and in the Septuagint the wife of Abraham originally had the identical name, Sara.[116] The description of Anna as being of the tribe of Asher, that is a daughter of that tribe, may therefore be an oblique reference to Sarah, the wife of Abraham.[117] Identical Greek names may have been enough for inclusion in Luke's sequence

---

111. In Num 26:46—26:30 in the Septuagint—in the context of the census on entering the promised land, and 1 Chr 7:30—Sore in the Septuagint—as part of genealogical information about the twelve tribes.

112. Wilcox, "Anna Bat Phanuel," 1575–79.

113. Brown, *Birth of the Messiah*, 688.

114. See the further close similarities of names as regards Mary and Elizabeth, noted in 6.4.1.

115. Sore in 1 Chr 7:30.

116. She had her name changed to Sarah (LXX Sarra) at God's command (Gen 17:15).

117. Wilcox notes the parallel between Serah and Sarah, and finds the two characters are confused in the rabbinic literature (Wilcox, "Anna Bat Phanuel," 1576).

of references, a suggestion given some support when the different, albeit similar, Hebrew names of the characters were linked by the rabbis. There is further co-textual evidence in the allusion in Luke 1:18[118] to the episode of Sarah's laughter (Gen 18:11–12), to which we refer in 6.3.7.[119] Although, on its own, the evidence for an allusion to Sarah is not strong, we believe that the mention of the tribe of Asher,[120] taken with the other allusions described in this section, is sufficient for it to merit consideration.

6.3.6 Anna's Age

There is disagreement as to whether Luke tells us that Anna was eighty-four years old, or had been a widow for eighty-four years and was therefore a great deal older. NRSV unambiguously makes Anna's age eighty-four and most current translations in English share this view.[121] The alternative view is that Anna, after the death of her husband was a widow for eighty-four years, and therefore her age was much more than eighty-four (see the calculation of her age below). This interpretation is found in Rieu and GNMM, and as a marginal alternative in many of the other translations, and is preferred by recent commentators.[122] The passage is better translated by Raymond Brown: "She had married as a young girl[123] and lived with her husband seven years, and then by herself as a widow[124] for eighty-four years."[125] He calculates her life-span as "about 103 years,"[126] but it is possible to be more

---

118. Identified by Litwak (*Echoes of Scripture*, 85–86).

119. See also the discussion of *rēma*, used in Genesis 18:14, in 6.4.3.

120. Bauckham, in "Anna of the Tribe of Asher," argues that Luke is referring to an actual person, and that she was of the tribe of Asher. But this does not explain why Luke described her at such length.

121. RSV, NEB, JB, TNT, NIV, and Barclay are cited by Marshall (*Gospel of Luke*, 123).

122. E.g., ibid., 123; Fitzmyer, *Luke I–IX*, 419; Johnson, *Gospel of Luke*, 54; and Brown, *Birth of the Messiah*, 467; but Joel Green, *Gospel of Luke*, 151, including n45, is not convinced because Luke is not explicit about either the age at which Anna married or her age when she encountered Jesus. His objection carries less weight if our interpretation, which sees Luke's text as literary and allusive, is correct.

123. Literally, "from her virginity"—Brown, *Birth of the Messiah*, 442.

124. Gaylin Eddy sees "Anna's status [as] given . . . in terms of her relation to or association with males" ("Contributing out of Her Poverty," 189) and that "great concern for her chastity was shown" (262). This may be so, but there is little evidence for a concern with chastity in Luke's depiction of other women. She may mean celibacy which would make more sense.

125. Brown, *Birth of the Messiah*, 436.

126. Ibid., 442.

precise, using the same information (which he drew from Jeremias).[127] After betrothal "usually entered into when the girl was between twelve and thirteen years old,"[128] the girl continued to live at her own family home, usually for about a year.[129] "Then took place the formal transfer . . . *in Galilee* . . . the wife had to be taken to her husband's home as a virgin."[130] So, Anna was betrothed at, say, 12½, living with her husband at 13½, a widow at 20½ and at the time of Luke's story, 104½. But Bauckham arrives at a similar age in a way which better fits our allusive literary reading:

> It is likely that the tradition Luke follows schematized her life in periods of seven years: two weeks of years before marriage, one week of years married, twelve weeks of years as a widow. This would make her age 105 years at the time of the event.[131]

On either calculation the closeness of the analogy with Judith, who "grew old in the house of her husband, one hundred and five years" (Jdt 16:23), seems to us inescapable.[132] Judith is discussed further in 6.3.7.5.

6.3.7 The Allusions to Women

We have identified the description of Anna as providing allusions to the fidelity and infidelity of Israel, including the reference to Huldah, and also to several women, Miriam, Deborah, Hannah, Sarah and Judith where the allusion has a different meaning. Before going on to the second half of the passage, we look more closely at these women to see what these allusions are intended to convey, taking the women in the order in which they appear in the history of Israel.

6.3.7.1 Sarah

Sarah is a very significant figure in the New Testament—she is mentioned in Romans (twice), Hebrews and 1 Peter[133]—but there are numerous ref-

---

127. Jeremias, *Jerusalem*.

128. Brown, *Birth of the Messiah*, 123.

129. Jeremias himself is more precise: the marriage "ordinarily took place one year after betrothal" (Jeremias, *Jerusalem*, 368).

130. Brown, *Birth of the Messiah*, 124.

131. Bauckham, "Anna of the Tribe of Asher," 186n78. Brown describes this as "a perfect married span and an even more perfect widowhood" (*Birth of the Messiah*, 689).

132. Brown notes that this parallel is "proposed by many scholars" (ibid., 689).

133. Rom 4:19; 9:9; Heb 11:11; 1 Pet 3:6.

erences throughout the New Testament to the children of Abraham, who, of course, in that context, were also her children. In the Septuagint she is presented as a woman of marked independence. Having passed the years of child-bearing, she gave her slave, Hagar, to Abraham: "See, the Lord has shut me off from giving birth; so go in to my slave-girl in order that you may beget children by her" (Gen 16:2). Here again the Septuagint differs from the standard version, which has: "It may be that I shall obtain children by her." The Septuagint version shows Sarah's motive as providing children for Abraham, not herself, making her action a form of *diakonia*; we have seen the importance attributed to a man having children in the stories of Tamar and the wise woman of Tekoa in 6.1.3.2.

Later, when the Lord told Abraham that she would bear a son, she was at first skeptical and laughed (Gen 18:12)—she was ninety years old (Gen 17:17)—but after the birth of Isaac she praised God in a canticle.[134]

> The Lord has made laughter for me,
> For anyone who hears will congratulate me . . .
> Who will report to Abraam that Sarra is nursing a child?
> For I have borne a son in my old age (Gen 21:6–7).

After her son, Isaac, was weaned Sarah again took the initiative, requiring Abraham to banish Ishmael, the son of her slave, Hagar, ensuring that her own son and his heirs would inherit. At this point the Lord told Abraham: "Whatever Sarra says to you, obey her voice" (Gen 21:12).[135] So, at a crucial moment in the story of Israel, Sarah acted decisively and successfully, on her own initiative (or at the interior prompting of God) and she also praised God in a short canticle.

6.3.7.2 Miriam

Miriam was the sister of Moses and Aaron—no other sister is mentioned in the genealogy of that family (Num 26:59). We are told how Pharaoh had instructed that all Israelite male children should be thrown into the Nile (Ex 1:22). After Moses was born his mother put him in the river in a papyrus basket and went away, but her daughter, Moses' sister Miriam, "was watching from a distance to learn what would happen to him" (Exod 2:4).

---

134. Although this passage is not usually translated as verse and is prose in NETS, in a commentary on the Hebrew version of Genesis, Speiser (*Genesis*, 153) so presents it, and JB shows the second part as verse. Nahum Sarna and the *JPS* translation treat v. 7 as verse (*Genesis*, 146) and Hermann Gunkel finds that "in form vv 6b, 7 are poetry" (*Genesis*, 225).

135. This is the incident referred to at length in Gal 3–4, specifically, 4:30.

At this point Pharaoh's daughter came and found the baby Moses on the banks of the Nile. Miriam, without any instruction from anyone, seized her opportunity and spoke to Pharaoh's daughter about the child (Exod 2:7). As a result Pharaoh's daughter arranged for Moses to be looked after by his mother (Exod 2:8–9), saving the child's life and ensuring that he was brought up knowing himself to be an Israelite (Exod 2:11). Without Miriam the Exodus story would not have been told, and her importance in that story is remembered in Micah 6:4: "For I brought you up from the land of Egypt, and redeemed you from a house of slavery, and I sent before you Moyses and Aaron and Mariam." Her importance was also recognized nearer Luke's time: Philo, who died about 50 CE, described the community of Therapeutrides, for whom: "[Miriam] is placed on equal footing with Moses as leader of the people: Moses leading men, Miriam leading women."[136]

We see Miriam again later, in the story of the crossing of the Red Sea, when she praised God in a short canticle:

> Let us sing to the Lord, for gloriously he has glorified himself.
>
> Horse and rider he threw into the sea (Exod 15:21).

Miriam also, at a decisive time, acted successfully on her own initiative and praised God in a canticle.

6.3.7.3 Deborah

Deborah was the judge of Israel and gave orders which were obeyed at a time when the Israelites had done "what was evil before the Lord" and were oppressed by the Canaanites, whose army was led by Sisera (Judg 4:1–3). Deborah summoned Barak and told him he was commanded by the Lord to gather an army and fight Sisera who would be given into his hand (Judg 4:6–7), but Barak was dubious and said that he would only do this if she accompanied him. Deborah did so, but told Barak that, because of his lack of faith, he would have no glory from his victory as "the Lord will give Sisera up in the hand of a woman" (Judg 4:9). Sisera's army was defeated, and he fled and was duly killed by a woman, Jael (Judg 4:17–22), and Deborah sang a long canticle of praise to the Lord, beginning:

> Hear, O kings; give ear, O mighty satraps;
> I will sing to the Lord.
> I will make music to the God of Israel (Judg 5:3).

---

136. Cohick, *Earliest Christians*, 253.

Deborah, like Sarah and Miriam, at a crucial moment for the people of Israel acted independently and successfully and praised God in a canticle.

6.3.7.4 Hannah

Next in the history of Israel comes Hannah. She was childless, and, rejecting the comforting words of her husband, prayed for a son, vowing to dedicate him to the Lord (1 Sam 1:2–18). She duly bore a son, Samuel, and refused to go with her husband to worship at Shiloh until her son was weaned (1 Sam 1:20–22), when she brought him to Shiloh and herself dedicated him to the Lord, leaving him there (1 Sam 1:24–28).[137] We are later told how Samuel anointed Saul as the first king of Israel (1 Sam 10:1), and, after Saul had failed to obey the Lord, anointed his successor David (1 Sam 16:13).

After she had dedicated Samuel, Hannah sang a canticle which provides much of the imagery for the Magnificat:

> My heart was made firm in the Lord;
> my horn was exalted in my god,
> My mouth was made wide against enemies,
> I was glad in your deliverance (1 Kgdms 2:1).

and

> The Lord makes poor and makes rich;
> he brings low, and he raises on high.
> He raises up the needy from the ground
> And lifts the poor from the dunghill,
> to make them sit with the mighty of the peoples,
> even making them inherit a throne of glory (1 Kgdms 2:7–8).

Hannah, like our other women, at a crucial moment acted decisively and successfully on her own initiative and praised God in a canticle.

6.3.7.5 Judith

The story of Judith tells how Nebuchadnezzar sought revenge on the lands from Cilicia (Southern Turkey) to Egypt, and sent an army led by Holofernes for that purpose. Holofernes destroyed the kingdom of Cilicia, and the nations of the coast of Palestine (Tyre and Sidon) surrendered to him

---

137. In the standard text Samuel's father is not named as a participant in the dedication of Samuel, whereas in the Septuagint he is so named (1 Kgdms 1:25), but it is clear that Hannah dedicated the child herself.

(Jdt 2:1—3:10). The people of Israel prepared to resist and the frontier town of Bethulia was besieged (Jdt 7:1-6). After days without water the people wanted to surrender and their leaders agreed to do so, subject to waiting for a further five days (Jdt 7:30–31). But Judith, a rich and childless[138] widow, summoned the leaders, rebuked them and told them to open the gates of the city for her so that she could go out (Jdt 8:10–36). She then made her way to the camp of Holofernes and, seizing her opportunity, decapitated him (Jdt 13:8), and returning to the city she masterminded the destruction of his army by the people of Israel (Jdt 14:1–5).

Before all this happened we are told that Judith fasted (Jdt 8:6) and that while it was happening she worshiped God (Jdt 10:8), references picked up by Luke in his description of Anna's worship and fasting (Luke 2:37). After the defeat of the enemy she sang a long canticle of praise to the Lord, beginning:

> Address my God with tambourines;
> sing to the Lord with cymbals.
> Adapt a tune and a song of praise for him;
> exalt and invoke his name (Jdt 16:1).

Like the other women, at a decisive moment Judith took independent and successful action and praised God in a canticle.

6.3.8 The Significance of the Women

Sarah, Miriam, Deborah, Hannah, and Judith are all, we suggest, specifically referred to in the description of Anna.[139] Each of them was a woman who took the lead in their episodes of the story of Israel, acting on their own initiative at crucial moments, decisively and successfully. We see Sarah active in procuring the expelling of Ishmael and ensuring the inheritance for Isaac, Miriam saving the life and Jewish heritage of Moses by persuading the daughter of Pharaoh to arrange for him to be looked after by his mother, and Deborah directing the defeat of the army of Sisera. Then we see Hannah petitioning God, resulting in the birth and dedication to God of Samuel, who anointed first Saul and then David as the first and second kings

---

138. We know she was childless as before she died she distributed her property to her husband's kin and her own (Jdt 16:24). Judith is a fictional narrative and the author may have made her childless to avoid the "widows and orphans" topos described in 6.1.3.

139. The references, with the exception of that to Sarah, are explicit.

of Israel, and Judith destroying Holofernes and his army.[140] This emphasis on women whom the Septuagint, Luke's intertext, considered important in Israel's history follows shortly after the nativity narrative, where Luke, and only Luke, portrays Mary as the most important woman in the story of Israel, the one who, without reference to her father or to Joseph, to whom she was betrothed, said: "Let it be with me according to your word" (Luke 1:38). This was another independent, decisive and successful action by a woman at the most crucial moment of all, and, like each of these women, Mary went on to praise God in a canticle, the Magnificat.[141] The description of Anna powerfully links Mary with the other women who, like her, had acted decisively and independently in the salvation history of Israel and who sang canticles in praise of God.

6.3.9 Widow

The mother of the seven brothers features in both 2 and 4 Maccabees, but especially in the latter, which "was probably written in Syria . . . in the first century,"[142] and could have been known to Luke. Although she does not fit the same pattern as the other women identified, she was seen as an important figure in the history of Israel. She is highly praised in both books: "The mother was especially admirable and worthy of honorable memory" (2 Macc 7:20), "one in soul as she was with Abraham" (4 Macc 14:20) and was "more noble than males in perseverance, more manly than men in endurance" (4 Macc 15:30). Beverly Gaventa[143] points out that the word (*odynoun*) used for the distress felt by the parents of Jesus when they could not find him (Luke 2:48) is used of the anguish felt by the mother over the death of her seven sons (4 Macc 18:9). Luke may have intended this allusion, thus linking her directly to Mary.[144] The mother's anguish is implicit in 2 Maccabees 7 and is described in 4 Maccabees 14:11–18:6, and it adds

---

140. The other two women identified as prophets by Wilcox following Talmudic usage, Abigail and Esther, did not sing a canticle. Also, Abigail (1 Sam 25) saved her husband and his household, not Israel, and Esther followed the instructions of Mordecai (Esth 4). Neither action fits the pattern we describe although Abigail was autonomous and both were agentic.

141. This reading of the Anna passage suggests that Luke may have had part of the Matthean infancy narrative as an antetext—this is discussed further in 6.3.12.

142. Saldarini, "Jewish Responses," 404.

143. Gaventa, *Glimpses of the Mother*, 68.

144. Although Luke may not have known 4 Maccabees, these parallels are suggestive.

resonance to Simeon's prophecy to Mary, that "a sword will pierce your own soul too" (Luke 2:35).

6.3.10 Anna's Own Actions

The second half of the passage describes the story of Anna herself, and we find that she too fits the pattern we have identified. We have already noted that the tribe of Asher worshiped at the temple as did Anna, and that Judith, like Anna, worshiped and fasted. It has often been assumed[145] that Anna was supported by the Temple, but we see no evidence of this in Luke's text—making her dependent, not autonomous, can be seen as an example of the patriarchal interpretation described in 6.1.

In this second section Anna began to praise God and to speak about the child—"the tense is imperfect: 'kept speaking.'"[146] She was a prophet, and we see her, without instruction and on her own initiative, like the other women, speaking publicly about the child before anyone else, man or woman.[147] Anna spoke as a prophet, was the first to proclaim Jesus[148] and, at the start of Luke's Gospel, she parallels Mary Magdalene, Joanna, Mary the mother of James, and the other women with them, who, at the end of the Gospel, were the first to speak about the Resurrection (Luke 24:10). We are not told in what way Anna spoke about the child, and there may be an allusion to the canticle of her namesake, Hannah. The ending of that canticle, which is not adapted and incorporated in the Magnificat, is as follows.

> The Lord ascended to the heavens and thundered.
> He will judge earth's ends
> and gives strength to our kings
> and will exalt the horn of his anointed, *christou* (1 Kgdms 2:10).

This Greek word for anointed was used about Jesus shortly before the Anna passage by both the angel of the Lord (Luke 2:11) and Simeon (Luke 2:26). Hannah's prophecy relates to the coming kingdom of Saul and David, to be inaugurated by her son. The same words are very appropriate for Anna to use about the child she has seen, a child of the house of David,[149] who

---

145. Spencer, "Neglected Widows," 722.
146. Brown, *Birth of the Messiah*, 442.
147. The shepherds did not do this. They "made known what had been told them about this child" to those present at Bethlehem (Luke 2:17).
148. "Simeon's function was to identify this particular child as Israel's redeemer to his parents, Anna spread the message more widely" (Seim, *Double Message*, 179).
149. Luke has told us this five times: Luke 1:27, 32, 69; 2:4, 11.

will himself bring about the kingdom of God. The description of Anna, seen as that epitome of a *florilegium* which we have described, provides a link to those words.

If Anna kept speaking about the child to "all who were looking for the redemption of Jerusalem," the narrator implies that not all were so looking. We are again reminded that some had accepted the covenant and some had not, and also that, as we have just been told by Simeon (Luke 2:34), some would accept Jesus and some would reject him.

6.3.11 To Sum Up

In 1.3.3.2 we identified four criteria which we required to be met in order to validate Septuagintal references, that is, volume, coherence, plausibility and satisfaction. We believe that the number of Septuagintal references, all similar in significance, in the Anna passage clearly meets the criterion of volume. As to the other criteria, the references which we have identified can be divided into two groups. The first group, related to the theme of faithfulness and the infidelity of Israel, meets two of the criteria, coherence and plausibility. The references are totally coherent with the prophetic statements of Mary and Simeon, referring to scattering and lifting up, to falling and rising, and to the description of Anna herself and those whom she addressed. This, taken with all the other references to fidelity and unfaithfulness in Luke-Acts, gives the theme satisfactory historical plausibility.

As regards the second theme, the autonomy and agentic faithfulness of women, our interpretation of the description of Anna is consonant with Luke's presentation of women, perhaps especially so with that of Mary, as we describe in 6.4. We consider other women in chapter 7 and argue that Luke usually presents women as autonomous and agentic, independently active in the bringing about of the kingdom of God. This is a theme explicit in our interpretation of the Anna story, and we shall also (in 7.6) consider historical plausibility. As to whether our interpretation is satisfying, or at least more satisfying than previous interpretations (insofar as they exist), that is for others to judge.

To summarize, this passage about Anna brings together from Luke's intertext, the Septuagint, a number of references to two themes of importance to Luke throughout his two-volume work. The first is the major theme of the contrasting faithfulness and infidelity of the people of Israel, brought together in Anna. The second, perhaps a less important theme for Luke, but very significant in itself, is the way that God's plans were taken forward by women, acting on their own initiative, independently of any male relatives, whether father, brother or husband. Anna herself did this, but the main thrust refers to Mary, to whom Anna spoke, who also, without any reference to Joseph, or any of her relatives, at the most crucial of moments, did what she was called upon to do in order to further God's plan, and who also praised God in a canticle.

6.3.12 A Matthean Antetext?

For many years there has been a near consensus on the solution to the synoptic problem, namely, that Matthew and Luke each used the same two written sources for their Gospels, Mark and a hypothetical document called Q. In recent years this consensus has been under attack by Mark Goodacre,[150] who has argued that a plausible solution is that Luke used two written sources, Mark and Matthew, both extant. Goodacre refers only briefly to the infancy narratives, but Raymond Brown has identified eleven points of similarity between the Matthean and Lukan versions,[151] of which ten occur in Matt 1:18—2:1. Whether or not Luke used Matthew as a source for the bulk of his Gospel, the possible use of this part of his infancy narrative is worth investigating. To do so does not necessarily imply that this part of Matthew, as we now have it, was a Lukan source. There may have been a common written source (analogous to Q) or an oral tradition, the essence of which is found in Matthew 1:18—2:1. However, pragmatically, we can here consider only how, if it had been available to him, Luke might have used the Matthean text:

> Now the birth of Jesus the Messiah took place in this way. When his mother Mary had been engaged to Joseph, but before they lived together, she was found to be with child from the Holy Spirit. Her husband Joseph, being a righteous man and unwilling to expose her to public disgrace, planned to dismiss her quietly. But just when he had resolved to do this, an angel of the Lord appeared to him in a dream and said, "Joseph, son of David, do not be afraid to take Mary as your wife, for the child conceived in her is from the Holy Spirit. She will bear a son, and you are to name him Jesus, for he will save his people from their sins." All this took place to fulfill what had been spoken by the Lord through the prophet:
>
>> "Look, the virgin shall conceive and bear a son,
>> and they shall name him Emmanuel,"

---

150. Goodacre, *Synoptic Problem*; *Case against Q*; and *Questioning Q*.
151. Brown, *Birth of the Messiah*, 34–35.

which means, "God is with us." When Joseph awoke from sleep, he did as the angel of the Lord commanded him; he took her as his wife, but had no marital relations with her until she had borne a son; and he named him Jesus (Matt 1:18–25).[152]

If Luke did have something like this passage as an antetext, his description of Anna can help to understand why he changed the antetext's description of the conception of Jesus. In Matthew's words: "When his mother Mary had been engaged to Joseph, but before they lived together, she was found to be with child from the Holy Spirit" (1:18). So, in this possible antetext Mary is not agentic nor is she shown to be autonomous. But the women alluded to in the Anna passage are very definitely both agentic and autonomous, and so are nearly all of the women who appear throughout the rest of Luke's two-volume narrative, described in 6.4 and chapter 7. The Lukan Mary, like the women referred to in the Anna story, acts without reference to her father, or to Joseph to whom she was betrothed, or any other man; she makes her own decision.

We see the description of Anna and Luke's version of the virginal conception as closely related, indeed, perhaps written to be read together. To summarize: Luke found, in Matthew, or a common source, the story of a virginal conception "from the Holy Spirit." He already knew, or perhaps deliberately devised,[153] the Anna description as a very specific series of allusions to the deeds, at crucial moments in salvation history, of women, each of whom acted independently and successfully, and who each then sang a canticle in praise of God. He reworked the Matthew narrative, and perhaps also reworked the Magnificat,[154] to show us Mary, at the most crucial moment of all, acting independently and successfully like the women referred to in the Anna narrative, and, like each of them, singing a canticle in praise of God.

---

152. Matt 2:1, not addressed here, shares with Luke only that the birth took place in Bethlehem during the time of Herod.

153. The Anna narrative, or the *florilegium* on which it could have been based, may have been written by a woman.

154. It has been argued that the Magnificat was originally put in the mouth of Elizabeth as it refers to "lowliness" (Luke 1:48) and as a whole is modeled on Hannah's canticle. This fits well with the speaker as a barren woman, rather than a virgin. For a full discussion, see Brown, *Birth of the Messiah*, 334–36.

6.4 MARY AND ELIZABETH

6.4.1 Mary and Elizabeth in the Nativity Story

The first two female characters in Luke's narrative are Mary and Elizabeth.[155] Both were prophets, people through whom God spoke. Elizabeth was "righteous before God" (Luke 1:5–6); after she conceived, she praised God (Luke 1:25) and later she "was filled with the Holy Spirit" and praised Mary and her child in a canticle (Luke 1:42),[156] showing that the Spirit had revealed Mary's circumstances to her. Luke devotes two verses (Luke 1:60–61) to emphasizing that Elizabeth's role fits our pattern. She, acting on her own initiative, ensured that the name given to her child was John, that chosen by the angelic messenger (Luke 1:13), so that she also is autonomous and agentic.

Mary accepted God's will of her own choice (Luke 1:38). The angel called her "favored one," told her that: "The Lord is with you" (Luke 1:28), and also that: "You have found favor with God" (Luke 1:30). Later, "in the powerful words of the Magnificat, she becomes not only a disciple but also a prophet."[157] Both women utter oracles, but that Mary "went with haste" to be with Elizabeth, who was in the latter part of her pregnancy, in the context of this narrative suggests that she also was a prophet in the sense of encouraging and strengthening, as described in 6.1.4. Elizabeth and Mary are both also mothers, providers of *diakonia*; that they were such providers is confirmed by the narrator, who tells us that Elizabeth's child "grew and became strong in spirit" (Luke 1:80) and that Mary's child "grew and became strong" (Luke 2:40).

Mary's economic status is shown by her ability to travel to see Elizabeth (Luke 1:39), and, after her marriage, by the sacrifice which she and Joseph offered at her purification in the temple (Luke 2:24), two young pigeons, that required of those who cannot afford the normal offering, a lamb (Lev 12:6, 8). That the cheaper offering was made means that the Lukan Joseph and Mary were poor, but had some resources—they were of the *penētes*. This is also how we are to understand Elizabeth—her husband was an ordinary priest, living not in Jerusalem but in the hill country of Judaea, so they were

---

155. In view of the use of similarity of names by Luke which we discussed in 6.3.3 and 6.3.5, it is perhaps no coincidence that in the Septuagint, *Elisabeth* was the wife of Aaron (Exod 6:23), and therefore sister-in-law to *Mariam* (Miriam—see 6.3.7.2), and in the Gospel *Elisabet*, Elizabeth, descended from Aaron (Luke 1:5), was a "relative" of *Maria*, Mary (Luke 1:36).

156. This is shown as verse in NA^{27}, although not in NRSV.

157. Gaventa, *Glimpses of the Mother*, 73.

not rich, and she was able to offer hospitality to Mary, so they were not destitute.

6.4.2 Mary in the Remainder of the Gospel and in Acts

We see Mary again in both Gospel and Acts. Luke tells us how the mother and siblings of Jesus sought to see him, and he told those around him that: "My mother and my brothers [and sisters] are those who hear the word of God and do it" (Luke 8:21). Luke has modified the version of this encounter in his antetext, Mark, in several important ways. First, he omits entirely the Markan introduction: "[His family] went out to restrain him" (Mark 3:21). He has also previously, in the story of the Nazareth synagogue (Luke 4:16-30), omitted the phrase in his antetext: "Prophets are not without honor, except . . . among their own kin, and in their own house" (Mark 6:4).[158] As a result, the Lukan intended reader, unlike the reader of Mark, is not predisposed to see a dispute between Jesus and his family. There is a further important change in that Mark concludes the scene:

> And looking at those who sat around him, he said, "*Here are my mother and my brothers*! Whoever does the will of God is my brother and sister and mother" (Mark 3:34-35, emphasis added).

That is, very explicitly, the Markan Jesus says that those around him, and not his relatives outside, are his family. Luke omits "looking at those who sat around him, he said, 'Here are my mother and my brothers'" and, as we have seen, amends the remainder of the saying to: "My mother and my brothers [and sisters] are those who hear the word, *logon*, of God and do it" (Luke 8:21). This has a different meaning to Mark's text, does not exclude his family outside, but it is also ambiguous. Fitzmyer[159] argues that Luke's version explicitly means that the mother and brothers of Jesus were among his disciples. This is a possible reading in Greek, as in English, that is: "My mother and my brothers [those people out there] are those who hear the word of God and do it." This view is rejected by Tannehill,[160] essentially on grammatical grounds.[161]

We would agree with Tannehill that the primary meaning is that Jesus described those then present and listening to him (who heard the word of

---

158. Noted in Seim, "Virgin Mother," 104n40.
159. Fitzmyer, *Luke I-IX*, 723.
160. Tannehill, *Narrative Unity*, 1:212-13.
161. Especially the absence of articles in Luke 8:21.

God and did it) as "his mother and his brothers," but would also see Jesus's words as alluding to the fact that Mary (and his brothers and sisters) did hear and do the will of God. We have seen Mary's own faith demonstrated in her assent when she heard the word of the angel sent by God (Luke 1:38), and Luke provides five reminders of her words of consent (see below). We will see her faith (and that of his siblings) again in Acts where the eleven "were constantly devoting themselves to prayer, together with certain women, including Mary, the mother of Jesus, as well as his brothers [and sisters]" (Acts 1:14). So, although this saying of Jesus primarily referred to those of his disciples to whom he was then speaking, we are to understand that Mary and his siblings also fitted the description.

6.4.3 Hearing and Doing the Word of God

Mary had demonstrated hearing and obeying when she said: "Let it be with me according to your word, *rhēma*" (Luke 1:38).[162] The narrator reminds us of this when Elizabeth, filled with the Holy Spirit, said: "Blessed is she who believed that there would be a fulfillment of what was spoken, *lelalēmenois*,[163] to her by the Lord" (Luke 1:45). We are given a second and then a third reminder when we are told that Mary "treasured all these words, *rhēmata*, and pondered them in her heart" (Luke 2:19) and again, "treasured all these things, *rhēmata*, in her heart" (Luke 2:51). As always for Luke, repetition is a way of emphasizing significance, and, indeed, there are two further reminders, the first described above—"My mother and my brothers [and sisters] are those who hear the word of God and do it" (Luke 8:21).

The second is when Luke later tells us that: "A woman in the crowd raised her voice and said to him, 'Blessed is the womb that bore you and the breasts that nursed you" (Luke 11:27), a form of testimony. Jesus responded in words close to those of Luke 8:21: "Blessed rather are those who hear the word (*logos*) of God and obey it" (Luke 11:28). *Logos*[164] and *rhēma*[165] both mean "word," so in both sayings there is a co-textual allusion to Mary's consent in the infancy narrative, which is also alluded to in Elizabeth's use of *laleō*, cited above.

---

162. Brown notes that: "The use of *rēma* rather than *logos* is not a meaningful difference. It was determined by the use of *rēma* in the preceding verse . . . which in turn was determined by Gen 18:14" (Brown, *Birth of the Messiah*, 318n64).

163. *Laleō*, "To utter words, *talk, speak*" (second meaning—BDAG, 582).

164. *Logos*, "A communication whereby the mind finds expression, word" (ibid., 599).

165. *Rhēma*, "That which is said, *word, saying, expression or statement*" (ibid., 905).

To recapitulate:

Mary said: "Here am I, the servant of the Lord; let it be with me according to your word, *genoito moi kata to rhēma sou*" (Luke 1:38).

Elizabeth said: "Blessed is she who believed that there would be a fulfillment of what was spoken to her by the Lord, *pisteusasa hoti estai teleiōsis lelalēmenois autē para kyriou*" (Luke 1:45).

Mary "treasured all these words and pondered them in her heart, *panta synetērei ta rhēmata tauta symballousa en tē kardia autēs*" (Luke 2:19).

Mary "treasured all these things in her heart, *dietērei panta ta rhēmata en tē kardia autēs*" (Luke 2:51).

Jesus said: "My mother and my brothers are those who hear the word of God and do it, *Mētēr mou kai adelphoi mou houtoi eisin hoi ton logon tou theou akouontes kai poiountes*" (Luke 8:21).

Jesus said: "Blessed rather are those who hear the word of God and obey it!, *Makarioi hoi akouontes ton logon tou theou kai phylassontes*" (Luke 11:28).

In these sayings the word of God is heard and also accepted, believed, treasured, done, or obeyed. The first four are specifically about Mary and the fifth, the first saying of Jesus, mentions his mother. The sixth is almost identical and it seems clear that Luke intends it also to refer to her. That is, Luke tells the story of the Annunciation and follows it with five reminders, more than for the conversion of Paul or the dream of Peter, emphasizing the importance to Luke of Mary's willing (autonomous and agentic) hearing and doing the word of God.

Luke does not tell us much about how Mary 'did' the word of God, and this is similar to his portrayal of other female characters, but we know that the child "grew and became strong." The care of Jesus and his brothers and sisters, including her share of the backbreaking toil of all peasant families, will have left Mary little time or energy to do more than ponder matters in her heart. But the care of children, including working in the fields to obtain food and shelter for them, is a classic example of *diakonia*, of loving service, and Luke's intended readers, like almost all his contemporaries other than the elites, were very well aware of the reality of grinding poverty.

We consider other women in Luke-Acts in the next chapter, and will then summarize our conclusions for the two chapters together.

CHAPTER 7

Other Women in Luke-Acts

7.1 INTRODUCTION

In the previous chapter we considered Luke's presentation of women in the introduction to the Gospel; in this chapter we examine the way in which he presented women in the remainder of Luke-Acts. We primarily use our tools of intertext and co-text, and, to a limited extent, context and antetext. 7.2 discusses the Hellenist widows in Jerusalem, arguing that the intertextual and co-textual evidence suggests to the intended reader that they were active in ministry, providers of *diakonia*, loving care. 7.3 considers a number of other women who were providers of *diakonia*, including Lydia, 7.4 looks at providers of witness or testimony and 7.5 at the remaining women in Luke-Acts, both those who were receptive to the message of Jesus but did not fall into any of the above categories, and those who did not respond. Some women have more than one role; we usually deal with them fully in the first relevant section, although Martha is considered with Mary in 7.5.1.1 and responsive members of local elites are discussed with the unresponsive elite of Pisidian Antioch in 7.5.2. In 7.6 we review contextual evidence to show that our interpretation of Luke's presentation of women is historically plausible in its setting in the Christian churches of the last quarter of the first century. We summarize our conclusions in 7.7.

7.2 THE HELLENIST WIDOWS

7.2.1 The Traditional View

> Now during those days, when the disciples were increasing in number, the Hellenists complained against the Hebrews because their widows were being neglected in the daily distribution of food.
> And the twelve called together the whole community of the disciples and said, "It is not right that we should neglect the word of God in order to wait on tables. Therefore, friends, select from among yourselves seven men of good standing, full of the Spirit and of wisdom, whom we may appoint to this task, while we, for our part, will devote ourselves to prayer and to serving the word" (Acts 6:1–4).

The problem in understanding the role of the Hellenist widows was described in the sixteenth century by John Calvin in a commentary on a Latin text:

> For when Luke says that the Greeks murmured, because consideration was not being given to their widows, he is reporting not something that actually did take place, but what they supposed happened . . . Also, the word *ministration* (*ministerium*) can be explained in two ways, actively or passively. For we know that widows were chosen for the diaconate of the Church at the beginning. However I myself am of the opinion that the Greeks were complaining because less generous provision was being given to their widows.[1]

Almost all subsequent commentators have taken the same view as Calvin, interpreting the widows as passive,[2] and receiving less generous provision.[3] Few mention the alternative, active, reading considered but not adopted by Calvin,[4] which is briefly raised, and rejected, by Gail O'Day:

---

1. Calvin, *Commentaries on the Acts of the Apostles*, 159.

2. Clarice Martin suggested that "the assumption [that 'all' widows were poor in pre-industrial, patriarchal, Greco-Roman and Jewish communities] may warrant further investigation" ("Acts," 781). 7.2.2 attempts that investigation.

3. Those taking this view include Bruce (*Acts*, 151), Haenchen (*Acts*, 260–62), Dillon ("Acts," 740), Tannehill (*Narrative Unity*, 2:82), Johnson (*Acts*, 105–6), Barrett (*Critical and Exegetical Commentary*, 1:306), Fitzmyer (*Acts*, 348), and Witherington (*Acts*, 248).

4. Barrett notes that: "1 Tim 5:9–13 may refer to an order of widows in a position to care for others as well as to widows in need of care" (*Critical and Exegetical Commentary*, 1:310).

"Women are the object of ministry in Acts 6:1–6, not agents of ministry."[5] This interpretation is also considered by Elisabeth Schüssler Fiorenza:

> The expression that they were "overlooked" or "passed over" in the daily *diakonia* or ministry could indicate either that they were not assigned their turn in the table service or that they were not properly served.[6]

She does not, as we understand her, attempt to resolve the issue, although Turid Karlsen Seim interprets her as arguing that:

> When the Hellenist widows are overlooked . . . this need not mean that they are not getting the daily ration to which the widows are entitled: rather, it suggests that these widows are passed over when it is their turn to preside at the daily meal.[7]

A few other scholars hold this view, including H. Kraft, who provides a more detailed description of widows in the early church:

> Care for widows is to be distinguished from the institution of widows who serve the community and are compensated (originally by food, etc.) . . . The official widows in the early Jerusalem church were responsible for collecting and preparing food for the meals taken communally in the various houses (Acts 6:1; 2:46). On this Jerusalem model there also arose in the churches of the first (Hellenistic) missions cooperatives of "saints," maintained by the "widows" ("saints and widows," 9:41). Tabitha, whom Peter brought back to life, was a disciple—a virgin or widow—in such an organization, and was responsible for making clothing.[8]

None of the scholars cited gives detailed evidence in support of their point of view. Haenchen suggests that:

> Perhaps the number of Hellenistic widows was relatively large, for many pious Jews in the evening of their days settled in Jerusalem so as to be buried near the Holy City; the widows of such

---

5. O'Day, "Acts," 308.
6. Schüssler Fiorenza, *In Memory of Her*, 166.
7. Seim, *Double Message*, 72–73. In support of her interpretation Seim cites Schüssler Fiorenza, *In Memory of Her*, 165, whom we interpret more ambiguously (see above). Seim herself views the widows as passive beneficiaries (see 234, 242).
8. Kraft, "Chēra," 466.

men had no relatives at hand to look after them and tended to become dependent on public charity.⁹

The only support cited for this suggestion is a "personal communication from K. H. Rengstorf,"¹⁰ but the theory has since become popular, having been picked up, for example, by Barrett, without Haenchen's "perhaps"¹¹ and Witherington.¹² We consider this further in 7.2.2.

Commentators¹³ also refer to the descriptions of widows in the Old Testament, for example, Ricci:

> Their sad state is confirmed by the frequent references the Old Testament makes to the condition of widows, either to confirm that they were under God's protection, or to show rules designed to alleviate their distress, or to deprecate the injustices of which they were victims.¹⁴

Ricci notes nineteen Old Testament references in support of her view, but we have argued in 6.1.3.1 that she also is mistaken. Spencer finds that the widows need to be understood in the light of the use of the term "widow" in the Gospel.¹⁵ However, he there finds that Anna "relies on [the temple] as her principal support system,"¹⁶ that the widow of Nain "faces a precarious future"¹⁷ and the widow before the unjust judge is "needy."¹⁸ We see each of these interpretations as mistaken.¹⁹

More recently, Reta Finger has considered this passage, coming to conclusions similar to ours, although her focus is historical, and on the nature of the meals rather than the status of the widows. She rejects the idea that there was an organized charitable distribution, and finds the idea of dependent widows implausible:

---

9. Haenchen, *Acts*, 261.
10. Ibid., 261n1.
11. Barrett, *Critical and Exegetical Commentary*, 1:310.
12. Witherington, *Acts*, 248.
13. E.g., Fitzmyer, *Acts*, 345.
14. Ricci, *Mary Magdalene*, 76.
15. Spencer, "Neglected Widows," 719.
16. Ibid., 722.
17. Ibid., 724.
18. Ibid., 726.
19. See 7.2.4.3 for both the widow of Nain and the widow before the unjust judge.

> Only when "the poor" are "the other"—the "charity cases," those "not like us"—can an organization relegate their care to a committee who hands them some alms on the side.[20]
>
> ... It hardly meant that [these widows] sat around lamenting their poverty and expecting handouts from the community ... Instead, they would have been given work within the community, the most obvious being meal preparation and serving.[21]

However, being "given work within the community" seems dubious. Most women, whether widows or not, would have found their own work, both within the community (*diakonia*) and outside it (in order to support themselves).

7.2.2 Context: Widows, Property, and Work

Richard Bauckham has described seven different ways in which a woman could obtain and hold property, even if she were a widow,[22] and there is a range of evidence that at least some widows did own property (see below).[23] The usual resource of a widow in Judaea was her *kettubah*, the amount guaranteed under her marriage contract. Such a contract[24] was "mentioned already in Tob 7:14,[25] dated as early as the beginning of the Second Temple period"[26] and was in essence a monetary arrangement between the bride and groom with the purpose of ensuring the bride's maintenance in the event of divorce or the husband's death.[27] Ilan notes that "the rabbis tried to find strictly legal ways to bestow property on a woman after the death of her husband[28] even if she was not his direct heir."[29]

---

20. Finger, *Widows and Meals*, 90.
21. Ibid., 262.
22. Bauckham, *Gospel Women*, 121–35.
23. See Finger, *Widows and Meals*, 211–14.
24. Léonie Archer does not think that this passage refers to a *kettubah* (Archer, *Beyond Rubies*, 172).
25. In NETS, 7:13.
26. Ilan, *Jewish Women*, 89.
27. Luise Schottroff suggests that the *kettubah* would enable a woman to maintain herself only if she also had full time employment (Schottroff, *Lydia's Impatient Sisters*, 95). This seems plausible as few households would have been able to support a woman who did not work.
28. Bauckham suggests that in Judaea a widow may also have inherited not only her *kettubah*, but also her dowry (*Gospel Women*, 127–30).
29. Ilan, *Jewish Women*, 168.

Evidence of women inheriting property is also found in Tobit, which "was probably written during the third century BCE"[30] where there is a:

> Stipulation that Tobias will receive the remainder of his property only after both [Raguel] and Edna have died (8:21). The implication is that if a husband dies first, the wife inherits.[31]

There is further evidence in the Babatha archive, dating from the Judaean desert in the early second century, which records four women who owned significant amounts of property, Babatha herself, her father's wife, her second husband's daughter and a neighbor.[32] We have also seen in chapter 2 that widows of the house of Herod (Salome, the sister of Herod, and Bernice) were wealthy[33] and that Salome inherited and bequeathed property.[34]

Widows could also work—Ruth gleaned the harvests (Ruth 2:7–23) and "after Tobit is blinded, [his wife][35] becomes the wage-earner and engages in 'women's work' outside the home."[36] In a city those with resources provided employment:

> The elite's devaluation of work, above all manual labor, makes a host of menials mandatory. Cooks, sweepers, carriers, drivers, nursemaids, valets are all indispensable to the effective functioning of the household.[37]

In strictly segregated households those who worked in the women's realm would have been predominantly, if not exclusively, other women. Indeed, the greater the segregation, the greater the employment opportunities for women. Sarah Pomeroy identifies over two dozen occupations for women (slaves and freedwomen) in Rome,[38] and a number of other occupations

---

30. Saldarini, "Jewish Responses," 295–96.
31. Bow and Nickelsburg, "Patriarchy with a Twist," 132.
32. Ilan, *Jewish Women*, 170, 171.
33. Ilan identifies Julia Crispina, a major figure in the Babatha archives, as the grand-daughter of Bernice from her marriage to Herod of Chalcis (*Integrating Women*, 217–33). The women who owned the property dealt with in the archive, however, were not of that family.
34. Herodias also had wealth of her own, and when her husband was deposed Gaius offered to let her retain it, but out of loyalty to her husband Antipas she refused (Josephus, *Ant* 18.253–54).
35. Not, of course, a widow but she supports herself and her family.
36. Bow and Nickelsburg, "Patriarchy with a Twist," 136.
37. Sjoberg, *Pre-Industrial City*, 203.
38. Pomeroy, *Goddesses, Whores*, 191–92.

for women born free.[39] However, their wages were probably very low; Luise Schottroff has found that women's wages were about half those of men.[40]

We should be aware that widows, like everyone else not of the elite, not only could but had to work. Some will have been fortunate and worked in the households of their fathers, brothers or children, carrying out domestic duties. But many, perhaps most, will have had to work outside the home.[41] How else were they to live? There was little organized almsgiving before the events described in Acts 2–6.[42] Widows in Luke-Acts should not automatically be assumed to be destitute, and, in particular, they cannot be assumed to be unable to work. Poor women had to do so, and their lifestyle was always very different from that of those with ample resources:

> Many urban lower-class and outcaste women are forced to some kind of gainful employment from time to time to keep the family going. If a woman loses her husband she can not always depend upon relatives for support—they are also struggling to make ends meet—and thus must make her own way in the community . . . Peasant women universally work in the fields alongside their husbands . . . How can women be cloistered when the whole family is crowded into a one- or two-room shanty? If seclusion of women is to be carried out, a large house is required with entirely separate living quarters and recreational areas.[43]

7.2.3 Widows in the Septuagint

We argued in 6.1.3.1 that widows in the Septuagint, except when associated with orphans, were never shown as destitute. In other instances they are seen to act decisively and effectively, especially where they are named.[44] What is more, their actions are always described favorably—each in her own way furthered God's purposes.

---

39. Ibid., 198–202.
40. Schottroff, *Lydia's Impatient Sisters*, 94–95.
41. See Bauckham, *Gospel Women*, 132–33.
42. For organized charity in Jerusalem, see 7.2.4.2.
43. Sjoberg, *Pre-Industrial City*, 169. He was writing about pre-industrial cities generally, but Jerusalem is unlikely to have differed greatly.
44. E. g., Tamar and Judith.

7.2.4 The Co-Text

We now turn to co-text, including further references to the intertext, to attempt to determine whether Luke saw the widows as active or passive, examining the following aspects:

1. The meaning of "complain" (7.2.4.1);
2. The description in Acts of charitable activities in Jerusalem, using as a model the well-known description of the "poor bowl" and "poor basket" by Joachim Jeremias (7.2.4.2);
3. The use of the term "*chēra*," "widow," in Luke's writings (7.2.4.3).

7.2.4.1 Complain

The Greek word translated as "complained" is *gongysmos*, a noun meaning "murmuring." There are several cognate words with similar meaning and of some forty instances of these words in the Septuagint, almost all are complaining about God, a meaning the intended reader will see as derogatory to those complaining. Most instances are in Exodus and Numbers, and relate to the Israelites in the desert, complaining about food, water or danger of some kind. Some of their complaints may have been formally directed against Moses and Aaron, but in reality, their complaints were against God.

> The Lord heard your complaining which you complain against us, then we, what are we? For not against us is your complaining, but rather against God (Exod 16:8).

In Exodus we are told that the Lord sometimes listened to the murmurings of the Israelites. So he provided water at Marah (Exod 15:25), and then provided manna (Exod 16), and again provided water in response to grumbling (Exod 17:2–6). At this point Moses:

> Called the name of that place Testing, *Peirasmos*, and Raillery, *Loidorēsis*, because of the railing of the sons of Israel and because they tested the Lord, saying, "Is the Lord among us or not?" (Exod 17:7).

The place became a byword: "You shall not tempt the Lord your God, as you tempted in the Temptation, *Peirasmōi*" (Deut 6:16).[45]

---

45. There are further similar references: Num 20:13, 24; 27:14; Deut 9:22; 32:51; Ps 81:7 (LXX 80:8); 106 (LXX 105):32 and 95 (LXX 94):8.

Again, at Numbers 11:1 we find that: "The people were muttering wicked things," but the muttering or complaint is clearly shown to be unjustified:

> The rabble among them craved with desire, and after they sat down, they wept—also the sons of Israel—and said, "Who shall feed us with meat? We remembered the fish that we used to eat in Egypt for nothing, and the cucumbers and the melons and the leeks and the onions and the garlic. But now our soul is parched; our eyes are toward nothing except the manna" (Num 11:4–6).

The rabble (*epimiktos*—motley group) complained about the lack of meat, but could not even say that they ate meat in Egypt; it was fish and the range of vegetables that they remembered. To confirm God's disapproval they were punished for their grumbling, at Num 11:1 and again at Num 11:19–20. Of the forty or so instances in the Septuagint, the only ones where no derogatory meaning is implied by *gongysmos* and its cognates are Judges 1:14[46] and Sirach 31:24,[47] to which should perhaps be added Joshua 9:18, where the congregation muttered against the leaders because those leaders had been tricked by the inhabitants of Gibeon. In these instances the use of *gongysmos* has nothing to do with God.

In Acts the Hellenists complain against the Hebrews, but the involvement of the apostles reminds the intended reader of the grumbling about Moses and Aaron cited above. There are six parallels between Numbers 11 and Acts 6:

1. In Numbers the people complained about the manna which was received daily (Num 11:9), in Acts about the daily distribution (Acts 6:1).
2. In Numbers there was a motley group, called a rabble in NETS (Num 11:4), in Acts, Hebrews and Hellenists (Acts 6:1).
3. Moses said that he could not carry the burden alone (Num 11:14), as did the apostles (Acts 6:2–4).
4. Both Moses and the apostles were helped by men to whom the Spirit had been given (Num 11:17; Acts 6:3–5).[48]

---

46. A daughter grumbling to her father about a dowry.
47. Grumbling about a man stingy with bread, contrasted with a generous one.
48. These four parallels (and others) were noted by Goulder (*Type and History*, 56, 170).

5. Moses did not choose the elders[49] but called together existing elders (Num 11:16, 24), the apostles did not choose the seven, but asked the people to choose them (Acts 6:3).

6. The Spirit was not restricted by the expectations of either Moses or the apostles; in Numbers the Spirit was received by two men not called by Moses (Num 11:26), and in Acts we see two of the seven who received the Spirit going on to do things other than that prescribed by the twelve (Acts 6:8–8:40).

The story of the widows, after identifying the seven men chosen by the community, tells that:

> They had these men stand before the apostles, who prayed and
> laid their hands on them, *epethēkan autois tas cheiras* (Acts 6:6).

NRSV, like most translations,[50] says it was the apostles who laid their hands on the men, but this is another example of patriarchal aggrandizement (in this case, of the role of the twelve):

> The whole company of believers, not the apostles alone, laid
> their hands on the seven men. There is no question that this is
> the grammatical meaning of Luke's words . . . if he meant something different he failed to express what he meant.[51]

This is a further parallel with Numbers where we are told that: "The sons of Israel shall place their hands, *epithēsousin hoi huioi Israēl tas cheiras*, on the Leuites" (Num 8:10). It is perhaps more likely that, following this precedent in Numbers, Luke did express what he meant,[52] and the whole company, in Acts men and women, laid on hands.

In view of the above, a reference to Numbers 11 in Acts 6 is probable, so that the word *gongysmos* in Acts has a similar connotation. This word and its cognates are also usually used in a derogatory way in the New Testament, that is, to describe people whose complaining or grumbling is without good grounds.[53] Luke uses these words to describe people complaining about

---

49. As he did in the version of the story at Exod 18:21–27. The people chose the elders at Deut 1:9–18.

50. A few translations are ambiguous.

51. Barrett, *Critical and Exegetical Commentary*, 1:315. He persuades Culy and Parsons on this point (*Acts*, 110).

52. In addition to the references to Numbers 11, Luke, in his description of the Baptist (Luke 1:15) referred to Num 6:3. We can be confident that he knew the Numbers 8 passage.

53. It is used neutrally at John 7:32 where it seems to mean muttering.

Jesus or his disciples,⁵⁴ and other New Testament writers also use them for this purpose, or with rebukes or injunctions not to grumble.⁵⁵ This usage, in both the Septuagint and the New Testament, taken with the parallels to Num 11 described above, confirms that the complaining in Acts 6 was unjustified.⁵⁶

The widows, therefore, complained without good reason, but it is difficult to reconcile this with their receiving less than their share of the daily distribution: to complain because you are deprived of food is hardly unjustified.⁵⁷ If, however, the complaining was about status, about not being offered a share in the active ministry described by Calvin, it could more readily be seen as unjustified, perhaps especially by male leaders of the church, which could account for the somewhat tetchy response of the apostles (Acts 6:2).

7.2.4.2 Charitable Activities in Jerusalem

Another approach to the question of the widows is to consider the meaning of the "daily distribution of food."⁵⁸ Jeremias described the daily and weekly charitable distributions performed at Jerusalem by Jewish almoners and compared them with this passage in Acts, seeing the distribution described in Acts 6:1 as a daily distribution made to the poor and especially widows.⁵⁹

> It is instructive to make a comparison between the two corresponding Jewish systems of . . . [the] "poor bowl" and . . . "poor basket." These may be distinguished as follows: The [poor bowl] was distributed daily among wandering paupers, and consisted of food (bread, beans and fruits, with the prescribed cup of wine at Passover). The [poor basket] was a weekly dole to the poor of the city and consisted of food and clothing.⁶⁰

---

54. Luke 5:30; 15:2; 19:7.

55. Matt 20:11; John 6:41, 43, 61; 7:12; 1 Cor 10:10; Phil 2:14; 1 Pet 4:9; Jude 16.

56. Koperski has identified a parallel between Acts 6:1–6 and Luke 10:38–42 (discussed in 7.5.1.1), which also supports this view, linking the complaining by Martha (for which she was rebuked by Jesus) to the complaining by the apostles.

57. The sons of Israel in the Numbers passage cited above complained about the menu, not the quantity.

58. There is no specific mention of food in the Greek text.

59. As do Haenchen (*Acts*, 261–62) and Barrett (*Critical and Exegetical Commentary*, 1:310).

60. Jeremias, *Jerusalem*, 131.

Brian Capper finds this application anachronistic[61] and sees the origin of the system "in the troubled times following the destruction of AD 70."[62]

> Jeremias argues that the Rabbinic "basket" and "tray," which are well attested only for the 2nd century, operated in pre-AD 70 Jerusalem. G. F. Moore is cautious about an early dating of the Rabbinic system, noting that there are only "scanty intimations" of it before the Hadrianic war, and nothing from the 1st century. D. Seccombe has shown that Jeremias' evidence for the early dating carries no weight and lists some evidence against. Accounts of the relief organized in two pre-70 famines make no mention of such a system . . . The origins of the Rabbinic system are later.[63]

Luke wrote Acts a number of years after AD 70, that is, at a time when Capper thought the rabbinic system might have been developing, and we suggest that it can help us to understand this passage. First, let us look more closely at the descriptions of charitable activities in chapters 2 and 4:

> All who believed were together and had all things in common; they would sell their possessions and goods and distribute the proceeds to all, as any had need. Day by day, as they spent much time together in the temple, they broke bread at home and ate their food with glad and generous hearts (Acts 2:44–46).

and

> There was not a needy person among them, for as many as owned lands or houses sold them and brought the proceeds of what was sold. They laid it at the apostles' feet, and it was distributed to each as any had need (Acts 4:34–35).

That they would "distribute the proceeds to all," that "day by day . . . they broke bread *at home*" and that "[the proceeds were] distributed to each as any had need" suggests a method of distribution similar in principle to the weekly dole, the poor basket, described by Jeremias, except that it seems to have occurred "as any had need" rather than weekly. The "proceeds"[64] distributed would probably be cash, and distributed is in the imperfect, suggesting an ongoing process. This, like Jeremias's poor basket, would be

---

61. A view shared by Fitzmyer (*Acts*, 348).
62. Capper, "Palestinian Cultural Context," 351.
63. Ibid., 351.
64. "Proceeds" at Acts 2:45 translates a pronoun "*auta*," referring to what was sold, and at Acts 4:34, "*timas*," meaning price as in 5:2.

appropriate for householders who could have obtained provisions for use in their own homes where "they broke bread" (Acts 2:46), perhaps with other members of the community.

By contrast the passage at Acts 6:1 refers to a daily distribution. Applying Jeremias's model, this would have been for "wandering paupers," and would have been administered by representatives of the community. If widows, as a group,[65] were involved, it would be as those representatives, in an active role. The text is compatible with this view. The Hellenist widows were neglected, *paretheōrounto*, but the prime meaning of *paratheōreō* is "overlook,"[66] or "pay insufficient attention."[67] If they were overlooked it was because the Hebrews, and perhaps the Hebrew widows, were monopolizing the task. Applying this model, the tables (*trapezais*) at which the apostles would not serve (Acts 6:2) were money-tables, and the phrase refers not to the daily distribution (of food) mentioned in Acts 6:1, but to the distribution "as any had need" described in Acts 2:44–46. This would include the supply of funds to those responsible for the daily distribution, that is, the group from which the Hellenist widows felt excluded. There is co-textual support for this interpretation in that *trapeza* is used elsewhere by Luke to mean "bank" (Luke 19:23).[68]

There is further co-textual support in the apostles' refusal to "wait, *diakonein*, on tables" (Acts 6:2). Luke uses that word with financial connotations on several occasions. Women "provided, *diēkonoun*, for them [Jesus and, perhaps, the disciples][69] out of their resources" (Luke 8:3). The disciples in Antioch decided to "send relief, *diakonian*" to the believers in Judaea (Acts 11:29) and in the same context Barnabas and Saul are described as "completing their mission, *diakonian*" (Acts 12:25).[70] So, Luke uses the noun twice, and the verb once in relation to financial services. It is, we believe, likely that he also used the verb in this sense in relation to the apostles and the widows. It may be because of these meanings of *trapeza* and *diakonein* that NRSV gives an alternative reading, "keep accounts," GNMM has "to handle finances" and The Message "help with the care of the poor."

---

65. Wandering paupers could, of course, include individual women, perhaps widows.

66. Balz and Schneider, "Paratheōreō," 22.

67. BDAG, 763.

68. He uses it more often in the ordinary meaning of table (Luke 16:21; 22:21, 30; Acts 16:34).

69. Textual witnesses disagree as to whether they provided for "him" or "them"—see 7.3.2.2.

70. The word group is also used by Paul in this sense: Rom 15:25, 31; 2 Cor 8:4, 19–20; 9:1, 12–13.

This application of the model makes, we suggest, better sense of the three passages in Acts, which then describe two different procedures. The passages in Acts 2 and 4 are linked to the donation of gifts and the sharing of the proceeds "as any had need," and the passage in Acts 6 to a daily distribution, using part of the proceeds for those, probably not householders, needing help on a daily basis. This may have been the view of Kirsopp Lake, who, without going into detail, commented on the relationship of these passages to the rabbinical system later described by Jeremias:

> The natural explanation of the story [of "communism" in Acts 4–6] is that the Christians formed a separate community in so far as they collected and distributed a "basket" and a "tray" independently of the rest of the Jewish population . . . It is clear that the organized charity implied in Acts vi is exactly similar to that described in Rabbinical writings.[71]

The model has been described as existing after the temple had been destroyed, some years after the time described in Acts. The Christians of Acts seem to have made their arrangements without reference to the temple, and given broadly equivalent attitudes to almsgiving, the practical solutions may have been similar. However, Finger sees it differently:

> Since meals are thus in view in 6:1–2, they must refer back to the daily bread-breaking and communal meals of 2:42, 46, which include *everyone* in various household situations. There is no indication whatsoever that "the needy" are singled out and given a daily sit-down meal at a table. Rather, there are no needy (4:34) because possessions are shared and meals are eaten in common.[72]

But Finger's view is compatible with our model. If, as she suggests, daily meals were eaten at home, that is where householders (including widows) would have invited one or more of those in need to share their meal. However, to give a daily distribution to householders does not seem sensible, which is why the rabbis ordered matters in a different way. The Christians' equivalent of the "basket" may have been distributed daily, but the householders would not come to the distribution every day, but only as they had need.

In Finger's interpretation the community invited guests to share their tables at home while in the more traditional view, the Christians ran a kind of daily soup-kitchen or food-bank for those in need. In either scenario,

---

71. Lake, "Communism," 149.
72. Finger, *Widows and Meals*, 257.

we see the main beneficiaries of the daily distribution undertaken by representatives of the community as the homeless and destitute, probably including non-Christians. Hellenist widows are mentioned, but they were not the beneficiaries, rather they aspired to be the representatives of the community who undertook the distribution of resources. Luke did not see widows as destitute or passive, nor would his intended audience have done so—they would probably have regarded such a suggestion as ridiculous for the reasons put forward by Finger (see 7.2.1).

7.2.4.3 Other Widows in Luke-Acts

In Luke's own writings widows are almost invariably shown as active in promoting the coming of the kingdom, so that they do not follow the Septuagint stereotype of the destitute described in 5.5.2 and there is very little evidence of destitution. We consider here those widows of whom Luke uses the word "*chēra*," seeking to set aside the "dominant negative" view of women as passive described in chapter 1.

We discussed Anna (Luke 2:36–38) in 6.3. We have no information on her economic circumstances[73] but she herself spoke about the child and, as we have shown, Luke in his description of her incorporated references to women notably active in the salvation history of Israel.

The widow of Nain (Luke 7:11–17) has traditionally been regarded as being destitute after the death of her son, her only means of support,[74] but there is no indication that she was dependent upon her son or was unable to work. Luke puts the emphasis in his story on her familial relation with her son, closely paralleling both the story of the daughter of Jairus (Luke 8:41–42, 49–56) and that of the widow of Zarephath (see below). In neither of these instances was the child a support for his or her mother. The son of the widow of Nain is called *neaniske*, a diminutive of *neanias*, both of which normally mean "youth, young man,"[75] but this does not mean that he was the support, much less the sole support, of his mother.

There is a close parallel between the story of the widow of Nain and that of the widow of Zarephath,[76] including an exact quotation, "and he gave

---

73. Despite this, commentators, for example, Spencer cited 7.2.1, have regarded her as being maintained by the temple. Such a view seems at variance with the avarice of the chief priests, described in 4.2.5, and Acts provides no evidence for it.

74. E.g., Marshall (*Gospel of Luke*, 283), Fitzmyer (*Luke I-IX*, 658). More recent commentators, e.g., Bock, *Luke 1*, 646–55, and Green, *Gospel of Luke*, 290–91, draw no such inference.

75. BDAG, 667.

76. Luke specifically mentions the widow of Zarephath (Luke 4:26). Klutz, *Exorcism*

him to his mother, *kai edōken auton tēi mētri autou*" (Luke 7:15; 3 Kgdms 17:23). The widow of Zarephath, as we saw in 6.1.3.1, was not destitute as it is normally understood. Although, like everyone else, she was suffering in the famine described in 1 Kings, she did, albeit with miraculous help, feed Elijah for the duration of the famine. Her son is described as *paidariōi*, a diminutive of *pais,* (3 Kgdms 17:21), so is not to be seen as a support for his mother.

If Luke had intended to present the widow of Nain as facing destitution following the death of her son, he could have followed the Septuagintal stereotype of widows and orphans by continuing with his model of the widow of Zarephath, who had young children (3 Kgdms 17:12, *teknois*, 13, 15). He went out of his way to reject that symbol in favor of an only child, emphasizing maternal affection. So, Luke did not intend his audience to see economic reliance upon her son as characteristic of the widow of Nain. Rather, like Jairus and his wife, she was a parent grieving for her only child.

The persistent widow in the parable prevailed on an unjust judge to give her justice (Luke 18:2–5). She was clearly active in her own cause, and although Jesus's story does not describe the nature of the dispute, "some kind of *economic* exploitation seems plausible."[77] In our view she had a claim upon resources of some kind,[78] and was being unjustly deprived of all or part of these. Reid summarizes the message of the parable, which does not imply destitution:

> When one doggedly resists injustice, faces it, names it, and denounces it until justice is achieved, then one is acting as God does.[79]

Similarly, the widows robbed by the scribes (Luke 20:47) must have owned something of which they could be robbed. They and the widow of the two small coins (Luke 21:1–4), the only demonstrably destitute widow in Luke-Acts, are described in two incidents which are very closely connected, in Luke as in his antetext (Mark 12:38–44).[80] Although the widow

---

Stories, 56–57, has also identified extensive parallels between her story and that of the man with an unclean spirit (Luke 4:31–37), see 56–57, and other parallels with the story of the Gerasene demoniac (8:26–39), see 109.

77. Spencer, "Neglected Widows," 725.

78. See 7.2.2 for possible claims of this kind.

79. Reid, "Beyond Petty Pursuits," 293. She adds that Luke "recasts [the widow] in a docile and acceptable role . . . There is nothing threatening about a widow who prays all day long" (293). This seems an idiosyncratic view—Holofernes would not agree.

80. This passage contains the only instances of *chēra* in Mark's Gospel. Matthew does not use it.

of the coins was very poor, she nevertheless, as Jesus says, "put in [to the treasury] more than all of them ... she out of her poverty has put in all she had to live on" (Luke 21:3–4). Despite her destitution she furthered God's kingdom.

In Acts we see the widows with the body of the deceased Tabitha (in Greek Dorcas) "weeping and showing tunics and other clothing that Dorcas had made while she was with them" (Acts 9:39). Fitzmyer, citing BDF in support, claims that:

> The middle [participle] *epideiknymenai* indicates that the widows were "showing themselves" in the robes that they were actually wearing, which Dorcas had made for them.[81]

However, what BDF actually says is that it "*can be* to show on oneself,"[82] a more tentative view shared by Bruce.[83] Stanley Porter has a different view of the middle voice:

> Most [grammarians] are agreed that a reflexive middle sense ("he washed himself"), in which the agent (subject) and recipient (object) of the action are the same, is *not* the predominant one in the Hellenistic period ... A better and more comprehensive description is that *the Greek middle voice expresses more direct participation, specific involvement, or even some form of benefit of the subject doing the action* ... The features of participation, involvement or benefit are not meant to convey only positive connotations, but to describe the heightened involvement of the subject in the event.[84]

The text, therefore, may be read, and, we believe, should be read, as the widows having heightened participation or involvement in the clothes, and as having made them with Dorcas,[85] not as wearing them. Further support for this view is found where Luke describes "clothing that Dorcas had made while she was *with them, met' autōn*" (Acts 9:39), emphasis added. The English phrase "with them" could mean while she was alive,[86] but the

---

81. Fitzmyer, *Acts*, 445. This interpretation is also found in BDAG, 370.
82. BDF, §316.1, emphasis added.
83. Bruce, *Acts*, 213.
84. Porter, *Idioms of Greek New Testament*, 67.
85. Barrett (*Critical and Exegetical Commentary*, 1:485) cites Delebecque (*Actes des Apôtres*, 48) as taking the text to mean that "Dorcas had had an ouvroir, a workshop, with the widows," which is similar to the description of widows by Kraft, cited in 7.2.1.
86. So Fitzmyer, *Acts*, 445, "still with them."

Greek, *meta*, does not so readily lend itself to such an interpretation,[87] and Luke conveys the concept elsewhere using a different preposition, *syn hymin* (Luke 24:44). *Meta* can mean:

1. "*in the midst of, among*" in a local sense;
2. a form of relationship . . . "the person in whose fellowship . . . something takes place," or "existence with someone";
3. "a common activity or experience" or "the joint activity of two parties" or "any other association of persons."[88]

Each of these meanings has Tabitha making the coats and garments in the company of the widows, and the most obvious interpretation of this is that they made them together, in a kind of sewing circle, so that the widows ministered to those in need, giving them the clothing which they had made together with Tabitha, an interpretation more consistent with Luke's other descriptions of widows as active in ministry.[89]

7.3 PROVIDERS OF DIAKONIA

7.3.1 Diakonia

Although *diakonia* and related words can carry a range of meanings, including acting as an intermediary, or providing cultic services (meanings prominent in Acts),[90] in the Gospel it always means personal service.[91] A great many of the women mentioned in Luke-Acts provide such personal service, to Jesus or to others, implicitly including, at the beginning of the Gospel, the care provided by Mary and Elizabeth to their sons. Provision of such service is generally seen in society as a subordinate function, but the Lukan Jesus says in an important passage (also discussed in chapter 5):

> The kings of the Gentiles lord it over them; and those in authority over them are called benefactors. But not so with you; rather the greatest among you must become like the youngest, and the

---

87. It may have such a meaning at John 13:33.
88. Radl, "Meta," 413.
89. Finger has a similar view: "Tabitha employed these women to work in the shop in her home as a way of helping them support themselves" (*Widows and Meals*, 260). But why see it as a matter of employment? Luke does not tell us that Aquila and Priscilla employed Paul (Acts 18:3).
90. Acts 1:17, 25; 6:4; 12:25 (about the collection for Jerusalem—see 11:29–30); 19:22; 20:24; 21:19.
91. Luke 4:39; 8:3; 10:40; 12:37; 17:8; 22:26, 27, also Acts 6:1, 2 (but see 7.2 above); 19:22.

leader like one who serves, *diakonōn*. For who is greater, the one who is at the table or the one who serves? Is it not the one at the table? But I am among you as one who serves (Luke 22:25–27).

This is a complete reassessment of the role of service:

> Jesus in His emphatic statement (*egō de* . . .) does not oppose to [the natural and especially Greek] view the general thought that serving is greater than being served. Instead, He points to the actuality: I am among you as a servant. This is said by the uncontested leader of the disciples, by the Son of Man who knows that He is Lord of the kingdom of God.[92]

Another example is in the parable of the watchful slaves, where: "The master . . . will fasten his belt and have them sit down to eat, and he will come and serve them" (Luke 12:37).[93] So, personal service is not in any way an inferior activity, and the women who serve are, apart from Jesus himself, the prime role models.[94] In 7.3.2 we examine women in the Gospel who provided *diakonia*, noting the way in which they did so, beginning at the start of the ministry of Jesus.

7.3.2 The Women in Galilee

7.3.2.1 *Disciples*

Before looking at the identified women in Galilee, we should consider whether there were others not specifically identified. The plural Greek word "*mathētai*," disciples, like *adelphoi*, siblings, discussed in 6.2.3, covers both genders, and, in itself, gives no indication of the gender of the people referred to except that they must include at least one male. At least some women were included among the *mathētai*, as Luke confirms in the account of the discovery of the empty tomb (see 7.3.2.2). Although we here consider only identified women, there is a specific instance where it seems probable that Luke intended the disciples not included in the twelve to be understood as gender inclusive, that is, as comprising both males and females.[95]

This is the sending out of the seventy-two, who, unlike the previous mission of the twelve (Luke 9:1–6), were sent out "in pairs" (Luke 10:1). There is no specific indication of gender in the passage and the word

---

92. Beyer, "Diakoneō," 84.
93. Discussed in Bailey, *Middle Eastern Eyes*, 365–77.
94. Peter and John prepare the Passover meal (Luke 22:13).
95. This is not to say that in other instances it meant only males.

mathētai is not used, but there are close parallels with the story of the "two . . . going to a village called Emmaus" (Luke 24:13) (where again the word *mathētai* is not used). The seventy-two were told: "Whatever house you enter, *eiselthēte* . . . remain, *menete*, in the same house eating and drinking whatever they provide" (Luke 10:5–7). In Emmaus, Jesus "went in, *eisēlthen*, to stay, *meinai*, with them" (Luke 24:29) and ate with them.[96] In issuing their invitation to Jesus, the two asked him to "Stay with us" (Luke 24:29) which suggests that the two share a house.[97] If so, the most likely explanation is that they were married. But if these "two" were man and woman, it is likely that at least some of the seventy-two "pairs" comprised a man and a woman. This possibility is supported by 1 Corinthians 9:5 which tells us that, in Paul's time, "the other apostles and the brothers of the Lord and Cephas" were "accompanied by a believing wife." For both the seventy-two and the other apostles, the joint mission by a man and a woman would have the practical effect of enabling men and women to be evangelized separately.

The sending of the seventy-two may provide another example of patriarchal amendment to the text. Early manuscripts differ as to the number, some giving seventy, others seventy-two. NA[27] chooses seventy-two, but indicates some doubt. Kurt Aland, dissenting from the expression of that doubt, finds that: "The opposing witnesses [for seventy] represent entirely an ecclesiastical normalizing . . . That they are in the majority is altogether understandable; if they are ancient, this only proves how early the normalizing process began to operate."[98]

Fitzmyer (who, following Aland, agrees with seventy-two) explains this choice as being because a change from seventy-two to seventy is more likely than vice versa, noting that seventy is frequently used in the Old Testament and is a round number,[99] but there is a further reason. Fitzmyer lists the possible references in the Old Testament[100] and the most relevant use of seventy is Moses' choice of those to assist him, stated as "seventy of Israel's elders" (Exod 24:1) or "seventy men, *andras*, from the elders of Israel" (Num 11:16, 24). There are no significant references in the Septuagint for seventy-two. Changing seventy-two to seventy gives a clear Septuagintal allusion suggesting that all of those sent out were men. In 7.6.6 we describe

---

96. *Eiselthēte* and *menete* (9:4) are also used in the instructions to the twelve, but there is no mention of eating and drinking.

97. Fitzmyer suggests that it was "the house that belonged to one of them" (*Luke X–XXIV*, 1567). This assumes that they were both men.

98. Note in Metzger, *Textual Commentary*, 127. The comment is on UBS[4], which has the same text and expression of uncertainty as NA[27].

99. Similarly Green, *Gospel of Luke*, 409n28.

100. Fitzmyer, *Luke X–XXIV*, 845–46.

a number of alterations to the wording of Acts which minimize the importance of women—this change may have a similar motivation.

7.3.2.2 Identified Women

After the cure of Simon's mother-in-law, she got up and began to serve, *diēkonei*, them (Luke 4:39), the first to serve Jesus in his ministry: "[Serve] could mean . . . to serve table or serve in a more generic sense."[101] Here it would seem to have its ordinary meaning, table-service.

Luke later tells us that "the twelve were with him as well as some women who had been cured of evil spirits and infirmities . . . who provided, *diēkonoun*, for them out of their resources" (Luke 8:1–3). There are variant readings: some manuscripts have "provided for him," i.e., Jesus.

> The better attested reading . . . is *autois*, "them." The singular is also suspect because it looks like a harmonization with Matt 27:55 or Mark 15:41.[102]

Carla Ricci has argued that the whole thrust of the passage concentrates on Jesus and the women, and that it is "more in harmony with what precedes it if it has *autōi*, 'for him,' as its object, referring back to its first subject, Jesus."[103] Robert Karris[104] is persuaded by her argument,[105] but there is a further problem. Whereas it has been plausible to explain the replacement of them (*autois*) by him (*autōi*),[106] it has been more difficult to explain a change in the opposite direction, and Ricci's attempt[107] is not altogether convincing. But, as we have seen, Luke's women are always autonomous, and he may have felt that their "providing for them" could subtly undermine such an understanding. If so, the wide-spread efforts to promote the subordination of women, described in 7.6, could have led to the adoption of the plural reading, as the replacement of "him" by "them" is comparable to some of the alterations to Acts (see 7.6.6).

---

101. Fitzmyer, *Luke I–IX*, 550.
102. Ibid., 698.
103. Ricci, *Mary Magdalene*, 157.
104. Referring to the Italian original.
105. Karris, "Women and Discipleship," 29.
106. As Fitzmyer, cited above.
107. Ricci, *Mary Magdalene*, 157–58.

These women included Mary Magdalene, Joanna, the wife of Herod's steward Chuza (who clearly came from a comfortable background, although not that of the Herodian elite),[108] and Susanna:

> The women's use of their property . . . permits the group around Jesus to be free of concern about what they shall eat or what they shall wear.[109]

But the women also illustrate the practical application of the teaching of Jesus.

> These women are thus characterized as . . . (2) persons who, like Jesus, "serve" others (cf. 22:24-27), and (3) exemplars of Jesus' message on faith and wealth . . . whose lives anticipate Luke's portrait of the early Christian community among whom "no one claimed private ownership of any possessions, but everything they owned was held in common" (Acts 4:32). In its current co-text, 8:1-3 thus parades these women (and not the twelve) as persons who both hear *and act* on the word of God (8:21; cf, 6:46-49).[110]

What these women did was described as *diēkonoun*, and it was provided not only by those with resources, but by all the women. Some of them were among those at the crucifixion (Luke 23:49, 55) and at the empty tomb preparing to embalm the body of Jesus, where Mary Magdalene and Joanna are again named, although again there were other women with them (Luke 24:10). Indeed, Luke implies that all the women who were with Jesus in Galilee were of the party (Luke 23:55), and we must also include them among the "certain women" with the apostles in Jerusalem (Acts 1:14). We see it as probable that Luke includes them whenever he refers to the disciples; this seems to be implicit in what was said to the women by the two men at the tomb:

> "Remember how he told you, while he was still in Galilee, that the Son of Man must be handed over to sinners, and be crucified, and on the third day rise again." Then they remembered his words (Luke 24:6-8).

---

108. Richard Bauckham argues that Chuza was "a very high ranking official at Herod's court" (Bauckham, *Gospel Women*, 136) and identifies Joanna with the apostle Junia of Romans 16:15 (165-98). Even if he is right about Junia, Chuza was not necessarily of high rank.

109. Seim, *Double Message*, 73-74.

110. Green, *Gospel of Luke*, 320.

This refers to words of Jesus in Galilee described at Luke 9:22, "with only the disciples near him" (Luke 9:18) and at Luke 9:44, also addressed to the disciples (Luke 9:43). As Seim points out,[111] Luke tells us three times that the women had followed him from Galilee (Luke 23:49, 55; 24:6), and the triple telling emphasizes its importance. These women, as well as witnessing the work of Jesus in Galilee, watched the crucifixion and found the empty tomb. Then, "returning from the tomb, they told all this to the eleven and to all the rest" (Luke 24:9):

> It can indeed be claimed that the women in Luke too, run immediately to the male disciples with the news . . . But this is a spontaneous action on their part. In Luke, no commission is given to the women to go and tell the other disciples that he is risen (Mt 28:7) and/or to tell them to meet him in Galilee (Mk 16:7, par. Mt). Instead, they are reminded of how Jesus told *them* . . . that the Son of Man must be handed over to the hands of sinners, be crucified, and rise again on the third day (24:6–7) . . . The women are themselves the first addressees of the resurrection message in a way that confirms their discipleship and the instruction they have received as disciples.[112]

That they acted without any commission reminds us of Sarah, Miriam, Deborah, Hannah and Judith, and indeed, in the Gospel itself, of Mary, Elizabeth, Anna and others. It contrasts sharply with the action of Peter, who, after seeing the empty tomb, "went home" (Luke 24:12).[113] What they have done is bear witness.

Subsequently, in Acts, they are not named as witnesses to the resurrected Jesus, but as a consequence they do not explicitly share in the disobedience of the apostles in choosing a replacement for Judas.[114] They, but not the women who were not present, hear the command of Jesus to "wait for the promise of the father" (Acts 1:4), repeated in Acts 1:8, but they decide, for their own reasons, to ignore the command of Jesus and fill the gap in their ranks. But these women, with Mary, the mother of Jesus and his sisters, are among the 120 who take part in the choosing of Matthias and subsequently they "were filled with the Holy Spirit and began to speak in other languages, as the Spirit gave them ability" (Acts 2:4).

---

111. Seim, *Double Message*, 148–49.
112. Ibid., 150–51.
113. See 6.1.2.2.
114. They do witness the risen Jesus and hear his command in Luke 24:49.

7.3.3 Other Providers of Diakonia

The other providers of *diakonia* are mostly well understood.[115] In Acts, Mary the mother of John Mark, assisted by her slave, Rhoda, provided hospitality, a form of *diakonia*, and perhaps leadership (Acts 12:12). Tabitha, whose story is discussed above in 7.2.4.3, provided a form of *diakonia*, and that she is described as a disciple, *mathētria* (Acts 9:36), suggests that she may have been among those who followed Jesus before the crucifixion, perhaps even from his time in Galilee[116]—if so, she would also have given witness. Priscilla, discussed in 7.4.5, also provided hospitality, as did Lydia as she urged Paul and his companions to "come and stay at my home" (Acts 16:15).

7.3.4 Lydia

If, as we have suggested, Luke was a child at the time of his first voyage, he would have been with one or both of his parents. He tells us nothing about them, but as they accompanied Paul, they should be regarded as fellow-missionaries of his, staying on[117] to continue his work in Philippi[118] when Paul was required to leave the city (Acts 16:39–40). We have argued that there were four heavenly interventions which resulted in Paul, Silas and Luke staying in the home of Lydia, Luke himself for some six years. The omniscient narrator indicates the reason, if we can understand him. There are two obvious explanations for Luke's stay in Philippi as part of the divine purpose, first, if he was a child, the getting of the education (of the kind described in 1.1.2.2) which enabled him to write his two volumes, and second, and perhaps more plausibly, whether child or adult, knowing Lydia herself. Luke tells us little about her but more can be deduced.

Philippi was a Roman colony. Its population would have been about 10,000,[119] including both Roman settlers and the original Macedonian inhabitants. The Christian community would appear to have been Greek-speaking, as Paul's letter to the Philippians is in Greek. There is little or no evidence of Jewish presence in the town and if Luke there received an educa-

---

115. Martha, much debated but not well understood, is discussed with Mary in 7.5.1.1.

116. The importance of such status, at least to those who shared it, is indicated by the story of the selection of Matthias, Acts 1:21–26.

117. As Paul left Priscilla and Aquila in Corinth (18:19).

118. "Luke was apparently left behind to continue the work in Philippi, where he reappears in [20:5]. His stay in Philippi may sufficiently account for his interest in the place" (Bruce, *Acts*, 323).

119. De Vos, *Church and Community Conflicts*, 238–39.

tion in "biblicizing Greek" as described by Alexander, it was probably from his parents. But there is no reason why this should not have happened—indeed, in the scenario we have described, with Luke as a child accompanying his parents as Christian missionaries in a gentile town, it would be the natural course.

There has been much disagreement about Lydia's economic status, the traditional view being that as a dealer in purple she must have been wealthy as purple cloth made from murex[120] was very expensive. However, more recent scholars[121] have noted that the purple associated with Thyatira, Lydia's place of origin (16:14), was made from the much cheaper madder,[122] used with woad.[123] Thyatira was in the province of Lydia, and Lydia may either be a personal name or mean "the woman from Lydia." Indeed, the name "Lydia" may have "been given [to her] while she was a slave"[124]—slave names could be based on the place where they were bought.[125]

In considering Lydia's probable economic status a good place to start is the source of the capital needed for her business. This would have been fairly substantial, whether she wove and dyed the material or was merely an importer.

> Dyeing . . . required an extensive plant and expensive materials, and an individual dyer would have been inhibited from working on his or her own.[126]

The most likely source[127] is a slave-owner, investing in the business of textiles, implying that Lydia was, or had been, a slave.[128] If the owner were in Thyatira, he or she would have sent Lydia to run a business in Philippi, while if the owner were in Philippi, Lydia, a skilled worker, would have been bought in Thyatira to run the business locally:

120. "A kind of shell-fish, the animal of which yields a purple dye" (*OED*, s.v. "murex").

121. Richter Reimer, *Women in Acts*, 104.

122. "A herbaceous climbing plant . . . cultivated . . . for the dye obtained from it" (*OED*, s.v. "madder").

123. Wild, "Dyeing," 499.

124. Barrett, *Critical and Exegetical Commentary*, 2:782. Although "Zahn conjectures that she was called 'the Lydian' to distinguish her from other merchants of purple . . . actually her name was either Euodia or Syntychē (Phil 4:2)" (cited Haenchen, *Acts*, 494n8). This is compatible with slave or ex-slave status.

125. Joshel, *Work, Identity and Legal Status*, 36.

126. Ibid., 135.

127. The only plausible alternative would be that she inherited it.

128. "This is a reasonable inference from both her name and her occupation" (Pervo, *Acts*, 403n25).

Beyond Rome, it is much less clear that local élites shared the same distaste for trade, with investments, frequently managed by their freedmen, in potteries, mines, textile production, and the like.[129]

If the slave-owner were Roman, a successful slave running a business would probably have been given freedom, but would have continued to operate the business in the interests of her former owner, who would take a substantial part of the profits.[130] If she were owned by a Greek, freedom would be less likely:

> At the top of the [slave] heap were the few hundreds of publicly owned slaves ... who served as a token police force or as other sorts of public functionary ... Below them were the privately owned, skilled slaves who "lived apart" ... in craft workshops established with start-up capital by their owners to whom they remitted a share of their profits ... The Athenian model of chattel slavery became widely diffused in the Greek world.[131]

However, even if her owner were Greek, the fact that her business was in the Roman colony of Philippi, where the commercial and legal systems would have been easier for a freedwoman to navigate, is a counter-argument. That she was able to offer hospitality to Paul and his companions does not necessarily mean that she was not a slave. A slave running a business, especially in a faraway city, would have to have considerable leeway, and the offering of hospitality need not have cost her owners anything.[132]

So she was probably not wealthy, but she had sufficient resources to offer hospitality to Paul, Silas, and the others in the group (including Luke himself) and sufficient personal authority to prevail upon them to accept it. Such authority is not negligible—apart from the Roman authorities the only other people in Acts to succeed in persuading Paul to do what they wanted him to do were James and the elders (Acts 21:20–26). After Paul was asked by the magistrates to leave Philippi, he did not do so until he had been to Lydia's home (Acts 16:40), another sign of her importance in Luke's narrative.

---

129. Paterson, "Trade, Roman," 1537.

130. "Numerous inscriptions from Philippi attest to [Augustales'] importance in that colony" (Hubbard, *Christianity in the Greco-Roman World*, 195). Augustales, wealthy freedmen, are described in 1.5.4.4.

131. Cartledge, "Slavery, Greek," 1415.

132. Paul boasted about paying for his keep (2 Thess 3:7–9).

The personal information given about Lydia, her name, her place of origin, and her profession, may be indications of servile origin.[133] Sandra Joshel tells us that family descent was of importance to freeborn Romans and was recorded in funerary inscriptions. As those of servile origins could not claim such status, their inscriptions gave name, place of origin[134] and profession,[135] together, in many cases, with the name of their owner or former owner. Luke rarely gives details of a person's family background, so its lack is not strong evidence for Lydia's status, but giving her place of origin and profession could suggest servile origins.

Luke spent six or seven formative years[136] in the household of Lydia, who very probably shared with Paul (and the freed men and women described by Joshel) a belief in the importance of working for a living. Such a belief was shared by Luke—see chapter 5—and the mention of Lydia's trade tells us of the importance, to Luke and to Lydia, of her work. Lydia's considerable personal authority may also have affected Luke's view of women and his presentation of them in Luke-Acts.

7.4 PROVIDERS OF WITNESS OR TESTIMONY

7.4.1 Introduction

Many women provided witness to Jesus. He raised the widow's son at Nain (Luke 7:11–15) and after this she was among those who "glorified God, saying, 'A great prophet has risen among us'" (Luke 7:16). Although, as we saw in 5.5.2, glorifying God is a stereotyped response to a cure, it is, nevertheless, a form of witness to Jesus. We discussed the economic status of the widow in 7.2.4.3 above, where we rejected the idea that Luke intended his reader to see her as a destitute widow dependent upon her son. She grieves for her only son, and has him restored to her arms.

---

133. So also Pervo, as noted above.

134. One element of the names would "generally reflect servile status: *natio* (origin), an indication of one's birthplace" (Joshel, *Work, Identity and Legal Status*, 40–41).

135. For freedmen "occupational title has a particular force. It shifts attention from birth and honor to productive activities and relations. From this perspective, the freedman with an occupational title no longer appears at the edges of Roman society" (ibid., 60).

136. Formative if he was a child, but the four heavenly interventions identified above suggest that Lydia was a major influence even if he was an adult.

7.4.2 The Woman with a Hemorrhage

The story of the daughter of Jairus is paired with another, in which a woman "who had been suffering from hemorrhages for twelve years" (Luke 8:43) took the initiative in seeking a cure from Jesus. She was originally endowed with some resources, for "she had spent all she had on physicians" (Luke 8:43), but was now dependent on what she could earn. She demonstrated faith as clearly as Jairus, and Jesus acknowledged this (Luke 8:48). This woman, albeit reluctantly, gave witness when "she declared in the presence of all the people why she had touched him, and how she had been immediately healed" (Luke 8:47). The courage shown in telling "all the people" about her illness, which had made her permanently unclean, should not be underestimated;[137] she did more than praise and glorify God.

7.4.3 The "Sinful" Woman

The sinful woman anointed Jesus with ointment, and Jesus told her: "Your sins are forgiven . . . Your faith has saved you"(Luke 7:48–50). What she did for Jesus could be seen as a form of *diakonia*, but is perhaps better regarded as witness, a testimony to Jesus's status.[138] Although Luke omits Mark's valuation of the jar of ointment at 150 *denarii*, the intended reader is no doubt as to its value as cheap ointment would not be kept in an alabaster jar (Luke 7:37).[139] So the woman was far from poor, and this argues against the traditional interpretation of her as a prostitute,[140] one driven to the last resort of those desperate to feed themselves and their children.[141] Nevertheless, the Pharisee expected that had Jesus known that she was a sinner, he would have rejected her; he did not do so.

This passage follows immediately on the story of the messengers from the Baptist (Luke 7:18–35), which included a distinction between sinners and Pharisees:

---

137. Further discussed in 6.1.6.

138. Jesus is the Christ, the anointed one, and Luke, like the other evangelists, shows us that he was anointed by a woman.

139. Pliny said that "the best ointment is preserved in alabaster," cited Witherington, *Women in the Ministry of Jesus*, 110.

140. For detailed arguments against this traditional view see Reid, *Choosing*, 115–17, and Hornsby, "Woman Is a Sinner," 124–29.

141. "Where explicit compulsion . . . was not in play, a primary motivation for women to enter prostitution was economic, that is, the desperation of poverty" (McGinn, *Economy of Prostitution*, 61). He notes that: "The ancient evidence is abundant" (ibid., 61n337).

> What distinguishes the two groups, according to the omniscient narrator, is that the sinners had been "baptized with the baptism of John" but the Pharisees had "rejected the purpose [*boulen*] of God for themselves, by not having been baptized by [John]" . . . The Baptist had preached a "baptism of repentance for the forgiveness of sins" (Luke 3:3) . . . Those who repent of sin . . . are forgiven . . . Since [the woman] has already been forgiven, she is able to recognize Jesus as the "one who comes."[142]

If the woman repented in response to the Baptist, it is in the Baptist's preaching that we should look for an understanding of her sinfulness:

> Even tax collectors came to be baptized, and they asked him, "Teacher, what should we do?" He said to them, "Collect no more than the amount prescribed for you." Soldiers also asked him, "And we, what should we do?" He said to them, "Do not extort money from anyone by threats or false accusation, and be satisfied with your wages" (Luke 3:12–14).

"Like the ancient prophets, Luke's Baptist defines righteousness in terms of social justice,"[143] so that sin is social injustice, as exemplified by the Baptist's injunctions to the tax collectors and soldiers, and the woman's ability to acquire expensive ointment tends to confirm this reading. Jesus's understanding of sin would be closely aligned with that of the Baptist, but Simon, who identified her as a sinner, would have had a different view. Perhaps, on the analogy of tax-collectors, her sinfulness for Simon was related to co-operation with pagan Romans or Greeks. It is not difficult to imagine such co-operation involving social injustice,[144] and therefore, for Jesus, sin.

Barbara Reid argues that "the imperfect verb *ēn* has the connotation 'used to be'; she is no longer the sinner she once was."[145] This seems unlikely—it is more probable that we should regard "sinner" as a Pharisee word, not a Jesus (or narrator) word.[146] The intended reader should understand that the woman had been previously forgiven, as Reid and others[147] interpret the passage, but this does not mean that she had ceased to be a

---

142. Darr, *Character Building*, 33–34.

143. Ibid., 72.

144. As in the story of Zacchaeus (Luke 19:8).

145. Reid, *Choosing*, 113.

146. For the use of "sinners" in the second temple period to describe "Jews who practised their Judaism *differently* from the writer's faction" see Dunn, *Jesus Remembered*, 528–32, this citation 530.

147. E.g., Marshall, *Gospel of Luke*, 314, Green, *Gospel of Luke*, 313–14.

"sinner."[148] There is no doubt but that Zacchaeus continued to be a tax-collector, and therefore a "sinner," at least for the Pharisees,[149] even after Jesus had brought salvation to his house.

7.4.4 Rhoda and Her Mistress, Mary

In Acts the slave, Rhoda, provided both *diakonia*, in going to the door, and a form of testimony, in telling what she had seen. That Rhoda is called a "maid," *paidiskē* (Acts 12:13), that is, a slave, and answered the door makes it clear that she belonged to the household of Mary, the mother of John Mark, who owned the house but her state of servitude is not emphasized:

> The master-slave relationship is not expressed in the story, in sharp contrast to Acts 16:16-19. The slave woman Rhoda behaves as if she were not a slave . . . [She] was not someone separate from the group of those who were gathered together.[150]

For Luke, she is more admirable than Mary and those praying inside: "They would rather believe that Peter is dead and so in the *inefficacy* of their prayer than heed the words of a female slave."[151] Although some scholars argue that this refusal to believe is a sign of Luke's low estimation of the importance of women, this is to misunderstand the authorial point of view. The blame for the failure of communication does not lie with the slave Rhoda but with those who do not believe her, including her owner, the Roman citizen.[152] Jesus was not believed.

7.4.5 Priscilla

Priscilla, with her husband Aquila, provided *diakonia* as they invited Paul to stay with them (Acts 18:3) and they worked together—the fact that Priscilla did this is one of the features of Luke's narrative removed by the Western text, as described in 7.6.6. Her main function was testimony; we are told how she and Aquila "took [Apollos] aside and explained the way of God to him more accurately" (Acts 18:26). She was the only woman in Acts who

---

148. "Her sins . . . were many" (Luke 7:47) but this does not tell us what they were.

149. That he no longer behaved extortionately would not, for the Pharisees, make him less of a "sinner."

150. Richter Reimer, *Women in Acts*, 242.

151. Chambers, "Knock, Knock," 94. But the reason for their incredulity is not given by Luke.

152. See 5.4.3.

provided instruction, *exethento*,[153] a form not only of testimony but also, as we saw in 6.1.4.3, of prophecy, and she was named before her husband, Aquila, indicating her greater importance in this role. Priscilla and Aquila worked for a living, but Luke does not tell us any more about their status unless it is implicit in their names. This is possible—it has been argued that these indicate that they were both freed slaves of the Acilius family.[154]

7.4.6 Summary

Most of the women discussed in this section belonged to the class of *penētes*, but Rhoda was a slave.[155] We have no information about the economic status of the widow of Nain, who provided a stereotypical response to healing.[156] The sinful woman was relatively rich as she bought expensive ointment, but, being a "sinner," she is not to be seen as belonging to the elite. It is possible that she worked at a despised trade so that she can be compared with Levi and Zacchaeus, and perhaps with Simon the tanner[157] (although his trade did not make him a "sinner"). But we can be sure that she was of the *penētes*.

7.5 OTHER WOMEN

7.5.1 Responsive Women

7.5.1.1 Martha and Mary

In this section we shall consider Mary (with Martha),[158] in 7.5.1.2, Sapphira, and in 7.5.1.3, Philip's prophesying daughters, all women who were responsive to the message of Jesus, but are not shown as providing either *diakonia* or testimony. There were many others, but they are mentioned only in pass-

---

153. Reid finds that Luke's use of *ektithēmi* rather than *didaskein* (used of teaching by male disciples, including Apollos, Acts 18:25) "seems a deliberate attempt by Luke to downplay Priscilla's teaching ministry, a ministry he considers more properly belonging to male disciples" (Reid, "Do You See," 118n28). But Luke makes it clear that Priscilla's *ektithēmi* is superior to the *didaskein* of Apollos, which she corrects.

154. Murphy-O'Connor, "Prisca and Aquila," 43–44. Luke gives their name, place of origin (for Aquila) and profession. As we saw above, these identifying data could indicate servile origins.

155. Luke's presentation of slaves is discussed in 7.5.2.

156. Although the destitute provide this stereotypical response, the converse is not necessarily true: the stereotypical response does not signify destitution.

157. All discussed in chapter 5.

158. Although Martha provided *diakonia*, this is not the point of the story.

ing, the only one in a major scene being the wife of Jairus, who, with her husband, was specifically told to "tell no one what had happened" (Luke 8:56). It is not clear why Luke includes this instruction, although it is, of course a "reformulation of the prohibition in Mark 5:43a,"[159] his antetext, but it is the reason that Jairus and his wife did not bear witness.

In the story of Martha and Mary, Martha is the more important character,[160] but there has been much scholarly disagreement about the role of each woman. Luke portrays Mary, the sister of Martha, as a disciple sitting and learning at the feet of her master (Luke 10:39); she does not provide either *diakonia* or witness. "But Martha was distracted, *periespato*, by her many tasks, *pollēn diakonian*" (Luke 10:40). It seems that: "As in Acts 6:1–6, the word is prioritized,"[161] but there is another way of looking at the story:

> In order to listen to the word (*logos*) of the Lord, Mary leaves (*kataleipō*) the serving (*diakoneō*) to Martha who complains. Similarly, the apostles assert that they should not have to leave (*kataleipō*) the word (*logos*) of God in order to serve (*diakoneō*) at tables.[162]

The co-textual parallels go further—Martha, who served, complained, the widows, who wanted to serve, complained, and, indeed, the apostles, who did not want to serve, complained. These parallels, especially the verbal parallels, suggest that Martha's complaining (like that of the apostles and perhaps of the widows) was not justified, and this is confirmed by Jesus's rebuke (Luke 10:41–42). But:

> 10:39 . . . includes an "also" or "and" (*kai*) not included by the NEB or the NAB. A more complete translation of the verse would read: "And Martha had a sister Mary *who also* having sat at the feet of Jesus was listening to/used to listen to his word."[163]

Even if D'Angelo's interpretation of the second *kai*, which is not shared by modern commentators, is incorrect, her understanding of Martha has other support:

159. Fitzmyer, *Luke I–IX*, 749.
160. Alexander, "Sisters in Adversity," 206.
161. Osiek and Balch, *Families in the New Testament World*, 141.
162. Koperski, "Luke 10:38–42," 517.

163. D'Angelo, "Redactional View," 454. She seems to have found no exegesis of the *kai* after Plummer, originally published in 1901, who suggests: "Mary joined in the welcome and also sat at his feet" (Plummer, *Luke*, 290–91). More plausibly, Young's Literal Translation reads: "Who also, having seated herself beside the feet of Jesus, was hearing the word." A similar view is taken by the McReynolds and Newberry interlinears and by the AV, OSB, and several other translations.

> The implication [*of perispaomai*] is that Martha wished to hear Jesus but was prevented from doing so by the pressure of providing hospitality.[164]

Hospitality, as we have seen, is *diakonia*, but did Jesus suggest that proclaiming, or listening to, the Word, was more important than *diakonia*? What he said, as we saw above, was: "For who is greater, the one who is at the table or the one who serves? Is it not the one at the table? But I am among you as one who serves" (Luke 22:27).

That both Martha and Mary had listened to Jesus should not be surprising as he had repeatedly emphasized the importance of listening:

> In the Sermon on the Plain he adjures his listeners to hear his words and do them (6:27, 47). In his explanation of the seed parable Jesus holds up as exemplary those who, "when they have heard the word, embrace it with a generous and good heart, and bear fruit through perseverance" (8:15). Jesus declares that whoever hears the word of God and does it is family to him (8:21). He proclaims blessed those who hear the word of God and obey it (11:28). Jesus uses the example of the queen of the South, who listened to the wisdom of Solomon, to emphasize how important it is to listen to him, for he is "greater than Solomon" (11:31). The command of the voice from the cloud at the transfiguration, "listen to him" (9:35), and the summons, "Whoever has ears to hear ought to hear" (8:8 and 14:35), epitomize the initial step of discipleship.[165]

To this one could add the important Isaian condemnation at the very end of Acts:

> For this people's . . . ears are hard of hearing . . . so that they might not . . . listen with their ears, and understand with their heart (Acts 28:27).

Jesus rebuked Martha but it is not clear why he did so. The idea that her ministry (whatever it might have been) was inferior to that of Mary does not seem plausible. If the differing activities of the sisters were the reason, Martha was rebuked for wanting to reduce her share of the work of *diakonia*, but this seems equally implausible. However, there may be another explanation. Looking at the immediate co-text, the explanation would seem to lie in Martha's speech (Luke 10:40), to which Jesus's rebuke was a response. The

---

164. Marshall, *Gospel of Luke*, 452. That is, she was "completely occupied" (Balz and Schneider, "Perispaomi," 76).

165. Reid, *Choosing*, 22.

speech is noteworthy for its egocentricity: of eighteen Greek words, three[166] are first person pronouns:

> She takes it for granted that priority belongs to the service she herself carries out . . . Martha's choice of words also refers continually back to herself: *adelphē mou, monēn me, moi.*[167]

This attitude, with its emphasis on the first person, is close to that of the Pharisee in the temple (Luke 18:11–12), also criticized by Jesus and discussed in 4.5.8; it also reminds us of the disciples chided by Jesus, whom Luke leaves unnamed (Luke 22:24–25). Martha, like the Pharisee in the parable and the other, unnamed, disciples, is faulted for her egocentricity;[168] her many tasks, *pollēn diakonian*, despite the importance Jesus gives to *diakonia*, are not sufficient to escape the (very gentle) rebuke by Jesus. On this reading the rebuke is not gender specific—Jesus rebukes Martha, a woman, and in the parable castigates the Pharisee, a man, for the same reason—self-importance.[169]

However, there is another possible, gender-specific, explanation for the rebuke. Martha asks Jesus to instruct Mary to help her. As we showed in 6.1.6, in Luke-Acts no-one tells a woman to do, or not do, anything. Martha's request is not acceptable to Jesus, and he tells her so.[170]

In his response, Jesus told Martha that: "There is need of only one thing. Mary has chosen the better part, which will not be taken away from her" (Luke 10:42). Most exegetes try to discover what the one thing is by examining the actions of either Martha or Mary. Especially if D'Angelo and Marshall[171] are correct in deducing that Martha had also either listened to or wished to listen to Jesus, it is possible that the "one thing" referred to them both. We may find it in the wider co-text summarized above by Reid, that is, to hear the word of God and do it. Martha, whatever her particular *diakonia* might have been, in her complaining was not doing the word of God but thinking of herself. Luke's story is about Martha who was rebuked, so that Mary, the minor character, is not shown to have been active, but

---

166. Four in NRSV.

167. Seim, *Double Message*, 103.

168. Three words out of eighteen, 17%. The Pharisee has five first-person verbs out of thirty-seven words, 14%.

169. Alexander also sees Martha's gender as relatively insignificant, for other reasons (Alexander, "Sisters in Adversity," 213).

170. This rebuke by Jesus can also be compared to that to the man who asked Jesus to tell his brother to divide the inheritance (Luke 12:13–14), see ibid., 209.

171. And the translations identified above.

Jesus commended her and the reader is to understand that, like the mother of Jesus (see 6.4), she, who had heard the word of the Lord, also *"did"* it.

7.5.1.2 Sapphira

Another woman who provided neither *diakonia* nor testimony was Sapphira:

> But a man named Ananias, with the consent of his wife Sapphira, sold a piece of property; with his wife's knowledge, he kept back some of the proceeds, and brought only a part and laid it at the apostles' feet (Acts 5:1–2).

Her husband was the leader in the action,[172] she allowed it and she too died for her fault. Richter Reimer explains:

> The husband does the action; the wife knows of it, but she does nothing to oppose this corrupt and corrupting deed. She takes her place within the patriarchal power system . . . In this story, women are shown an opportunity for liberation from death-dealing structures. They may—indeed they must—distance themselves from any such corrupt and corrupting decisions of their husbands. They are offered an opportunity for active disobedience.[173]

This is fully consonant with the role of women as seen by Luke and shown in the description of Anna and the action of Mary, that is, that they should make their own decisions, not follow their husband or father. Sapphira did not make her own decisions, did not take the opportunity to dissent, and paid the penalty.

7.5.1.3 Philip's Prophesying Daughters

Luke tells us that he was part of Paul's party when:

> We went into the house of Philip the evangelist, one of the seven, and stayed with him. He had four unmarried daughters, *thugateres . . . parthenoi*, who had the gift of prophecy (Acts 21:8–9).

---

172. "The verbs which describe this action are all third person singular, not plural, implying that this was Ananias's plan for the most part" (Thomas, *Devil, Disease and Deliverance*, 240).

173. Richter Reimer, *Women in Acts*, 24.

As Luke tells us nothing about the daughters of Philip except that they had the gift of prophecy, the question arises: why tell us? Also, Luke tells us that he stayed there only "for several days" (Acts 21:10), so how did he know about this gift? This first visit would have been about 57 and Luke began his third voyage from Caesarea in 59. He does not tell us what he was doing between the time of his first visit shortly before Paul was arrested and the start of the voyage from Caesarea to Rome, but in view of his interest in Paul, it seems likely that he spent some part, perhaps a great part, of that time in Caesarea, near Paul (who was there for two years). If so, he may intend the reader to infer that he again stayed, or at least spent time, there with Philip and his daughters.

We can also consider the likely age of the daughters of Philip. They are described as *parthenoi*,[174] of marriageable age. Jewish girls married "between thirteen and twenty years of age,"[175] but, especially in referring to four sisters, Luke may have used the term loosely. Information given in Acts about Philip can help us to estimate the age of his daughters, as understood by Luke's intended readers, who shared, or could be told about, Luke's understanding of the time-scale.

Philip was driven from Jerusalem in the persecution of the Hellenists, which Dunn dates about 31–32,[176] albeit tentatively.[177] He spent time in Samaria and then set out for Gaza (Acts 8:4–26). After his meeting with the Ethiopian eunuch:

> The Spirit of the Lord snatched Philip away; the eunuch saw him no more, and went on his way rejoicing. But Philip found himself at Azotus, and as he was passing through the region, he proclaimed the good news to all the towns until he came to Caesarea (Acts 8:39–40).

It seems unlikely that he arrived in Caesarea before 34. Because the Spirit "snatched," *hērpasen*, Philip, it is very likely that Luke is telling us that he was alone at the time of that event, and therefore probably unmarried. If he married after arriving in Caesarea, his eldest daughter is unlikely to have been older than 20 when Luke first stayed with them in 57, and she could have been younger. Her sisters certainly would have been.[178]

---

174. "A young woman of marriageable age [with] or without focus on virginity" (BDAG, 777).

175. Cohick, *Earliest Christians*, 57.

176. Dunn, *Beginning from Jerusalem*, 503, 512.

177. Or 35, if Jesus was crucified in 33.

178. Seim ("Virgin Mother," 97) claims to "have argued that . . . Philip's virgin daughters . . . may be young," citing Seim, *Double Message*, 180–83, but she does not

They are described as having the gift of prophecy. The importance and meaning of prophecy is discussed in 6.1.4—as prophets they provided encouragement and strengthening. They are also described as *parthenoi*. Seim reads this as "virgins," and argues that:

> Of the seven concrete cases of prophesying women who are mentioned in Luke-Acts—Elizabeth, Mary, Anna and Philip's four daughters—six are said to be chaste [*sic*—she seems to mean celibate] . . . with the exception of Elizabeth . . . all the named female prophets are virgins or widows.[179]

But Elizabeth is not celibate, the primary meaning of *parthenos* is not virgin but unmarried girl, and Mary's virginity (Luke 1:34) has to do with the conception of Jesus (Luke 1:35), not with her prophesying. Luke's mention of the brothers and sisters[180] of Jesus refutes the idea that he thought Mary lived celibately with Joseph after the birth of Jesus. Philip's daughters were unmarried when Luke met them around 56, but in his narrative he gives no reason to suppose that he expected them to remain so, nor that, once married, they would no longer have the gift of prophecy. Seim's analysis of prophecy and "chastity" draws on second-century Christian sources.[181] If Luke lived in the first century, as he claims, it is in writings of that time that we should look for the background to his understanding of the daughters of Philip.

7.5.2 Unresponsive Women

We listed the unresponsive women in chapter 6. As we have seen, Herodias, Drusilla and Bernice all were, or had been, queens and the women at Antioch were of high standing. The other two, discussed below, were slaves. Bernice, indeed, was no more unresponsive than Agrippa, but whereas Agrippa's indifference was shared with most men, especially wealthy men, in Luke-Acts, Bernice's indifference was unusual for a Lukan woman. But it was not unusual for a wealthy woman; we see a similar response in Herodias and Drusilla, who, like Bernice, were members of the ruling elite. We saw in chapter 2 that both Herodias (2.2.4) and Drusilla (2.2.6) divorced their husbands and entered into new marriages in order to increase their status,

---

there address their age.

179. Seim, *Double Message*, 180, 184.

180. Luke 8:20-21; Acts 1:14.

181. Acts of Paul and Thecla, Montanism, and sources drawn upon by Eusebius (Seim, *Double Message*, 180-81).

wealth and power. Bernice, also, left her husband and later was attracted to the even greater status, wealth and power of Titus (2.2.6). She lived with him and hoped to marry him. These women sought to share in the status and authority of their men (as we have seen, bestowed by the devil—Luke 4:6)[182] and did not respond to Jesus.

As we discussed in 5.2.2, Sergius Paulus came from Pisidian Antioch, represented in the senate in Luke's time by the high-flying senator Caristanius Fronto, as well as either the first or the second senator Sergius Paulus, which leads the intended reader to see representatives of that very wealthy city as being linked to the senatorial ruling elite. If so, the "devout women of high standing" joining the persecution of Paul in Pisidian Antioch were not just local elite status, but rather of wealth and status similar to that of Herodias, Bernice and Drusilla.[183]

Not all rich women were hostile or indifferent; in Thessalonica "not a few of the leading women" joined Paul (Acts 17:4) and in Beroea "not a few Greek women . . . of high standing" believed (Acts 17:12). These were members of local elites, as perhaps was Damaris in Athens (Acts 17:34) as she is mentioned in the same breath as Dionysius, whom we so placed in 5.2.2. Like the male members of these elites, some were responsive, some were not, but the unresponsive women described by Luke were in the very wealthy city of Pisidian Antioch and, very possibly, close to the senatorial family of Paulus.

At the other end of the social scale two female slaves were unresponsive. The first was the servant girl in the house of the high priest (Luke 22:56), perhaps because no one associated with the chief priests is shown as responsive. The second was the slave with the spirit of divination who was exorcised by Paul (Acts 16:16–18). We are not told in any way that she, herself, had been reached by Paul, either before or after the exorcism, nor are we given an explanation of this. Both the slave of the high priest and the slave with the spirit of divination acted in accordance with the wishes of their owners. But this should not surprise us—Luke tells us of several people who were converted, together with their households.[184] These households would have included slaves, for, as we saw in 1.5.4.1, a substantial majority of those living above subsistence level owned slaves. In Luke's narrative

---

182. See 2.4.1.

183. Herod the Great or Agrippa I might regard themselves as of greater status than an ordinary senator, but this would not be so plausible of Antipas or Agrippa II.

184. Members of the households of Cornelius (Acts 11:14), Lydia (Acts 16:15), the jailer at Ephesus (Acts 16:31), and Crispus (Acts 18:8).

unnamed household slaves, like these two women and Rhoda,[185] always follow their owners in accepting or rejecting Jesus.

An explanation for this may lie in the less individualistic and more group centered approach to behavior of people in the Mediterranean world. This is described in a behavioral grid as "strong group person":[186]

> Group-oriented persons internalize and make their own what others say, do, and think about them because they believe it is necessary, if they are to be human beings, to live out the expectations of others.[187]

If such were the pressures on free individuals, it would seem plausible that the pressures on slaves would be considerably greater, and the expectations in question would be those of their owners. We saw in 7.3.4 that matters considered important for freed slaves in Rome included information about their former owners—Pliny tells us that "the house provides a slave with a country and a sort of citizenship."[188]

Nearly all of the other women in Luke-Acts whose social or economic status can be determined fell between these extremes. They were *penētes*, they worked for a living, but they were not by any means destitute. Almost all of them are shown as responding to the message of Jesus, and those described at any length were active in promoting God's purposes.

7.6 THE PLAUSIBILITY OF OUR INTERPRETATION

7.6.1 Paul

In this section we shall consider whether our interpretation of Luke's presentation of the role of women as independent and active in ministry is plausible in the light of Luke's context in the early Christian churches. To understand that context we examine Christian writings, dated either before or within some twenty-five years after Luke wrote, including the variant readings of the Western text of Acts, and also examine the Gospels themselves. The earliest extant writings are the authentic letters of Paul[189] and there are indicators in those letters of the way in which he saw the role of women, the

---

185. Discussed in 7.4.4.
186. Malina and Neyrey, "First Century Personality," 72–76.
187. Ibid., 73.
188. Pliny, *Letters*, 8.16.
189. 1 Thess, 1 & 2 Cor, Gal, Rom, Phil, and Phlm, probably written between 50 and 58.

best evidence we have of their role in the first decades of the church (during Paul's lifetime) to about 60 CE. Paul spoke of women prophesying (see the citation from Barclay in 7.6.3.2), and his general view is given in the baptismal formula: "There is no longer male and female; for all of you are one in Christ Jesus" (Gal 3:28). That Paul was serious in believing that gender distinctions were unimportant is confirmed by the number[190] and status in the churches[191] of women mentioned in his letters:

> In Romans 16 Paul calls Prisca a co-worker (v. 3), then commends Mary, Tryphaena, Tryphosa, and Persia for "working" or "laboring" (vv. 6, 12), a verb (*kopian*) Paul uses to characterize his own evangelizing and that of these women. He names Phoebe a *diakonos* (a "minister," v. 1) and Junia an "apostle" (v. 7). In Philemon, Apphia is a "sister" (v. 2). In Philippians, Paul writes that the women Euodia and Syntyche have "struggled beside me in the work of the gospel, together with Clement and the rest of my co-workers" (4:3).[192]

These writers also take the view that 1 Cor 14:33b–34 telling women to be silent in the churches, is an interpolation.[193] This is discussed in 7.6.3.2 but even if that passage is by Paul himself it cannot take away the actual role of women as described in the letters. Paul referred to women prophets and also said: "Do we not have the right to be accompanied, *periagein*, by a believing [sister] wife, *adelphēn gynaika*, as do the other apostles and the brothers of the Lord and Cephas?" (1 Cor 9:5).[194] These "believing wives" accompanied the apostles, but we are to take it that they shared in the work of evangelization, were co-workers[195] like Phoebe (Rom 16:1) and Apphia (Phlm 2),[196] each of whom is also called *adelphē*. The reference in *Codex*

---

190. "The named individuals Paul greets among the Christians of Rome in Romans 16:3–15 comprise nine women and sixteen men" (Bauckham, *Gospel Women*, xxi).

191. Status in the churches does not necessarily relate to status in society generally. "The public acknowledgement of Prisca's prominent role in the church, implicit in the reversal of the secular form of naming the husband before his wife, underlines how radically egalitarian the Pauline communities were" (Murphy-O'Connor, "Prisca and Aquila," 40–42).

192. Osiek and Balch, *Families in the New Testament World*, 117.

193. Ibid., 117. NRSV shows the whole passage (33b–36) as an aside. Other scholars see this as the view of the Corinthians—see Omanson, *Textual Guide*, 349.

194. On this see Barrett, *Commentary 1 Corinthians*, 203–4.

195. Apollos is co-worker, *synergoi* ("working together" in NRSV) at 1 Cor 3:5–9, brother at 1 Cor 16:12, Epaphroditus is both at Phil 2:25, and Philemon is co-worker at Phlm 2, and brother at Phlm 7, 20.

196. Said probably to be *co-workers* by Beutler, "Adelphos," 30.

Bezae to the wives and children of the apostles (see 7.6.6) confirms that such an idea was plausible, and also supports the idea that the apostolic missionaries often evangelized as married couples,[197] perhaps like the seventy-two. Paul shows that many women were active in the work of the early church—Osiek, as we saw above, identified the names of ten women whose activity in the church is described, and if, as Paul states, other apostles and the brothers of the Lord were accompanied by their wives as fellow-evangelists,[198] this is evidence of many more such women.

7.6.2 The Order of Widows

A number of scholars have also suggested that in the very early church there were groups of women engaged in religious works of some kind, who are sometimes referred to as the "order of widows":

> Evidence for an order of widows in the early church is astonishingly widespread . . . The overall picture is of celibate women, often but not always or exclusively older women, who seem to have lived in groups and carried out works of prayer and charitable endeavor, as well as teaching.[199]

Luke himself refers in the Gospel to groups of women, perhaps including widows, engaged in good works, those "who provided for 'him' or 'them'[200] out of their resources" (Luke 8:2–3)[201] and who "prepared spices and ointments" after Jesus was laid in the tomb (Luke 23:56). We also see such groups in Acts, where the Hellenist widows were neglected (Acts 6:1) and where Tabitha and the widows made garments (Acts 9:39). We have argued that the description of the widow Anna is a sequence of references to women in the Septuagint who acted independently, and we have suggested that the description may be an epitome of a *florilegium*. Such a *florilegium* could have been prepared by or for a group of this kind.

---

197. We would see Luke's parents as such a couple.

198. Paul does not confine the term "apostle" to the twelve; apart from frequently claiming it for himself he applies it to Andronicus and Junia (Rom 17:7).

199. Maloney, "Pastoral Epistles," 371. So members of such an order may not all have been actual widows.

200. Discussed in 7.3.2.2.

201. Of the three named, one (Joanna) is said to be married, but the other two named may have been widows, as may some of the other women in the group.

7.6.3 The Pseudonymous Pauline Letters

7.6.3.1 The Deutero-Pauline Letters

The deutero-Pauline letters[202] show a reaction against the role of women[203] described above, starting a trajectory which is followed in the Pastorals and 1 Peter, expressed in particular in the household codes. These emphasize the authority to be exercised by the head of a household over his wife, children, and slaves, and their respective duties. Taking the relevant passages[204] in the probable order of their composition, we find:

> Wives, be subject to your husbands, as is fitting in the Lord (Col 3:18).

> Wives, be subject to your husbands as you are to the Lord. For the husband is the head of the wife just as Christ is the head of the church, the body of which he is the Savior. Just as the church is subject to Christ, so also wives ought to be, in everything, to their husbands (Eph 5:22–24).

> Wives, in the same way, accept the authority of your husbands, so that, even if some of them do not obey the word, they may be won over without a word by their wives' conduct, when they see the purity and reverence of your lives (1 Pet 3:1–2).

7.6.3.2 An Interpolation in 1 Corinthians?

There is nothing of this kind in the authentic Pauline letters, except the passage requiring women to be silent in church (1 Cor 14:33b–36), referred to in 7.6.1. It is not surprising that there is a body of scholarly opinion which believes that this is an interpolation,[205] perhaps by those responsible for the later pseudonymous letters.[206]

> The next paragraph . . . seems to place a total ban on women's speech in church, which is strangely inconsistent with Paul's permission in 11:2–16 that (veiled) women could pray and

---

202. Col and Eph.
203. And of slaves.
204. I.e., those relating to wives.
205. For a broader view of the possibilities see Omanson, *Textual Guide*, 349.
206. See Osiek and Balch, *Families in the New Testament World*, 117.

prophesy . . . Either Paul is truly inconsistent here, reacting against a threat of "unruly" women by forbidding their verbal participation, despite what he had earlier allowed. Or this passage is an interpolation into the letter by a later editor, one who took the opportunity of the surrounding context to introduce the restrictive ethos of the Pastoral letters (e.g., 1 Tim 2:8–15, part of a letter generally regarded as written by a later Paulinist, not by Paul himself). This latter option is favoured by many commentators, and it is given slight textual support by the fact that some manuscripts place vv. 34–5 at the end of the chapter, rather than in their present location; that might indicate that they were once a marginal gloss which was inserted by scribes at varying points into the original text . . . But as it stands the passage seems to presuppose that women in all Paul's churches were wholly silent, which hardly fits what we know of women leaders in Pauline congregations (e.g., Rom 16:1–2, 3–5, 7; Phil 4:2).[207]

Jerome Murphy O'Connor is more explicit: "The verses contradict 11:5. The injunctions reflect the misogynism of 1 Tim 2:11–14 and probably stem from the same circle."[208] That passage is indeed very similar:

Let a woman learn in silence with full submission. I permit no woman to teach or to have authority over a man; she is to keep silent. For Adam was formed first, then Eve; and Adam was not deceived, but the woman was deceived and became a transgressor (1 Tim 2:11–14).

7.6.3.3 The Pastoral Letters

In the Pastoral letters there are, in addition to those previously cited, a number of passages which suggest that women should be subordinate to male authority.[209] Included in these is evidence of disagreement between a group of widows of the kind described above and the writer of the Pastorals in 1 Timothy (5:3–16), a work probably dating from "the very beginning of the second century."[210] It is clear that these widows were active in ministry, but the writer sees a need to control them and to exclude from their number widows who were not "real widows left alone" (1 Tim 5:5). By a "real widow" he seems to have in mind the destitute, a definition like that of *almanah*

---

207. Barclay, "1 Corinthians," 1130.
208. Murphy-O'Connor, "First Corinthians," 811.
209. 1 Tim 2:8–15; 3:11; 4:7; 5:3–16; 2 Tim 3:6–7; Titus 2:3–5.
210. Kümmel, *Introduction*, 387.

which we have seen in 6.1.3.1, so it is clear that among the group he refers to there were some who were not "real widows," that is, not destitute. The author is trying to reduce the cost to the church of widows, but also seems to be attempting to control what they do, as when he criticizes them for "gadding about" (1 Tim 5:13). This passage is almost as misogynistic as that from the same work cited above.

7.6.4 Ignatius

The importance of "widows" in the churches at this time is confirmed by the letter of Ignatius to the Smyrnaeans, dating from about 107,[211] which sent greetings to "the virgins who are called widows, *tas parthenous tas legomenas chēras*."[212] We rather read this letter as indicating that groups of "widows" active in ministry were widespread in the church and that the instructions of 1 Timothy, if known, had not been obeyed, so that "widows" still ministered in a group which included the never (or not yet) married.

There is further evidence of an attempt to control widows in Ignatius's letter to Polycarp, the bishop of Smyrna. In a prominent position, at the beginning of a section about social order, he says:

> Do not let the widows be neglected. After the Lord, you be their guardian. Let nothing be done without your consent, nor do anything yourself without God's consent.[213]

The first sentence, that widows be not neglected, etc., could mean that they were recipients of alms, but, if the following sentence refers to the widows,[214] it seems more likely to refer to them as active ministers to be supervised, a reading supported by the reference to "the virgins who are called widows" in the letter to Smyrna, cited above. If it does so refer to the widows it is a complementary instruction to that included in most of Ignatius's other letters, to the effect that each congregation should obey its bishop,[215] in some instances extended to include obedience to its (male) presbyters. This is another form of patriarchalism.

---

211. Staniforth, *Early Christian Writings*, 64.

212. Ign. *Smyrn.* 13.1.

213. Ign. *Pol.* 4.1.

214. William Schoedel, assuming that the widows are beneficiaries, sees this sentence as relating to the funds required for their support (Schoedel, *Ignatius of Antioch*, 269).

215. Specifically, Ign. *Eph.* 2.2; 20.2; Ign. *Magn.* 3.2; 13.2; Ign. *Trall.* 2.1; 13.2; Ign. *Phld.* 7.1, 2; Ign. *Smyrn.* 8.1; 9.1; Ign. *Pol.* 6.1. See Schoedel, *Ignatius of Antioch*, 113-14.

7.6.5 Reinterpretation of the Septuagint

There is also evidence of attempts to control widows (and women generally) by changing or re-interpreting scriptural texts, including some of those to which we referred in our analysis of the Anna passage in chapter 6. Clement wrote from Rome about the year 96[216] and described the ideal for women:

> Let us guide our women toward that which is good: let them display a disposition to purity worthy of admiration; let them exhibit a sincere desire to be gentle; let them demonstrate by their silence the moderation of their tongue; let them show their love, without partiality and in holiness, equally toward all those who fear God.[217]

Although expressed more moderately than the pastorals, this represents a similar ideal, especially shown by the reference to their silence. Clement later in the letter described admirable women:

> Many women, being strengthened by the grace of God, have performed many manly deeds. The blessed Judith, when the city was under siege, *asked the elders to permit her* to go to the enemy's camp. So she exposed herself to peril and went out for love of her country and of her besieged people, and the Lord delivered Holophernes into the hand of a woman.[218]

But if we turn to the book of Judith in the Septuagint, we find no reference to Judith begging permission from the elders. On the contrary:

> Judith's summons of Chabris and Charmis [the elders of her city—Jdt 8:10] inaugurates a series of events that demonstrate an assurance of her authority among the elders of Bethulia.[219]

She rebuked them sternly (Jdt 8:11–27), told them that she was about to leave the city (Jdt 8:32–33) and said: "Only, do not try to find out what I am doing; for I will not tell you until I have finished what I am about to do" (Jdt 8:34). No request for permission!

> Approximately one quarter of *1 Clement* is given over to quotations from the Jewish scriptures—about 75 in total—and there appear to be many allusions as well . . . [which] suggests that he knew the Greek Jewish scriptures very well. At the same time he

---

216. Staniforth, *Early Christian Writings*, 17.
217. *1 Clem.* 21.6–7.
218. Ibid., 55:3–5—emphasis added.
219. Elder, "Judith," 459.

is creative in his approach to these writings, and not afraid to present them in a novel way in order to support the argument that he advances.[220]

Clement's description of Judith asking permission is certainly novel. He has been described as generally loose in his use of scripture,[221] but his misleading reference to Judith's begging permission from the elders is surely intended to promote female subordination,[222] and could fairly be described as a lie.

Clement also, like Ignatius, promoted episcopal authority. He appears to have been the first to describe what has become known as the apostolic succession:

> The apostles received the gospel for us from the Lord Jesus Christ; Jesus the Christ was sent forth from God. So then Christ is from God, and the apostles are from Christ . . . So, preaching [the good news] both in the country and in the towns, they appointed their first fruits . . . to be bishops and deacons for the future believers.[223]

and

> They appointed the leaders mentioned earlier and afterwards they gave the offices a permanent character; that is, if they should die, other approved men, *andres*, should succeed to their ministry.[224]

The apostolic succession did not have to be patriarchal—as we have seen at least one woman was called "apostle," the seventy-two were sent out two by two, and Cephas, the other apostles and the brothers of the lord were accompanied by their wives as fellow preachers. But Clement, by his use of *andres*, made it clear that by apostolic succession, he meant dodecanal succession, based on the Twelve. Women are excluded from leadership positions, as in the Pastorals. The leadership role Clement describes could readily become patriarchalist, as is shown in the letters of Ignatius described above.

---

220. Gregory, "1 Clement," 29.
221. Staniforth, *Early Christian Writings*, 22.
222. Although Schüssler Fiorenza notes Clement's praise of Judith, she does not comment on the alleged request for permission (Schüssler Fiorenza, *In Memory*, 118).
223. *1 Clem.* 42.1–4.
224. Ibid. 44.2.

There may be a similar attempt to bolster masculine authority where 1 Peter,[225] in an extension of the household code cited in 7.6.3.1, tells us that "Sarah obeyed Abraham and called him Lord" (1 Pet 3:6). There is no reference to Sarah obeying Abraham in either NRSV or the Septuagint; on the contrary, as we have seen, God told Abraham: "Whatever Sarra says to you, obey her voice" (Gen 21:12). Moreover, she never calls him "Lord" in either standard bibles or the Septuagint, and although she refers to him (within herself) as "my lord" (LXX Gen 18:12, "husband" in NRSV), this is a sarcastic passage which does not suggest that she actually so thought of him.

If our interpretation of the Anna passage was shared by women who read or heard it in Luke's time, Judith and Sarah may have been seen as role models by the "widows." However, Clement and the author of 1 Peter may have sought, by changing the understanding of scriptural texts which perhaps were not widely available to women, to diminish their role and bolster male ecclesiastical authority. The texts reflect an attitude to women which is similar to that we have seen in the near contemporary 1 Timothy, very different to that reflected in the authentic Pauline letters. Luke probably wrote after the deutero-Pauline letters and some years before 1 Peter and the Pastorals, but his presentation of women as we understand it is much closer to that of Paul, the protagonist of the second half of Acts and a man whom he claims to have accompanied on his apostolic missions.

7.6.6 Alterations to Acts

At about the same time a number of textual alterations were made in copies of Acts, collectively known as the Western text,[226] a "broad stream of textual tradition"[227] which Kümmel finds "as old as the 'Egyptian' [i.e., standard] text."[228] Most scholars would agree that the alterations to the original text were very early, and Strange finds that "there is a unity of approach . . . shown in the similar types of reading favored by the copyists responsible for the Western witnesses."[229] Witherington demonstrates that:

> At the points in Acts where Luke gives or appears to give noticeable attention to women (and particularly prominent women),

---

225. Probably dating from 90–95 (Kümmel, *Introduction*, 425).
226. The best known version being *Codex Bezae*.
227. Strange, *Problem of the Text of Acts*, 37.
228. Kümmel, *Introduction*, 187.
229. Strange, *Problem of the Text of Acts*, 37.

the Western text attempts to tone down or eliminate such references.[230]

He finds alterations to the story of Priscilla[231] particularly obvious, citing J. H. Ropes, who said: "The desire to reduce the prominence of Priscilla seems to have been at work in a number of places in this chapter."[232] Ivoni Richter Reimer has detailed the changes in this story,[233] summarizing them as follows:

> The [Western text] three times inserts the name of Aquila without mentioning Priscilla, and attempts to create a stronger relationship between Paul and Aquila. It not only thrusts Priscilla out of her craft position, but out of the missionary work as well.[234]

Witherington notes a number of other changes in a similar direction, including "the addition of *kai teknois* and children at 1:14 by Codex Bezae so that women are no longer an independent group but are simply the wives of the apostles."[235] He summarizes his findings:

> It appears that there was a concerted effort by some part of the Church, perhaps as early as the late first century or beginning of the second, to tone down texts in Luke's second volume that indicated that women played an important and prominent part in the early days of the Christian community.[236]

If Strange is right in thinking that a number of copyists were responsible for the Western tradition, such an effort was fairly wide-spread and we have identified prominent promoters of these ideas. As a number of such changes to Acts have already been identified, it is possible that there are others, in Acts or Luke. One such is the story of the women in Galilee who "provided for him" or "provided for them," discussed in 7.3.2.2. This tendency provides a reason for copyists to have replaced "him" by "them," making the

---

230. Witherington, "Anti-Feminist Tendencies," 82. This tendency had been noted many years before by Ropes (see below) and by Bruce, *Acts*, 352.

231. Identified by Adolf von Harnack in 1900, whose findings are summarized in Heine, *Women and Early Christianity*, 43–44. Heine herself describes it as "an interest in making women vanish" (44).

232. Ropes, *Text of Acts*, 178, note on v. 26.

233. Richter Reimer, *Women in Acts*, 197–99.

234. Ibid., 198.

235. Witherington, "Anti-Feminist Tendencies," 82.

236. Ibid., 83. The assumption that "women and children" must refer to the wives of the apostles may be part of the ideology fostered by these copyists.

women subordinate to the Twelve, and therefore to the male hierarchy of the post-Lukan church, in order to bolster patriarchal authority. As noted in 7.3.2.1 the changing of the seventy-two into seventy may also have been due to this tendency.

7.6.7 The Gospels

7.6.7.1 *The Synoptic Gospels*

We have above considered Paul, from the period before Luke wrote, and a number of writings from after Luke's time. However there are writings more contemporary with Luke: the Gospel of Mark was written in the early 70s, and the Gospel of Matthew around 80. Luke's Gospel and Acts were written at about the same time as Matthew and the Gospel of John perhaps ten years later. Some support for our theory that there was a fairly widespread attempt around the end of the first century to subordinate women to men in the church is to be found in the Gospels, which date from an earlier time.

In the Gospels of both Mark and Matthew, the earthly Jesus, that is, Jesus before his death and resurrection, never instructs a woman to do something, or not to do something. The apparent exceptions are not such instructions—for example, Jesus says to the daughter of Jairus: "Little girl, get up" (Mark 5:41), but Jesus is not some stage hypnotist demonstrating his power. What he is saying is something like: "You are cured. Go, live your life."[237] In intention it differs little from Jesus's words shortly before to the woman suffering from hemorrhages: "Go in peace, and be healed of your disease" (Mark 5:34), and, indeed, can be regarded as stylistic variation.[238] In Matthew there is not even the appearance of a command in the corresponding stories. The Matthean Jesus does not speak to the daughter of the leader of the synagogue (Matt 9:25) and his words to the woman healed of a hemorrhage are very similar to those in Mark cited above. However, after the resurrection, the Matthean Jesus tells the women who go to the tomb: "Do not be afraid; go and tell my brothers to go to Galilee; there they will see me" (Matt 28:10). But this instruction is given by the risen Jesus—before his death the Matthean Jesus never told a woman to do, or not do, anything.

In Luke's writings neither Jesus nor any of the apostles give instructions to a woman. But, Luke goes further: no-one at all, whether man or

---

237. This also applies to other cured people, for example, the cured paralytic man (Mark 2:10–11). See 6.1.6.

238. In another variation the daughter of the Syro-Phoenician woman (Mark 7:29) is healed with no command.

woman, in either Luke or Acts tells a woman to do, or not do, anything, and, as we saw in 6.1.6, he omitted three instances in his Markan antetext where a woman was told, explicitly or implicitly, to do something.

We see this as a deliberate choice on Luke's part—that Jesus issues no instructions in the Markan and Matthean examples may not be significant as they feature few women and there is little opportunity for them to portray Jesus giving instructions to a woman. But Luke has ample opportunity, and does not avail of it. Indeed, he often shows women telling men what to do, from Elizabeth (explicitly) and Mary (implicitly) deciding on the names of their sons, to Lydia prevailing on Paul and his companions to stay in her house.[239]

7.6.7.2 The Gospel of John

In the Gospel of John Jesus said to the Samaritan woman: "Give me a drink" (John 4:7). As the Fourth Gospel was written a decade or so after Luke, towards the end of the first century, if this were a command it might be seen as evidence for our argument, but, although Jesus's speech has the appearance of an instruction, it should rather be regarded as a request.[240] The polite circumlocutions of English were not used in Greek and the early commentators agree that Jesus *asked* for water.[241]

Also in the Gospel of John, the post-resurrection Jesus instructs Mary Magdalene:

> Do not hold on to me, because I have not yet ascended to the Father. But go to my brothers and say to them, "I am ascending to my Father and your Father, to my God and your God" (John 20:17).

As for Matthew, the post-resurrection Jesus is not to be regarded in the same way as Jesus during his life on earth.

---

239. Elizabeth names the child (Luke 1:57–63); Mary names the child (Luke 2:21); Jesus obedient to his parents (Luke 2:51); Martha asking Jesus to tell her sister to help her (Luke 10:38–42); the woman with the hemorrhage touching Jesus (Luke 8:43–48); the parable of the woman confronting the unjust judge (Luke 18:2–8); Lydia prevailing upon Paul (Acts 16:14–15) and Priscilla instructing Apollos (Acts 18:26).

240. "Will you give me a drink" (NIV); "Please give me a drink" (NLT, NCV, ISV); "Would you give me a drink of water" (The Message); "asked her to give him a drink" (Rieu).

241. Maximus of Turin, Ephrem the Syrian, Theodore of Mopsuestia, Chrysostom, Augustine, in Elowski, *Ancient Christian Commentaries, John 1–10*, 147–48.

However, there is one command by Jesus. He said to the woman taken in adultery: "Neither do I condemn you. Go your way, and from now on do not sin again" (John 8:11). This is unambiguously the earthly Jesus telling the woman not to do something, and the only instance of this kind in the Gospels. However, it seems clear that this pericope was not part of the original version of the Gospel, but was a later addition: "It is only from ca. 900 that it begins to appear in the standard Greek text,"[242] although there are earlier witnesses from the third century.[243] As a later addition, it is not evidence against our observation that Jesus never tells women to do, or not do, anything in the original versions of the four Gospels, and, indeed, could provide some additional support for our hypothesis that there was a later attempt to impose patriarchal authority.

Many commentators think that the pericope is an authentic oral memory of Jesus, added to the Gospel at a later date.[244] However, the actual command, "from now on do not sin again, *apo tou nun mēketi hamartane*" (8:11), may not have been in the earliest tradition. It is at the end of the passage, the pericope makes perfect sense without it, and it repeats the words of John 5:14, "*mēketi hamartane*."[245] Andrew Lincoln discusses the origins of the story,[246] describing two third/fourth-century partial versions, dealing with a woman who had sinned. In one Jesus concludes the passage by saying: "Go then, neither do I condemn you" and the other[247] with: "He who has not sinned, let him take a stone and cast it."[248] Neither includes the command to sin no more. It is certainly possible, and in our view probable, that this final command was not part of any first century tradition. Indeed, the earliest full version of the story is in *Codex Bezae*, dating from the fifth century, and, as we have seen in 7.6.6, the Bezan text of Acts includes changes designed to reduce the importance of women.

It has been suggested that: "The ease with which Jesus forgave the adulteress was hard to reconcile with the stern penitential discipline in vogue in the early Church."[249] If this was the reason the story was rejected, it is plausible that "*mēketi hamartane*" was added to overcome the patriar-

---

242. Brown, *John 1*, 335.

243. Ibid., 335.

244. Ibid., 335.

245. This has similarities to the reason given by Fitzmyer, cited in 7.3.2.1, for rejecting the idea that the women in Luke 8:1–3 provided for "him."

246. Lincoln, *John*, 524–28.

247. Didymus the Blind. For the text see Ehrman, *Didymus the Blind*, 145.

248. Lincoln, *John*, 526.

249. Brown, *John 1*, 335. E.g., Augustine (Elowski, *Ancient Christian Commentaries*, 272).

chalists' distaste for the apparent condoning of adultery. If, as many scholars argue, the original story was more Lukan in character,[250] this is the more likely. The Lukan Jesus did not tell those he healed not to sin again, not the sinful woman (7:50), not Zacchaeus (19:9–10), not Peter.

7.7 SUMMARY: CHAPTERS 6 AND 7

In these two chapters we have examined the presentation of women in Luke-Acts and have found that very many traditional interpretations are questionable, in that they minimize the importance of women in Luke's narrative. Some of our specific interpretations are arguable, but others are supported by substantial evidence, for example the story of the selection of Matthias. But we do not see Luke merely as recognizing that women have a role to play, rather, he tells us that that role is of very great importance. This is demonstrated at the beginning of the Gospel in the description of Anna, which brings to mind the autonomous and agentic women who played a significant part in the salvation history of Israel, and each of whom sang a canticle in praise of God. Then Mary, at the most important moment of all, was also autonomous and agentic, not consulting anyone, but saying yes to the request of God. A very small number of women are not responsive to Jesus: nearly all of these are exceptionally rich, and the others are slaves of rich people. One woman, initially responsive, fell away because she colluded in deception with her husband, probably in obedience to him. But in both Gospel and Acts, other women are always portrayed as autonomous, often agentic, and usually work to bring about the kingdom of God by *diakonia*, prophecy and witness.

We see Luke's view of women as being to a large extent due to spending a substantial part of his formative years in the household of Lydia, probably a freed slave managing the textile business of her former owner. Her importance to Luke is shown by a sequence of four heavenly interventions leading him to spend six or seven years living in her household in Philippi. There, we suggest, he received a Greek education while learning the scriptures, that is, the Septuagint, from his parents, Christian missionaries.

Our view of the women in Luke-Acts differs from generally accepted views. We describe some of the reasons for these views, for, example, the belief that widows in the early first-century church (and in the Septuagint) were dependent on the charitable support of others. We show that this was not the case. Another reason is the acceptance of the authority of the apostles, including Peter's decision that the successor to Judas must be male.

250. Brown, *John 1*, 336; Perkins, "John," 965.

We have shown that Luke's intention was to contrast the self-seeking pre-Pentecost Peter with the post-Pentecost exemplary Christian missionary. However, even in the post-Pentecost church, the apostles are flawed—they abandon *diakonia*, to concentrate on preaching the Word. In a similar way, we see Luke's portrait of Paul as nuanced. Like the pre-Pentecost Peter, he too could be impulsive, irascible and too clever by half.

However, we see the most important explanation of the traditional views as the development of a patriarchal ideology, absent from all the Gospels and from the authentic Pauline letters. There are indications of its emergence in the deutero-Pauline letters and it appears in full flower in the Pastorals and the letter of Clement which, indeed, incorporates a lie about an episode in scripture. This ideology also led to many alterations to the text of Acts and to the mistaken interpretations of Luke-Acts described in these two chapters. Our view is similar to that of Elizabeth Schüssler Fiorenza who describes the development of "ecclesial patriarchalization" after "the genuine Pauline letters,"[251] including some of the examples cited above, and also the later work of Tertullian. She finds:

> It is clear, however, that such a patriarchal leadership structure was advocated in conflict with a more egalitarian church practice, which it sought to replace. It goes hand in hand with an ideological legitimation of the exclusion of women from church leadership.[252]

But Luke had no part in this patriarchalization, indeed, shows no awareness of a patriarchal structure. His protagonists are all male, but they do not treat women as subordinate.

---

251. Schüssler Fiorenza, *Discipleship of Equals*, 171.
252. Ibid.

CHAPTER 8

Summary and Conclusions

8.1 INTRODUCTION

This study aims to understand the way in which Luke presented the men and women who met Jesus and the apostles in both his Gospel and in the Acts of the Apostles. It is a socio-historical literary study which attempts to read Luke's narrative, in particular his portrayal of characters or character groups of differing socio-economic categories, in the way that he intended and in the light of the circumstances of his time. He says that he decided "to write an orderly account for you—so that you may know the truth concerning the things about which you have been instructed" (Luke 1:3–4). We have worked on the assumption that he did just that, telling the story in a way which he saw as orderly and intending to present the truth as he saw it.

The tools which we see as of greatest utility in achieving such understanding include the examination of *context*, that is, the social, economic and political world shared by Luke and his intended readers, *intertext*, the Jewish scriptures, and co-*text*, the way in which one part of Luke's work can help his intended readers understand another. We also compare Luke's narrative with his known written sources, his *antetext*. Where Luke has changed the antetext, identifying and analyzing the change can help us to understand his intentions.

We argue that he and his intended readers shared not only a general knowledge of the history and culture of the first century, but also a particular knowledge of the Septuagint and some knowledge of the house of Herod, whose members play an important part in his narrative. His work was intended to be read aloud; not all of the audience would have the same knowledge of, for example, the Septuagint, as Luke himself or those to whom he sent copies of his manuscript, his first actual readers. Reading was usually to groups of people and, in the case of Luke, probably in a Christian context—Luke specifically writes for those "who have been instructed." The auditors will usually have discussed the reading amongst themselves, sharing their understanding of the text, the lector probably taking the lead. Much could have been explained.

We primarily assess the portrayal of both individuals and group characters in the narrative by considering the way in which they respond to Jesus and the apostles, an important indication of the point of view of the narrator which is aligned with that of the Lukan Jesus. Several passages in the Gospel are especially helpful in understanding that viewpoint. One of the more important, widely recognized by scholars, is Jesus's citation of Isaiah in his statement of his mission in Nazareth, including: "The Spirit of the Lord has anointed me to bring good news to the poor," its importance confirmed when he said: "Today this scripture has been fulfilled in your hearing" (Luke 4:18–21). Other important passages near the beginning of the Gospel are the devil's claim to "authority over all the kingdoms of the world" (Luke 4:5–6) and the description of Anna (Luke 2:36–37), which we see as a celebration of autonomous and agentic women in the history of Israel. Towards the end of the Gospel, the Lukan Jesus explains the importance of service (Luke 22:26–27), contrasting it with the authority prized by secular rulers. This was almost the last thing he said to his disciples, which gives it special significance, and we see it as a crucial aid to understanding Luke's presentation of men and of women.

For the purposes of our analysis we classified Luke's characters (including group characters) into broad categories based upon their function in the society of the Roman empire, and compared the characters in each category, one with another, and also with characters in other categories. We found that Luke's presentation of characters within each category was not consistent, but varied depending on other circumstances, although there is a clear distinction between Luke's presentation of men and his presentation of women.

Having first described our methodology, our survey considered the house of Herod and then the Roman governors, the ruling elites of the Roman empire, those men of great wealth and status who feature in his narrative, together with the soldiers and others who served them. We next turned to the Jewish authorities, comprising both the chief priests in Jerusalem, who were the local elite for that city, and the Pharisees, who were not of elite status but carried a substantial degree of religious authority. Luke's attitude towards the chief priests is colored by his theological need to understand the destruction of the city and the temple, a defining event which had taken place about ten years before he wrote Luke-Acts.

We also assessed other groups, including the local elites, whose members were less rich and powerful but had significant status in their own cities. Of much lower status were the *penētes*, people who had to work for a living and were despised by all those in the elite classes. Most of the men we meet in Luke-Acts fall into this group, including centurions and soldiers, Pharisees and tax collectors. Other characters described are of an even lower status, the destitute, *ptōchoi*, beggars and day laborers, including most of those who were sick. The other major classes in the Roman empire were slaves and freedmen, but only a few slaves feature in Luke-Acts, and they are invariably shown as responding to Jesus and the apostles in the same way as their owners. The only clearly identifiable freedman, Felix, was a member of the ruling elite and is dealt with as such. Women are examined separately.

Although such categorization provided a useful approach to the wide range of Lukan characters, it is not the only clue to understanding how Luke intended the reader to evaluate them—for this their response to the Lukan Jesus is more important, and the advice of the Baptist to soldiers and tax-collectors is also relevant. Our conclusions below partly cross these boundaries, drawing together those whom the narrator presents in a similar way, although again men are considered separately from women. We also consider the utility of our methodology, the presentation of Peter and Paul in the parts of the narrative which we consider, and the church around the end of the first century. Our conclusions may be analyzed under the following headings:

1. 8.2 The methodology used in the study;
2. 8.3 The author of Luke-Acts;
3. 8.4 The male characters covered in the study;
4. 8.5 The female characters covered in the study;
5. 8.6 Peter and Paul;
6. 8.7 The church around the end of the first century;
7. 8.8 In conclusion.

Some of our conclusions are firm. We have examined the evidence in Luke-Acts about men of the ruling elite, the local elite, the chief priests and the non-elite, and about women, and regard most of our conclusions about them as well supported. Others are extremely tentative—for example, there is a great deal of information in Luke-Acts about Peter and Paul, only a small part of which is included in this study, so our conclusions about Luke's presentation of Peter and of Paul are valid, if at all, only for those sections of Luke-Acts here covered.

8.2 METHODOLOGY

One of the fundamental assumptions made for the purposes of our argument was that Luke was a skilled writer, able to communicate effectively that which he wished to communicate. Some 2,000 years later it may be difficult to understand what that was, but an attempt can be made by using the concept of the intended reader, that is, the way in which the reader (or auditor) envisaged by Luke would have been expected to understand his words. To achieve this we have used four principal tools, listed above, context, intertext, co-text and antetext; we have made a further assumption, that is, that the Lukan narrator attempted to align his views with those of the Lukan Jesus. This approach has suggested new ways of understanding Luke's presentation of the characters whom we consider, why he said things in a particular way, supported by evidence in the Lukan text and through the use of our investigative tools. We conclude that the methodology of the study is shown to be fruitful.

The methodology requires a view on the date of the text, to ensure that it is considered against the background of a particular time and place. We have followed most scholars in dating it to around the early years of Domitian, that is, the early 80s. Taking into account events which could plausibly have been known to the intended reader at that time has helped to clarify Luke's intentions, an important example being Paul's change of name and the immediately following journey to Antioch by Paul and Barnabas.

8.3 THE AUTHOR

Luke tells us that he "investigated everything carefully from the very first" (Luke 1:3). This and other autobiographical material in Acts can provide useful information about Luke's life and we have argued that the best explanation for the information available in the text is that Luke was a child when he first met Paul. He tells us that he spent some half a dozen years in the Roman colony of Philippi, in the household of Lydia, a trader in cloth. If at that time he was an adolescent he could have received the education in the effective but non-classical Greek which has been identified in his writings; he could also have developed an understanding of the Roman public moral code, which may account for aspects of his portrayal of Roman soldiers and administrators. He spent some time in the company of Paul before arriving at Philippi, and if he was indeed a child, this will have been with his parents who were Christian missionaries. They could have provided him with the knowledge of the Septuagint so evident in his work. However, this hypothesis is a by-product of our study and in no way fundamental to our other conclusions set out below.

Luke tells us that he knew Paul well, and that he knew James, the brother of Jesus, and the elders of Jerusalem. He also tells us that he stayed with Philip, whom he shows as an important figure in the early church, and with Mnason, who was an early disciple. These men could have been among those who provided information about events "from the very beginning." He also tells us that he knew Julius, who, we argue, was an eye-witness to Paul's interrogation before Agrippa. Moreover, it may be that he knew almost all of the identified Christian women about whom he wrote in Acts as he tells us that he visited the cities in which they were based: Jerusalem for Mary, the mother of Mark and Rhoda, Philippi for Lydia, Caesarea for the daughters of Philip, and Rome for Priscilla (and perhaps Joanna).

In chapter 1 we explained that, for the purposes of the study, we would assume Luke's historical reliability, in particular, that he was present at the events described in the "we" passages, and in our conclusions consider whether this was a tenable viewpoint. We have found no reason to doubt this assumption, and the fruits of our examination give good reason to accept it.

8.4 THE MALE CHARACTERS

8.4.1 The Ruling Elite

Luke's presentation of his male characters can best be understood by dividing them into major socio-economic categories, the ruling elite, including the house of Herod, the local elites, the *penētes*, and the *ptōchoi*. The Jewish chief priests, because of their religious significance, are presented separately, but none of the other groups is treated monolithically. The most important factor in the presentation is the character's attitude to Jesus or the apostles, but there are other differences. These can often be understood by examining the words of the Lukan Jesus, especially those noted above, or by the love of money, linked to the devil and idolatry. Other factors, such as the words of the Baptist, can also explain differences in presentation.

Almost all of the extremely rich members of the house of Herod and the Roman governors are presented as evil. Herod the Great was notorious, and Luke mentions him only briefly. Archelaus, who killed many, is obliquely referred to and the evil deeds of Antipas and Agrippa I, both of whom Luke calls "Herod," are described in the text. Philip and Agrippa II are exceptions. Philip is referred to, but is not called "Herod," and Jesus finds refuge from Antipas in his territory. The description of him by Josephus suggests a man who took his duties seriously.

Agrippa II is described in more detail. He listened to and accepted Paul's defense and referred ironically to becoming a Christian himself. He provided the military escort for Paul's conveyance to Rome, including the centurion Julius who treated Paul well. Luke tells us no ill of him. The Baptist told tax-collectors and soldiers, the latter being gentiles in the employment of the house of Herod, to do their duty and shun extortion. Both Philip and Agrippa II would have cleared this low bar, and Luke may have required no more from these men who, like the tax-collectors and soldiers in the Baptist's audience, were in the service of rulers who owed their authority to the devil.

Turning to the Roman governors, Pilate and Felix are also shown to be evil men. Pilate condemns a man whom he has three times declared to be innocent, and frees an insurrectionist and murderer; Luke shows that he was not a faithful servant of the emperor. Felix is venal, and both he and Pilate, for their own purposes, seek to curry favor with the Jewish leaders. Gallio does little—he does not even prevent violence before his own tribunal. There is nothing praiseworthy about these men.

Sergius Paulus, we are told, believed. Under his influence Saul changed his name to Paul and both he and Barnabas left Cyprus to travel hot-foot to the home town of Sergius, Pisidian Antioch. Here their mission was initially successful, but eventually the leading families turned on them and drove them out. The patronage of Sergius Paulus was not enough, which raises questions in the mind of the intended reader, aware of the power of the senatorial class, as to how enduring his belief was. We argue that the status of the senatorial families of Antioch in Luke's time was known to Luke's intended audience—he tells his readers about one of them—and would be taken into account in their understanding of Luke's narrative. Thus they would see the episode as a partial failure on the part of Paul and Barnabas, caused by their fawning at the feet of power. Their behavior can be contrasted with that of the Lukan Jesus in his dealings with Antipas and Pilate.

The final governor seen is Porcius Festus, whose activities are described at some length. Luke presents him as a conscientious servant of the emperor, all of his actions reflecting his duty as governor. He sought to please the Jewish leaders, undoubtedly part of his job, but did not allow them to railroad him into sending Paul for trial in Jerusalem, instead asking Paul what he thought and accepting his appeal to Caesar. In this he acted as a governor should, in accordance with the moral code of the Roman ruling classes as shown in the writings of the younger Pliny. We found parallels with the teachings of Jesus, but it is by remembering the words of the Baptist that we see that the actions of Felix are acceptable to the Lukan narrator. He did not, of course, become a Christian and, as he died in office, Luke could not have looked for his future conversion. Even in the service of one whose authority was bestowed by the devil, Festus could, like the soldiers and tax-collectors and in accordance with his own moral code, meet the requirements of the Baptist.

8.4.2 The Local Elites

The most important of the local elites for Luke is that in Jerusalem, the chief priests, sharply differentiated from other local elites and from the other religious group, the Pharisees. They do not appear in Luke's story until near the end of the journeying of Jesus, as he nears Jerusalem, and they are unremittingly murderous and hostile to Jesus, eventually procuring his death, and subsequently hostile to the apostles and Paul. There are no mitigating factors in Luke's account, and he expects the reader, familiar with the Septuagint, to see parallels with the previous destruction of the city and the temple described in 2 Kings. The chief priests are entrusted with a special responsibility by the nature of their religious status, which they abuse—Jesus condemns them in the parable of the vineyard. The only leaders of the Jerusalem Sanhedrin who do not seek to destroy Jesus and then the apostles are Joseph of Arimathea, who was neither a priest nor from Jerusalem, and Pharisees (including Gamaliel), whom Luke always carefully distinguishes from the chief priests. The chief priests and their associates, who perished in the destruction of the city and the temple, carry all the responsibility.

Local elites in other cities varied in their response to Jesus or the apostles, and Luke rarely gives explanations for this. In the Gospel the rich ruler is left undecided—Luke does not tell us whether he follows the command of Jesus to give away all his possessions or not. In Acts there are many more elites, including the magistrates in various towns. Some accept and some reject Jesus, but rejection is most pronounced in Pisidian Antioch, an extremely rich town which was exceptional in the eastern empire in providing, by Luke's time, three senators. The city, led by a small group of ambitious leading families, did not provide fertile ground for the growth of the gospel. But in most cities, and especially in cities which were the seats of the Roman governors, there was little or no opposition to the apostles and some members of these elites responded to the good news.

8.4.3 The Penētes

Most of the characters in the Gospel and Acts are of the *penētes*, including Pharisees, centurions, soldiers, and many of the residents of the towns evangelized by the apostles.

The Pharisees were too obtuse to recognize Jesus but never attempted to harm him; they engaged with him in various ways, continually argued with him, often invited him to dinner, and, in the Gospel, showed signs of listening to what he had to say. In Acts we see some, including Paul, become Christians. Others, first Gamaliel and then an un-named group, do not oppose the apostles but save them, and later save Paul, from the murderous hostility of the chief priests. Centurions and soldiers are also presented favorably. Centurions are generous, one recognizes Jesus as innocent, another is converted and yet another is kind to Paul. Although soldiers crucify Jesus, they are following orders, and Luke removes the gratuitous cruelty of the Markan account; soldiers also on several occasions rescue Paul.

Many other *penētes* accepted Jesus, including the tax-collectors, Levi and Zacchaeus, Jairus and all of the apostles whose status can be identified in Luke's text. In Acts again, the missionaries, Simon the tanner, Aquila, Apollos, and others were of this status.

Those *penētes* who rejected the message, Judas, Ananias, Simon Magus, Bar Jesus and others were led astray by money, which is always, in Acts, linked to the devil, or magic, or false gods, and we saw that these three are themselves closely linked. However, even those who serve the devil can be brought to repent and follow Jesus, as is shown by the book-burning magicians of Ephesus who abandoned magic and by Simon Magus who repented.

8.4.4 The Ptōchoi

The destitute are healed by Jesus but in the Gospel they play no part in his ministry, and Luke amends his antetext to show that blind Bartimaeus, the last major healing in the Gospel, fulfils the Septuagintal role as one of the destitute, dependent upon God, not acting independently. However, in Acts the followers of Jesus use their resources wisely, so that there are no needy among them and all can play their part in spreading the good news, including the man born lame, the first major healing in Acts, active in supporting Peter and John.

8.5 THE FEMALE CHARACTERS

We have argued that traditional interpretations of Luke's presentation of women have followed a patriarchal ideology; even those who reject that ideology have accepted it as an explanation of Luke's words. We have identified three major sources of this misinterpretation: the story of the selection of Matthias, the belief that, in the Septuagint and therefore in Luke-Acts, widows are symbols of destitution, and the understanding of prophecy as involving the utterance of oracles, so that Lukan women, who do not utter oracles, are not prophets. By examining and rejecting these arguments, a clearer understanding of Luke's intentions is possible. Luke does not believe that the successors to the apostles must be male, widows in Luke-Acts are almost never destitute, and women are presented as prophets, although, like men, their prophetic activity is described very rarely. Our review also gives attention to Lydia, recognizing that there were not three, but four heavenly interventions sending Paul, and Luke, to Philippi and the household of Lydia, where Luke stayed for six or seven years. The honor paid to Lydia when Luke tells us that "the Lord opened her heart" (Acts 16:14), an intervention otherwise only afforded to those most significant in Luke's story, shows how Luke intended the reader to value her.

Luke always shows women as autonomous, altering his Markan antetext three times to remove instances where women were not so seen. He has prepared in the description of Anna a summary of references to women autonomous in the history of Israel, who were also agentic in promoting God's purposes, each of whom sang a canticle in praise of the Lord. We have argued that the description of Anna, with its references to autonomous and agentic women, is a reflection, amplification, or, indeed, explanation, of the story of the annunciation, when Mary also acted autonomously and agentically in saying "Yes" to God, and sang a canticle, the Magnificat. The autonomy of Lukan women extends to their relationship with the Lukan Jesus, who never instructs a woman to do, or not to do, anything, and similarly to their relationship with Peter and Paul.

Women are nearly all receptive to the message, and act to bring about the kingdom, usually by *diakonia*, or by prophecy in the form of witness or encouragement. Jesus emphasized the importance of service, of *diakonia*, "I am among you as one who serves" (Luke 22:27), and we interpret this as guidance to the apostles as to how they should act in their apostleship. Luke depicts many women as models of that service.

8.6 PETER AND PAUL

This study did not set out to examine Luke's presentation of Peter or of Paul, but in attempting to understand why our interpretation of Luke's portrayal of women differed so substantially from that of other scholars, we discovered that a major factor was the story of the selection of Matthias to replace Judas among the twelve apostles. The traditional interpretation ignores the evidence; we conclude that Luke intended the story to provide a contrast between the behavior of Peter before Pentecost, and his very different behavior afterwards, when he had "turned back" to strengthen his brothers. Luke's description of Pentecost provides an extremely vivid picture of that turning. We see Peter turn again after the intervention of the Spirit, in the story of the conversion of Cornelius—that story could also be described as the second conversion of Peter.

We also examined the journey by Paul and Barnabas from Cyprus to Antioch. Saul changes his name to Paul in honor of the patronage of Sergius Paulus and then goes directly to his home city where, like any senator, he had great influence. After some initial success Paul and Barnabas were driven from Antioch and then from Iconium, but more importantly, the reader is left with the clear impression that the leading families of Antioch (including that of Sergius Paulus) rejected the Gospel. Although there were converts in Antioch, they were not of the local elite.

Luke shows the faults of both Peter and Paul. Peter has to be persuaded to respond to Cornelius, and Paul is shown as both quarrelsome and headstrong. His dash to Antioch fails of its purpose, and this may also be true of Paul's clever defense in Jerusalem and his decision to appeal to Caesar; this results in Paul losing a good two years of missionary activity—Luke recounts none on the journey to Rome—and once arrived there Paul continued to be constrained. His activities should be contrasted with those of the Lukan Jesus, who did not look for the patronage of the great or attempt to manipulate legal processes.

8.7 THE CHURCH AFTER LUKE'S TIME

To corroborate the plausibility of our interpretation of the presentation of women in Luke-Acts we examined writings from the time before Luke wrote up to about twenty-five years later. We found substantial evidence of a change in the portrayal of women, from Paul saying there is no male or female and the four Gospels which in their original form, never showed any living man telling any individual woman to do or not to do anything. Later we see patriarchal and misogynistic passages in the deutero-Pauline letters, the Pastorals, 1 Peter, and the letters of Clement and Ignatius, and also in alterations to the text of Acts and perhaps of 1 Corinthians. Most of this evidence is of the kind which detective stories describe as circumstantial, not conclusive and with each instance being open to other explanations, but there is one "smoking gun." When Clement describes how "the blessed Judith" asked permission from the elders, it is difficult to see this as other than a deliberate lie. As such, it adds considerable weight to the other evidence identified, the extent and variety of which add substantial support to our interpretation.

8.8 IN CONCLUSION

Luke was an extremely skilled and subtle writer. His narrative describes the birth, life, death, and teaching of Jesus, and how his teaching was carried forward by his followers after his death and resurrection. Our study has not considered that major aspect, but has looked at minor characters, to further understand the Lukan viewpoint. His writings have, as regards many of the people dealt with in our study, been misinterpreted; in the case of his presentation of women, grossly so. We attribute this to a general desire among church leaders around the end of the first century to impose a patriarchal structure on the church, similar to the structure of the society in which they lived. This structure is seen not only in the subordination of women but also in seeing some men as possessing patriarchal authority. This patriarchal structure is buttressed by an ideology which has been used to interpret Luke-Acts, both by misinterpreting Luke's presentation of women and interpreting the portraits of Peter and Paul in Acts as models for episcopal authority in the growing church.

Examples raised in this study are the failure to consider whether the resurrected Jesus might have appeared to Simon the Zealot, not to Simon Peter, and whether the story of the selection of Matthias is a further example of the pre-Pentecostal obtuseness of the disciples. We also regard the idea that the apostles were justified in excusing themselves from *diakonia* and that they, not the people, laid hands on the Seven as examples of such patriarchal interpretation. The recent discovery that the family of Sergius Paulus was resident in Pisidian Antioch raises questions about Paul which could have an important bearing on both Lukan and Pauline studies.

We see Luke as rejecting totally the imperial structures of the Roman empire of his time and promoting two alternative approaches to authority. The first is the autonomy of women; the women in Luke-Acts are nearly all agentic in the bringing into being of God's kingdom, primarily doing this through loving service, *diakonia*, of which they are exemplars. Lukan women do not seek power and authority, what they do is work tirelessly in prophecy, that is, the building up and strengthening of the church, and they are autonomous, not directed by any man but only by God.

The second approach, more evident in Luke's text, is to realize that the imperial ruling structures, the formal basis of Greco-Roman society, derive from the devil, the source of the power and authority of earthly rulers, including those who seek to kill first Jesus and then the apostles. The devil also, through idolatry, magic, and the love of money, corrupts many others, not only members of the ruling elite. The Lukan Baptist tells those in the service of that diabolical system to be satisfied with their wages, not to seek money by extortion, and the Lukan Jesus tells one ruler, part of that ruling structure, to give away all that he has. Others, not part of that structure, are repeatedly told to give alms, to support the poor, and in the beginning of Acts we see that this leads to a situation where "there was not a needy person among them" (Acts 4:34) so that all could play their full part in bringing about the kingdom of God. But our examination of writings around the end of the first century suggests that there was a wide-spread and largely successful drive by church leaders, increasingly manifest in promoting obedience to bishops and the subordination of women, to bring the governance of the church into line with the structures of that devil-bestowed imperial authority.

Appendix I

Members of the House of Herod Significant for Luke

In the following list each individual is shown with Hanson's identifying number. Lukan references are shown where appropriate and Markan or Matthean references are given where there is no mention in Luke. Descendants of the Hasmonean royal family (that is, of Mariamme I) are marked (H).

Herod I (the Great). Called King Herod by Luke (1:5).

Archelaus. Matt 2:22. Son of Herod I. Possible references at Luke 2:1-2; 19:12-15.

Herod Philip. Mark 6:17. Son of Herod I. First husband of Herodias. Called Philip by Mark and Matthew (Matt 14:3).

Herod Philip I. Ruler of Ituraea and Trachonitis (Luke 3:1). Son of Herod I. First husband of Salome. Called Philip by Luke.

Herod Antipas. Son of Herod I. (Luke 3:1, 19-20; 8:3; 9:7-9; 13:31-32; 23:7-15; Acts 4:27; 13:1). Called Herod the Tetrarch[1] or Herod by Luke.

Herodias (H). (Luke 3:19; see Mark 6:17-28).

Salome III (H). Mark 6:22-28. Called "Herodias" or "daughter of Herodias" by Mark, "daughter of Herodias" by Matthew (Matt 14:6).

Agrippa I (H). (Acts 12:1-4, 19-23). Called "King Herod" or "Herod" by Luke.

---

1. Ruler in NRSV.

Agrippa II (H). (Acts 25:13—26:32). Son of Agrippa I. Called "King Agrippa" or "Agrippa" by Luke.

Berenice III (H). (Acts 25:13, 23; 26:30). Daughter of Agrippa I. Called "Bernice" by Luke.

Drusilla (H). (Acts 24:24). Daughter of Agrippa I. Married to Felix.

Felix. (Acts 23:24; 23:33—24:27; 25:14). A freedman. Husband of Drusilla.

Herod IV of Chalcis (H). Brother of Agrippa I. Second husband of Berenice III.

Aristobulus IV (H). Son of Herod of Chalcis. Second husband of Salome III.

Appendix II

Chēra (widow) and cognates in the Septuagint

CHĒRA (WIDOW)

Gen 38:11, of Tamar.

Exod 22:22 (LXX 22:21), Widows and orphans.

Exod 22:24 (LXX 22:23), Punishment.

Lev 21:14, A chief priest shall not marry a widow.

Lev 22:13, If the daughter of a priest is a widow without offspring she shall return to her father's house.

Num 30:10, The vow of a widow shall bind her.

Deut 10:18, Widows and orphans.

Deut 14:29, Widows and orphans.

Deut 16:11, Widows and orphans.

Deut 16:14, Widows and orphans.

Deut 24:17, Widows and orphans.

Deut 24:19, Widows and orphans.

Deut 24:20, Widows and orphans.

Deut 24:21, Widows and orphans.

Deut 26:12, Widows and orphans.

Deut 26:13, Widows and orphans.

Deut 27:1, Widows and orphans.

2 Sam 14:5, The wise woman of Tekoa.

2 Sam 20:3, David's concubines live as widows, i.e., celibately.

1 Kgs 7:14, Hiram son of a widow.

1 Kgs 11:26, Jeroboam son of a widow.

1 Kgs 17:9, Widow of Zarephath commanded to feed Elijah.

1 Kgs 17:10, Widow of Zarephath.

1 Kgs 17:20, Widow of Zarephath.

Tob 1:8, Widows and orphans.

Jdt 9:4, Judith.

Jdt 9:9, Judith.

Job 22:9, Widows and orphans.

Job 24:3, Widows and orphans.

Job 27:15, Punishment.

Job 29:12–13, Widows and orphans.

Job 31:16–17, Widows and orphans.

Ps 68:5 (LXX 67:6), Widows and orphans.

Ps 78:64 (LXX 77:64), Punishment.

Ps 94:6 (LXX 93:6), Widows and orphans.

Ps 109:9 (LXX 108:9), Punishment.

Ps 146:9 (LXX 145:9), Widows and orphans.

Prov 15:25, The Lord . . . maintains the widow's boundaries.

Wis 2:10, Let us not spare the widow.

Sir 35:14–15 (LXX 35:17–18), Widows and orphans.

Zech 7:10, Widows and orphans.

Mal 3:5, Widows and orphans.

Isa 1:17, Widows and orphans.

Isa 1:23, Widows and orphans.

Isa 9:17, Punishment.

Isa 10:2, Widows and orphans.

Isa 47:8, Punishment.

Isa 49:21, Punishment (bereaved in NRSV).

Jer 5:28, Widows and orphans (orphans only in NRSV).

Jer 7:6, Widows and orphans.

Jer 15:8, Punishment.

Jer 18:21, Punishment.

Jer 22:3, Widows and orphans.

Jer 49:11 (LXX 30:4), Punishment (widows and orphans in NRSV).

Bar 4:12, Punishment.

Bar 4:16, Punishment.

Lam 1:1, Punishment.

Lam 5:3, Punishment.

Let Jer 37, Widows and orphans.

Ezek 22:7, Widows and orphans.

Ezek 22:25, Punishment.

Ezek 44:22, Priests shall not marry a widow . . . but only a widow who is the widow of a priest.

2 Macc 3:10, Widows and orphans.

2 Macc 8:28, Widows and orphans.

2 Macc 8:30, Widows and orphans.

4 Macc 16:10, Mother of the seven brothers.

CHĒREIA (WIDOWHOOD)

Mic 1:16, Punishment (not in NRSV).

Isa 47:9, Punishment.

Isa 54:4, Punishment.

CHĒREUEIN (TO BE WIDOWED)

2 Sam 13:20, Tamar to live as a widow, i.e., celibately (desolate in NRSV).

Jdt 8:4, Judith.

Jer 51:5 (LXX 28:5), Punishment (forsaken in NRSV).

CHĒREUSIS (WIDOWHOOD)

Gen 38:14, Tamar.

Gen 38:19, Tamar.

Jdt 8:5, Judith.

Jdt 8:6, Judith.

Jdt 10:3, Judith.

Total number 77, widows and orphans 34, punishment 19, identified individuals 15, other references 9.

Note: References are to NRSV. Septuagint, where different, shown in brackets. Variants are excluded.

Bibliography

Achtemeier, P. J. "'Omne Verbum Sonat': The New Testament and the Oral Environment of Late Western Antiquity." *Journal of Biblical Literature* 109 (1990) 3-27.
Alexander, Loveday. "Acts." In *OBC*, 1028-61.
———. *Acts in Its Ancient Literary Context*. London: T. & T. Clark, 2007.
———. "Ancient Book Production and the Circulation of the Gospels." In *TGAC*, 71-111.
———. "Sisters in Adversity: Retelling Martha's Story." In *FCL*, 197-213.
Applebaum, S. "The Legal Status of the Jewish Communities in the Diaspora." In *The Jewish People in the First Century*, edited by S. Safrai and M. Stern, 1:420-63. Assen, Netherlands: Van Gorcum, 1974.
Archer, L. J. *Her Price Is beyond Rubies: The Jewish Woman in Graeco-Roman Palestine*. Sheffield, UK: JSOT, 1990.
Ascough, Richard S. *Lydia: Paul's Cosmopolitan Hostess*. Collegeville: Liturgical, 2009.
Bacote, Vincent E. "Justice." In *Dictionary for Theological Interpretation of the Bible*, edited by Kevin J. Vanhoozer, 415-16. Grand Rapids: Baker, 2005.
Bailey, Kenneth E. *Jesus through Middle Eastern Eyes: Cultural Studies in the Gospels*. London: SPCK, 2008.
———. *Poet and Peasant (Bound with through Peasant Eyes)*. Grand Rapids: Eerdmans, 1983.
Balz, H. "Anoia." In *EDNT*, 1:105.
———. "Hou." In *EDNT*, 2:539.
Balz, H., and G. Schneider. "Paratheoreō." In *EDNT*, 3:22.
———. "Perispaomi." In *EDNT*, 3:76.
———. "Spēlaion." In *EDNT*, 3:264.
Barclay, John. "1 Corinthians." In *OBC*, 1108-33.
Barrett, C. K. *A Commentary on the First Epistle to the Corinthians*. 2nd ed. London: Black, 1971.
———. *A Critical and Exegetical Commentary on the Acts of the Apostles*. 2 vols. Edinburgh: T. & T. Clark, 1994-1998.
Bauckham, Richard. "Anna of the Tribe of Asher (Luke 2:36-38)." *Revue Biblique* 104 (1997) 161-91.
———. "For Whom Were Gospels Written?" In *TGAC*, 9-48.
———. *Gospel Women: Studies of the Named Women in the Gospels*. Edinburgh: T. & T. Clark, 2002.
———. "John for Readers of Mark." In *TGAC*, 147-71.

Beutler, J. "Adelphos." In *EDNT*, 1:28–30.
Beyer, H. W. "Diakoneō." In *TDNT*, 2:81–93.
Bock, D. L. *Luke*. Vol. 1. Grand Rapids: Baker, 1994.
Bond, Helen K. *Pontius Pilate in History and Interpretation*. Cambridge: Cambridge University Press, 1998.
Bovon, Francois. *Luke 1: A Commentary on the Gospel of Luke, 1:1–9:50*. Translated by Christine M. Thomas. Minneapolis: Fortress, 2002.
———. *Luke 3: A Commentary on the Gospel of Luke, 19:28–24:53*. Translated by James Crouch. Minneapolis: Fortress, 2012.
Bow, Beverly, and George W. E. Nickelsburg. "Patriarchy with a Twist: Men and Women in Tobit." In *Women Like This: New Perspectives on Jewish Women in the Greco-Roman World*, edited by Amy-Jill Levine, 127–43. Atlanta: Scholars, 1991.
Braudel, Fernand. *The Mediterranean and the Mediterranean World in the Age of Philip II*. Vol. 1. Translated by Siân Reynolds. London: Fontana, 1975.
Brawley, R. L. "The God of Promises and the Jews in Luke-Acts." In *Literary Studies in Luke-Acts: Essays in Honor of Joseph B. Tyson*, edited by R. P. Thompson and T. E. Phillips, 279–96. Macon, GA: Mercer University Press, 1998.
Bremen, Riet van. *The Limits of Participation: Women and Civic Life in the Greek East in the Hellenistic and Roman Periods*. Amsterdam: Gieben, 1996.
Brodie, T. L. "Towards Tracing the Gospel's Literary Indebtedness to the Epistles." In *Mimesis and Intertextuality in Antiquity and Christianity*, edited by Dennis R. MacDonald, 104–16. Harrisburg, PA: Trinity, 2001.
Broshi, Magen. *Bread, Wine, Walls and Scrolls*. Sheffield, UK: Sheffield Academic, 2001.
Brown, Raymond E. *The Birth of the Messiah*. 2nd ed. London: Chapman, 1993.
———. *The Death of the Messiah*. 2 vols. London: Chapman, 1994.
———. *The Gospel according to John (I–XII)*. London: Chapman, 1971.
Bruce, F. F. *The Acts of the Apostles*. 2nd ed. London: Tyndale, 1952.
Burridge, Richard A. "About People, by People, for People: Gospel Genre and Audiences." In *TGAC*, 113–45.
Cadbury, H. J. *The Making of Luke-Acts*. London: SPCK, 1958.
Calvin, J. *Commentaries on the Acts of the Apostles*. Vol. 1. Translated by J. W. Fraser and W. J. G. McDonald. Edinburgh: Oliver & Boyd, 1965.
Campbell, J. B. *The Emperor and the Roman Army 31 BC–AD 235*. Oxford: Clarendon, 1984.
Capper, B. "The Palestinian Cultural Context of Earliest Christian Community of Goods." In *The Book of Acts in Its Palestinian Setting*, edited by R. Bauckham, 323–56. Grand Rapids: Eerdmans, 1995.
Cartledge, P. A. "Slavery: Greek." In *OCD*, 1415.
Cassidy, R. J. *Society and Politics in the Acts of the Apostles*. Maryknoll: Orbis, 1987.
Chambers, Kathy. "Knock, Knock—Who's There? Acts 12:6–17 as a Comedy of Errors." In *FCAA*, 89–97.
Cheesman, G. L. *The Auxilia of the Roman Imperial Army*. Oxford: Clarendon, 1914.
———. "The Family of the Caristanii at Antioch in Pisidia." *Journal of Roman Studies* 3 (1913) 253–66.
Christol, M., and Thomas Drew-Bear. "Les Sergii Pauli et Antioche." In *Actes Du Ier Congrès International Sur Antioche De Pisidie*, edited by Thomas Drew-Bear et al. Paris: de Boccard, 2002.

Cohen, Chayim. "Widow: Biblical Period." In *Encyclopaedia Judaica*, 16:487–91. Jerusalem: Keter, 1971.
Cohick, Lynn H. *Women in the World of the Earliest Christians: Illuminating Ancient Ways of Life.* Grand Rapids: Baker Academic, 2009.
Conzelmann, H. *Acts of the Apostles: A Commentary on the Acts of the Apostles.* Translated by J. Limburg et al. Philadelphia: Fortress, 1987.
Corbier, Mireille. "Family Behavior of the Roman Aristocracy, Second Century BC–Third Century AD." Translated by Ann Cremin. In *Women's History and Ancient History*, edited by S. B. Pomeroy, 173–96. Chapel Hill: University of North Carolina Press, 1991.
———. "Male Power and Legitimacy through Women: The *Domus Augusta* under the Julio-Claudians." In *Women in Antiquity: New Assessments*, edited by R. Hawley and B. Levick, 178–93. London: Routledge, 1995.
Cornell, Tim J. "Police." In *OCD*, 1204–5.
Culy, Martin M., and M. C. Parsons. *Acts: A Handbook on the Greek Text.* Waco, TX: Baylor University Press, 2003.
D'Angelo, M. R. "The Anēr Question in Luke-Acts: Imperial Masculinity and the Deployment of Women in the Early Second Century." In *FCL*, 44–69.
———. "(Re)Presentations of Women in the Gospel of Matthew and Luke-Acts." In *Women & Christian Origins*, edited by Ross Shepard Kraemer and M. R. D'Angelo, 171–95. Oxford: Oxford University Press, 1999.
———. "Women in Luke-Acts: A Redactional View." *Journal of Biblical Literature* 109 (1990) 441–61.
Darr, J. A. "Irenic or Ironic? Another Look at Gamaliel before the Sanhedrin (Acts 5:33–42)." In *Literary Studies in Luke-Acts: Essays in Honor of Joseph B. Tyson*, edited by R. P. Thompson and T. E. Phillips, 121–39. Macon, GA: Mercer University Press, 1998.
———. *On Character Building: The Reader and the Rhetoric of Characterization in Luke-Acts.* Louisville: Westminster John Knox, 1992.
Degenhardt, H.-J. *Lukas Evangelist der Armen: Besitz und Besitzverzicht in den lukanischen Schriften.* Stuttgart: Katholisches Bibelwerk, 1965.
Delebecque, E. *Les Actes des Apôtres.* Paris: Société d'édition "Les belles lettres," 1982.
Delling, G. "Magos." In *TDNT*, 4:356–59.
DeSilva, D. A. *Honor, Patronage, Kinship, and Purity: Unlocking New Testament Culture.* Downers Grove: InterVarsity, 2000.
Dillon, R. J. "Acts of the Apostles." In *NJBC*, 722–67.
Dines, Jennifer M. *The Septuagint.* London: T. & T. Clark, 2004.
The Divine Office: The Liturgy of the Hours according to the Roman Rite. Vol. 1. London: Collins, 1974.
Duncan-Jones, Richard. *The Economy of the Roman Empire: Quantitative Studies.* Cambridge: Cambridge University Press, 1974.
———. *Money and Government in the Roman Empire.* Cambridge: Cambridge University Press, 1994.
Dunn, J. D. G. *Beginning from Jerusalem.* Grand Rapids: Eerdmans, 2009.
———. *Jesus Remembered.* Grand Rapids: Eerdmans, 2003.
Eddy, Gaylyn Elaine Ginn. "Contributing out of Her Poverty: A Study of the Widow in Luke-Acts." PhD diss., Vanderbilt University, 1999.

Edwards, D. "The Socio-Economic and Cultural Ethos of the Lower Galilee in the First Century." In *The Galilee in Late Antiquity*, edited by L. I. Levine, 53–73. New York: Jewish Theological Seminary of America, 1992.
Ehrman, Bart D. *Didymus the Blind and the Text of the Gospels*. Atlanta: Scholars, 1986.
Elder, L. B. "Judith." In *STS*, 2:455–69.
Elliott, J. K. "Anna's Age (Luke 2:36–37)." *Novum Testamentum* 30 (1988) 100–102.
Elowski, Joel C. *Ancient Christian Commentary on Scripture: New Testament, John 1–10*. Downers Grove: InterVarsity, 2006.
Esler, P. F. *Community and Gospel in Luke-Acts: The Social and Political Motivations of Lucan Theology*. Cambridge: Cambridge University Press, 1987.
Evans, C. A. *Jesus and His World: The Archaeological Evidence*. London: SPCK, 2012.
Fiedler, P. "Euschēmōn." In *EDNT*, 2:86.
Finger, Reta Halteman. *Of Widows and Meals: Communal Meals in the Book of Acts*. Grand Rapids: Eerdmans, 2007.
Finley, M. I. *The Ancient Economy*. London: Chatto & Windus, 1973.
Fitzmyer, J. A. *The Acts of the Apostles*. New York: Doubleday, 1998.
———. *The Gospel according to Luke, I–IX*. Garden City, NY: Doubleday, 1981.
———. *The Gospel according to Luke, X–XXIV*. Garden City, NY: Doubleday, 1985.
Fleddermann, H. "A Warning about the Scribes (Mark 12:37b–40)." *Catholic Biblical Quarterly* 44 (1982) 52–67.
Foerster, W. "Daimōn." In *TDNT*, 2:1–20.
———. "Diaballō." In *TDNT*, 2:71–73, 75–81.
Fokkelman, J. P. *Reading Biblical Narrative: An Introductory Guide*. Louisville: Westminster John Knox, 1999.
Franklin, Eric. "Luke." In *OBC*, 922–59.
Freyne, S. *Galilee from Alexander the Great to Hadrian, 323 BCE to 135 CE: A Study of Second Temple Judaism*. Wilmington, DE: Glazier, 1980.
———. *Jesus, a Jewish Galilean: A New Reading of the Jesus Story*. London: T. & T. Clark, 2004.
———. "Urban-Rural Relations in First Century Galilee: Some Suggestions from the Literary Sources." In *The Galilee in Late Antiquity*, edited by L. I. Levine, 75–91. New York: Jewish Theological Seminary of America, 1992.
Friesen, Steven J. "Poverty in Pauline Studies: Beyond the So-Called New Consensus." *Journal for the Study of the New Testament* 26 (2004) 323–61.
Gabba, Emilio. "The Social, Economic and Political History of Palestine 63 BCE–CE 70." In *The Early Roman Period*, edited by William Horbury et al., 94–167. Vol. 3 of *The Cambridge History of Judaism*. Cambridge: Cambridge University Press, 1999.
Garnsey, P. *Cities, Peasants and Food in Classical Antiquity: Essays in Social and Economic History*. Cambridge: Cambridge University Press, 1998.
———. "The *Lex Iulia* and Appeal under the Empire." *Journal of Roman Studies* 56 (1966) 167–89.
———. *Social Status and Legal Privilege in the Roman Empire*. Oxford: Clarendon, 1970.
Gaventa, B. R. *Mary: Glimpses of the Mother of Jesus*. Edinburgh: T. & T. Clark, 1999.
Gench, Frances Taylor. *Back to the Well: Women's Encounters with Jesus in the Gospels*. Louisville: Westminster John Knox, 2004.
Gibson, Jeffrey B. *The Temptations of Jesus in Early Christianity*. Sheffield, UK: Sheffield Academic, 1995.

Giesen, H. "Hypokrisis." In *EDNT*, 3:403.
Gillespie, Thomas W. *The First Theologians: A Study in Early Christian Prophecy*. Grand Rapids: Eerdmans, 1994.
Gilliam, J. F. *Roman Army Papers*. Amsterdam: Gieben, 1986.
Goodacre, Mark. *The Case against Q: Studies in Markan Priority and the Synoptic Problem*. Harrisburg, PA: Trinity, 2002.
———. *The Synoptic Problem: A Way through the Maze*. London: T. & T. Clark, 2001.
Goodacre, Mark, and Nicholas Perrin. *Questioning Q*. London: SPCK, 2004.
Goodman, Martin. *Rome & Jerusalem: The Clash of Ancient Civilizations*. London: Penguin, 2008.
———. *The Ruling Class of Judaea: The Origins of the Jewish Revolt against Rome AD 66–70*. Cambridge: Cambridge University Press, 1987.
Goodman, M., and J. Sherwood. *The Roman World 44 BC–AD 180*. London: Routledge, 1997.
Goulder, M. D. *Luke: A New Paradigm*. Vol. 1. Sheffield, UK: Sheffield Academic, 1989.
———. *Type and History in Acts*. London: SPCK, 1964.
Grant, Michael. "Translator's Introduction." In *Tacitus: The Annals of Imperial Rome*, xvii–xxxviii. London: Folio, 2006.
Green, J. B. *The Gospel of Luke*. Grand Rapids: Eerdmans, 1997.
Gregory, Andrew. "1 Clement: An Introduction." In *The Writings of the Apostolic Fathers*, edited by Paul Foster, 21–31. London: T. & T. Clark, 2007.
Gowler, David B. *Host, Guest, Enemy and Friend: Portraits of the Pharisees in Luke and Acts*. Eugene, OR. Wipf & Stock, 2007.
Gunkel, Hermann. *Genesis*. Translated by Mark E. Biddle. Macon, GA: Mercer University Press, 1997.
Haacker, K. "Gallio." In *ABD*, 2:901–3.
Haenchen, E. *The Acts of the Apostles*. Oxford: Blackwell, 1971.
Hamel, Gildas. *Poverty and Charity in Roman Palestine, First Three Centuries C.E.* Berkeley CA: University of California Press, 1990.
Hanse, Hermann. "Echō." In *TDNT*, 2:816–32.
Hanson, K. C. "The Herodians and Mediterranean Kinship, Part 1: Genealogy and Descent." *Biblical Theology Bulletin* 19 (1989) 75–84.
———. "The Herodians and Mediterranean Kinship, Part 3: Economics." *Biblical Theology Bulletin* 20 (1990) 10–21.
Hanson, K. C., and Douglas E. Oakman. *Palestine in the Time of Jesus: Social Structures and Social Conflicts*. Minneapolis: Fortress, 1998.
Harrington, D. J. "Antiochus." In *EDB*, 68–69.
Hays, Richard B. *Echoes of Scripture in the Letters of Paul*. New Haven: Yale University Press, 1989.
———. "The Liberation of Israel in Luke-Acts: Intertextual Narration as Countercultural Practice." In *Reading the Bible Intertextually*, edited by Richard B. Hays et al., 101–17. Waco, TX: Baylor University Press, 2009.
Heine, Susanne. *Women and Early Christianity*. Translated by J. Bowden. London: SCM, 1987.
Herodotus. *The Histories*. Translated by Aubrey de Sélincourt. London: Folio, 2006.
Hill, David. *New Testament Prophecy*. Basingstoke, UK: Marshall Morgan & Scott, 1985.
Hoehner, Harold W. *Herod Antipas*. Cambridge: Cambridge University Press, 1972.

Holmberg, Bengt. *Sociology and the New Testament: An Appraisal*. Minneapolis: Fortress, 1990.

Hopkins, K. *Conquerors and Slaves: Sociological Studies in Roman History*. Vol. 1. Cambridge: Cambridge University Press, 1978.

———. "Élite Mobility in the Roman Empire." In *Studies in Ancient Society*, edited by M. I. Finley, 103–20. London: Routledge and Kegan Paul, 1974.

Hopkins, K., and Graham Burton. "Ambition and Withdrawal: The Senatorial Aristocracy under the Emperors." In *Death and Renewal*, edited by K. Hopkins, 120–200. Cambridge: Cambridge University Press, 1983.

Hornsby, Teresa J. "The Woman Is a Sinner/The Sinner Is a Woman." In *FCL*, 121–32.

Horsley, R. A. *Archaeology, History and Society in Galilee: The Social Context of Jesus and the Rabbis*. Harrisburg, PA: Trinity, 1996.

———. *Galilee: History, Politics, People*. Valley Forge, PA: Trinity, 1995.

———. "The Pharisees and Jesus in Galilee and Q." In vol. 1 of *When Judaism and Christianity Began: Essays in Memory of Anthony J. Saldarini*, edited by Alan J. Avery-Peck et al., 117–45. Leiden: Brill, 2004.

Hubbard, Moyer V. *Christianity in the Greco-Roman World: A Narrative Introduction*. Peabody, MA: Hendrickson, 2010.

Ilan, Tal. *Integrating Women into Second Temple History*. Peabody, MA: Hendrickson, 2001.

———. *Jewish Women in Greco-Roman Palestine*. Peabody, MA: Hendrickson, 1996.

Isaac, Benjamin. *The Limits of Empire: The Roman Army in the East*. Rev. ed. Oxford: Clarendon, 1992.

———. *The Near East under Roman Rule: Selected Papers*. Leiden: Brill, 1998.

Jeremias, J. *Jerusalem in the Time of Jesus*. London: SCM, 1969.

Johnson, L. T. *The Acts of the Apostles*. Collegeville: Liturgical, 1992.

———. *The Gospel of Luke*. Collegeville: Liturgical, 1991.

Jones, A. H. M. *The Herods of Judaea*. Oxford: Clarendon, 1938.

Jones, B. W. *Domitian and the Senatorial Order: A Prosopographical Study of Domitian's Relationship with the Senate A.D. 81–96*. Philadelphia: American Philosophical Society, 1979.

———. *The Emperor Domitian*. London: Routledge, 1992.

Jones, C. P. *The Roman World of Dio Chrysostom*. Cambridge: Harvard University Press, 1978.

Joshel, S. R. *Work, Identity, and Legal Status at Rome: A Study of the Occupational Inscriptions*. Norman: University of Oklahoma Press, 1992.

Karris, Robert J. "The Lukan Sitz im Leben: Methodology and Prospects." In *SBL Seminar Papers, 1976*, edited by George MacRae, 219–33. Missoula, MT: Scholars, 1976.

———. "Women and Discipleship in Luke." In *FCL*, 23–43.

Kearsley, R. A. "Asiarchs." In *ABD*, 1:495–97.

Kim, K.-J. *Stewardship and Almsgiving in Luke's Theology*. Sheffield, UK: Sheffield Academic, 1998.

King, Helen. "Women." In *OCD*, 1623–24.

Klauck, Hans-Josef. *Magic and Paganism in Early Christianity*. Translated by Brian McNeil. Edinburgh: T. & T. Clark, 2000.

Klutz, Todd. *The Exorcism Stories in Luke-Acts: A Sociostylistic Reading*. Cambridge: Cambridge University Press, 2004.

Koenig, J. *New Testament Hospitality: Partnership with Strangers as Promise and Mission.* Philadelphia: Fortress, 1985.
Kokkinos, Nikos. *The Herodian Dynasty: Origins, Role in Society and Eclipse.* Sheffield, UK: Sheffield Academic, 1998.
Koperski, V. "Luke 10:38–42 and Acts 6:1–7: Women and Discipleship in the Literary Context of Luke-Acts." In *The Unity of Luke-Acts,* edited by J. Verheyden, 517–44. Leuven: Leuven University Press, 1999.
Kraemer, Ross Shepard. "Jewish Women and Women's Judaism(s) at the Beginning of Christianity." In *Women & Christian Origins,* edited by Ross Shepard Kraemer and M. R. D'Angelo, 50–79. Oxford: Oxford University Press, 1999.
Kraft, H. "Chēra." In *EDNT,* 3:465–66.
Kümmel, W. G. *Introduction to the New Testament.* Rev. ed. Translated by H. C. Kee. London: SCM, 1975.
Laffey, Alice L. "Ruth." In *NJBC,* 553–57.
Lake, Kirsopp. "The Communism of Acts II and IV–VI and the Appointment of the Seven." In vol. 5 of *The Beginnings of Christianity: The Acts of the Apostles,* edited by K. Lake and H. J. Cadbury, 140–51. London: Macmillan, 1933.
Levick, B. *Roman Colonies in Southern Asia Minor.* Oxford: Clarendon, 1967.
———. "Senators, Patterns of Recruitment." In *OCD,* 1387–88.
Levine, L. I. *Caesarea under Roman Rule.* Leiden: Brill, 1975.
Levinskaya, I. *The Book of Acts in Its Diaspora Setting.* Carlisle, UK: Paternoster, 1996.
Ligt, L. de. *Fairs and Markets in the Roman Empire: Economic and Social Aspects of Periodic Trade in a Pre-Industrial Society.* Amsterdam: Gieben, 1993.
Lincoln, A. T. *The Gospel according to St. John.* London: Continuum, 2005.
Litwak, Kenneth Duncan. *Echoes of Scripture in Luke-Acts: Telling the History of God's People Intertextually.* London: T. & T. Clark, 2005.
Lust, J. E., et al. *A Greek-English Lexicon of the Septuagint.* Vol. 1. Stuttgart: Deutsche Bibelgesellschaft, 1992.
MacMullen, Ramsay. *Roman Social Relations 50 B.C. To A.D. 284.* New Haven: Yale University Press, 1974.
Malina, Bruce J. *The New Testament World: Insights from Cultural Anthropology.* 3rd ed. Louisville: Westminster John Knox, 2001.
Malina, Bruce J., and J. H. Neyrey. "First Century Personality: Dyadic, Not Individual." In *The Social World of Luke-Acts: Models for Interpretation,* edited by J. H. Neyrey, 67–96. Peabody, MA: Hendrickson, 1991.
Malina, Bruce J., and Richard L. Rohrbaugh. *Social Science Commentary on the Synoptic Gospels.* Minneapolis: Fortress, 1992.
Maloney, L. M. "The Pastoral Epistles." In *STS,* 2:361–80.
Mandell, Sara R. "Hasmoneans." In *EDB,* 555–56.
Mantel, Hilary. "The War against Women." In *The Observer* [from *The New York Review of Books*] April 19, 2009, 3–4.
Marshall, I. Howard. *The Gospel of Luke.* Exeter, UK: Paternoster, 1978.
———. "Who Is a Hypocrite?" *Bibliotheca Sacra* 159 (2002) 131–50.
Martin, C. J. "The Acts of the Apostles." In *STS,* 2:763–99.
Martin, Thomas W. "Paulus, Sergius." In *ABD,* 5:205–6.
Mason, Steve. *Josephus and the New Testament.* 2nd ed. Peabody, MA: Hendrickson, 2003.

———. *Josephus, Judea, and Christian Origins: Methods and Categories*. Peabody, MA: Hendrickson, 2009.
McGinn, T. A. J. *The Economy of Prostitution in the Roman World: A Study of Social History & the Brothel*. Ann Arbor: University of Michigan Press, 2004.
Meeks, W. A. *The First Urban Christians: The Social World of the Apostle Paul*. 2nd ed. New Haven: Yale University, 2003.
———. "The Social Level of Pauline Christians." In *Social-Scientific Approaches to New Testament Interpretation*, edited by David G. Horrell, 195–232. Edinburgh: T. & T. Clark, 1999.
Meggitt, J. J. *Paul, Poverty and Survival*. Edinburgh: T. & T. Clark, 1998.
Meister, Klaus. "Nicolaus of Damascus." In *OCD*, 1041–42.
Merkel, H. "Telōnēs." In *EDNT*, 3:348–50.
Millar, F. *The Emperor in the Roman World (31 BC–AD 337)*. London: Duckworth, 1977.
———. *The Roman Near East: 31 BC–AD 337*. Cambridge: Harvard University Press, 1993.
Mitchell, Stephen. "Antioch of Pisidia." In *ABD*, 1:264–65.
———. "Geographical and Historical Introduction." In *Pisidian Antioch: The Site and Its Monuments*, edited by Stephen Mitchell and Marc Waelkens. London: Duckworth, 1998.
Momigliano, Arnaldo, and Miriam T. Griffin. "Annaeus Novatus." In *OCD*, 95.
Moulton, J. H., and G. Milligan. *Vocabulary of the Greek Testament*. Peabody, MA: Hendrickson, 1997.
Mowery, Robert L. "Paul and Caristanius at Pisidian Antioch." *Biblica* 87 (2006) 223–42.
Moxnes, H. *The Economy of the Kingdom: Social Conflict and Economic Relations in Luke's Gospel*. Philadelphia: Fortress, 1988.
Moyise, Steve. "Intertextuality and the Study of the Old Testament in the New Testament." In *The Old Testament in the New Testament: Essays in Honour of J. L. North*, edited by Steve Moyise, 14–41. Sheffield, UK: Sheffield Academic, 2000.
Mullins, Michael. *The Gospel of Luke*. Dublin: Columba, 2010.
Murphy-O'Connor, J. "The First Letter to the Corinthians." In *NJBC*, 798–815.
———. "Prisca and Aquila: Travelling Tentmakers and Church Builders." *Bible Review* 8 (1992) 40–51, 62.
Neusner, Jacob. *Judaism in the Beginning of Christianity*. Philadelphia: Fortress, 1984.
Oakman, Douglas E. *Jesus and the Economic Questions of His Day*. Lewiston, NY: Mellen, 1986.
O'Day, Gail R. "Acts." In *The Women's Bible Commentary*, edited by Carol A Newsom and Sharon H. Ringe, 305–12. London: SPCK, 1992.
Ó Fearghail, F. "The Imitation of the Septuagint in Luke's Infancy Narrative." *Proceedings of the Irish Biblical Association* 12 (1989) 58–78.
Omanson, Roger L. *A Textual Guide to the Greek New Testament*. Stuttgart: Deutsche Bibelgesellschaft, 2006.
Osiek, C. "Women in House Churches." In *Common Life in the Early Church: Essays Honoring Graydon F. Snyder*, edited by Julian V. Hills, 300–315. Harrisburg, PA: Trinity, 1998.
Osiek, C., and D. L. Balch. *Families in the New Testament World: Households and House Churches*. Louisville: Westminster John Knox, 1997.

Paltiel, Eliezer. *Vassals and Rebels in the Roman Empire: Julio-Claudian Policies in Judaea and the Kingdoms of the East*. Brussels: Latomus, 1991.
Parsons, M. C. *Luke: Story Teller, Interpreter, Evangelist*. Peabody, MA: Hendrickson, 2007.
Paterson, J. J. "Trade: Roman." In *OCD*, 1537–38.
Pearson, B. W. R. "Antioch (Pisidia)." In *Dictionary of New Testament Background*, edited by C. A. Evans and S. E. Porter, 31–34. Downers Grove: InterVarsity, 2000.
Penner, Todd. "Madness in the Method? The Acts of the Apostles in Current Study." *Currents in Biblical Research* 2 (2004) 223–93.
Perkins, Pheme. "The Gospel According to John." In *NJBC*, 942–85.
Pervo, Richard I. *Acts: A Commentary*. Minneapolis: Fortress, 2009.
Peterson, David G. *The Acts of the Apostles*. Grand Rapids: Eerdmans, 2009.
Philips, Thomas E. *Paul, His Letters, and Acts*. Peabody, MA: Hendrickson, 2009.
———."Reading Recent Readings of Issues of Wealth and Poverty in Luke and Acts." *Currents in Biblical Research* 1 (2003) 231–69.
Pleket, H. W. "Urban Elites and Business in the Greek Part of the Roman Empire." In *Trade in the Ancient Economy*, edited by P. Garnsey et al., 131–44. London: Chatto & Windus, 1983.
Pliny. *A Self-Portrait in Letters*. Translated by Betty Radice. London: Folio, 1978.
Plümacher, E. "Luke." Translated by Dennis Martin. In *ABD*, 4:397–402.
Pollard, Nigel. *Soldiers, Cities, and Civilians in Roman Syria*. Ann Arbor: University of Michigan Press, 2000.
Pomeroy, S. B. *Goddesses, Whores, Wives, and Slaves*. New York: Schocken, 1995.
Porter, Stanley E. *Idioms of the Greek New Testament*. 2nd ed. Sheffield, UK: Sheffield Academic, 1994.
Potter, D. S. "Quirinius." In *ABD*, 5:588–89.
Rabinowitz, Peter J. *Before Reading: Narrative Conventions and the Politics of Interpretation*. Ithaca: Cornell University Press, 1987.
———. "Whirl without End: Audience-Oriented Criticism." In *Contemporary Literary Theory*, edited by G. Douglas Atkins and Laura Morrow, 81–100. London: Macmillan, 1989.
Radl, W. "Meta." In *EDNT*, 2:413–14.
———. "Poieō." In *EDNT*, 3:123–26.
Reid, B. E. "Beyond Petty Pursuits and Wearisome Widows." *Interpretation* 56 (2002) 284–94.
———. *Choosing the Better Part? Women in the Gospel of Luke*. Collegeville: Liturgical, 1996.
———. "Do You See This Woman? A Liberative Look at Luke 7:36–50 and Strategies for Reading Other Lukan Stories against the Grain." In *FCL*, 106–20.
———. "The Power of the Widows and How to Suppress It (Acts 6:1–7)." In *FCAA*, 71–88.
Reynolds, Joyce. "Cities." In *The Administration of the Roman Empire (241 BC–AD 193)*, edited by David C. Braund, 15–51. Exeter, UK: University of Exeter, 1988.
Ricci, C. *Mary Magdalene and Many Others: Women Who Followed Jesus*. Translated by P. Burns. Tunbridge Wells, UK: Burns & Oates, 1994.
Richardson, Peter. "Herod." In *EDB*, 579–84.
———. *Herod: King of the Jews and Friend of the Romans*. Edinburgh: T. & T. Clark, 1999.

Richter Reimer, Ivoni. *Women in the Acts of the Apostles: A Feminist Liberation Perspective*. Translated by Linda M. Maloney. Minneapolis: Fortress, 1995.

Rius-Camps, Josep, and J. Read-Heimerdinger. *The Message of Acts in Codex Bezae: A Comparison with the Alexandrian Tradition*. Vols. 2 & 3. London: T. & T. Clark, 2006–2007.

Rogers, Guy MacLean. *The Sacred Identity of Ephesus: Foundation Myths of a Roman City*. London: Routledge, 1991.

Ropes, J. H. *The Text of Acts*. Vol. 3, pt. 1 of *The Beginnings of Christianity: The Acts of the Apostles*, edited by F. J. Foakes-Jackson et al. London: Macmillan, 1926.

Roth, Jonathan. "The Army and the Economy in Judaea and Palestine." In *The Roman Army and the Economy*, edited by Paul Erdkamp, 375–97. Amsterdam: Gieben, 2002.

Roth, S. John. *The Blind, the Lame, and the Poor: Character Types in Luke-Acts*. Sheffield, UK: Sheffield Academic, 1997.

Saddington, D. B. *The Development of the Roman Auxiliary Forces from Caesar to Vespasian, 49 BC–AD 79*. Harare: University of Zimbabwe, 1982.

Safrai, Z. *The Economy of Roman Palestine*. London: Routledge, 1994.

Saldarini, A. J. "Jewish Responses to Greco-Roman Culture, 332 BCE to 200 CE." In *The Cambridge Companion to the Bible*, edited by H. C. Kee et al., 288–440. Cambridge: Cambridge University Press, 1997.

———. *Pharisees, Scribes and Sadducees in Palestinian Society: A Sociological Approach*. Grand Rapids: Eerdmans, 2001.

———. "Scribes." In *ABD*, 5:1012–16.

Sanders, E. P. *Jesus and Judaism*. London: SCM, 1985.

———. *Judaism: Practice and Belief, 63 BCE–66 CE*. London: SCM, 1992.

Sarna, Nahum M. *Genesis*. Philadelphia: Jewish Publication Society, 1989.

Sartre, Maurice. *L'Orient Romain*. Paris: Éditions du Seuil, 1991.

Sawyer, J. F. A. *The Fifth Gospel: Isaiah in the History of Christianity*. Cambridge: Cambridge University Press, 1996.

Schaberg, Jane. "Luke." In *The Women's Bible Commentary*, edited by Carol A Newsom and Sharon H. Ringe, 275–92. London: SPCK, 1992.

Schalit, Abraham. "Berenice." In *Encyclopaedia Judaica*, 4:601–2. Jerusalem: Keter, 1971.

Schaper, Joachim. "The Pharisees." In *The Early Roman Period*, edited by William Horbury et al., 402–27. Vol. 3 of *The Cambridge History of Judaism*. Cambridge: Cambridge University Press, 1999.

Schenk, W. "Nomizō." In *EDNT*, 2:470.

Schmidt, T. E. *Hostility to Wealth in the Synoptics*. Sheffield, UK: JSOT, 1987.

Schmithals, W. "Lukas—Evangelist der Armen." *Theologia Viatorum* 12 (1973–74) 153–67.

Schneider, G. "Akoloutheō." In *EDNT*, 1:49–52.

———. "Apostomatizō." In *EDNT*, 1:146.

Schnider, F. "Prophētēs." In *EDNT*, 3:183–86.

Schoedel, William R. *Ignatius of Antioch: A Commentary on the Letters of Ignatius of Antioch*. Philadelphia: Fortress, 1985.

Schottroff, L. *Lydia's Impatient Sisters: A Feminist Social History of Early Christianity*. Louisville: Westminster John Knox, 1995.

Schürer, Emil. *The History of the Jewish People in the Age of Jesus Christ (175 B.C.–A.D. 135)*. Vol. 2. Edited by G. Vermes et al. Edinburgh: T. & T. Clark, 1979.

Schüssler Fiorenza, E. *Discipleship of Equals: A Critical Feminist Ekklēsia-Logy of Liberation*. Translated by Barbara Martin Rumscheidt. London: SCM, 1993.

———. *In Memory of Her: A Feminist Theological Reconstruction of Christian Origins*. 2nd ed. London: SCM, 1994.

Schwartz, D. R. *Agrippa I: The Last King of Judaea*. Tübingen, Germany: Mohr, 1990.

Seccombe, D. P. *Possessions and the Poor in Luke-Acts*. Linz, Austria: Fuchs, 1982.

Seim, T. K. *The Double Message: Patterns of Gender in Luke-Acts*. Translated by Brian McNeil. Edinburgh: T. & T. Clark, 1994.

———. "Feminist Criticism." In *Methods for Luke*, edited by J. B. Green, 42–73. Cambridge: Cambridge University Press, 2010.

———. "The Gospel of Luke." In *STS*, 2:728–62.

———. "The Virgin Mother: Mary and Ascetic Discipleship in Luke." In *FCL*, 89–105.

Sherwin-White, A. N. *The Roman Citizenship*. 2nd ed. Oxford: Oxford University Press, 1973.

———. *Roman Society and Roman Law in the New Testament*. Oxford: Clarendon, 1963.

Sherwin-White, A. N, et al. "Colonization, Roman." In *OCD*, 364–65.

Sjoberg, Gideon. *The Pre-Industrial City: Past and Present*. New York: Free Press, 1960.

Spaul, John. *Cohors 2: The Evidence for and a Short History of the Auxiliary Infantry Units of the Imperial Roman Army*. Oxford: Archaeopress, 2000.

Speidel, M. P. *Roman Army Studies*. Vol. 2. Stuttgart: Steiner, 1992.

Speiser, E. A. *Genesis*. Garden City, NY: Doubleday, 1964.

Spencer, F. S. *Journeying through Acts: A Literary-Cultural Reading*. Grand Rapids: Baker Academic, 2010.

———. "Neglected Widows in Acts 6:1–7." *CBQ* 56 (1994) 715–33.

Staniforth, M. *Early Christian Writings: The Apostolic Fathers*. Harmondsworth, UK: Penguin, 1968.

Stegemann, Ekkehard W., and Wolfgang Stegemann. *The Jesus Movement: A Social History of Its First Century*. Translated by O. C. Dean. Edinburgh: T. & T. Clark, 1999.

Stegemann, W., and L. Schottroff. *Jesus and the Hope of the Poor*. Translated by M. J. O'Connell. New York: Orbis, 1986.

Stern, M. "Nero." In *Encyclopaedia Judaica*, 12:964–65. Jerusalem: Keter, 1971.

———. "The Province of Judaea." In *The Jewish People in the First Century*, edited by S. Safrai and M. Stern, 1:308–76. Assen, Netherlands: Van Gorcum, 1974.

Strange, James F. *Beth-Saida*. *ABD*, 1:692–93.

Strange, W. A. *The Problem of the Text of Acts*. Cambridge: Cambridge University Press, 1992.

Suetonius, Gaius. *The Twelve Caesars*. Translated by Robert Graves. London: Folio, 1964.

Sullivan, Richard D. *Near Eastern Royalty and Rome, 100–30BC*. Toronto: University of Toronto Press, 1990.

Syme, Ronald. "Antonius Pallas, Marcus." In *OCD*, 116–17.

Tacitus. *The Annals of Imperial Rome*. Translated by Michael Grant. London: Folio, 2006.

Talbert, C. H. *Reading Luke-Acts in Its Mediterranean Milieu*. Leiden: Brill, 2003.

Tannehill, Robert C. "'Cornelius' and 'Tabitha' Encounter Luke's Jesus." *Interpretation* 48 (1994) 347–56.

———. "Freedom and Responsibility in Scripture Interpretation with Application to Luke." In *Literary Studies in Luke-Acts: Essays in Honor of Joseph P. Tyson*, edited by R. P. Thompson and T. E. Phillips, 265–78. Macon, GA: Mercer University Press, 1998.

———. *The Narrative Unity of Luke-Acts: A Literary Interpretation*. Vol. 1, *The Gospel according to Luke*. Philadelphia: Fortress, 1986.

———. *The Narrative Unity of Luke-Acts: A Literary Interpretation*. Vol. 2, *The Acts of the Apostles*. Minneapolis: Fortress, 1994.

———. "Should We Love Simon the Pharisee? Hermeneutical Reflections on the Pharisees in Luke." *Currents in Theology and Mission* 21 (1994) 424–33.

Tate, Georges. "The Syrian Countryside During the Roman Era." Translated by Lisa Hall. In *The Early Roman Empire in the East*, edited by Susan E. Alcock, 55–71. Oxford: Oxbow, 1997.

Telford, W. R. *The Theology of the Gospel of Mark*. Cambridge: Cambridge University Press, 1999.

Thayer, J. H. *A Greek-English Lexicon of the New Testament*. Grand Rapids: Baker, 1977.

Theissen, G. *The Social Setting of Pauline Christianity: Essays on Corinth*. Edinburgh: T. & T. Clark, 1982.

Thiede, Carsten Peter. *The Cosmopolitan World of Jesus: New Light from Archaeology*. London: SPCK, 2004.

Thomas, John Christopher. *The Devil, Disease and Deliverance: Origins of Illness in New Testament Thought*. Sheffield, UK: Sheffield Academic, 1998.

Thompson, Michael B. "The Holy Internet: Communication between Churches in the First Christian Generation." In *TGAC*, 49–70.

Thucydides. *The History of the Peloponnesian War*. Translated by Rex Warner. London: Folio, 2006.

Thurston, Bonnie. "Who Was Anna? Luke 2:36–38." *Perspectives in Religious Studies* 28 (2001) 47–55.

Tracey, Robyn. "Syria." In *The Book of Acts in Its Graeco-Roman Setting*, edited by David W. G. Gill and C. Gempf, 223–78. Carlisle, UK: Paternoster, 1994.

Trebilco, Paul. "Asia." In *The Book of Acts in Its Graeco-Roman Setting*, edited by David W. J. Gill and C. Gempf, 291–362. Grand Rapids: Eerdmans, 1994.

Tuckett, C. M. "Mark." In *OBC*, 886–922.

Völkel, M. "Hodos." In *EDNT*, 2:491–93.

Vos, C. S. de. *Church and Community Conflicts: The Relationships of the Thessalonian, Corinthian, and Philippian Churches with Their Wider Civic Communities*. Atlanta: Scholars, 1999.

Walaskay, Paul W. *And So We Came to Rome: The Political Perspective of St. Luke*. Cambridge: Cambridge University Press, 1983.

Wallace, Sherman LeRoy. *Taxation in Egypt from Augustus to Diocletian*. Princeton, NJ: Princeton University Press, 1938.

Walton, Steve. "The State They Were In: Luke's View of the Roman Empire." In *Rome and the Bible in the Early Church*, edited by Peter Oakes, 1–41. Carlisle, UK: Paternoster, 2002.

Watson, G. R. *The Roman Soldier*. London: Thames & Hudson, 1969.

Weiser, A. "Diakoneō." In *EDNT*, 1:302–4.

Wells, Colin M. "Roman Empire." In *ABD*, 5:801-6.
White, L. Michael. "Urban Development and Social Change in Imperial Ephesos." In *Ephesos, Metropolis of Asia: An Interdisciplinary Approach to Its Archaeology, Religion, and Culture*, edited by Helmut Koester, 27-79. Valley Forge, PA: Trinity, 1995.
Whittaker, C. R. *Land, City and Trade in the Roman Empire*. Aldershot, UK: Variorum, 1993.
Wifstrand, Albert. "Septuagint." In *Epochs and Styles*, edited by L. Rydbeck and S. E. Porter, 28-45. Tübingen, Germany: Mohr/Siebeck, 2005.
Wilckens, U. "Hypokrinomai." In *TDNT*, 8:559-71.
Wilcox, M. "Luke 2:36-38: Anna Bat Phanuel of the Tribe of Asher, a Prophetess . . . A Study in Midrash in Material Special to Luke." In *The Four Gospels*, edited by F. Van Segbroek et al., 2:1571-79. Leuven: Leuven University Press, 1992.
Wild, J. P. "Dyeing." In *OCD*, 499.
Williams, Margaret H. "Palestinian Jewish Personal Names in Acts." In *The Book of Acts in Its Palestinian Setting*, edited by R. Bauckham, 79-113. Grand Rapids: Eerdmans, 1995.
Wills, L. M. "Methodological Reflections on the Tax Collectors in the Gospels." In *When Judaism and Christianity Began: Essays in Memory of Anthony J. Saldarini*, edited by Alan J. Avery-Peck et al., 1:251-66. Leiden: Brill, 2004.
Winter, B. W. "Official Proceedings and the Forensic Speeches in Acts 24-26." In *The Book of Acts in Its Ancient Literary Setting*, edited by B. W. Winter and A. D. Clarke, 305-36. Grand Rapids: Eerdmans, 1993.
Winter, Paul. *On the Trial of Jesus*. Berlin: de Gruyter, 1961.
Witherington, B. *The Acts of the Apostles: A Socio-Rhetorical Commentary*. Grand Rapids: Eerdmans, 1998.
———. "The Anti-Feminist Tendencies of the 'Western' Text in Acts." *Journal of Biblical Literature* 103 (1984) 82-84.
———. *Women in the Ministry of Jesus: A Study of Jesus' Attitude to Women and Their Roles as Reflected in His Earthly Life*. Cambridge: Cambridge University Press, 1984.
Wright, A. G. "The Widow's Mites: Praise or Lament?—A Matter of Context." *Catholic Biblical Quarterly* 44 (1982) 256-65.
Wright, N. T. *The Resurrection of the Son of God*. London: SPCK, 2003.
Yamazaki-Ransom, Kazuhiko. *The Roman Empire in Luke's Narrative*. London: T. & T. Clark, 2010.
Zeller, D. "Aphrosynē." In *EDNT*, 1:184-85.
Zmijewski, J. "Asthenēs." In *EDNT*, 1:170-71.

Scripture Index

OLD TESTAMENT

Genesis

16:2	225
17:15	222
17:17	225
18:11–12	223, 225, 284
18:14	223
21:6–7	225
21:12	225, 284
22:12	126
38	201
38:11	201
46	222
46:4	126
46:17	222
48:14	126
48:17	126
49:23	140

Exodus

1:22	225
2:4	225
2:7	226
2:8–9	226
2:11	226
5:4	92
6:23	234
7:4	126
15:20	219
15:21	226
15:25	245
16	245
16:8	245
17:2–7	245
18:21–27	247
24:1	257

Leviticus

12:6	234
12:8	234

Numbers

6:3	87, 247
8:10	247
11	246, 247
11:1	246
11:4–6	246
11:9	246
11:14	246
11:16	247, 257
11:17	246
11:19–20	246
11:24	247, 257
11:26	247
20:13	245
20:24	245
26:30 (LXX)	222
26:46	222
26:59	225
27:14	245

Deuteronomy

1:9–18	247
6:16	245
9:22	245
32:16–17	174
32:51	245

Joshua

9:18	246

Judges

1:14	246
4:1–3	226
4:4	219
4:6–7	226
4:9	226
4:17–22	226
5:3	226
8:8–9	221
8:17	221

Ruth

1–4	200
2:7–23	243
2:14	87

1 Samuel/1 Kingdoms

1:2	220
1:2–18	227
1:20–22	227
1:24–28	227
1:25	227
2:1	227
2:1–10	219
2:7–8	227
2:10	230
10:1	227
16:13	227
25	200, 229

2 Samuel/2 Kingdoms

11	200
14	201
14:7	201
18:12	126

1 Kings/3 Kingdoms

12:25–33	221
17	201
17:12–23	201, 253
17:13	253
17:15	253
17:21	253
17:23	253
18:17	92

2 Kings/4 Kingdoms

21:20	220
22:14	219
22:16–17	220
22:19–20	220
23:24	174
23:29	220
23:32	220
23:34	220
23:37	220
24:9	220
24:19	220

1 Chronicles

4:4	221
7:30	222
8:25	221

2 Chronicles

30:10–11	221
33:22	220
34:22	219
36:2	220

36:4–5	220	**2 Maccabees**	
36:9	220		
36:12	220	4:6	135
		4:40	135
		5:25	141
Judith		6:21	141
		6:24	141
2:1—3:10	228	6:25	141
7:1–6	228	7	202, 229
7:30–31	228	7:20	229
8:6	228	9:9	71
8:7	202	14:5	135
8:10	282	15:33	135
8:10–36	228		
8:11–27	282		
8:32–33	282	**3 Maccabees**	
8:34	282		
10:8	228	3:16	135
13–14	201	3:20	135
13:8	228		
14:1–5	228		
16:1	228	**4 Maccabees**	
16:23	224		
16:24	228	6:15	141
		6:17	141
		8–18	202
Esther		14:11—18:6	229
		14:20	229
A:13	126	15:30	229
4	229	16:9	202
6:2	126	18:9	229
Tobit		**Psalms**	
7:14	242	2	71
8:21	243	2:2	67
		21:2 (LXX)	135
		80:8 (LXX)	245
1 Maccabees		80:15 (LXX)	126
		81:7	245
1:21–24	71	94:8 (LXX)	245
1:54	71	95:8	245
1:57	71	105:32 (LXX)	245
14:35	57	106:32	245
		108 (LXX)	200
		108:6–19 (LXX)	197

Proverbs

14:8	135
15:25	202
22:15	135

Ecclesiastes

11:10	135

Song of Songs

2:15	66

Job

33:23	135

Wisdom

2:6–20	202
15:18	135
19:3	135

Sirach

31:24	246

Micah

6:4	226

Isaiah

5:25	126
8:3	219
11:14	126
14:11	71
14:14	71
53:7–8	107, 176
56:1	107
56:4–7	176

Baruch

4:7	174

Jeremiah

7:6	127
7:9–11	127–128
18:18	140
18:21	200

Daniel

2:2–4	174
9:21	71
11:27	71
11:31	71
11:36	71

NEW TESTAMENT

Matthew

1:18—2:1	8, 232
1:18–25	232–233
1:25	213
2:1	233
4:8–9	64
4:18–20	164
5:17	210
7:15	13
8:5–13	89
9:3	132
9:8	132
9:10	165
9:11	133
9:14	133
9:25	286
10:34	210
12:2	133

12:10	134	2:10–11	286
12:14	134	2:12	132
14:1	61	2:13–14	112
14:3	61	2:15	165
14:13	65	2:16	133
16:6	141	2:18	133
16:11	141	2:23–24	133
16:21	150	3:2	134
18:23–25	36	3:6	134
19:16	157	3:21	235
19:20	157	3:31–32	217
19:22	157, 158	3:34–35	235
19:24	158	5:20	184
19:28	195	5:30	212
20:10	210	5:32	212
20:11	248	5:34	286
20:20–28	173	5:41	286
21:23	136	5:43	269
21:32	136	6:4	235
22:14	143	6:14	61, 70
22:15–16	125	6:14—8:26	61
22:35	125	6:16–17	61
23:1–36	138	6:17–28	190
23:13	141	6:19–29	61
23:15	141	6:24	212
23:23	141	6:31–32	65
23:25	138, 141	6:46	65
23:27–29	141	7:1–22	61–62
24:51	142	7:6	141
26:6–13	136	7:29	286
26:14–16	168	8:15	141
26:31	11	8:31	150
27:15	94	10:17	157
27:19	93	10:22	157, 158
27:25	93	10:25	158
27:27–31	87	10:35–45	173
27:34	87	10:52	182
27:54	89	11:15–17	127
27:57	130	12:13	125
28:7	212, 260	12:15	141
28:10	212, 286	12:28	125
		12:38—13:2	128
		12:38–40	126
Mark		12:38–44	253
		12:42	154
1:16–20	164	12:43	154
1:20	112	14:3–9	136
2:1–12	132	14:10–11	168

Mark (continued)

14:13	182
14:56	129
15:6	94
15:14	93
15:16–20	87
15:21	14
15:26	87
15:36	87
15:39	89
15:40	27
15:43	130
16:7	195, 212, 260

Luke

1–4	21
1:1	24
1:1–4	4, 14
1:3	1, 24, 47, 294
1:3–4	291
1:4	74
1:5	25, 65, 234
1:5–6	234
1:6	130
1:8	148
1:13	234
1:15	247
1:15–25	215
1:18	223
1:25	234
1:26–56	215
1:27	230
1:28	234
1:30	234
1:31	213
1:32	230
1:34–35	274
1:36	234
1:38	229, 234, 236, 237
1:39	234
1:40–45	215
1:42	234
1:45	236, 237
1:46–55	219
1:48	233
1:51–52	166
1:51–53	179
1:53	166, 179
1:57–63	213, 287
1:57–66	215
1:60–61	234
1:69	230
1:80	234
2:1–2	25, 69
2:2	45, 160
2:4	230
2:5–7	215
2:8	11
2:11	230
2:15	11
2:16–19	215
2:17	230
2:18	11
2:19	236, 237
2:20	11, 183
2:21	213, 287
2:21–35	215
2:24	234
2:25	130
2:26	230
2:32	102
2:34	231
2:35	230
2:36	220
2:36–37	292
2:36–38	189, 215, 218, 252
2:37	222, 228
2:38	204
2:39–51	215
2:40	234
2:44	114, 210
2:46	123
2:48	229
2:51	213, 236, 237, 287
3:1	14, 52, 53, 63, 65, 68
3:1–2	25
3:3	266
3:7	164
3:10	164
3:11	164, 183
3:12	77, 164
3:12–14	62, 266
3:13	116

3:14	38, 87, 102, 164	6:1–5	133
3:15	164	6:6–11	133–134, 182
3:16–17	204	6:7	123, 143
3:18	164	6:14	194
3:19	61, 62, 215	6:14—8:26	61
3:19–20	65, 68	6:15	194
3:21–22	65	6:16	23
3:23	210	6:20–21	180
3:30	222	6:24–26	166
4:5–6	64, 292	6:27	270
4:6	29, 77, 275	6:42	142
4:9–12	68	6:46–49	259
4:13	172	6:47	270
4:16	98	7:2–10	81, 182
4:16–30	235	7:3	89, 122
4:17	25, 98	7:3–5	166
4:18–19	179	7:6	89
4:18–21	292	7:8	87
4:21	25	7:11–15	264
4:23–24	68	7:11–16	182
4:25–27	102	7:11–17	252
4:26	252	7:12–15	215
4:26–28	184	7:15	253
4:31	25	7:16	183, 264
4:31–37	253	7:18–35	65, 265–266
4:33–35	182	7:21	138
4:33–37	181	7:22	180
4:38–39	183, 215	7:25	163
4:39	255, 258	7:26	204
5:3–12	179	7:30	123, 136, 138
5:5	164	7:31	136
5:8	26	7:34	136
5:9	164	7:36	136
5:10–11	164	7:36–50	215
5:12–14	182	7:37	26, 265
5:17	120, 123, 124, 132, 135, 157	7:39	136
5:17–26	132	7:44–46	136
5:18–26	182	7:47	267
5:21	123, 124, 132	7:48–50	265
5:25	183	7:49	137
5:26	132, 137, 151, 183	7:50	289
5:27	77, 165	8:1–3	258, 259, 288
5:28–29	165	8:2	138, 170
5:29–32	133	8:2–3	183, 216, 278
5:30	123, 136, 248	8:3	16, 62, 63, 64, 74, 154, 250, 255
5:32	150		
5:33	136	8:4–15	104
5:33–39	133	8:8	270

Luke (continued)

Verse	Pages
8:15	270
8:19	197
8:19–21	215, 217
8:20–21	274
8:21	235, 236, 237, 259, 270
8:26	25
8:26–39	253
8:27	179
8:39	183, 184
8:41	167
8:41–42	216, 252
8:41–56	182
8:43	179, 265
8:43–48	183, 216, 287
8:44	214
8:45–46	212
8:47–48	265
8:49–56	216, 252
8:54	213
8:56	213, 269
9:1–6	256
9:4	257
9:7	61
9:7–9	61, 65, 68
9:9	22, 73
9:10	65
9:18	260
9:22	123, 126, 149–150, 260
9:33	92, 196
9:35	270
9:37–43	182
9:43–44	260
9:46	196
9:62	126
10:1	98, 256
10:5–7	257
10:8–12	146
10:25	123, 125, 137
10:28–29	137
10:29	125, 131, 146
10:35	163
10:36–37	137
10:38–42	216, 248, 287
10:39	269
10:40	213, 255, 269, 270
10:41–42	269
10:42	271
11:13	138
11:14	182
11:16	68
11:20	146
11:26	138, 170
11:27	236
11:27–28	216
11:28	236, 237, 270
11:29	138
11:29–30	68
11:31	176, 270
11:34	138
11:38	138, 139
11:39	144–145, 146
11:39–52	138
11:40	135, 139
11:41	139, 180
11:42	146
11:42–52	124–125
11:43	122, 128, 145, 147, 166, 196
11:44	142
11:45	123, 139
11:46	138
11:53	123, 125, 140
11:53–54	139
11:54	143
12:1	140, 196
12:1–3	142
12:13–14	271
12:19	163
12:21	163
12:32	11
12:33	163, 180
12:33–34	159
12:35–40	164
12:37	255, 256
12:41–48	164
12:46	142
12:56	142
12:58	104
13:1	92
13:10–13	182
13:10–17	142–143
13:11–13	216
13:13	183
13:15	142
13:25–30	164

Scripture Index   331

13:31	66, 68, 143	18:27	158, 167
13:32	68	18:28	158, 196
13:32–33	66	18:31–33	208
13:33	143	18:32	68
14:1	143	18:33	88
14:1–6	182	18:35–43	182
14:3	123, 143	18:43	182, 183
14:4	143	19:1–10	158, 165
14:12–14	183	19:2	77, 167
14:15	143	19:4–5	167
14:16–24	164	19:7	167, 248
14:24	143	19:8	116, 180, 266
14:26–32	158	19:8–10	167
14:33	158	19:9–10	289
14:35	270	19:11–27	69, 164
15:2	123, 144, 248	19:23	250
15:3–10	153–154	19:39–40	146
15:25	163	19:45	128, 176
15:29	163	19:45–46	127
15:30	144	19:46	107
16:1–13	164	19:47	123, 124, 126, 130, 146
16:13	144, 174	20:1	123–124
16:14	144, 145, 158, 166	20:1–2	126
16:15	131, 145	20:9–16	66, 164
16:16–19	267	20:19	66, 124, 126, 130
16:19	163	20:20	125, 131, 142, 143
16:19–31	113, 145	20:20–22	126
16:21	250	20:26	126
16:28–31	163	20:39	123, 124
17:7	11	20:45–47	126–127
17:8	255	20:46	122, 166, 175
17:11–19	182	20:46–47	124
17:14	213	20:47	253
17:15–19	183, 213	21:1–4	253
17:18–19	184	21:2	154
17:20	145	21:2–4	216
18:2–5	253	21:3	154
18:2–8	214, 287	21:3–4	254
18:9	125, 131, 146	21:5–6	128
18:11	146	21:12–13	68
18:11–12	271	21:16	217
18:12	146	22:2	124, 126
18:14	122, 146, 175	22:2–5	128
18:18–19	157	22:3	168, 172, 173, 174
18:22	157, 183	22:5	168
18:23	158	22:13	256
18:24–25	103	22:21	250
18:25	158, 179	22:21–23	173

Luke (continued)

22:24	195, 196
22:24–25	271
22:24–27	21, 122, 259
22:24–32	172–173
22:25	42
22:25–27	255–256
22:26	255
22:26–27	175, 292
22:27	191, 199, 214, 255, 270, 299
22:28–30	195
22:30	250
22:31–32	194
22:35–38	173
22:37	140
22:45	196
22:47–53	128
22:52	124
22:56	275
22:56–57	216
22:57–58	192
22:60	192
22:66	93, 124
22:66–71	128
23:1	93
23:1–5	128
23:2	92, 126
23:3	68
23:4	69, 93
23:5	93
23:7–12	67, 68
23:8–9	73
23:9	68
23:10	70, 124, 128
23:12	67, 71
23:13	93, 157
23:13–25	128
23:15	69
23:16	93
23:18	126
23:21	126
23:22	93
23:23	93, 126
23:24	93, 100
23:25	93, 94
23:27–31	216
23:28	66, 213
23:35	128, 157
23:36–38	87
23:47	89, 131
23:49	259, 260
23:50	131
23:50–51	130
23:51	25
23:53	98
23:55	216, 259, 260
23:56	278
24:6–7	260
24:6–8	259
24:9	260
24:9–10	193
24:10	216, 230, 259
24:11	196
24:12	192, 260
24:13	25, 257
24:20	126, 128, 157
24:23	193
24:24	193
24:28	98
24:29	257
24:32–33	193
24:33–35	193
24:34	194
24:36–53	195
24:44	255
24:49	193, 260
26:3	73

John

4:7	287
4:46–53	89
5:14	288
6:41	248
6:43	248
6:61	248
7:12	248
7:32	247
8:11	288
10:16	11
13:33	255
20:17	287

Acts

1:1	4, 14
1:4	260
1:4–5	193
1:8	194, 260
1:13	98, 194
1:14	215, 216, 236, 259, 274, 285
1:15	198
1:15–26	191–192
1:17	255
1:18	168
1:21–26	261
1:25	255
2–6	244
2:1–4	198
2:2	98
2:4	260
2:10	47
2:14—4:22	198
2:17–18	203, 216
2:23	94
2:42	251
2:44–46	175, 249, 250
2:45	185, 249
2:46	185, 240, 250, 251
3:2	179
3:8	185
3:11	185
3:13	94
3:17	128–129, 135, 157
4–6	251
4:1	124
4:3	129
4:5	124, 157
4:5–7	129
4:8	157
4:9	185
4:10	94
4:13	197
4:14	185
4:16–17	129
4:21	129
4:23	124
4:24–30	94
4:26	157
4:26–27	67
4:27	94
4:31	67, 169
4:32	259
4:32–37	175
4:34	185, 249, 251, 302
4:34–35	249
4:36	204
4:36–37	178
4:37	158
5:1–2	272
5:1–11	12, 216
5:2	249
5:3	174
5:3–4	168–169
5:14	216
5:17	124
5:17–18	129
5:33	129
5:34	123, 147
5:37	69
5:38	147
5:38–39	148
6:1	175, 185, 216, 240, 246, 248, 250, 255, 278
6:1–2	251
6:1–4	239
6:1–6, 240	248, 269
6:2	250, 255
6:2–4	246
6:3	247
6:3–5	246
6:4	255
6:6	247
6:7	120, 148
6:8—8:40	247
6:10	198
6:11–14	129
6:12	124
6:31	101
7:25	210
7:27	157
7:29	98
7:35	157
7:52	94
7:54—8:1	12
7:55	158, 211
7:56	204
7:58	104, 129
8:1	129, 147

Acts *(continued)*

8:1–3	129	10:2	90
8:2–3	12	10:6	177
8:3	147, 216	10:7	88, 156
8:4	177, 198	10:9	177
8:4–26	273	10:10	177
8:9	169	10:13	211
8:12	216	10:17	177
8:17	169	10:22	22, 89, 90
8:17–19	29	10:23	177
8:20	210	10:24	90
8:22	169	10:26	174
8:24	148, 169	10:30–32	22
8:26	177	10:30–33	90
8:26–29	198	10:34–35	101
8:27	176, 216	10:43	204
8:30–35	25	10:44	88
8:32–33	107	11:13–14	22, 90
8:39	176, 211	11:14	90, 275
8:39–40	177, 273	11:19–21	198
8:40	107, 177	11:26	155
9:1–2	129	11:27–28	204
9:1–19	22	11:28	207
9:2	143, 216	11:29	250
9:4–18	198	11:29–30	255
9:5–6	211	11:30	123, 155
9:10–16	211	12:1	70, 82
9:14	129	12:1–3	198
9:21	129	12:1–19	12
9:23–24	106	12:1–23	68
9:23–25	12	12:2–3	70, 129
9:24	143	12:4	70
9:29	24	12:12	98, 261
9:30	154–155	12:12–13	178
9:32	177	12:12–17	216
9:33–34	184	12:13	267
9:36	261	12:19	70, 88
9:36–39	177	12:20–23	174–175
9:36–41	216	12:23	56, 70
9:36–42	184	12:25	250, 255
9:38	25	13:1	16, 62, 64, 74, 159, 204
9:39	185, 254, 278	13:1–3	107
9:41	240	13:2–4	29
9:43	177	13:6	12, 170
10:1	81, 82, 90	13:6–12	107
10:1–6	22	13:7	32, 103, 160, 169
10:1–8	90	13:7–12	45
		13:8	169
		13:8–12	12

13:9	160	16:10–17	3
13:10	170	16:11–40	4
13:12	103	16:12	4, 5, 25, 42, 211
13:13–14	47, 160	16:13	5, 98, 209, 210
13:14–52	47	16:13–15	216
13:16	160	16:14	7, 209, 210, 262, 299
13:26	160	16:14–15	287
13:27	135	16:15	211, 214, 261, 275
13:27–28	94	16:16	170, 210
13:43	160–161	16:16–18	184, 216, 275
13:44	166	16:16–19	267
13:45	12, 166	16:19	170
13:46	162	16:19–23	104–105
13:48	166	16:19–24	12
13:50	12, 106, 130, 161, 166, 216	16:20–21	170
14:1	166	16:21	102
14:2	12, 166	16:22–24	178
14:5	12, 104, 162	16:27	88
14:8–10	184	16:31	275
14:8–18	167	16:31–34	156
14:11–18	175	16:33	106
14:15	174	16:34	250
14:19	12, 106, 167, 210	16:35–40	104–105
14:21–23	162	16:37	178
14:21–24	47	16:39–40	261
14:22	204, 206	16:40	4, 5, 204, 211, 263
14:23	123	17:4	160, 167, 217, 275
14:24	47	17:5	167
14:26–28	107	17:5–9	12, 105
14:27	210	17:9	177
15:1	120, 157	17:12	130, 160, 167, 217, 275
15:1–2	12	17:13	12, 106, 167
15:2	123, 148	17:18–32	175
15:4	123	17:21	160
15:5	12, 120, 148	17:29	210
15:6	123	17:32	160
15:14	194	17:34	106, 159, 217, 275
15:22	123, 148, 151	18:1–11	107
15:23	123	18:2	177
15:29	175	18:2–3	217
15:30–39	107	18:3	177, 178, 255, 267
15:32	204	18:6	12
15:38	47	18:7	178
15:39	29	18:8	167, 275
15:40	4	18:12	167
16:1	216	18:12–17	12, 84
16:4	123	18:13	102
16:6–12	209	18:17	103

Acts (continued)

18:18	177
18:18–19	217
18:19	261
18:21	206
18:23	206
18:24	177, 206
18:24–28	217
18:25	268
18:26	27, 177, 207, 214, 267, 287
18:26–28	149
18:27	177
18:32	206
19:1–20	107
19:7	204
19:9	12
19:12	138
19:13	24, 138
19:13–16	170
19:15–16	138
19:17–20	171
19:21	99
19:22	255
19:23–40	12
19:24–25	172
19:26	172
19:27	140, 172
19:28–41	106
19:31	42, 106, 160
19:35	41
20:1	204
20:2	107
20:3	106
20:3–5	4
20:4	5, 178
20:5	261
20:5–6	5
20:5–15	3, 4
20:6	211–212
20:7–11	6
20:7–12	206
20:8	98
20:9–12	184
20:17	123
20:17–35	11
20:18–38	206
20:24	255
20:28	11
20:34–35	180
21:1	47
21:1–18	3
21:1–25	4
21:3–4	207
21:4	204
21:5	6, 205
21:5–6	217
21:8	107, 176, 178
21:8–9	272
21:8–14	107
21:9	203, 204, 217
21:10	273
21:10–11	204, 207
21:11	207–208
21:12–14	6
21:16	178
21:18	4, 123
21:19	255
21:19–25	4
21:20–26	263
21:23–24	178
21:25	175
21:27—26:32	12
21:28	95, 167
21:29	167, 178, 210
21:32	88, 90, 93
21:32–33	91
21:33	88, 91
21:35	88
21:37	91
21:39	120, 178
22:3	123, 147, 149
22:4	217
22:5	124, 129
22:6–16	22
22:10	91
22:22–23	149
22:24	88, 90, 93
22:24—23:30	34
22:25	178
22:25–26	90
22:26–27	91
22:28	83
22:29	91
22:30	124
23:2	129, 149

23:6	120, 149	25:24–27	99
23:6–9	124	25:25	99, 101
23:7–10	149	25:26–27	75
23:8	124	25:30–32	75
23:9	123, 149	26:1	73
23:10	88, 91	26:2	74
23:11	99	26:5	123, 149
23:12–13	129	26:7	74
23:12–15	149	26:12–18	22
23:14	123, 124, 129	26:13	74
23:16	217	26:19	74
23:16–33	129	26:24	101
23:17	90	26:25	47
23:23	90, 91, 100	26:26–27	74
23:26	47	26:27–29	74
23:26–30	91	26:28	76
23:29	91, 95, 97	26:29	76, 151, 161
23:33–34	97	26:30–31	100, 217
24:1	93, 123, 124, 129	26:31	74, 75
24:5–6	95	26:32	74, 90, 100
24:6	99	27–28	21
24:7	95	27:1	16, 63, 82, 90
24:10	71	27:1—28:16	3, 4
24:19	98	27:3	90
24:22	71, 72, 74	27:5	47
24:24	217	27:12	25
24:24–27	72	27:13	6
24:26	87, 95	27:15–17	6
24:27	70, 100	27:32	88
25:2	93, 129	27:37	6, 159
25:3	96, 97, 98, 129	27:42–43	88
25:5	98	27:43	89
25:6	86	28:3–6	175
25:7	86, 98, 129	28:7	106, 159
25:8	97	28:8	184
25:9	70, 96, 97, 98, 100	28:10	159
25:10	97, 98	28:14	98
25:10–11	98	28:16	5, 89
25:11	99	28:27	270
25:12	86, 99, 101	28:30–31	72, 89
25:13	217	28:31	90, 108
25:15	97, 124		
25:16	98		
25:18–19	97		
25:20	98		
25:21	99	4:19	224
25:23	75, 82, 86, 98, 217	9:9	224
25:24	99	15:25	250

Romans

Romans (continued)

15:31	250
16:1	277
16:1–7	280
16:3–15	277
16:7	63
16:15	259
17:7	278

1 Corinthians

3:5–9	277
5:6–8	142
7:26	210
7:36	210
9:5	165, 257, 277
9:7	11
10:10	248
10:20	174
11:2–16	279
11:5	205, 280
14:3–5	205
14:12	205
14:17–18	205
14:24–25	205
14:26	205
14:31	205
14:33b–34	277
14:33b–36	279
14:34–35	280
15:5	194
15:24	64

2 Corinthians

8:4	250
8:19–20	250
9:1	250
9:12–13	250

Galatians

3:28	277
4:30	225

Ephesians

5:5	175
5:22–24	279

Philippians

2:14	248
2:25	277
4:2	262, 280

Colossians

3:5	175
3:18	279

2 Thessalonians

3:7–9	263

1 Timothy

2:8–15	280
2:11–14	280
3:11	280
4:7	280
5:3–16	280
5:9–13	239
5:13	281
6:5	210

2 Timothy

3:6–7	280

Titus

2:3–5	280

Philemon

2	277
7	277
20	277

Hebrews

11:11	224

James

2:1–4	145

1 Peter

3:1–2	279
3:6	224, 284
4:9	248
5:2	11
5:3	11

Jude

16	248

Revelation

9:20	174